I0715326

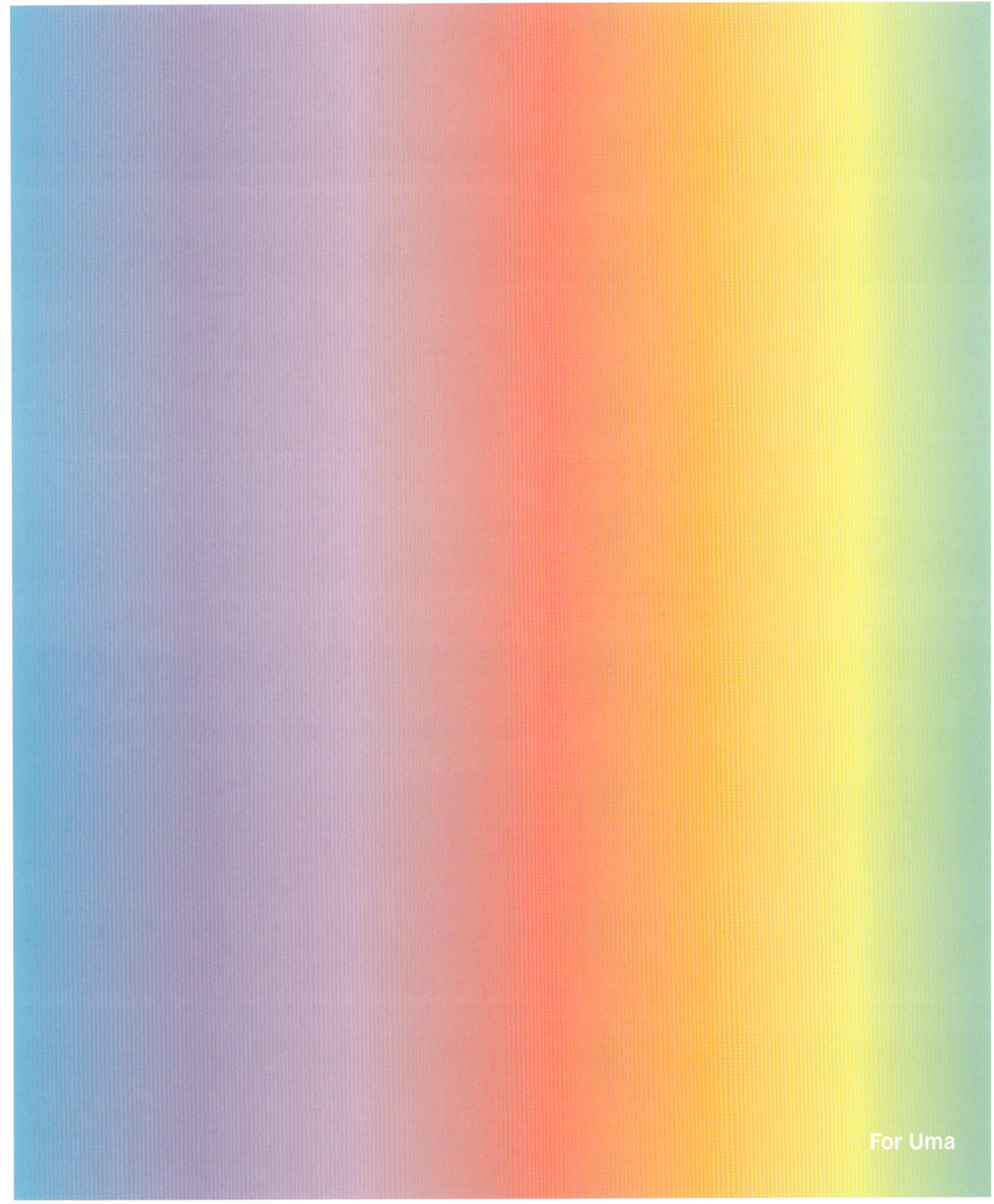
For Uma

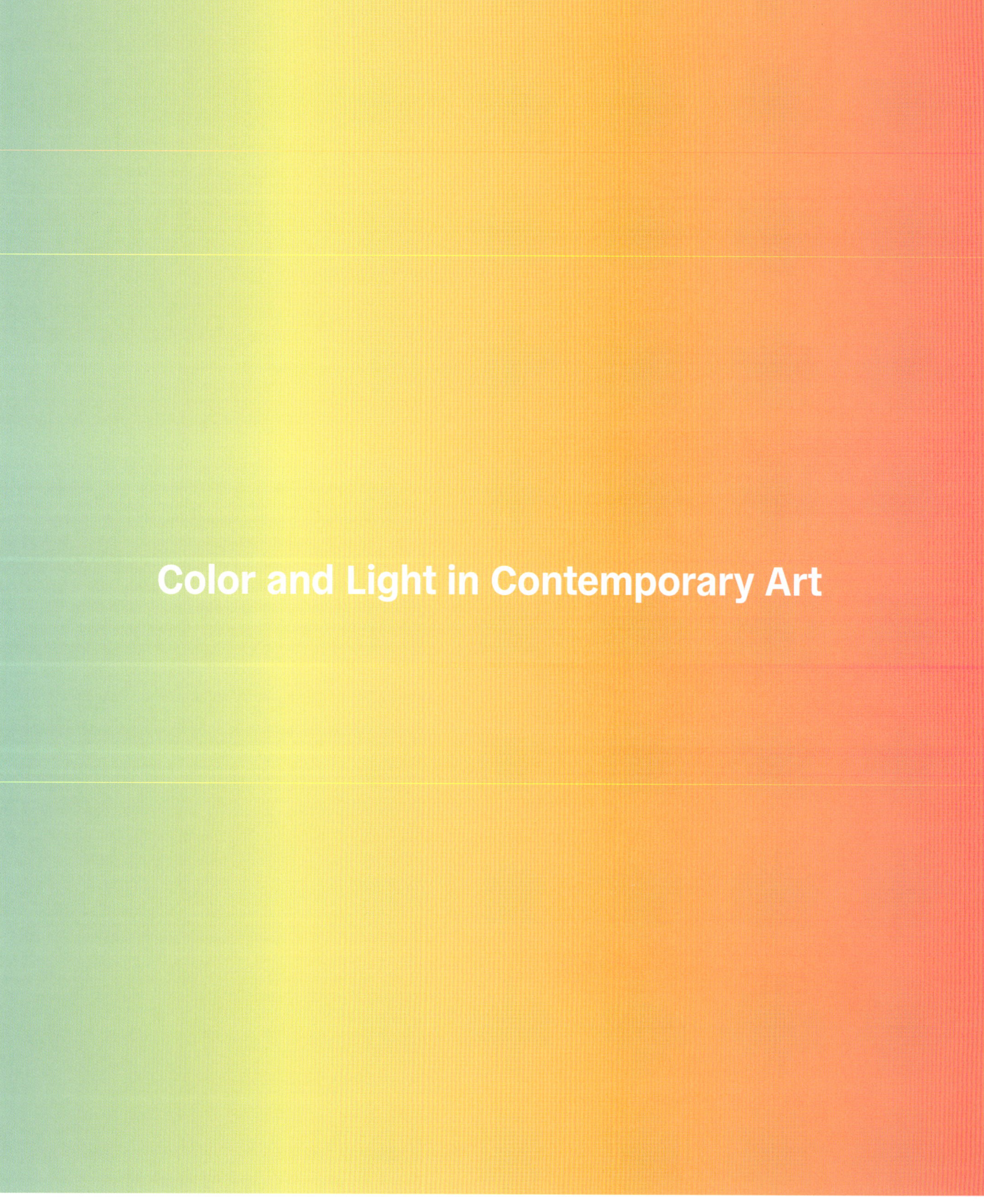
Color and Light in Contemporary Art

Rainbow Dreams

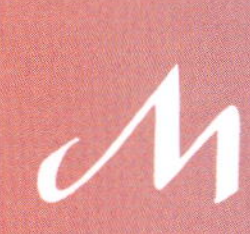

OLGA REI   **VALENTINE UHOVSKI**

Introduction
OLGA REI & VALENTINE UHOVSKI   6

Artworks   8 — 243

MICKALENE THOMAS on Color   77

JUDY CHICAGO and SARAH THORNTON in Conversation   155

I've Been Walking   242
SHANTELL MARTIN

Index of Artists and Works   244
Image Credits   254
Acknowledgments   256

Introduction

OLGA REI & VALENTINE UHOVSKI

Be a rainbow in somebody else's cloud.
—Maya Angelou

Welcome to *Rainbow Dreams*, the ultimate celebration of artists who use color and light to create powerful symbols of optimism, resilience, and community.

We live in interesting and unpredictable times, and the emotions they stir are many. Yet among them, we choose to highlight hope, joy, and the beauty of color. Rainbows, in their timeless simplicity, remind us of the miracle of existence. They can serve as a visual antidote to life's complexities or as a gentle reminder of how beauty always finds its way through.

The idea for this book first took root when a friend envisioned a physical museum dedicated to rainbows in Iceland. But by 2020, the vision had expanded into something greater: not just a place, but an ideology. At a time when the world seemed clouded, it became apparent that humanity needed hope, color, and beauty more than ever.

From this realization came Rainbow Contemporary, a collective we've formed to bring joy through the vibrant language of art. What began as conversations soon evolved into collaborations, as artists united across mediums and geographies to create collectibles that benefited fantastic causes. What bound us all was a simple truth: color has the power to heal, to connect, and to inspire. And for us, it created a five-year curatorial journey in which we often traveled far and wide to see these installations in person.

We weren't alone in turning to rainbows. During the global lockdowns of COVID-19, children everywhere painted them on windows as symbols of hope. Damien Hirst released rainbow-inspired editions. Lauren Halsey used color to pay tribute all at once to the beauty, loss, and change of her South Central Los Angeles neighborhood. Fred Tomaselli's collages, set against jarring *New York Times* headlines, were poetic reminders of the power of color to unite humanity. *Seven Magic Mountains* by Ugo Rondinone, first installed in 2016, grew into an even more powerful symbol for those who made the trek to the desert to interact with it and contemplate the intersection of human creation and nature.

Seeing so much powerful work expressed through the rainbow wasn't unique to that moment, however. Throughout history, rainbows have captivated the human imagination, standing as symbols of hope, renewal, and the beauty found in the marriage of colors. They're accessible, calming, unifying, and stimulating. Artists have employed them to evoke, explore, and amplify.

One of the earliest depictions of a rainbow can be found in a thirteenth-century Persian illustrated manuscript by Zakariya ibn Muhammad Qazwini, in which the rainbow represents divine presence on earth. In the fifteenth-century *Annunciation* by Jan van Eyck, the rainbow spectrum represents the redemption of humankind. John Constable incorporated a rainbow in his 1831 painting, *Salisbury Cathedral from the Meadows,* as a symbol of hope and optimism after losing his wife, the mother of his seven children. Modern artists such as Georges Seurat, Marc Chagall, Paul Klee, and Josef Albers have applied the full spectrum of color toward more abstract ends. "Color provokes a psychic vibration," wrote Wassily Kandinsky in 1911. "Color hides a power still unknown but real, which acts on every part of the human body."

In curating this book of contemporary art, we were constantly inspired by the different ways artists from around the world have utilized the spectrum of the rainbow. While some incorporate the theme as an aesthetic exploration, others employ it symbolically to represent themes like peace and harmony—both personal and political. This range of approaches reminds us that rainbows are cultural touchstones that surpass the restrictions of borders and languages.

The editing of this book unfolded against the backdrop of a world still marked by uncertainty, conflict, and crisis. Loss and suffering are parts of everyone's life, and no amount of color can banish them. But rainbows can cut through darkness, offering a lens for repair and renewal.

Paul Cézanne is said to have remarked that "we live in a rainbow of chaos." Perhaps that contradiction captures our world best: the light with the dark, beauty with disorder, color with ambiguity. Rainbows help to tell the story of the human experience: our longing for light, our resilience amid turmoil, our ability to create beauty even in fractured times. That is the essence of *Rainbow Dreams*. Through these pages, we invite you to journey across a spectrum of imagination. May the works within mesmerize, inspire, and above all, remind you of the enduring promise always surrounding us in an array of scintillating hues.

Always, with Rainbow Dreams,
Olga & Valentine

Ellsworth Kelly

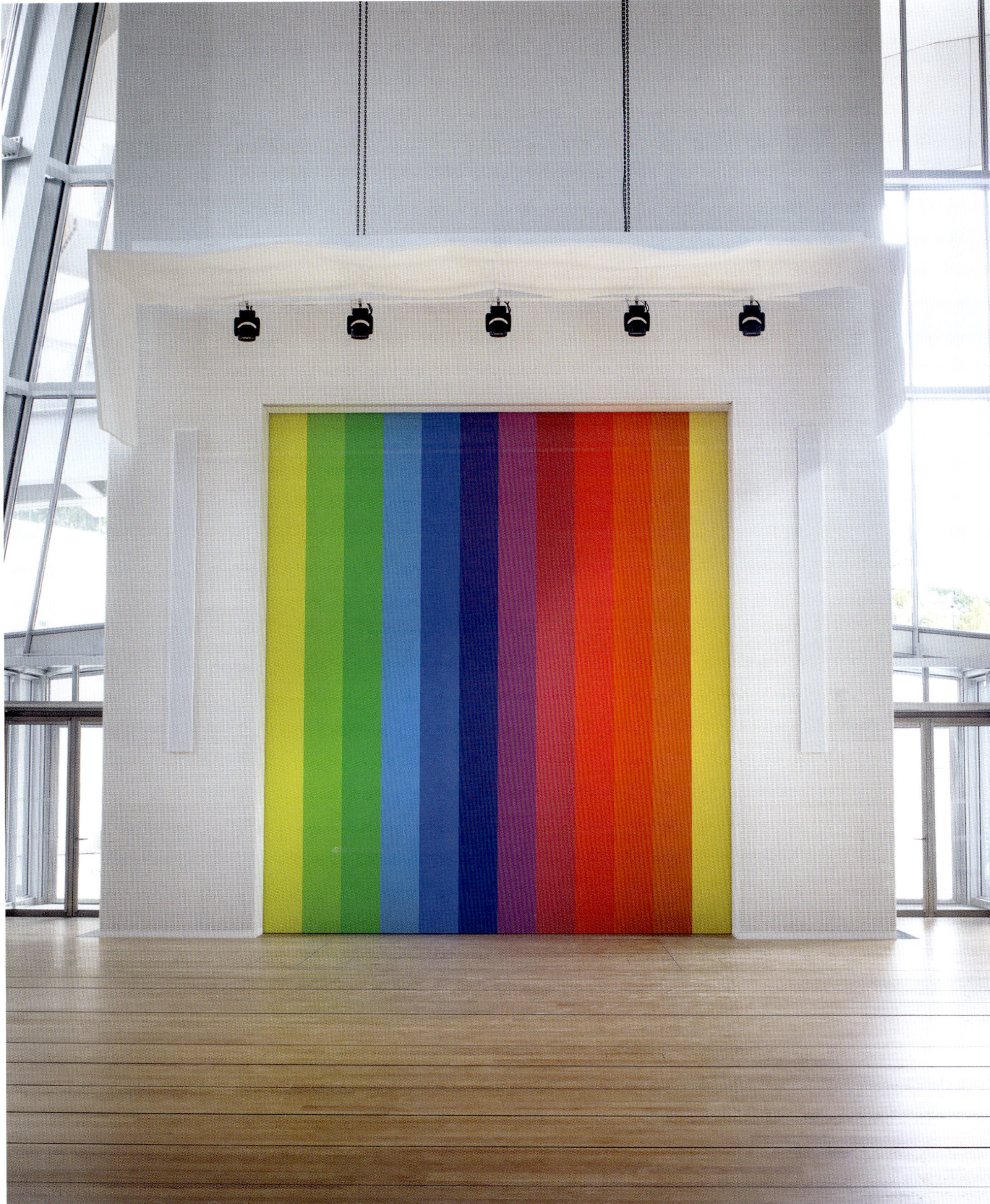

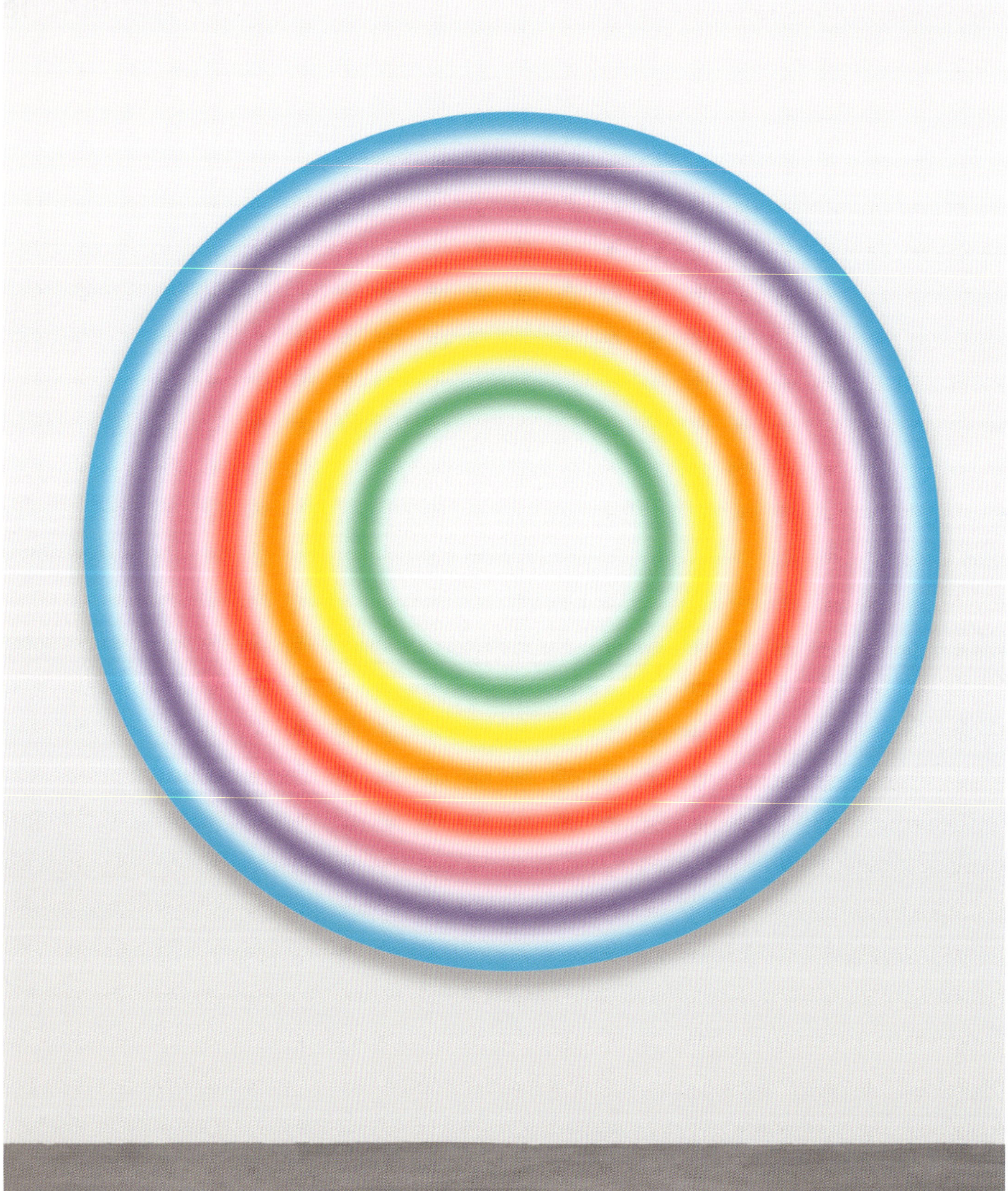

Ugo Rondinone

Love invents us 1999

pp. 12–13 Installation view: *seven magic mountains* 2016
pp. 14–15 *clockwork for oracles* 2008

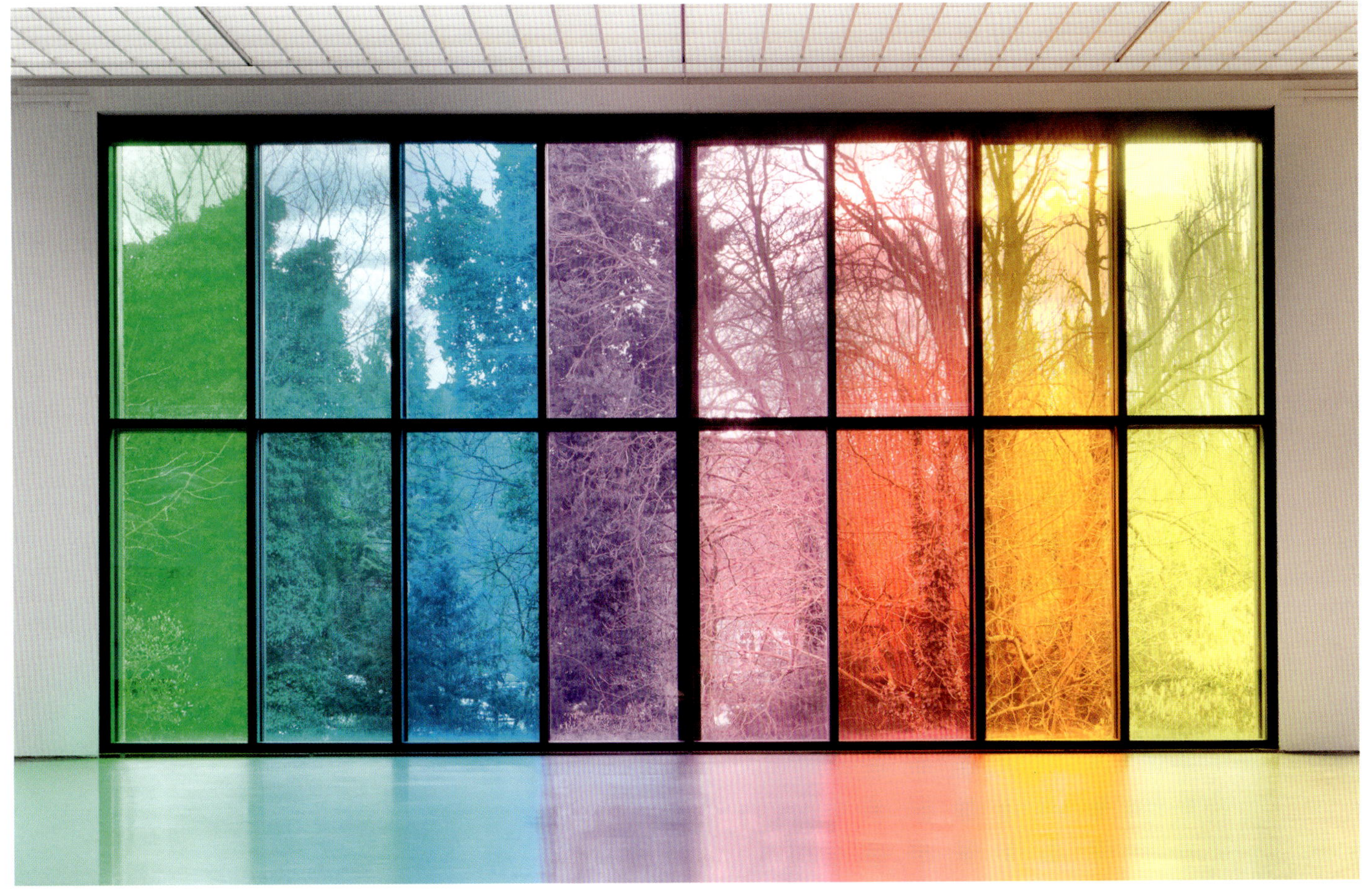

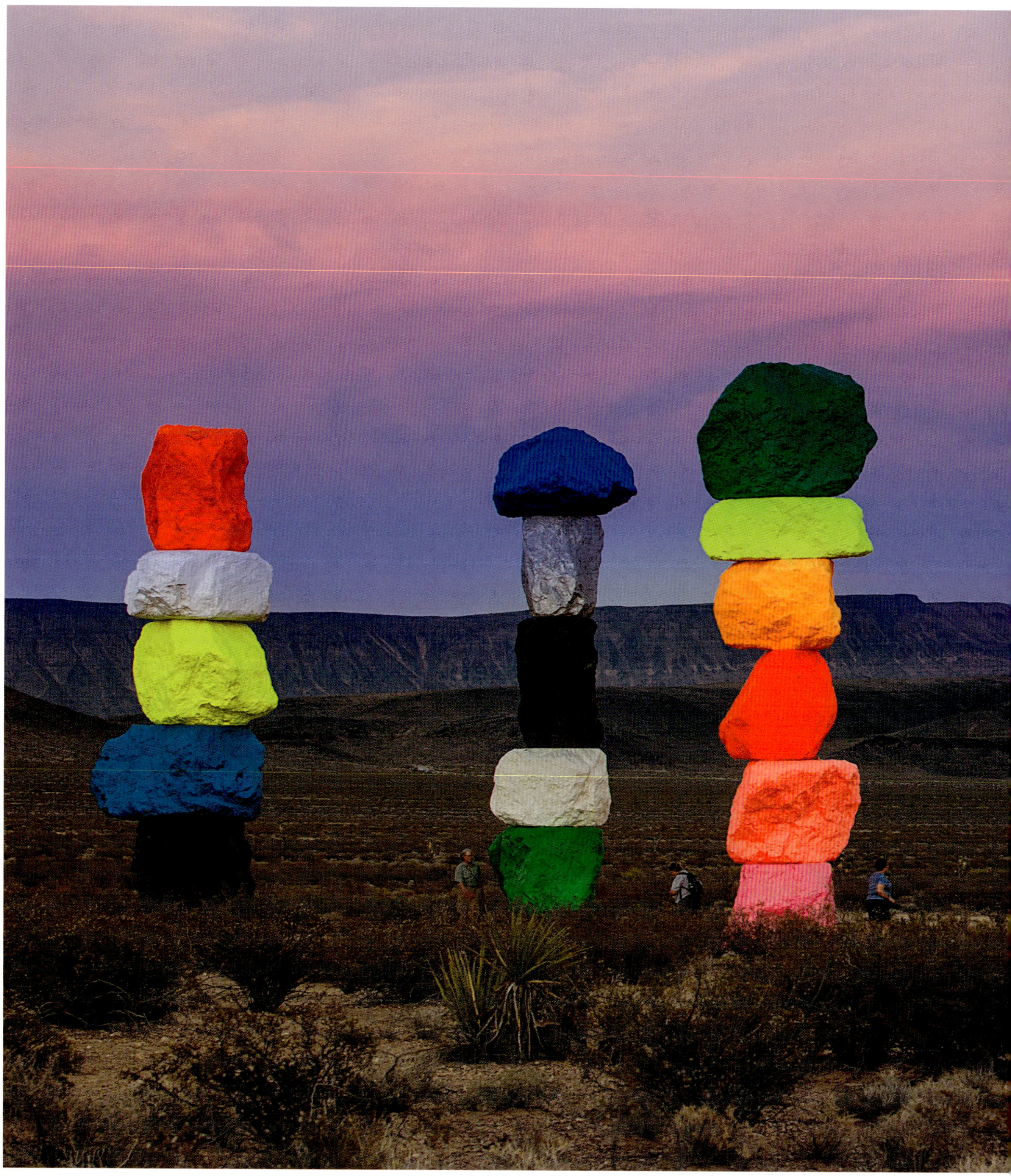

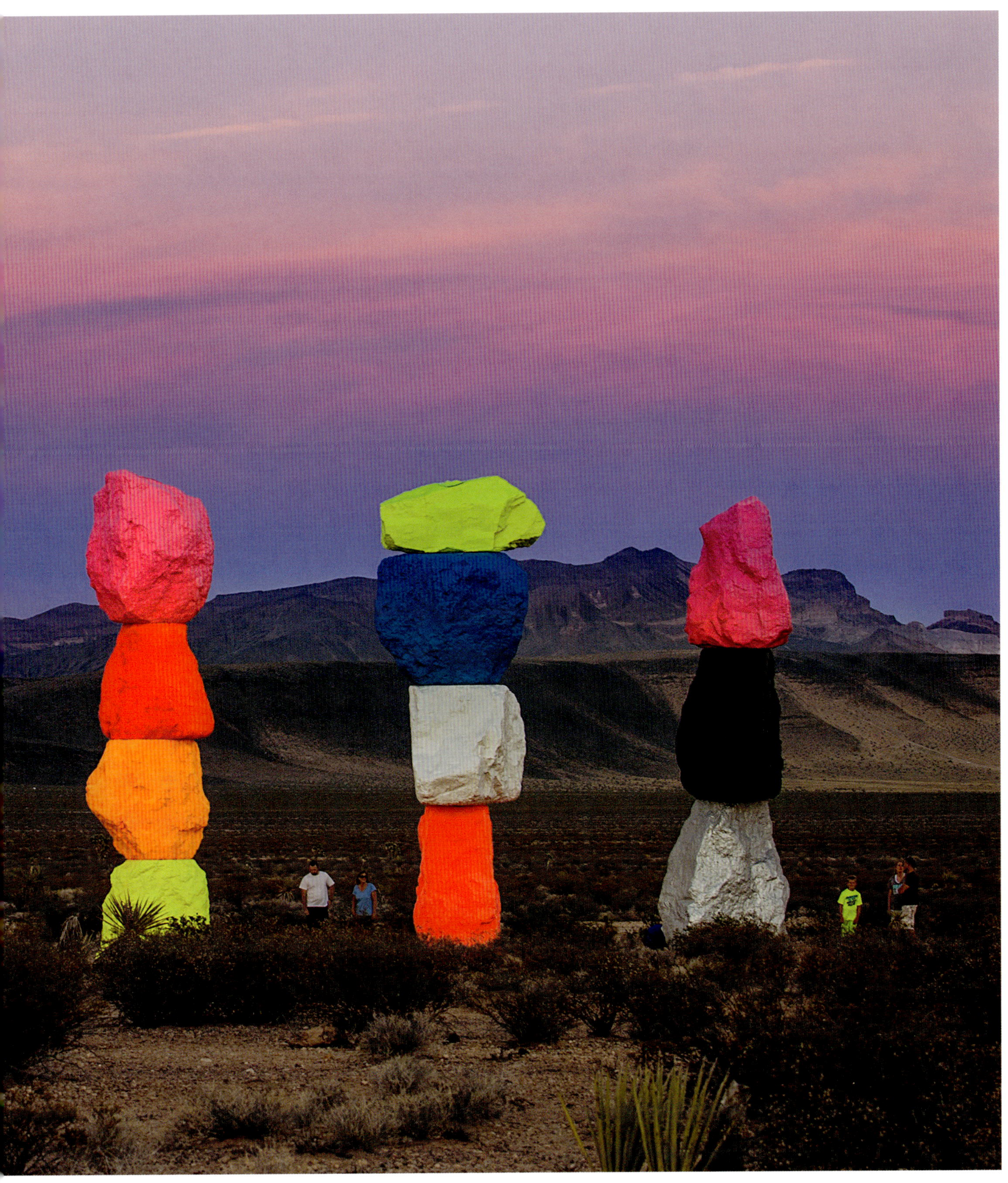

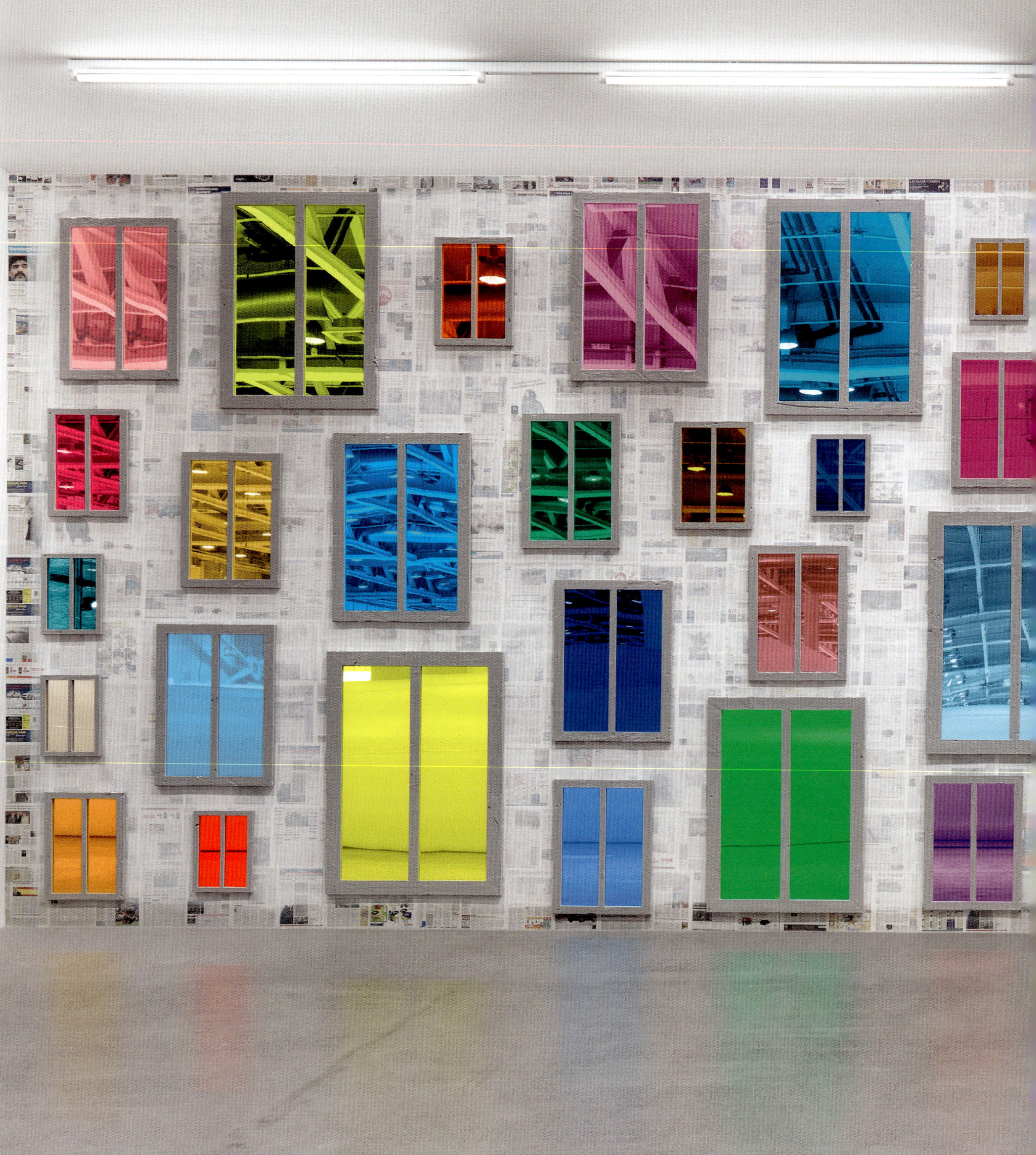

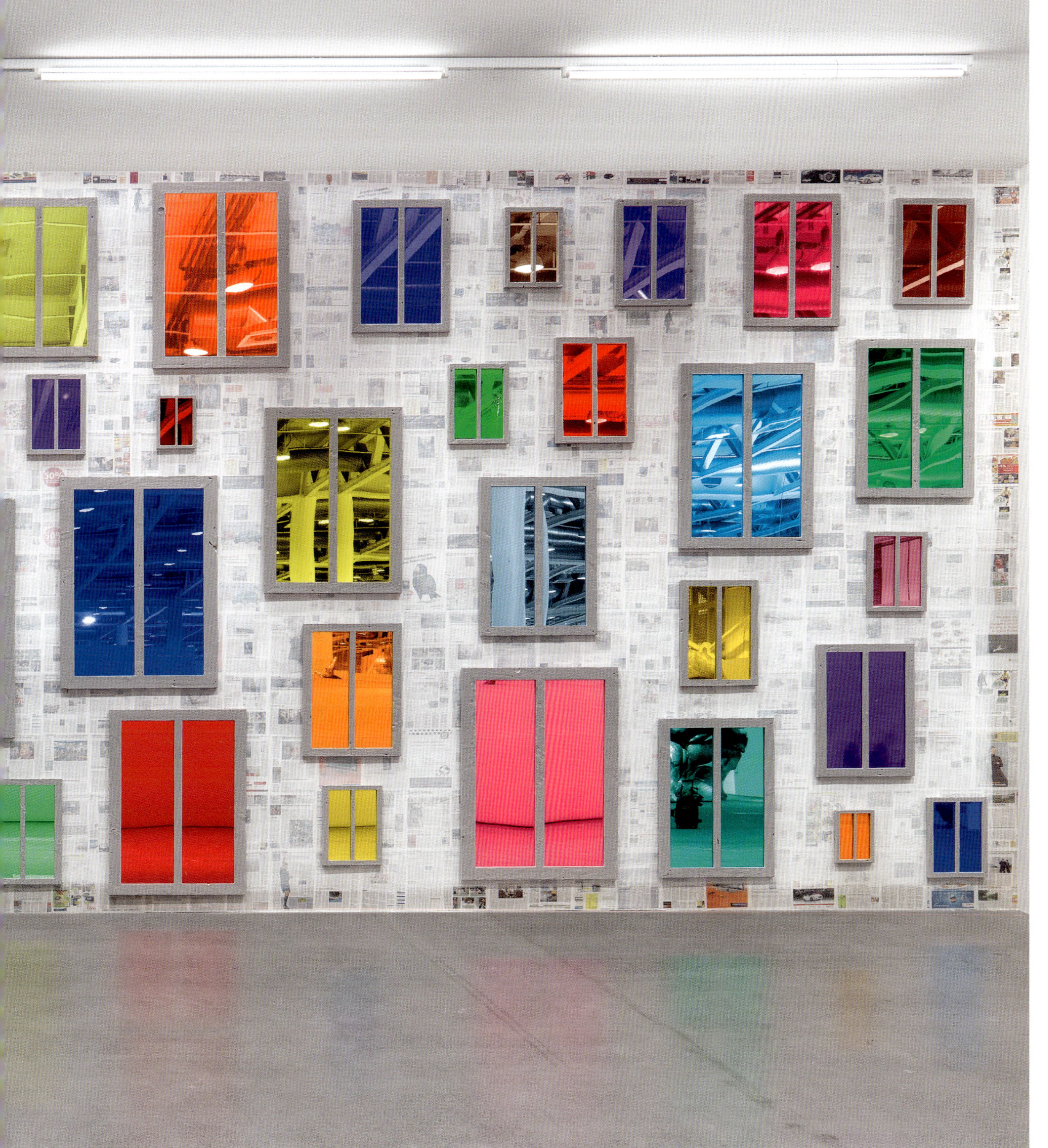

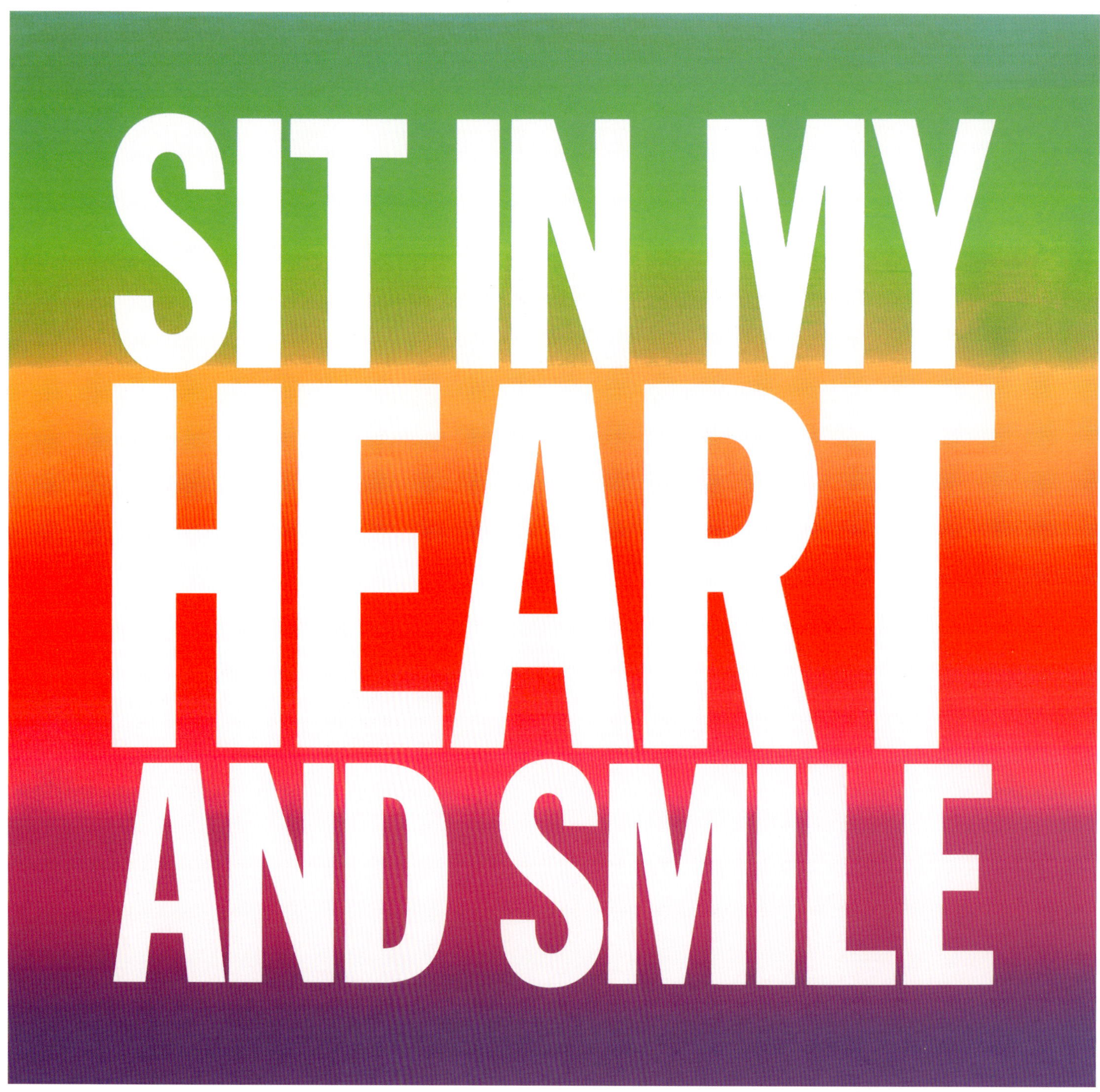

SIT IN MY HEART AND SMILE   2019

John Giorno

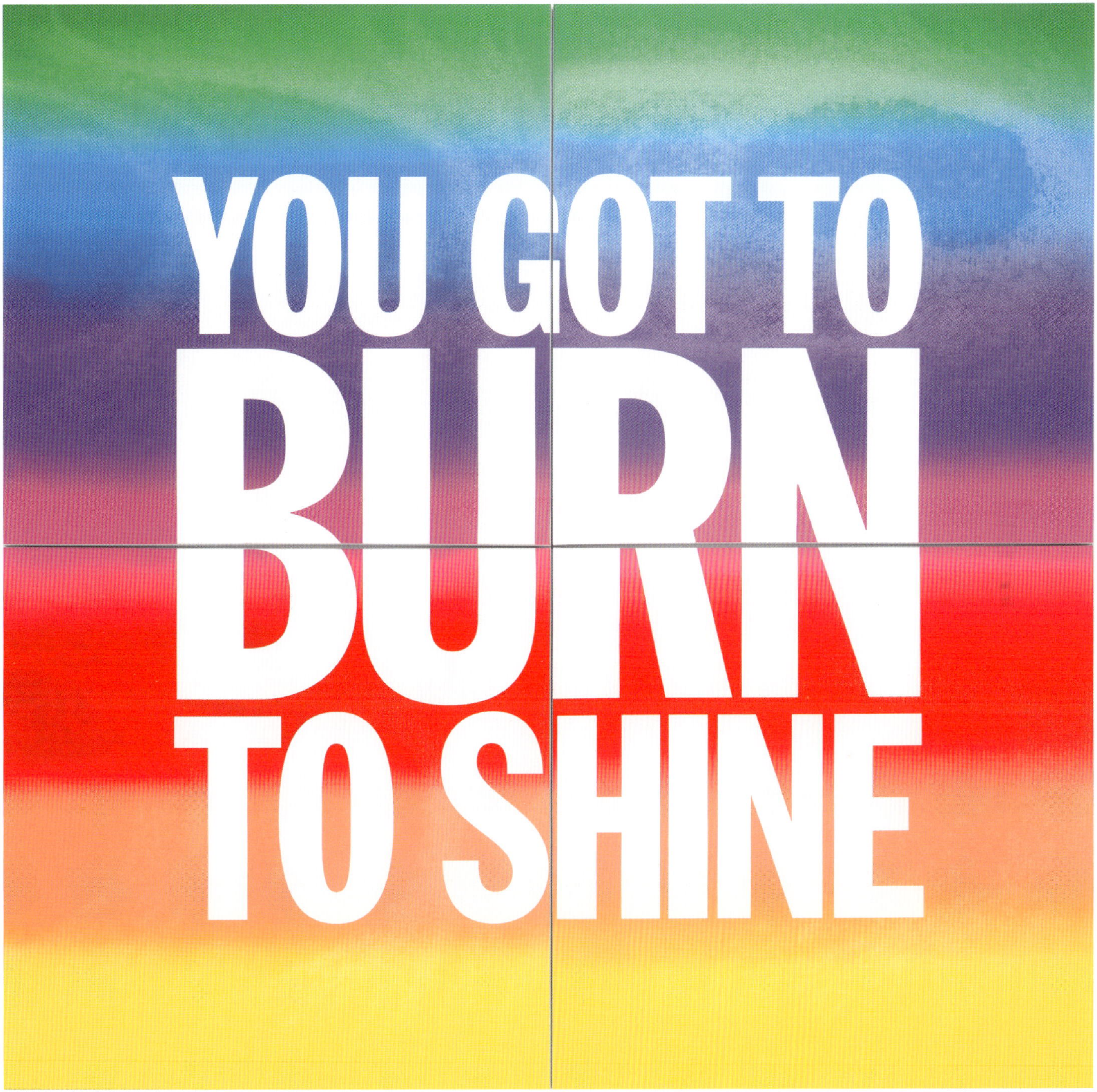

YOU GOT TO BURN TO SHINE 2018

Carlos Cruz-Diez

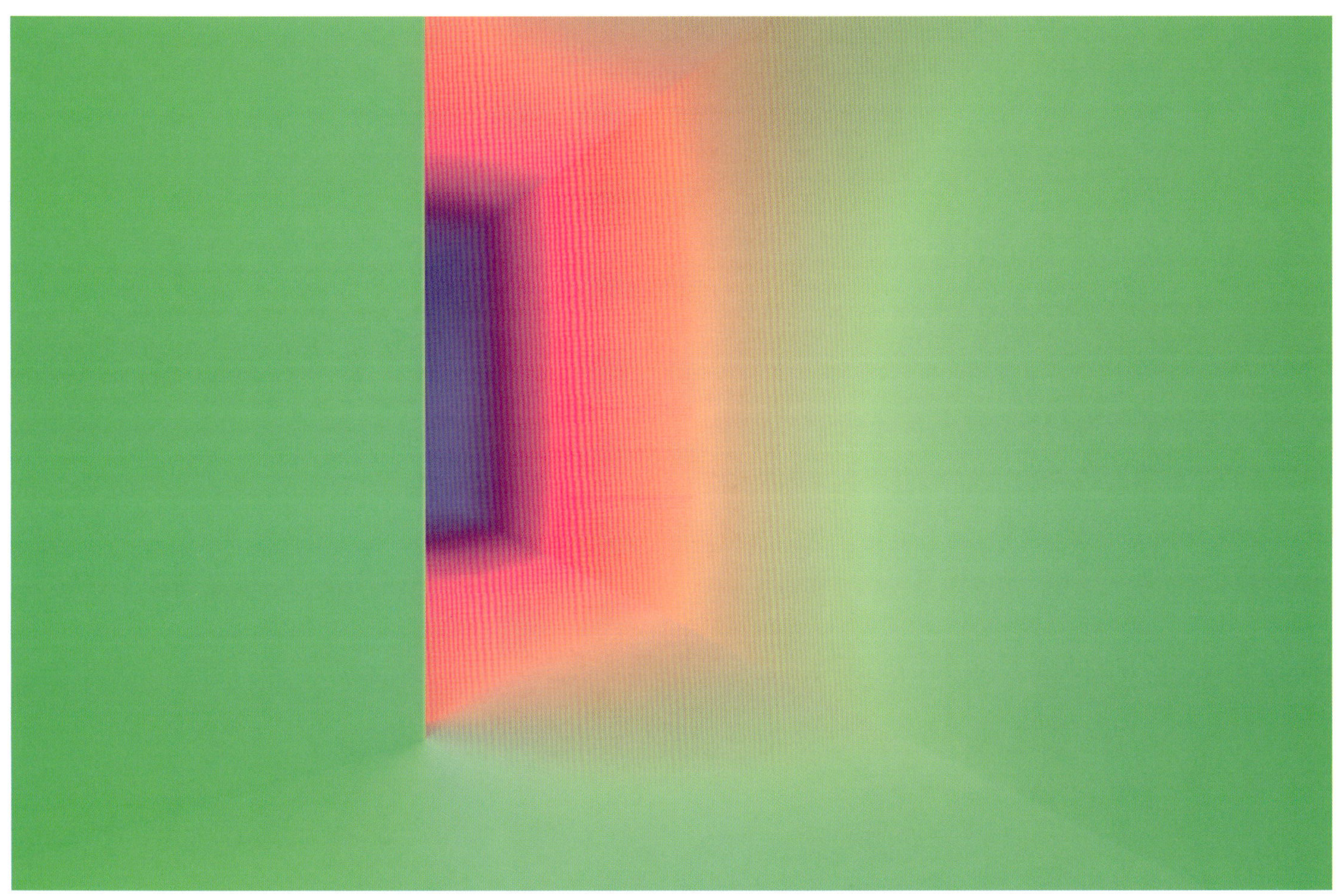

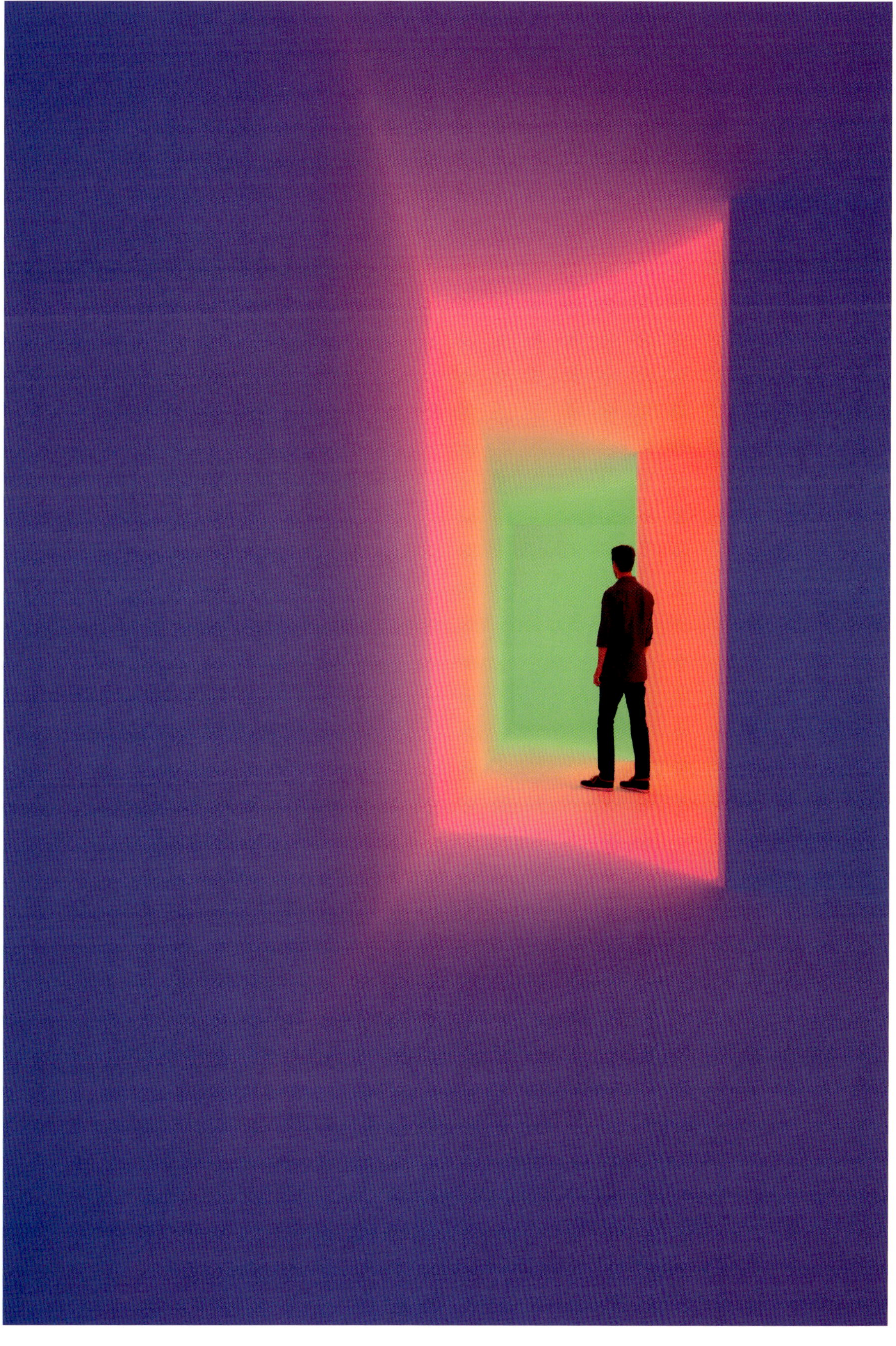

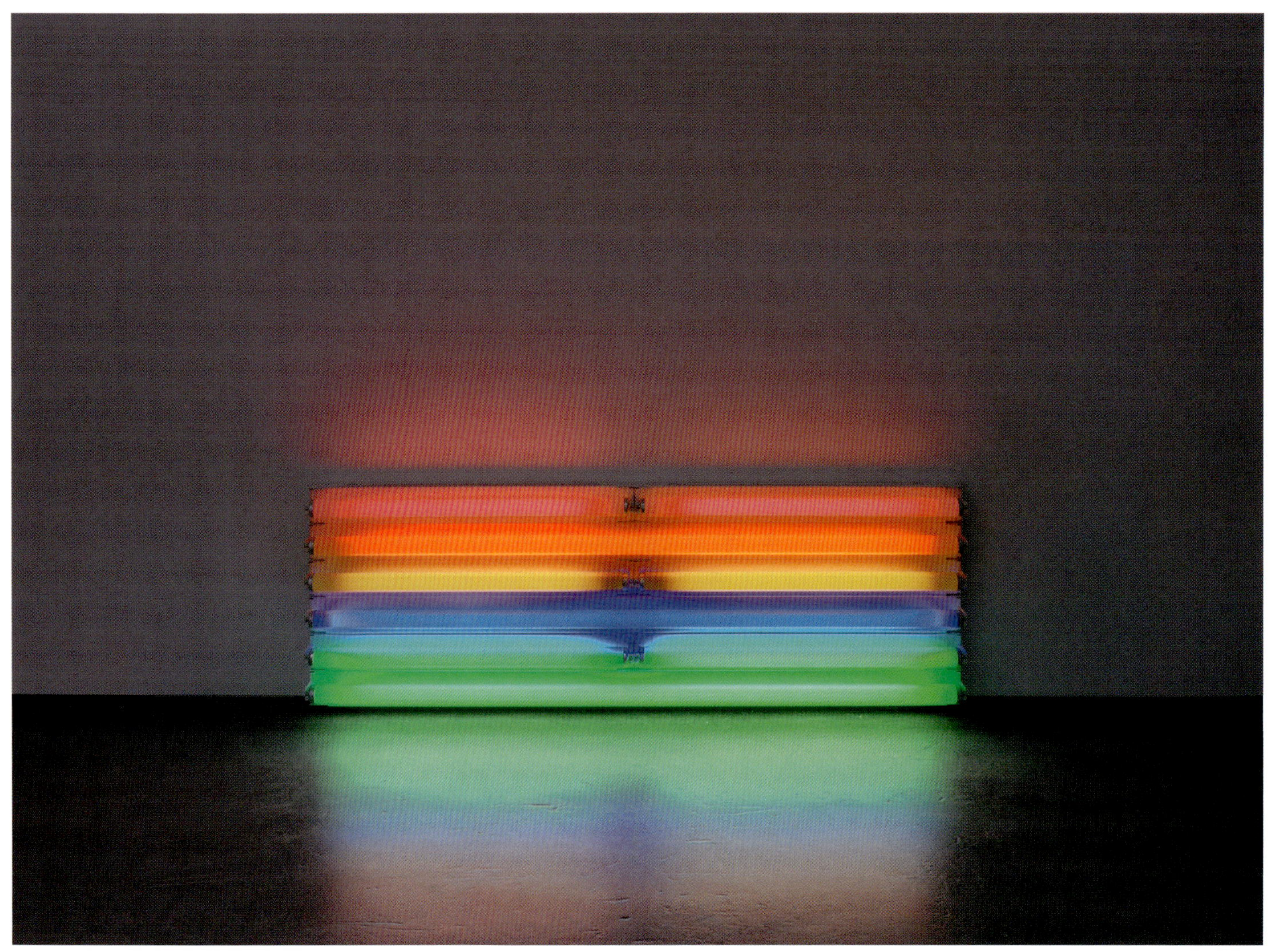

untitled (for Ad Reinhardt) 2h 1990

untitled (in honor of Harold Joachim) 3 1977

Dan Flavin

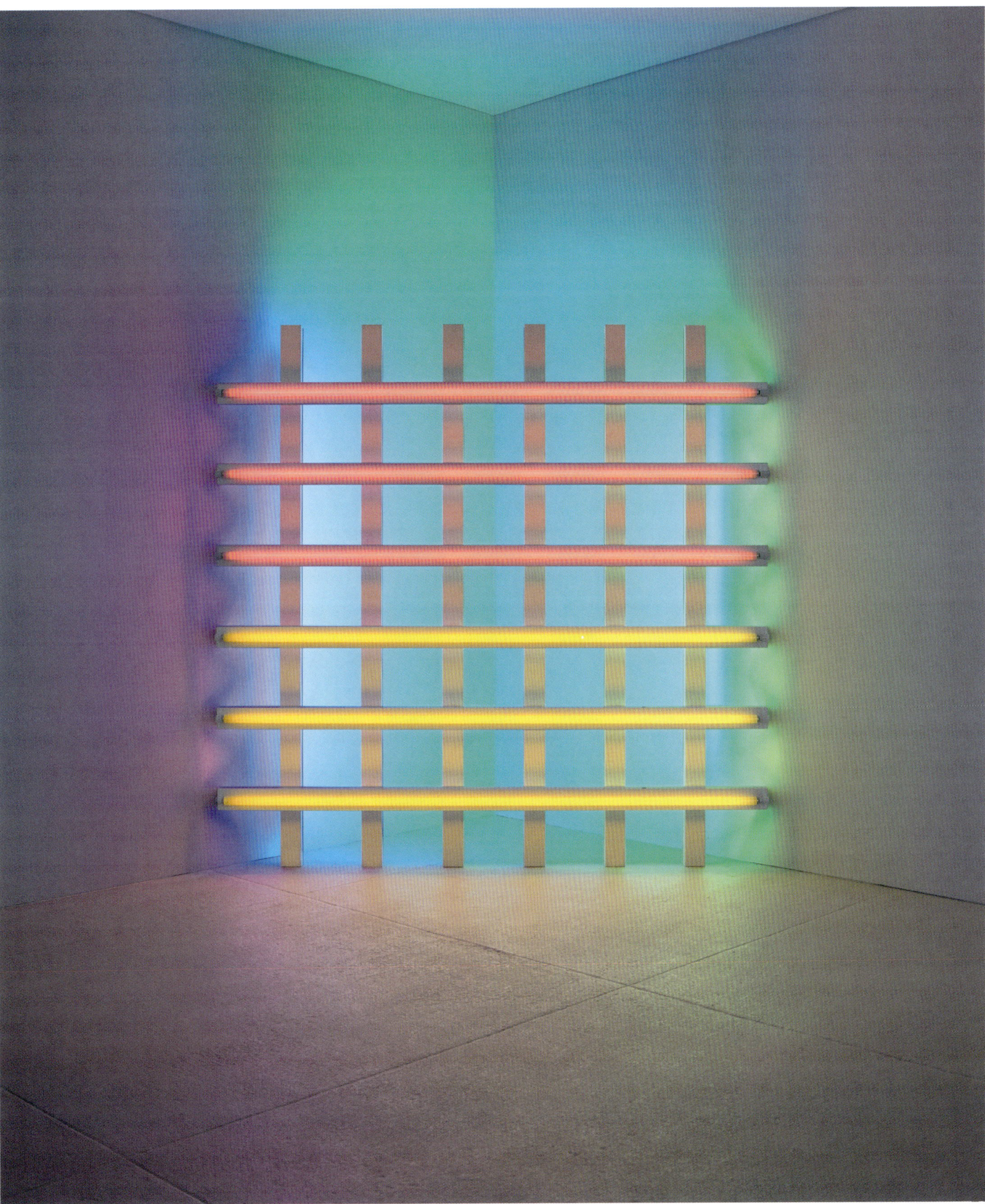

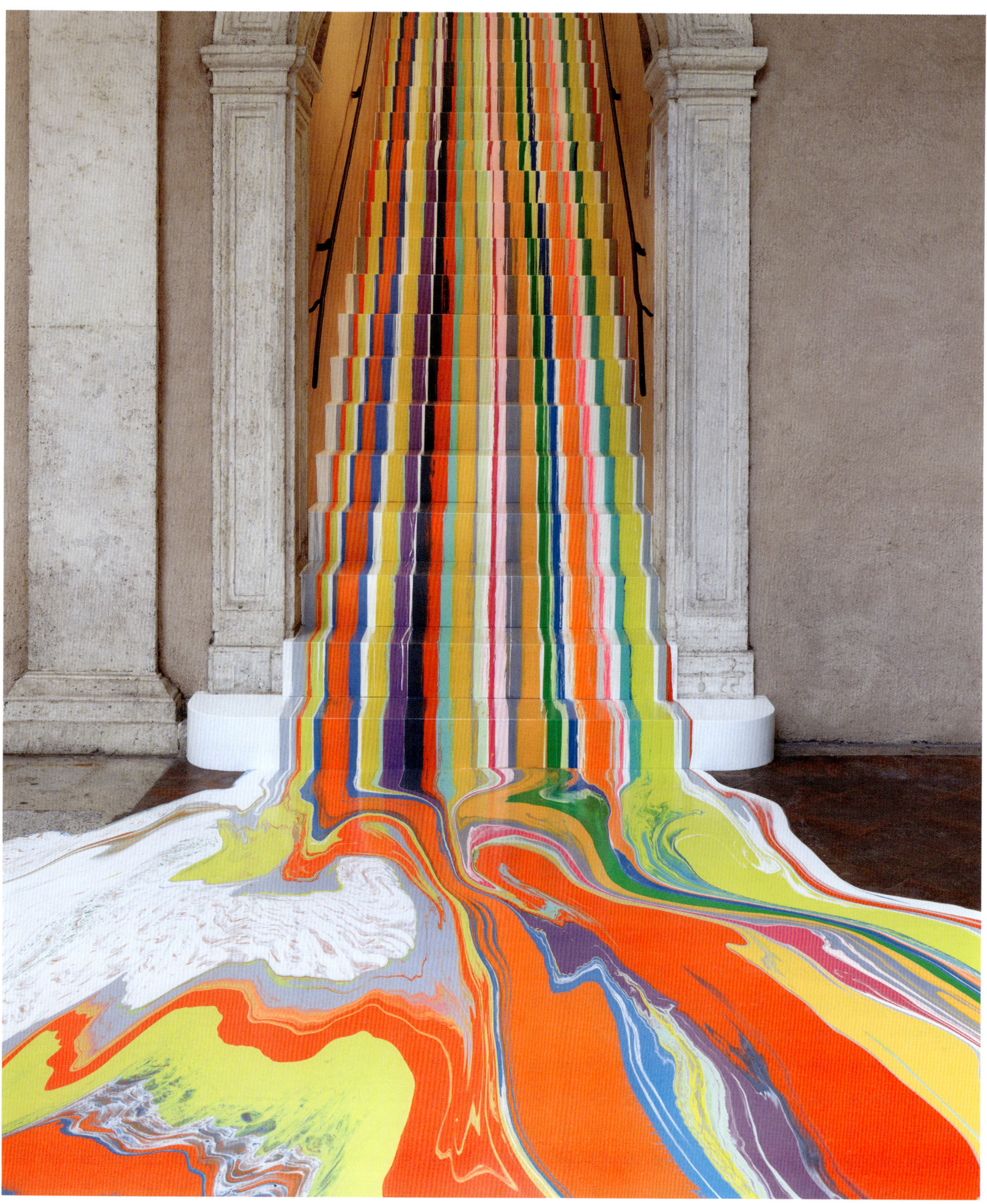

Ian Davenport

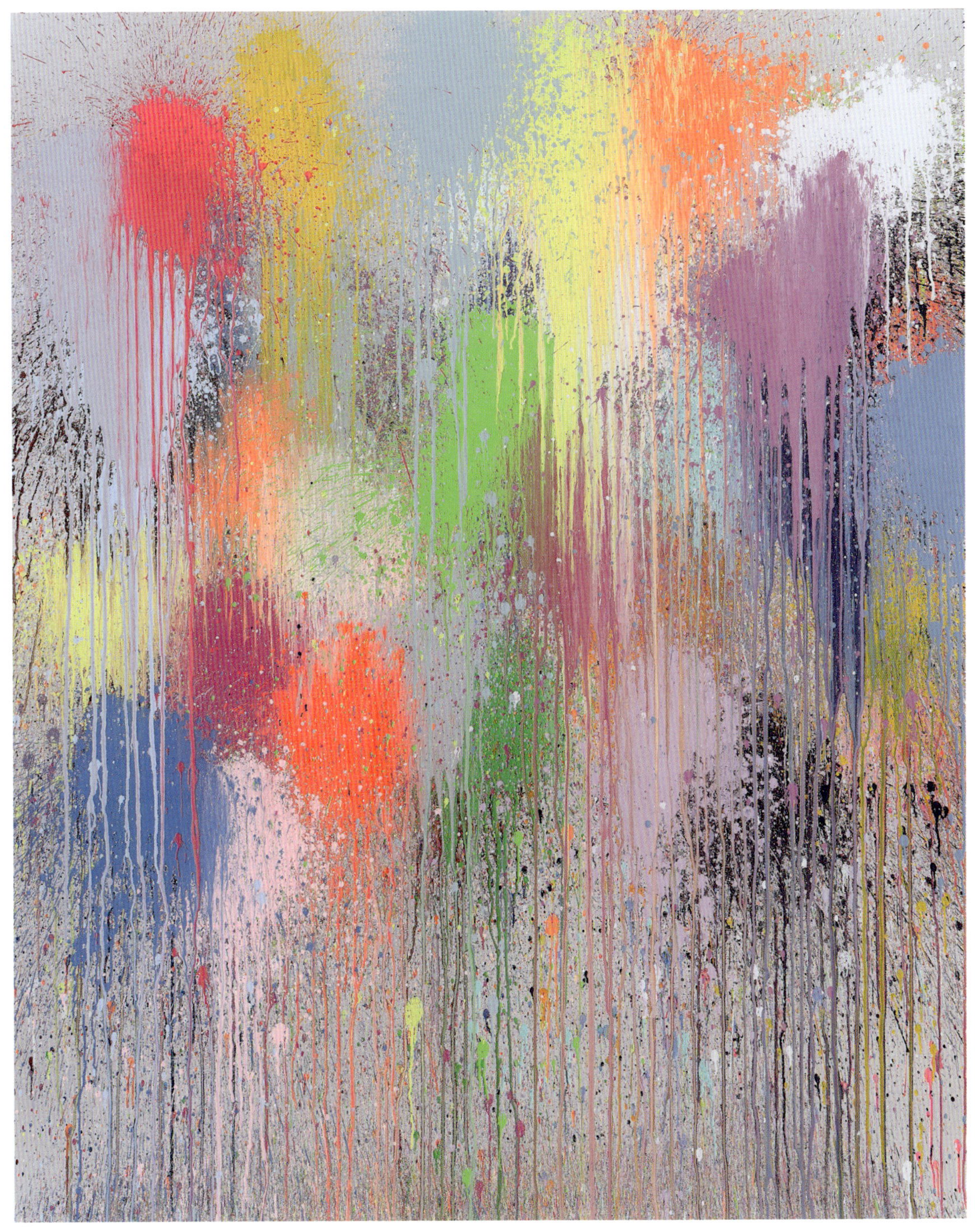

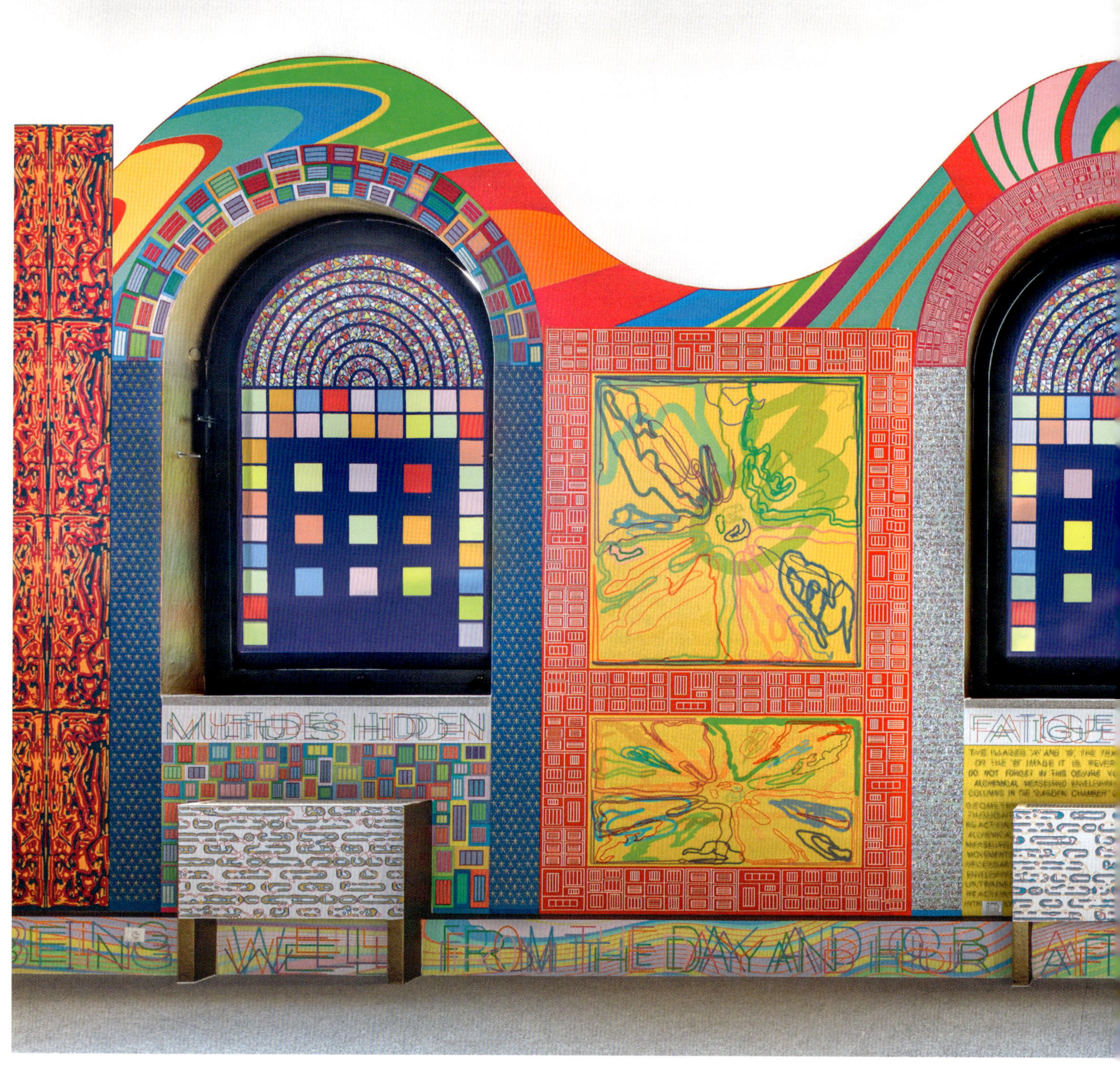

Peter Halley

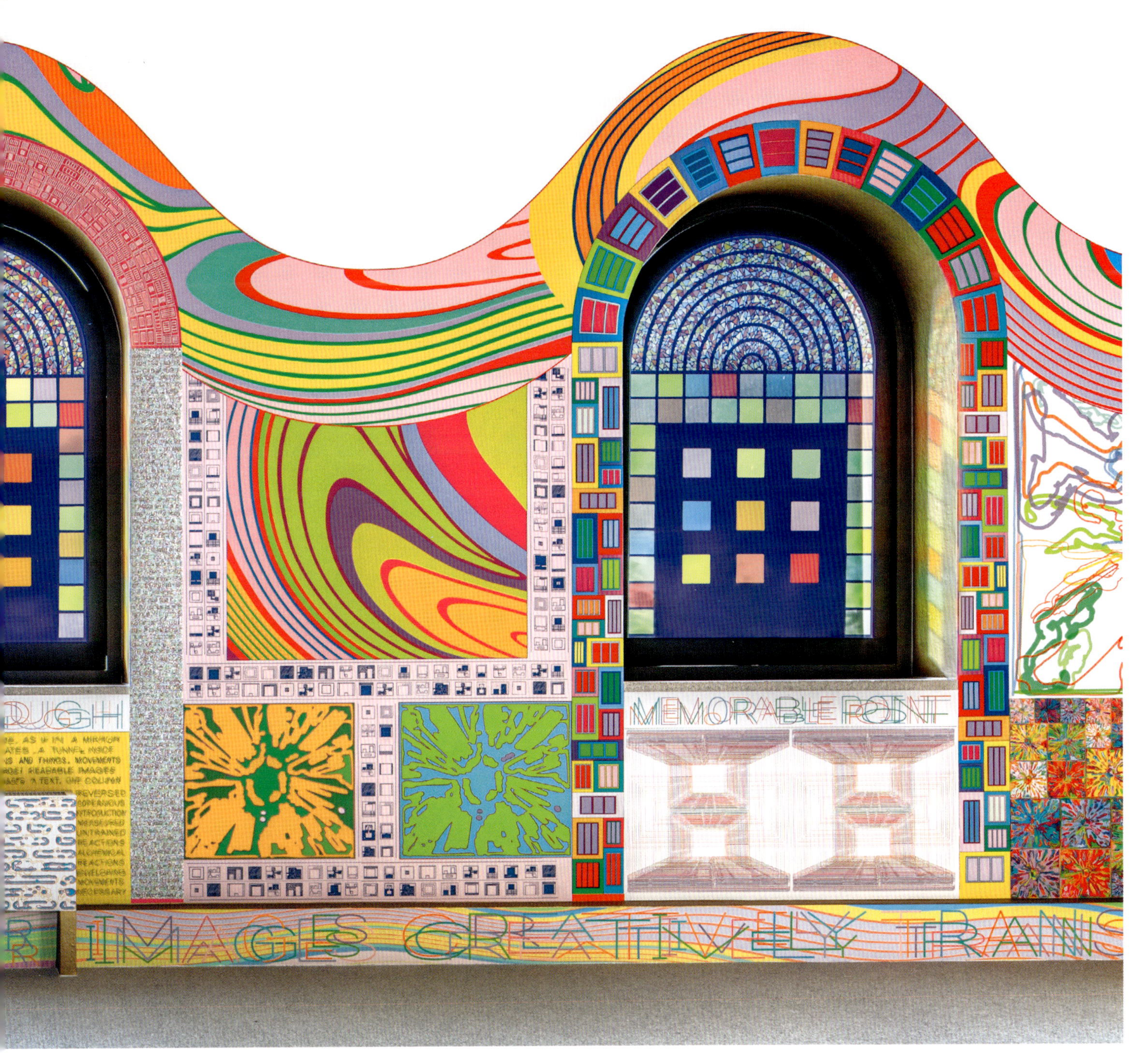
MEMORABLE POINT
IMAGES CREATIVELY TRANS

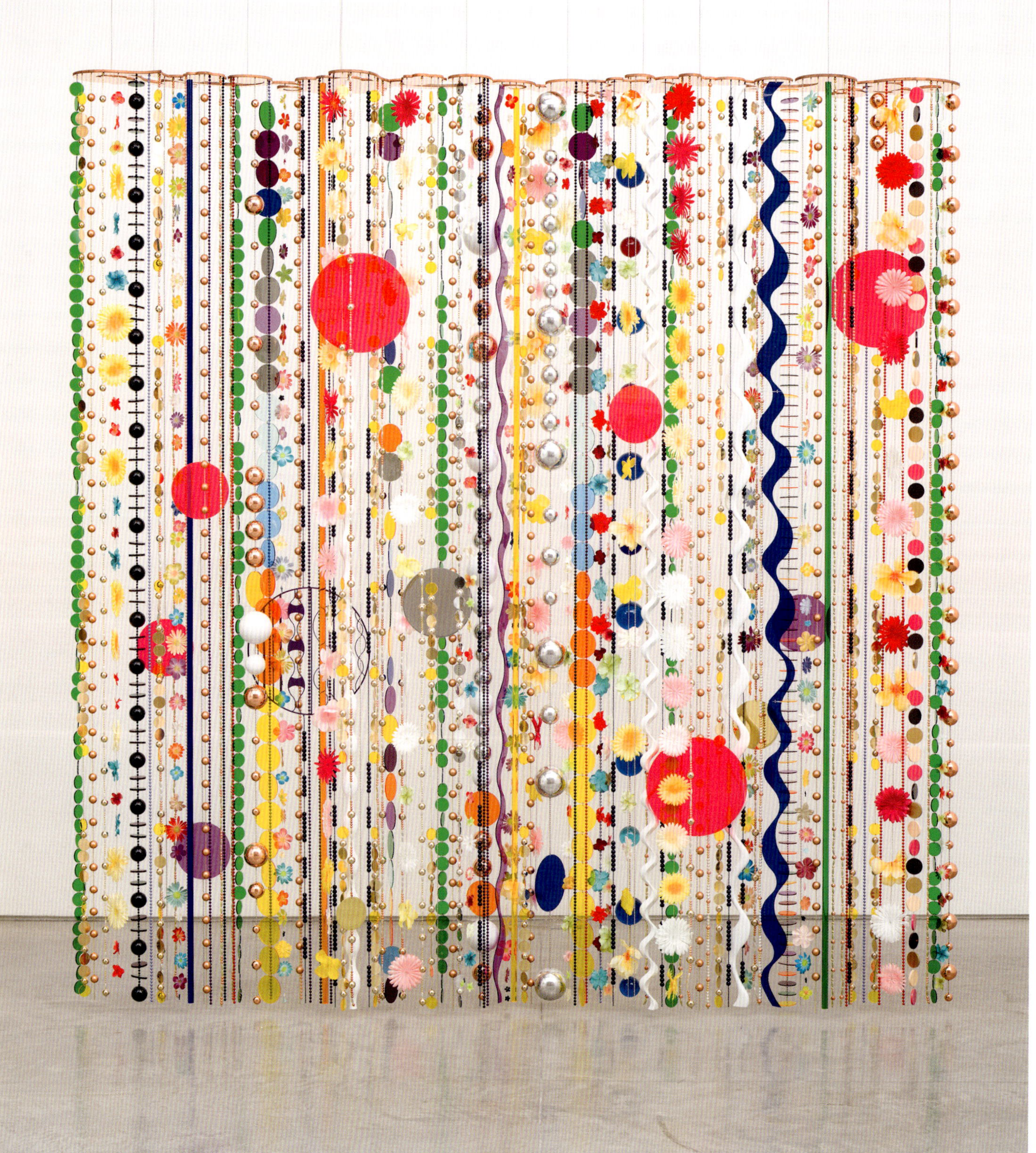

Beatriz Milhazes

O Esplendor 2023

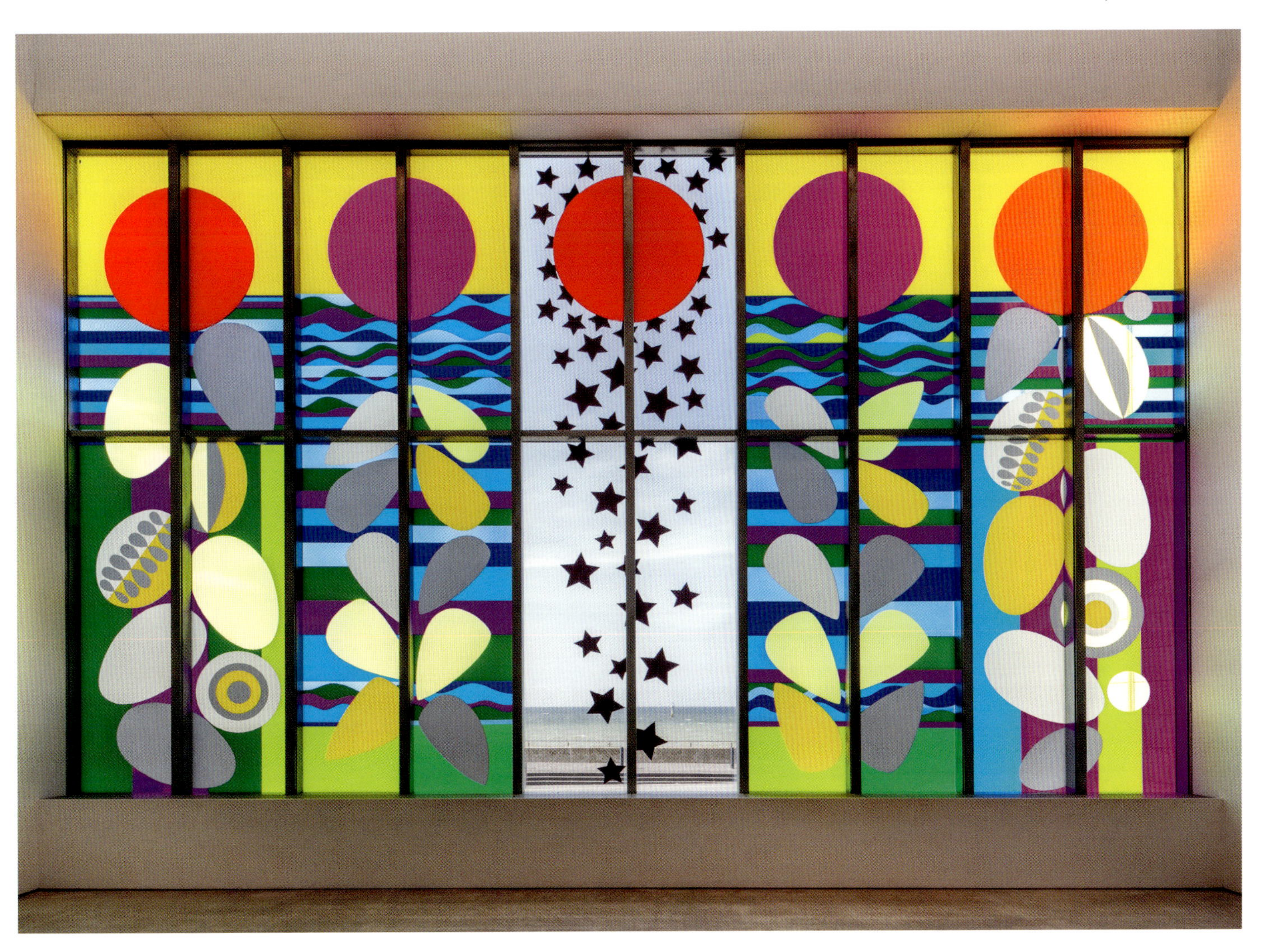

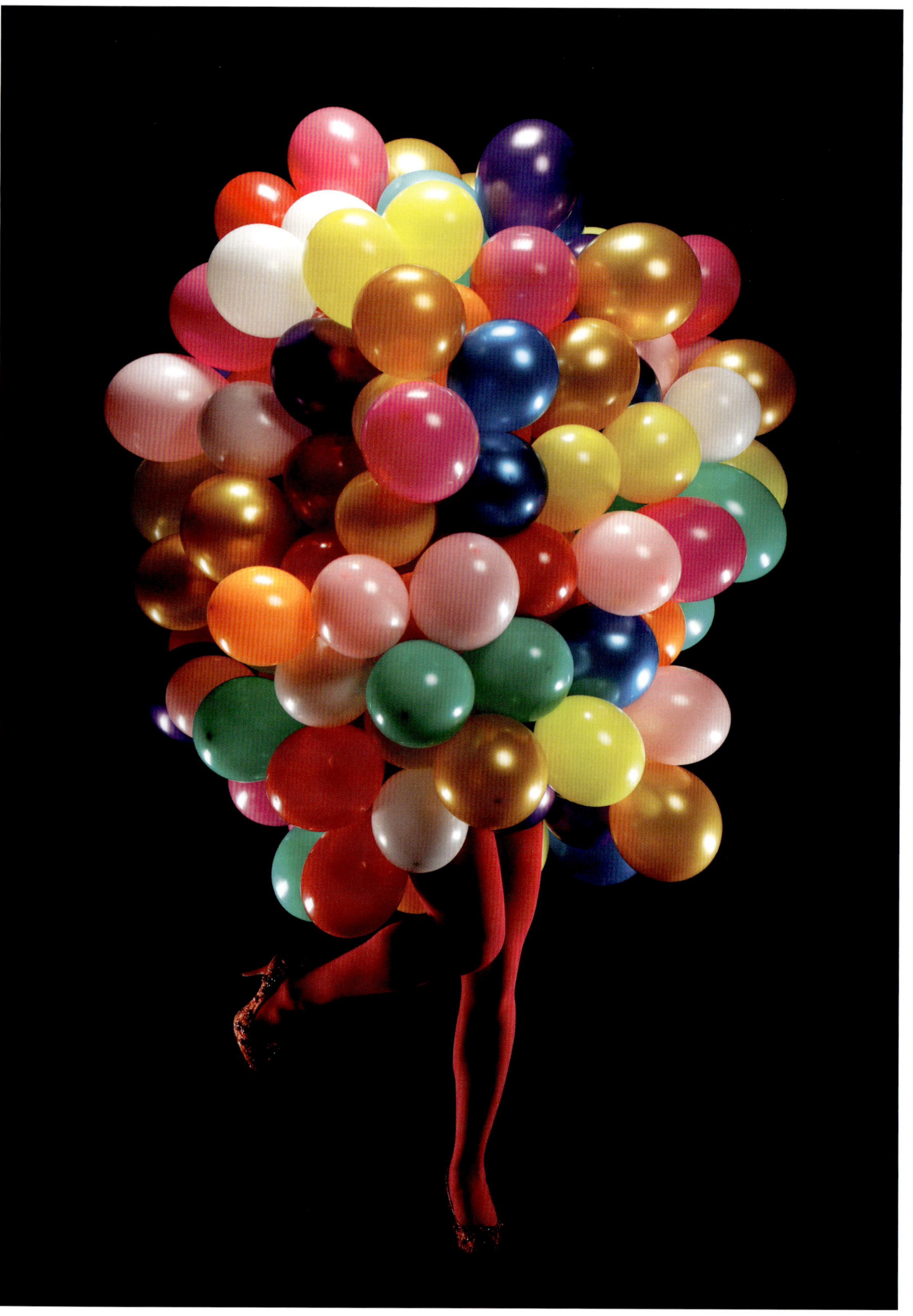

Athi-Patra Ruga

Thud of a Snowflake (detail) 2013

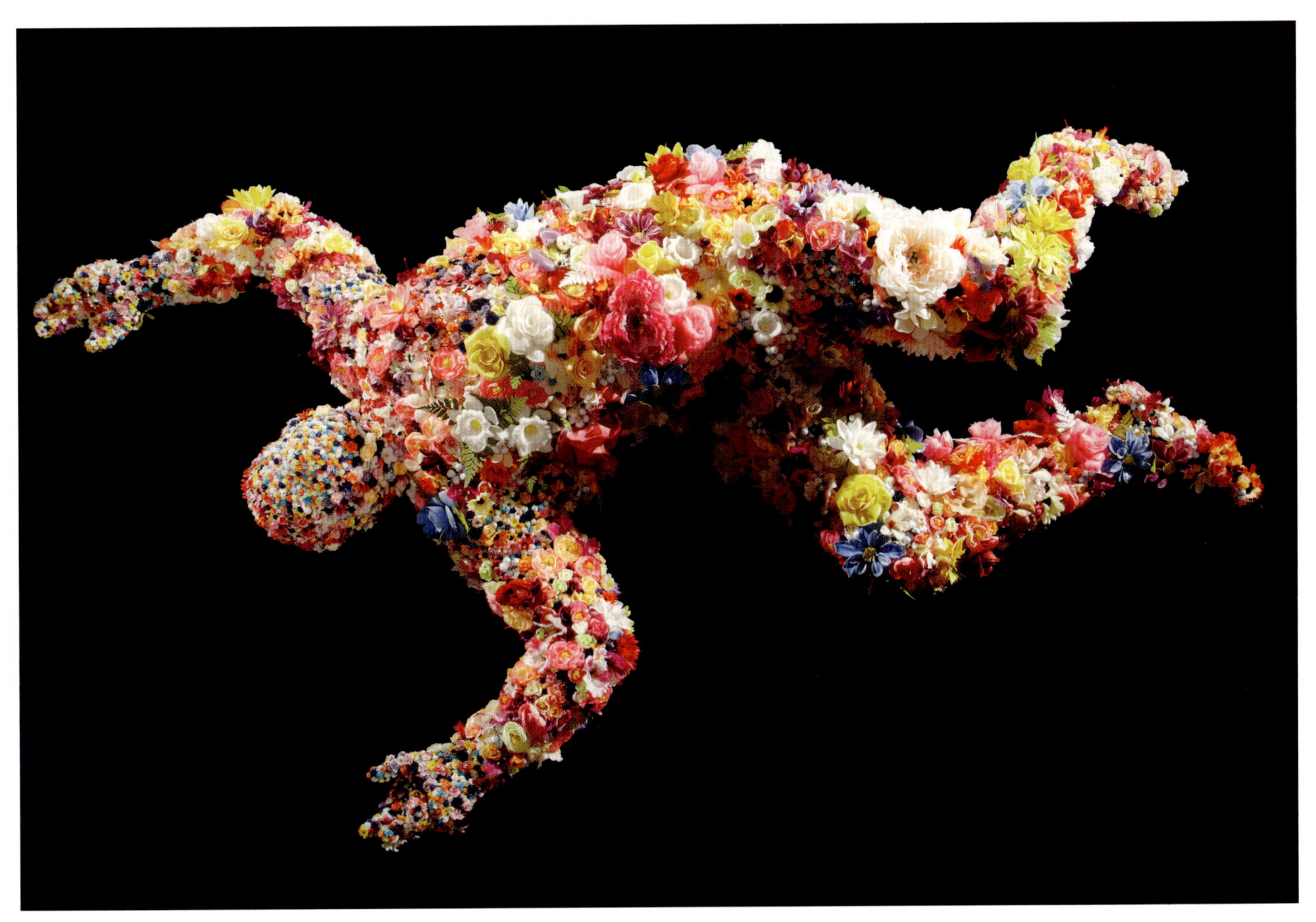

Fred Tomaselli

March 16, 2020   2020

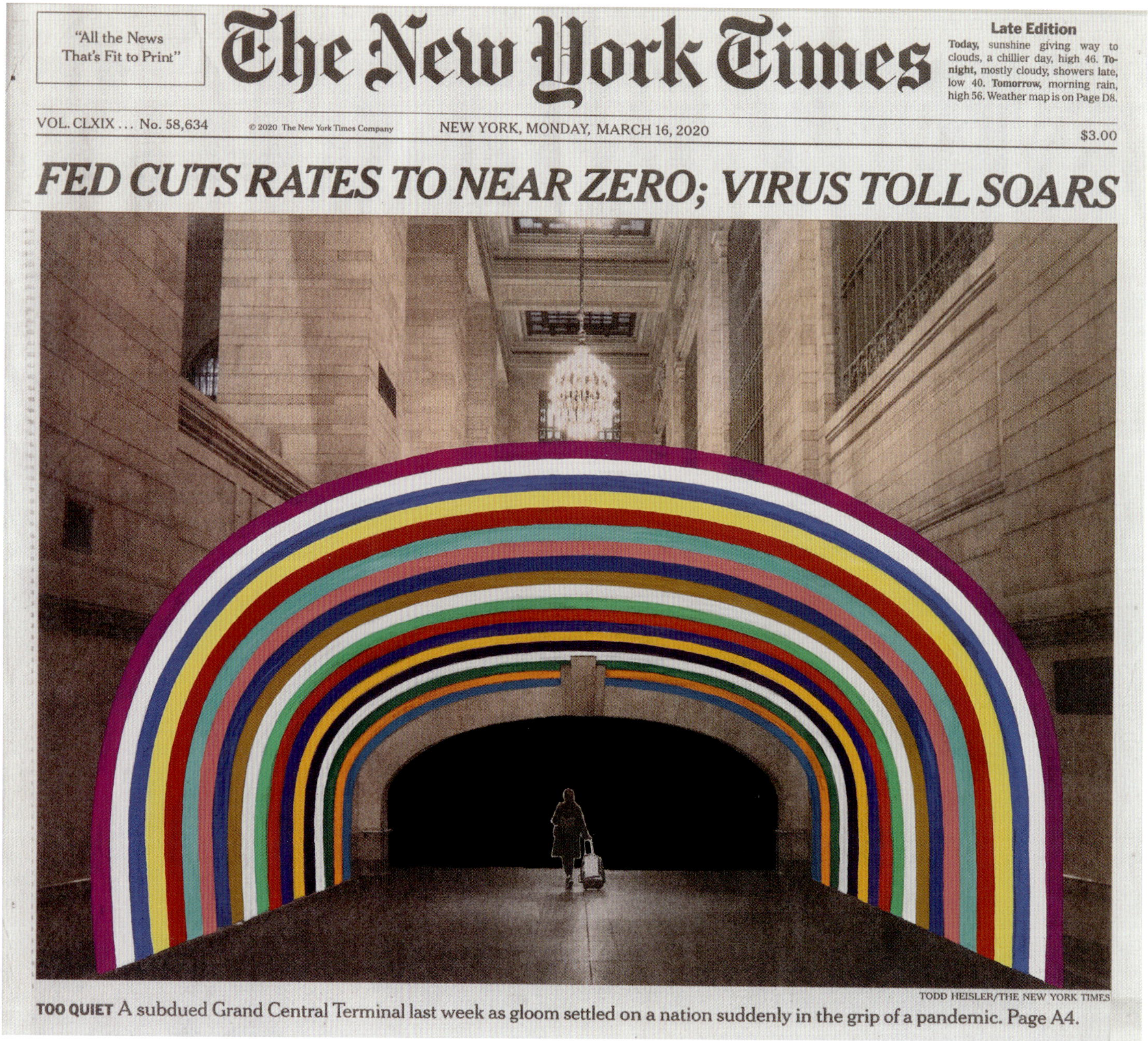

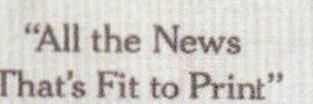

The New York Times front page, March 16, 2020.

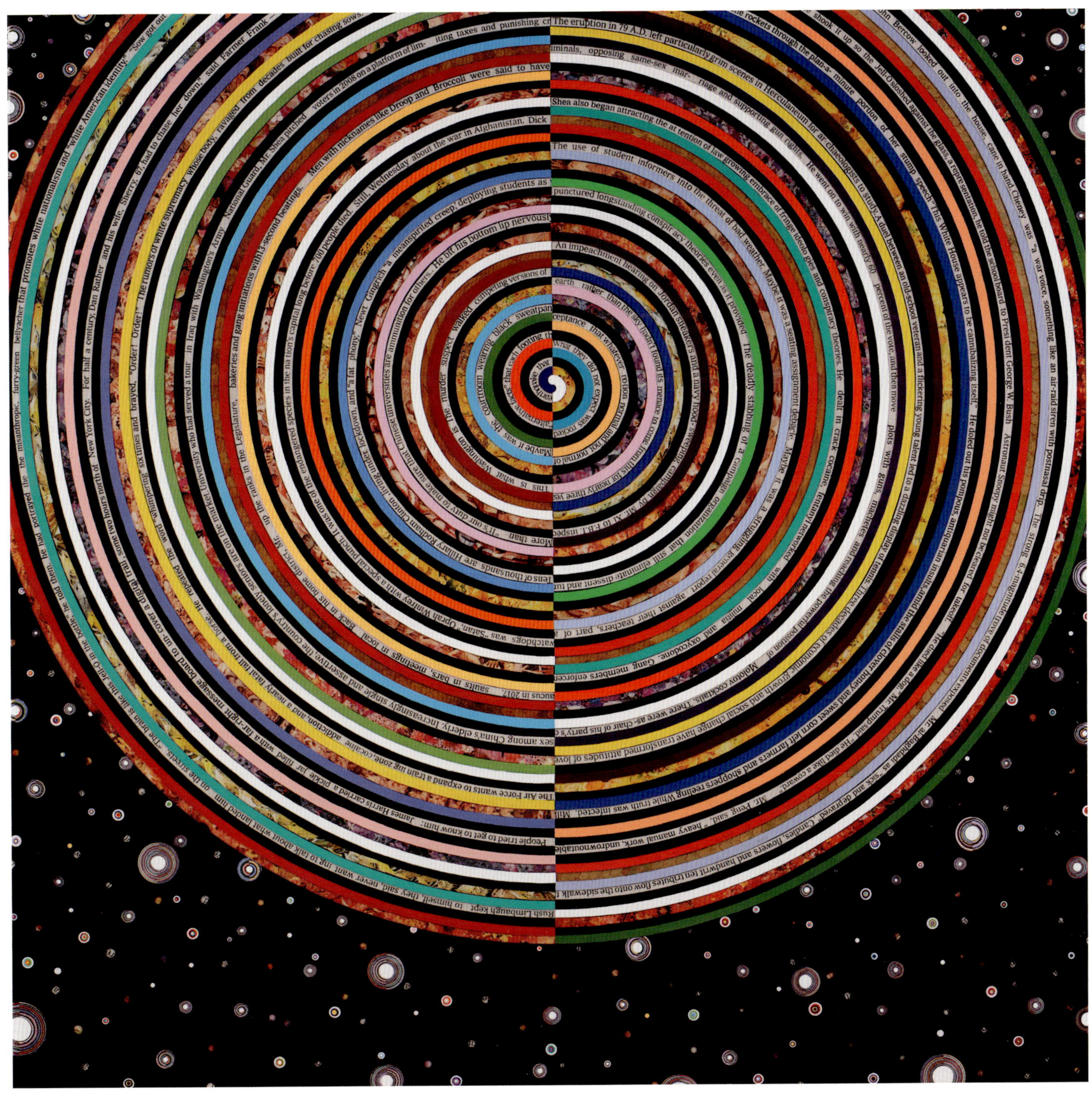

Untitled 2020

Astrid Krogh

ORNAMENT 2003

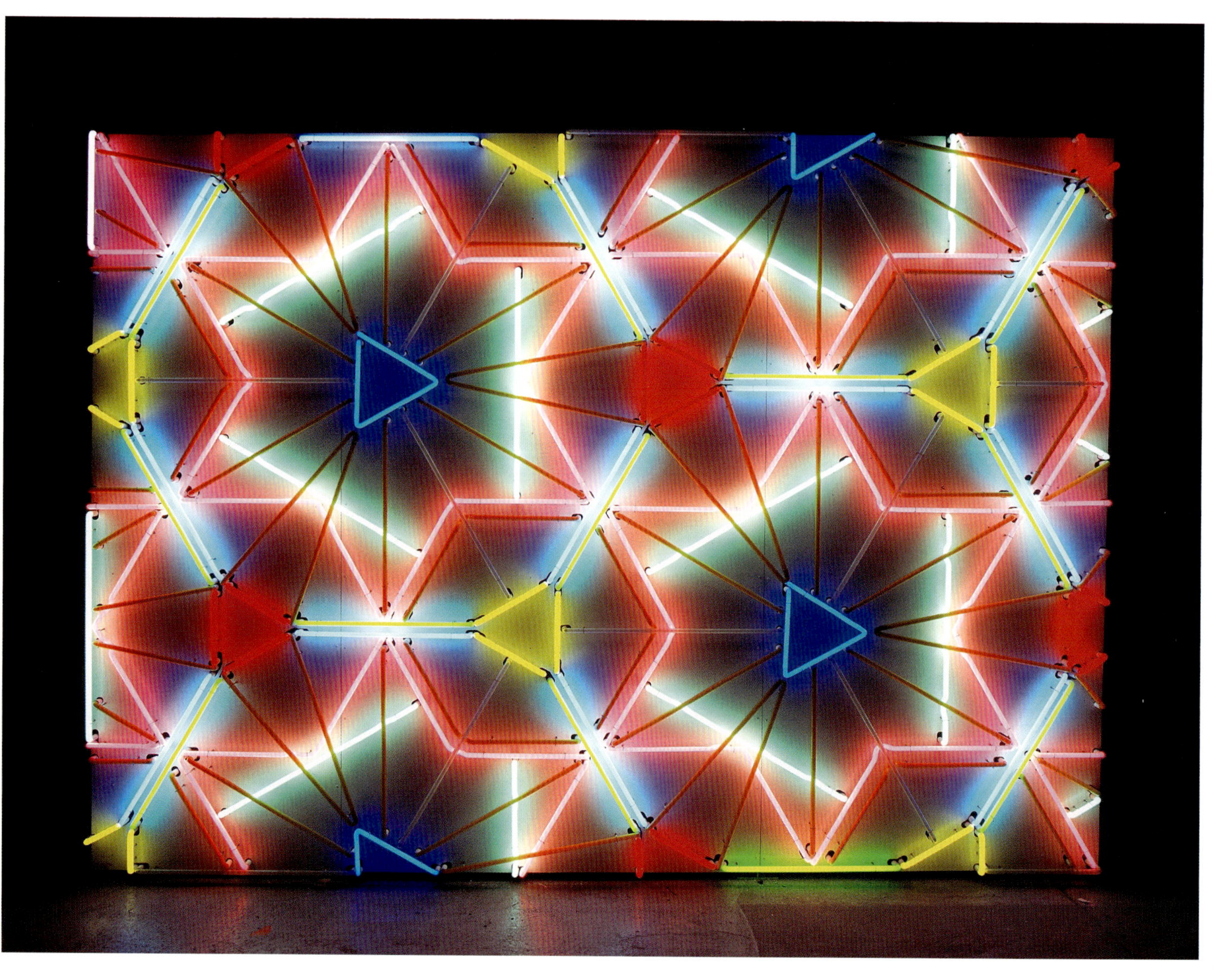

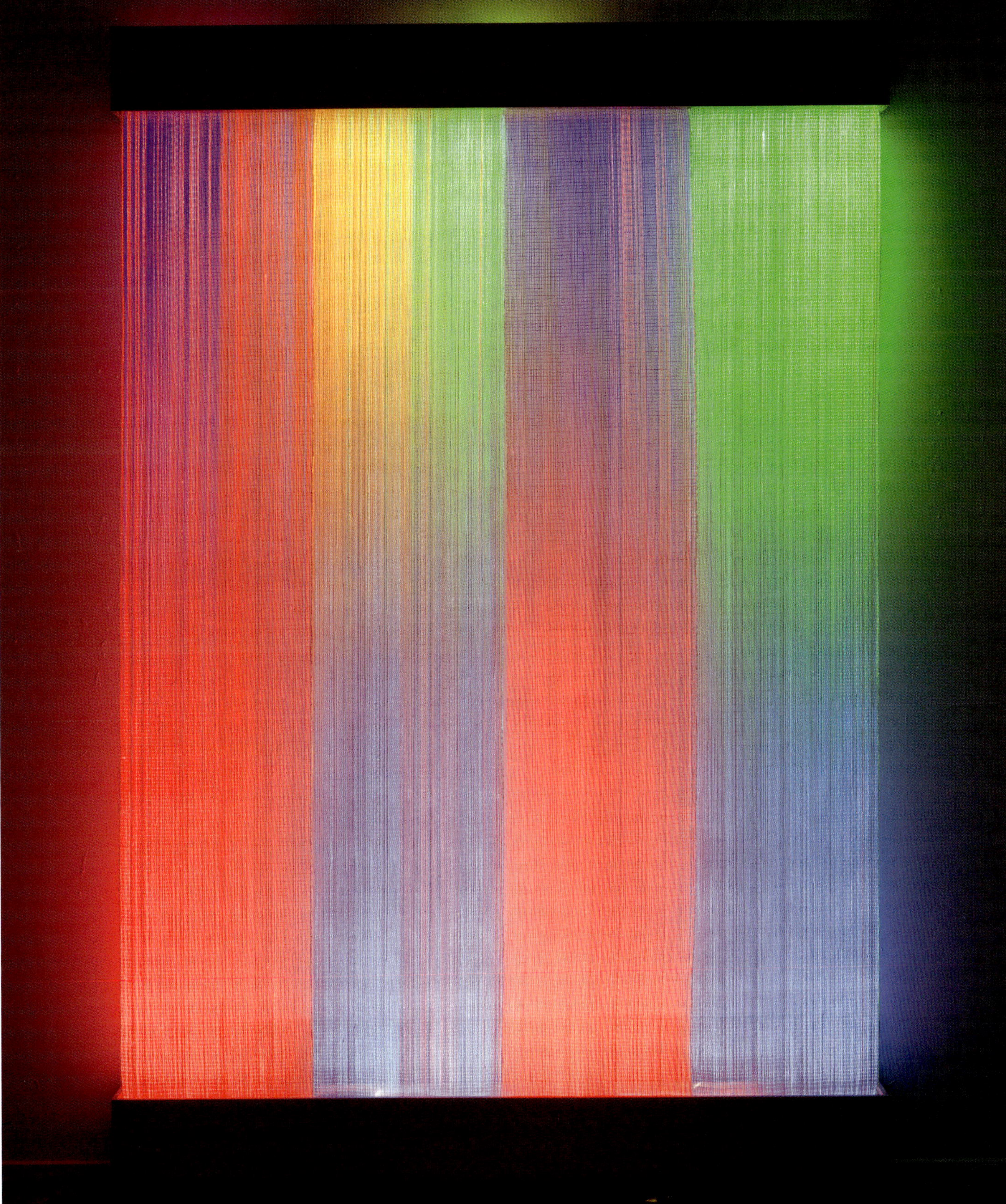

Liz West

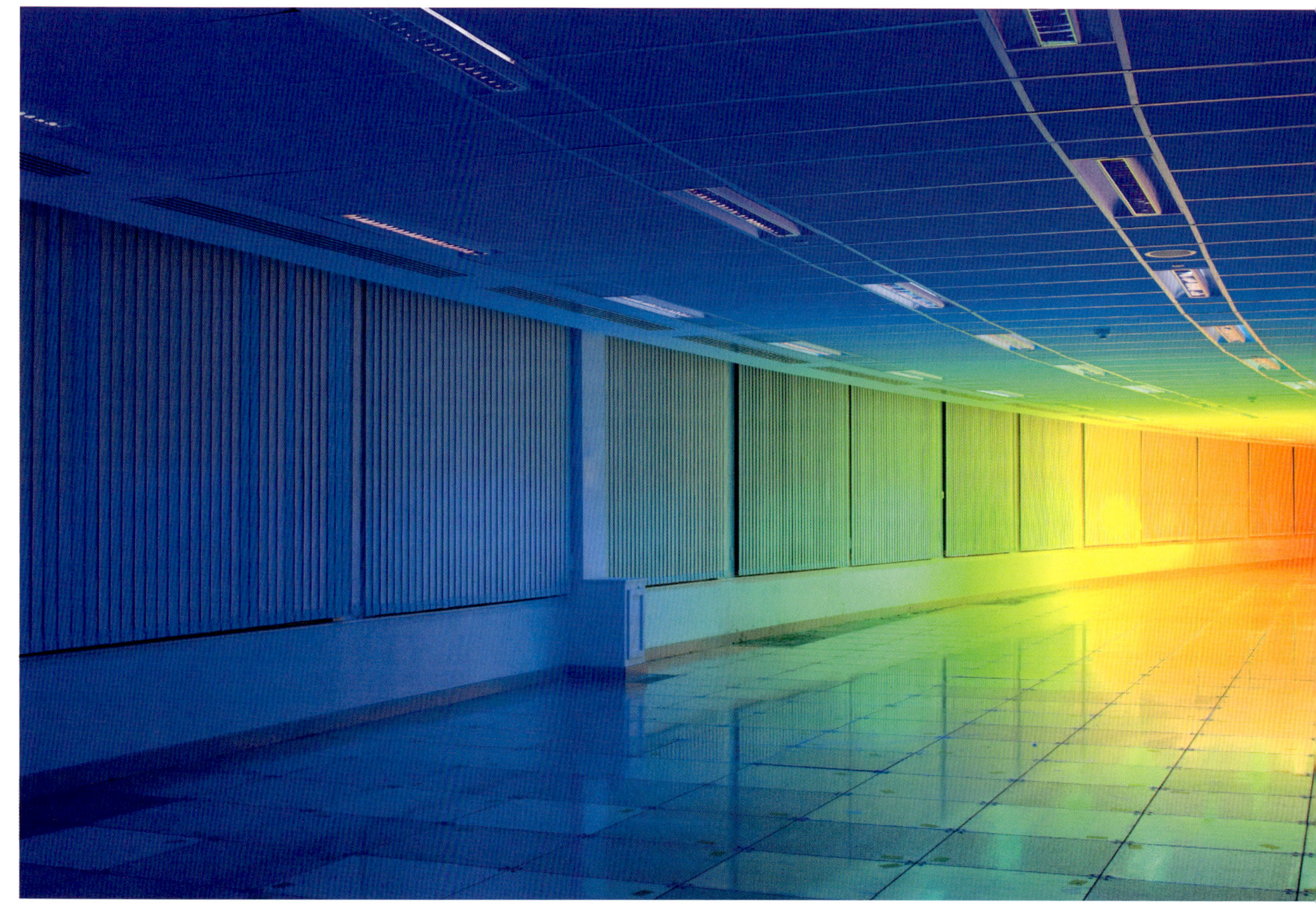

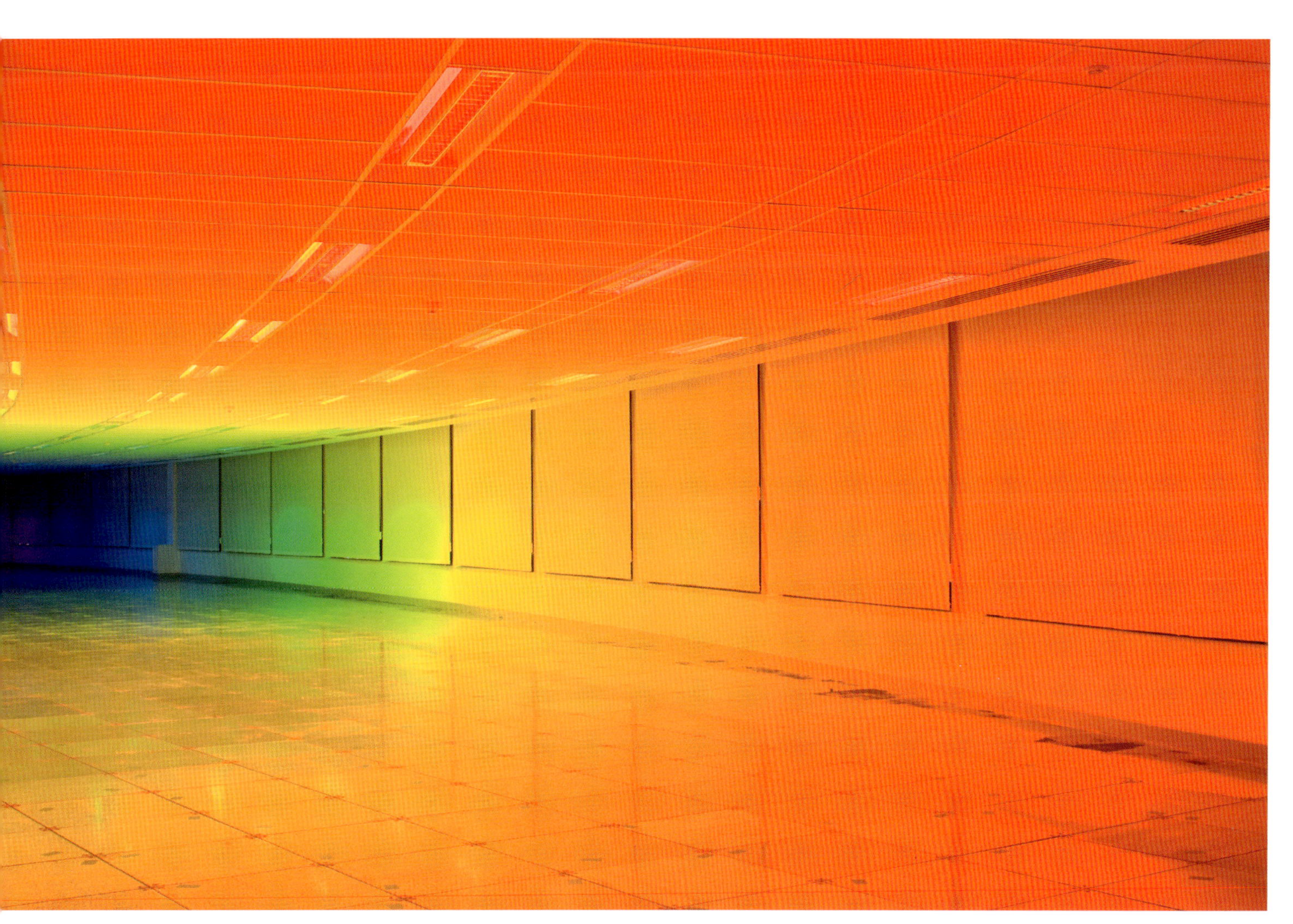

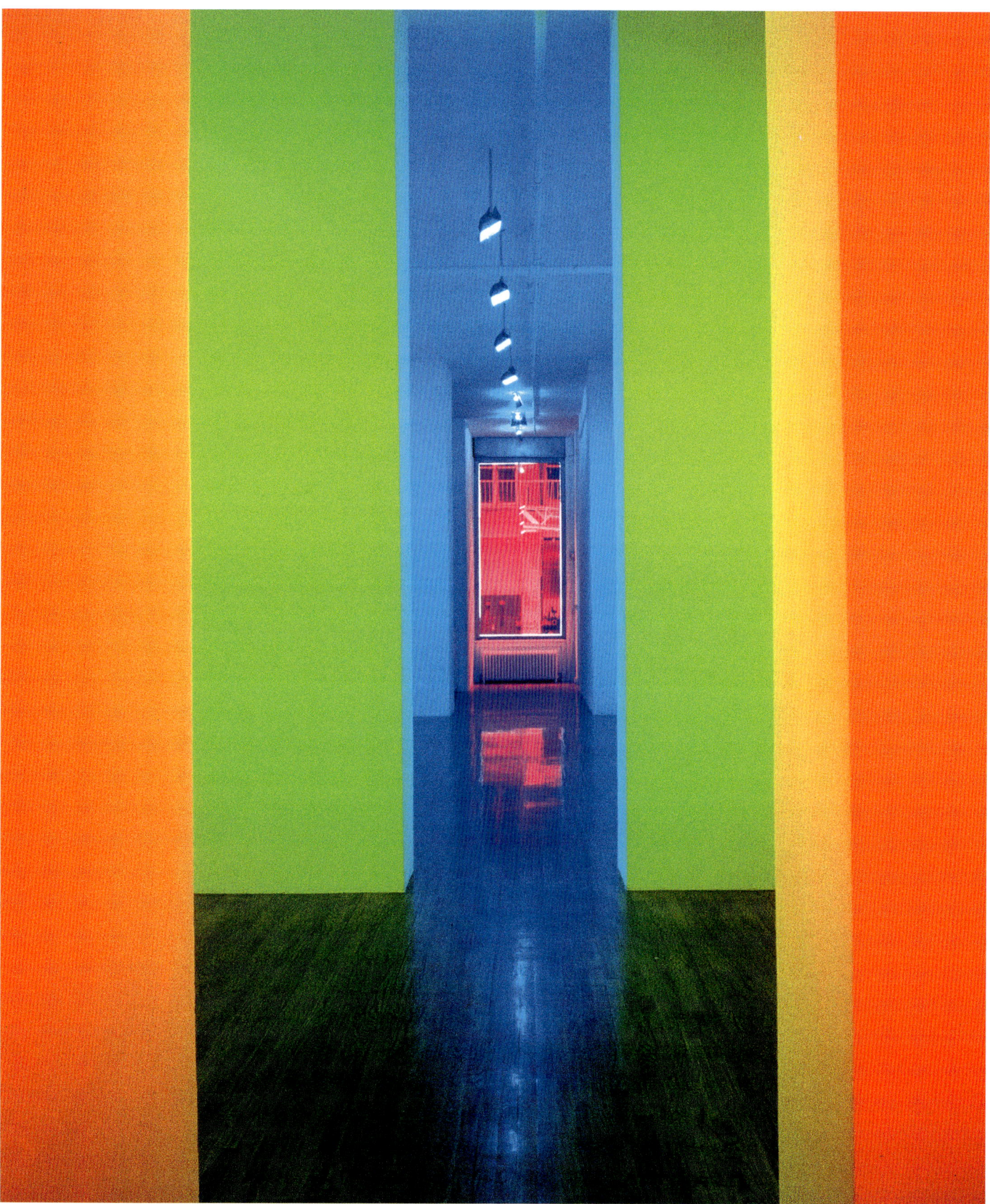

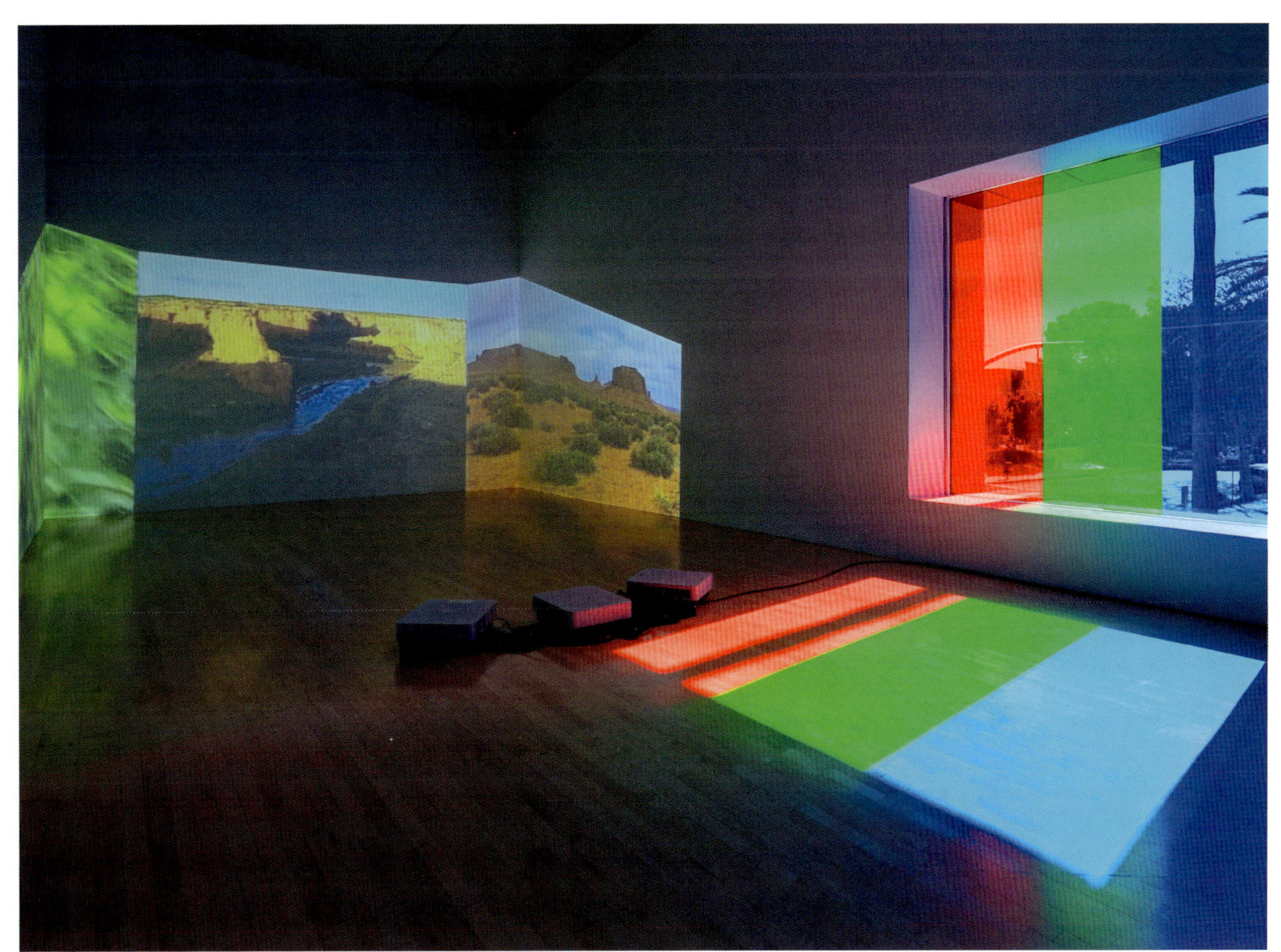

Abyss of Light   1993

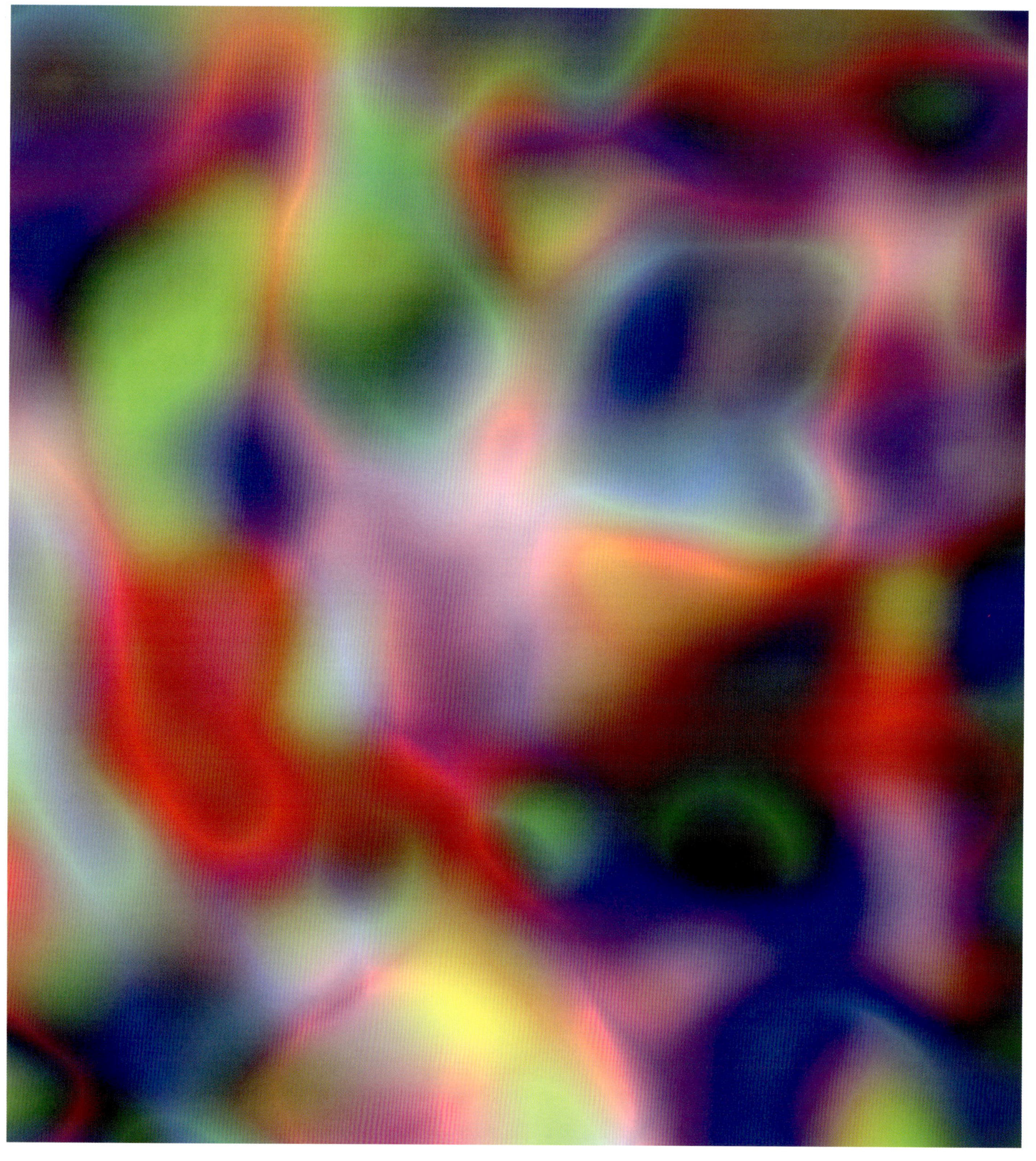

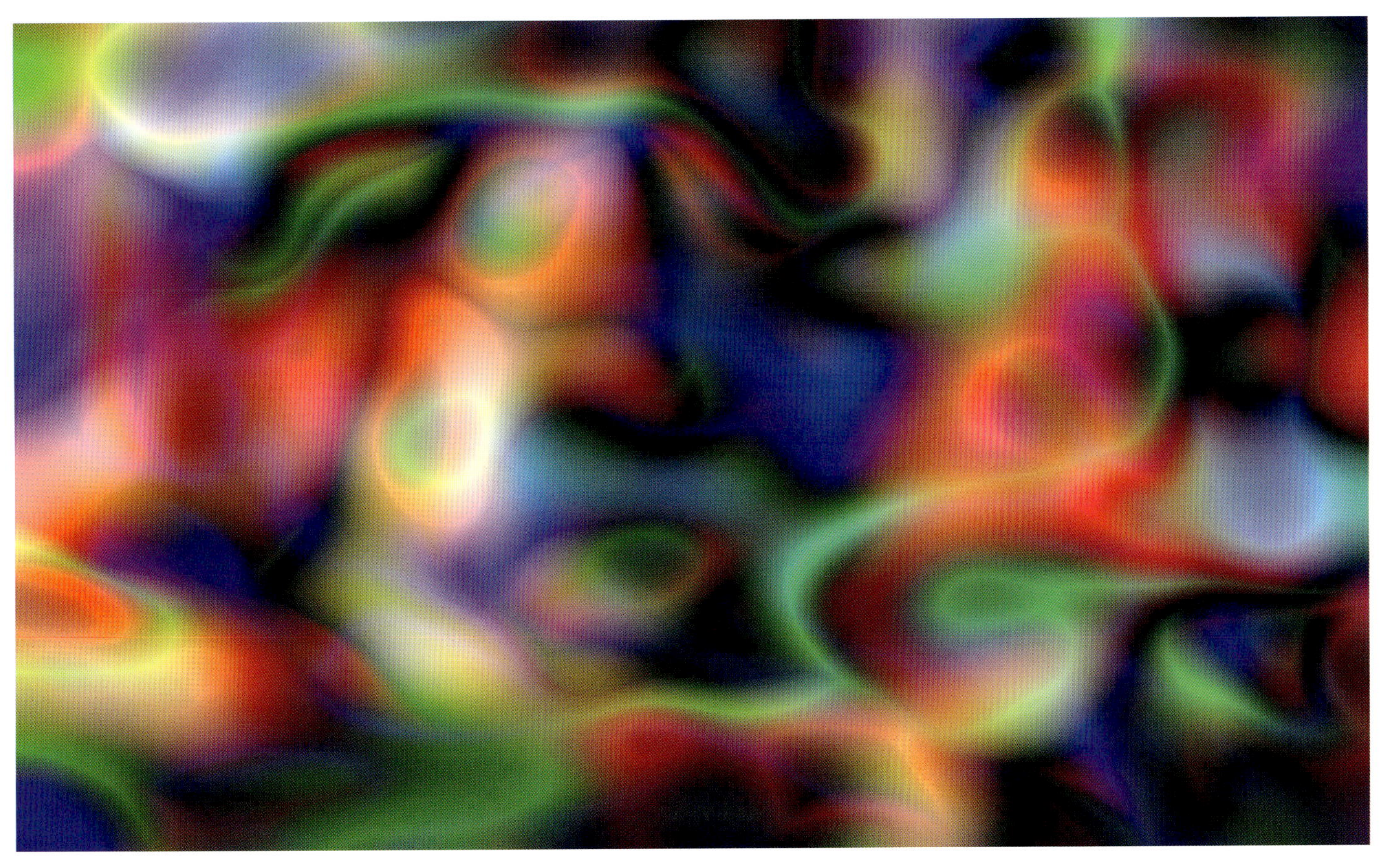

James Clar

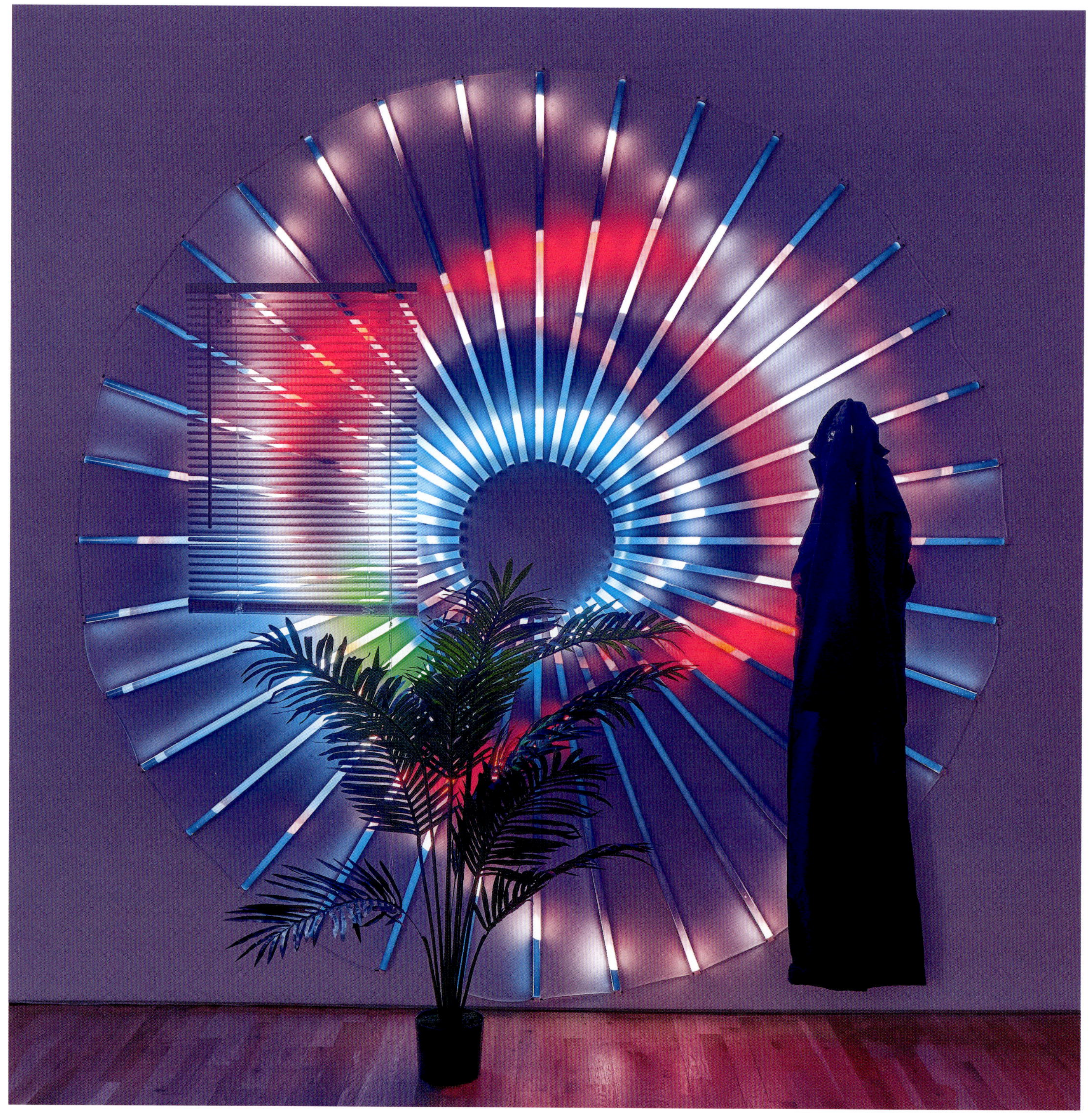

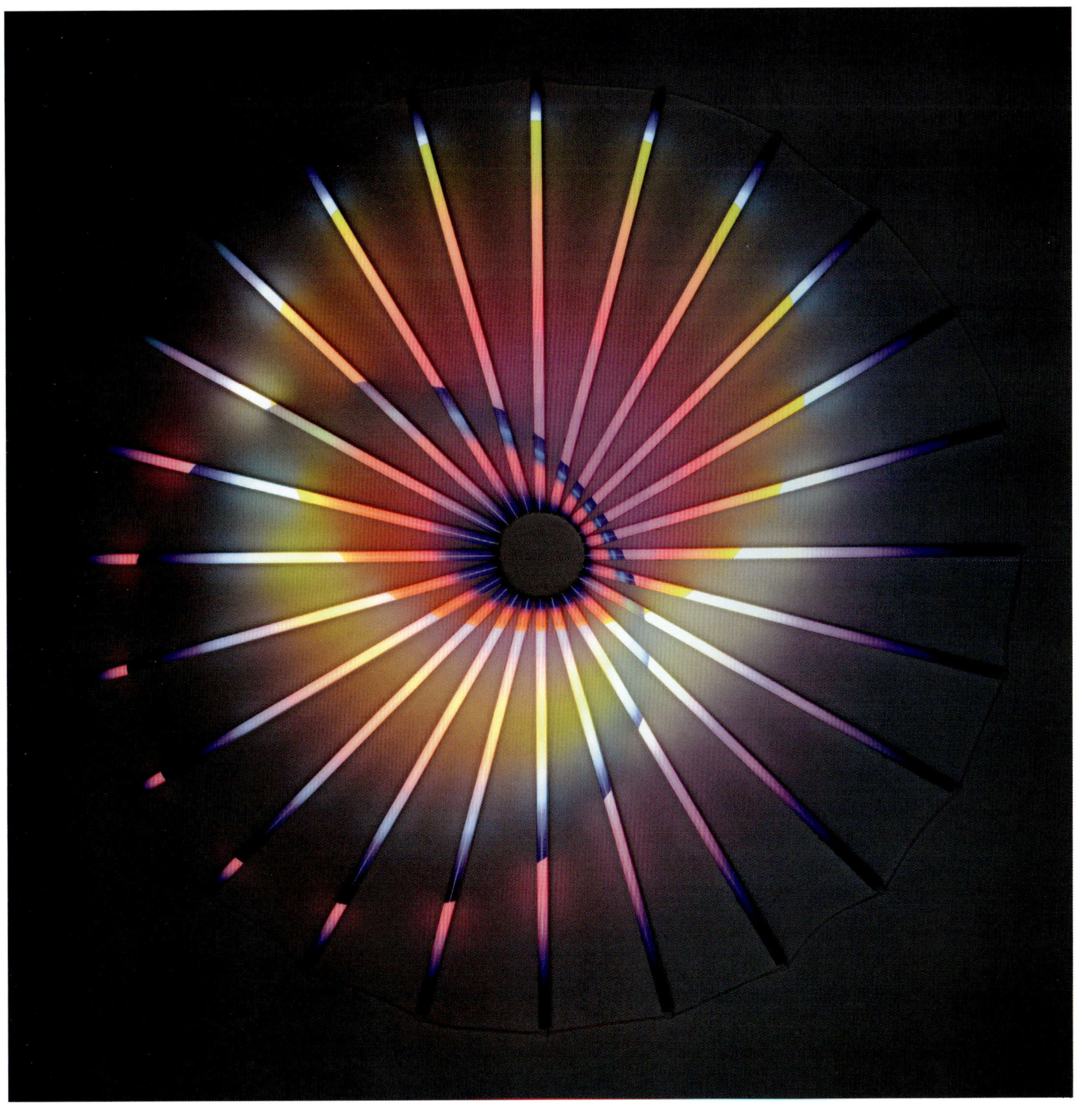

Binary Star 2016

Ann Veronica Janssens

yellowbluepink 2015

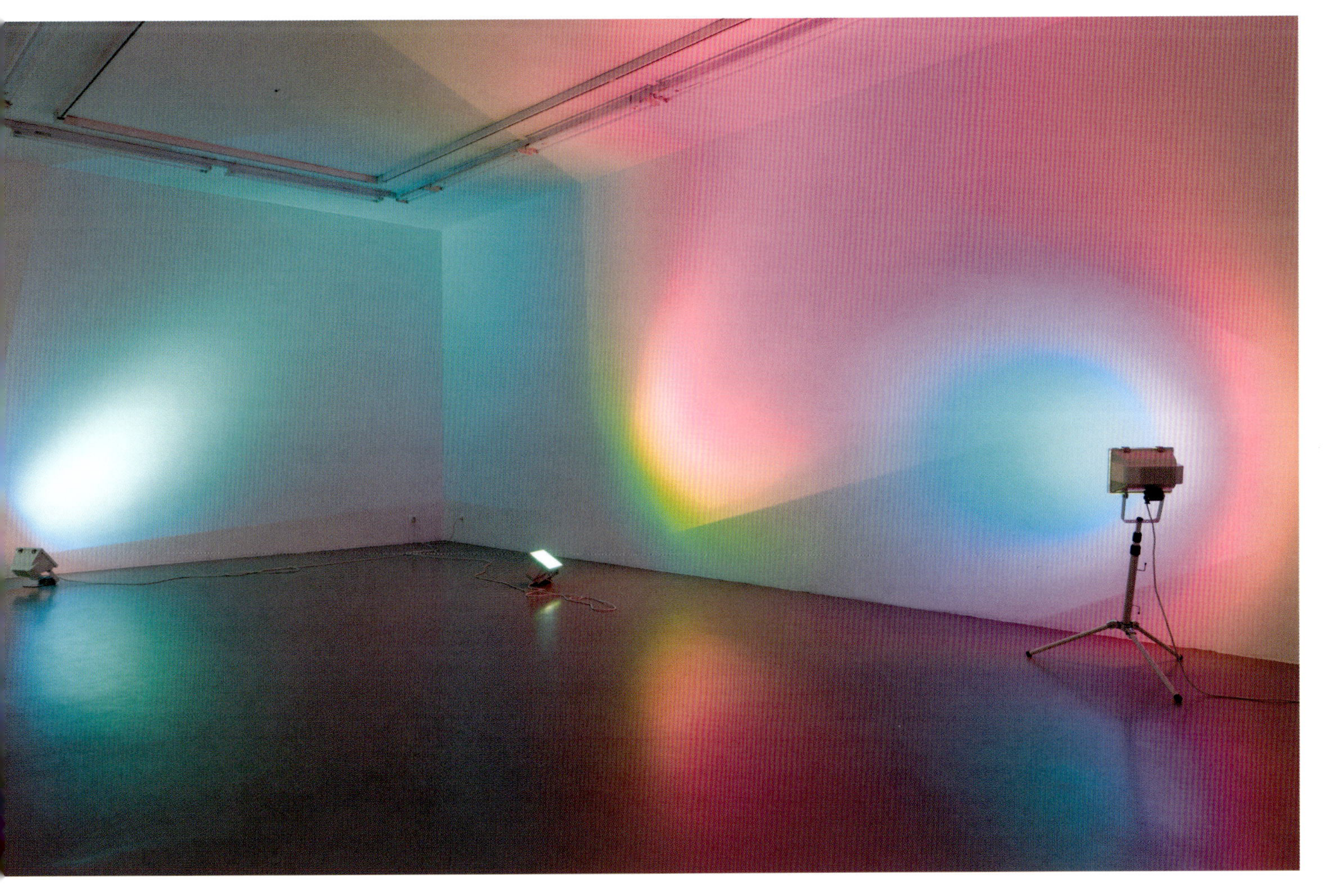

Left: *Peacock Blue*   2017
Right: *Hot Pink Turquoise*   2006

Taisuke Koyama

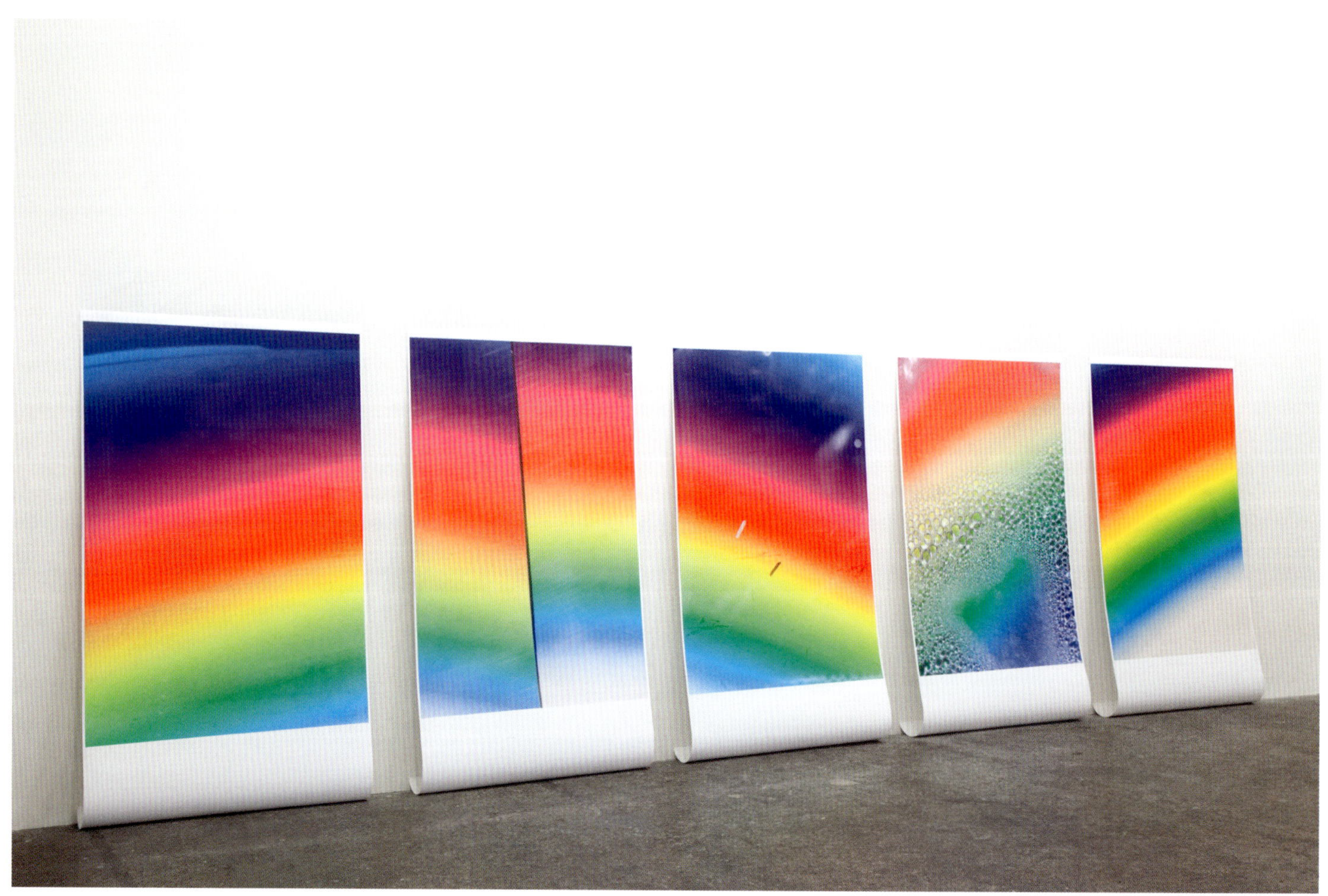

Installation view: *THE EXPOSED #4*   2009

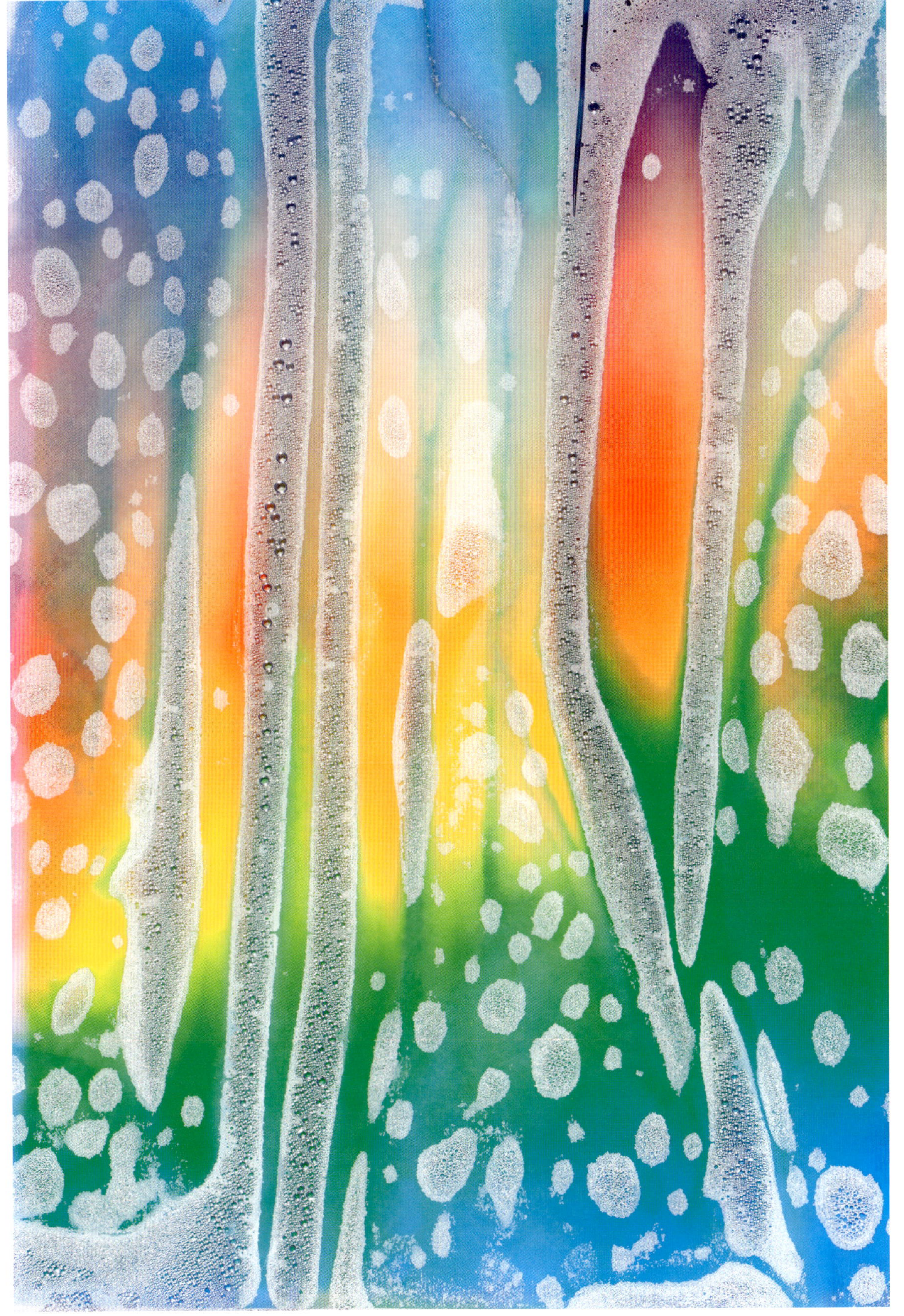

Loie Hollowell

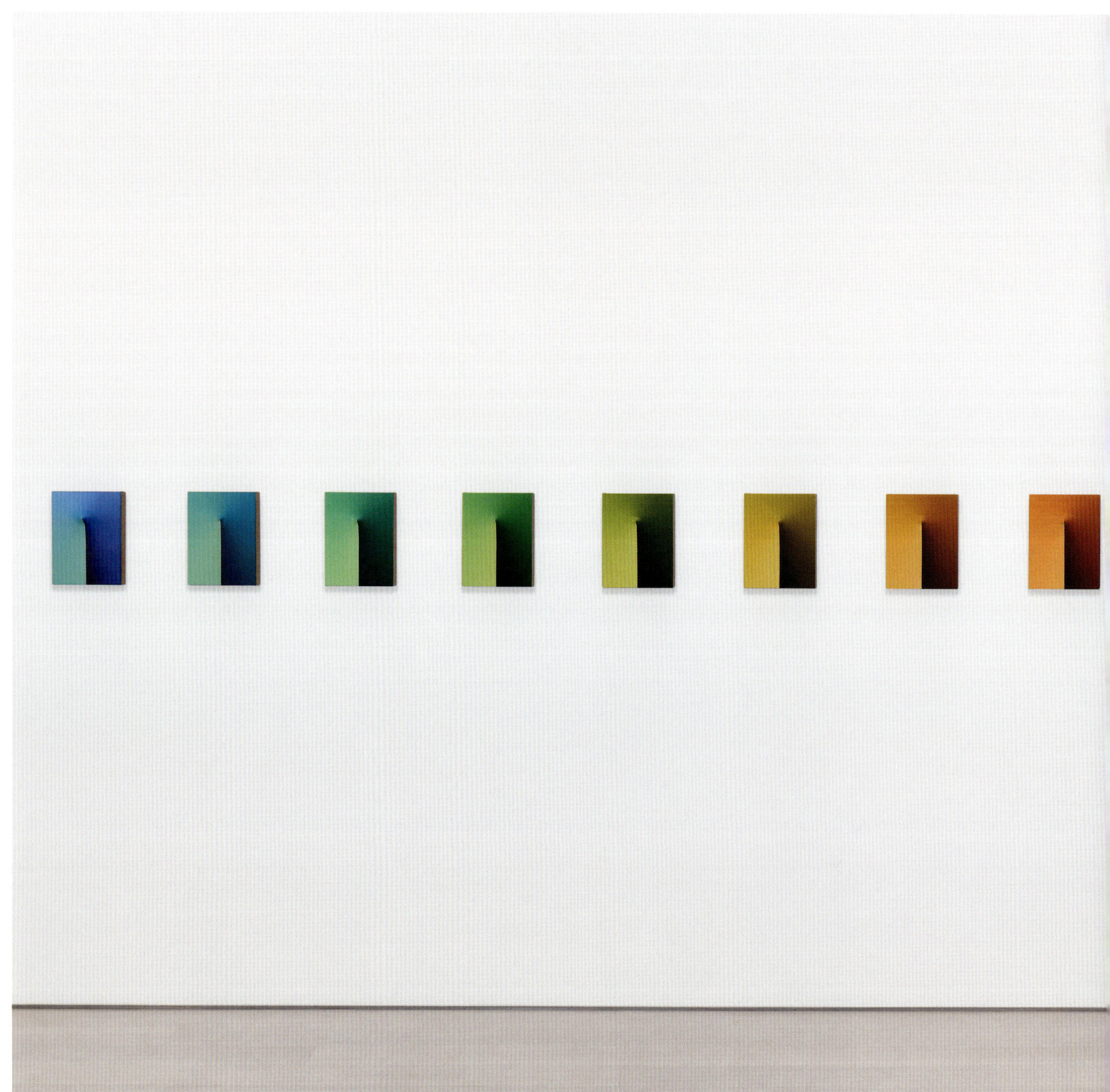

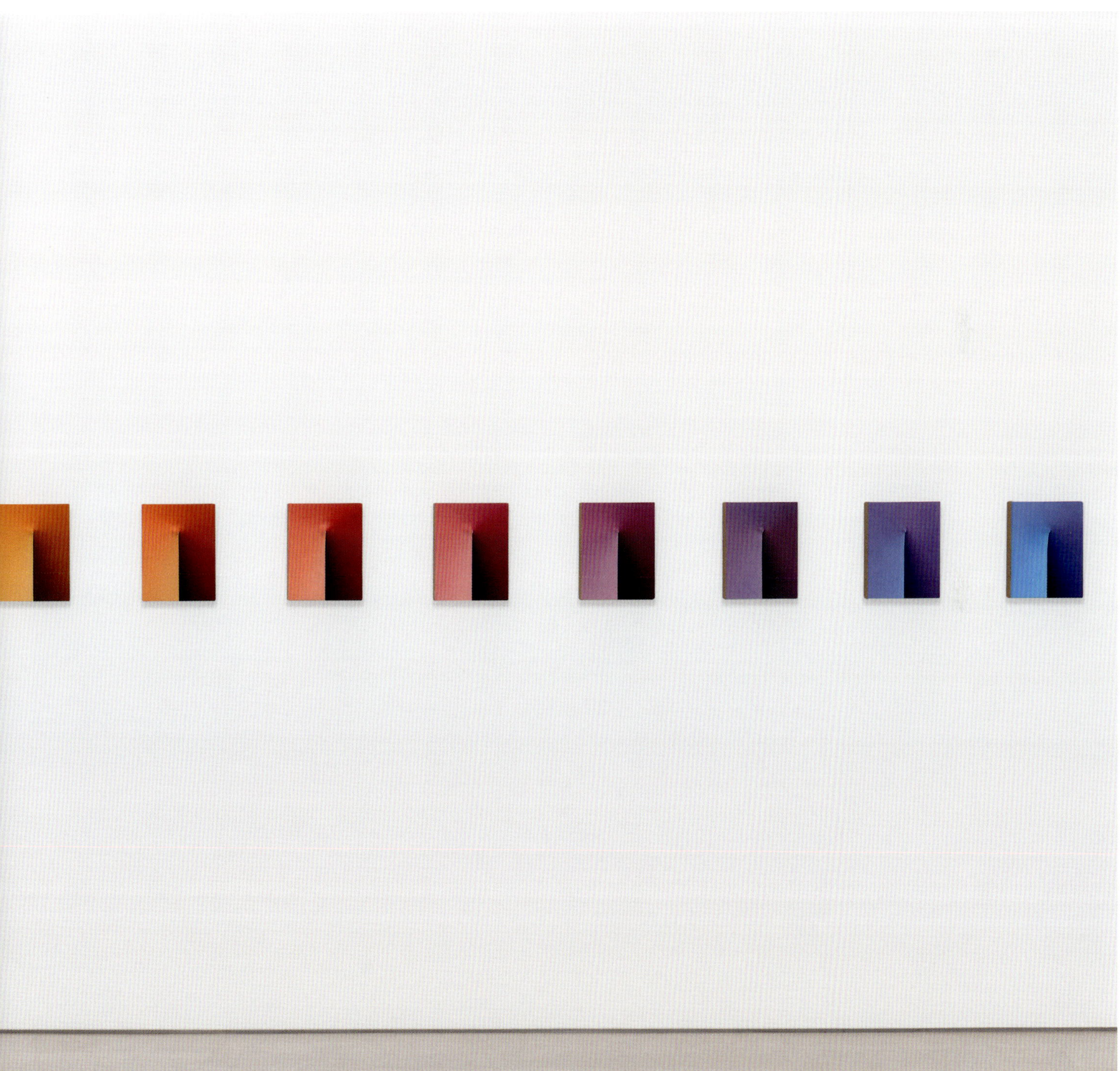

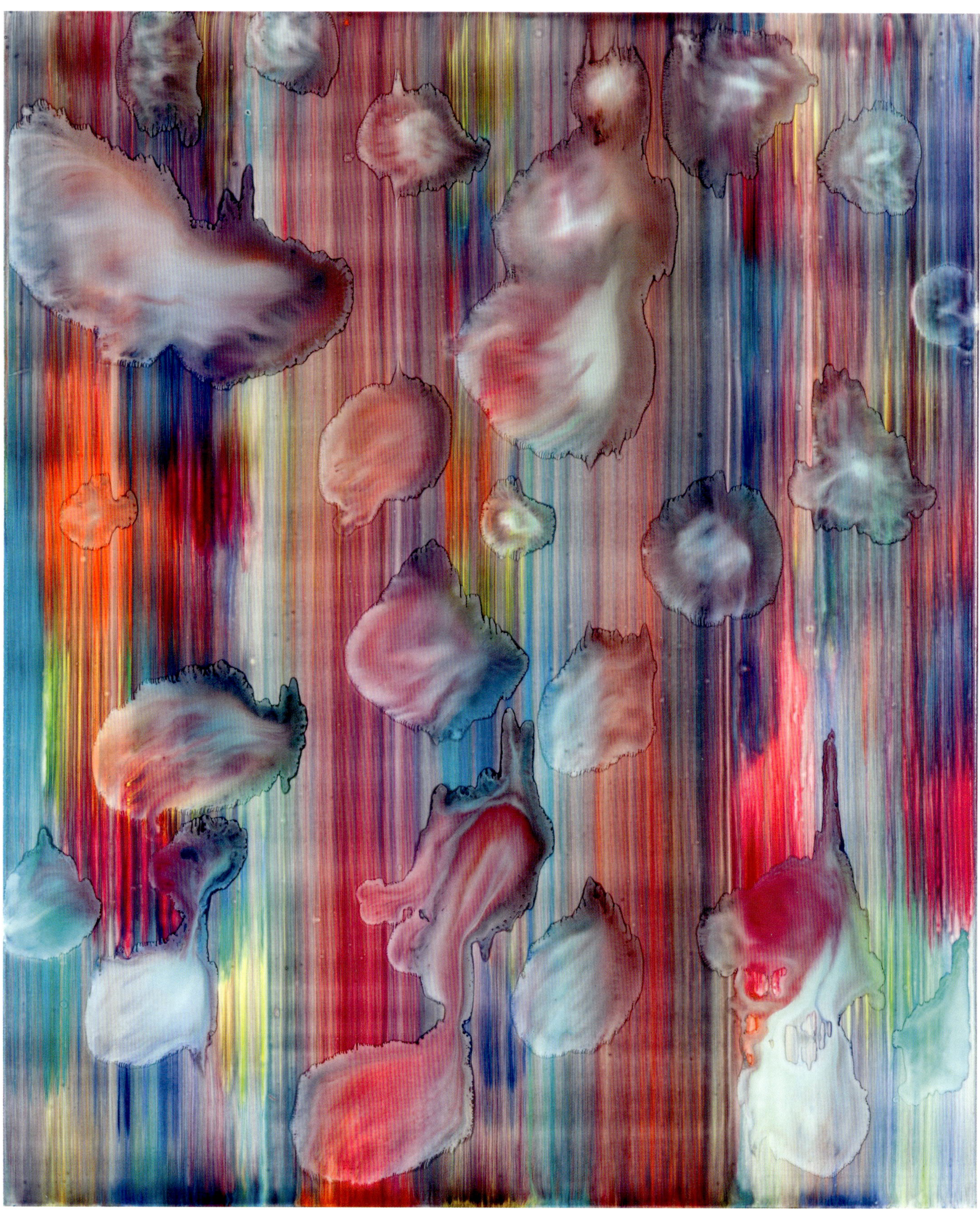

Bernard Frize

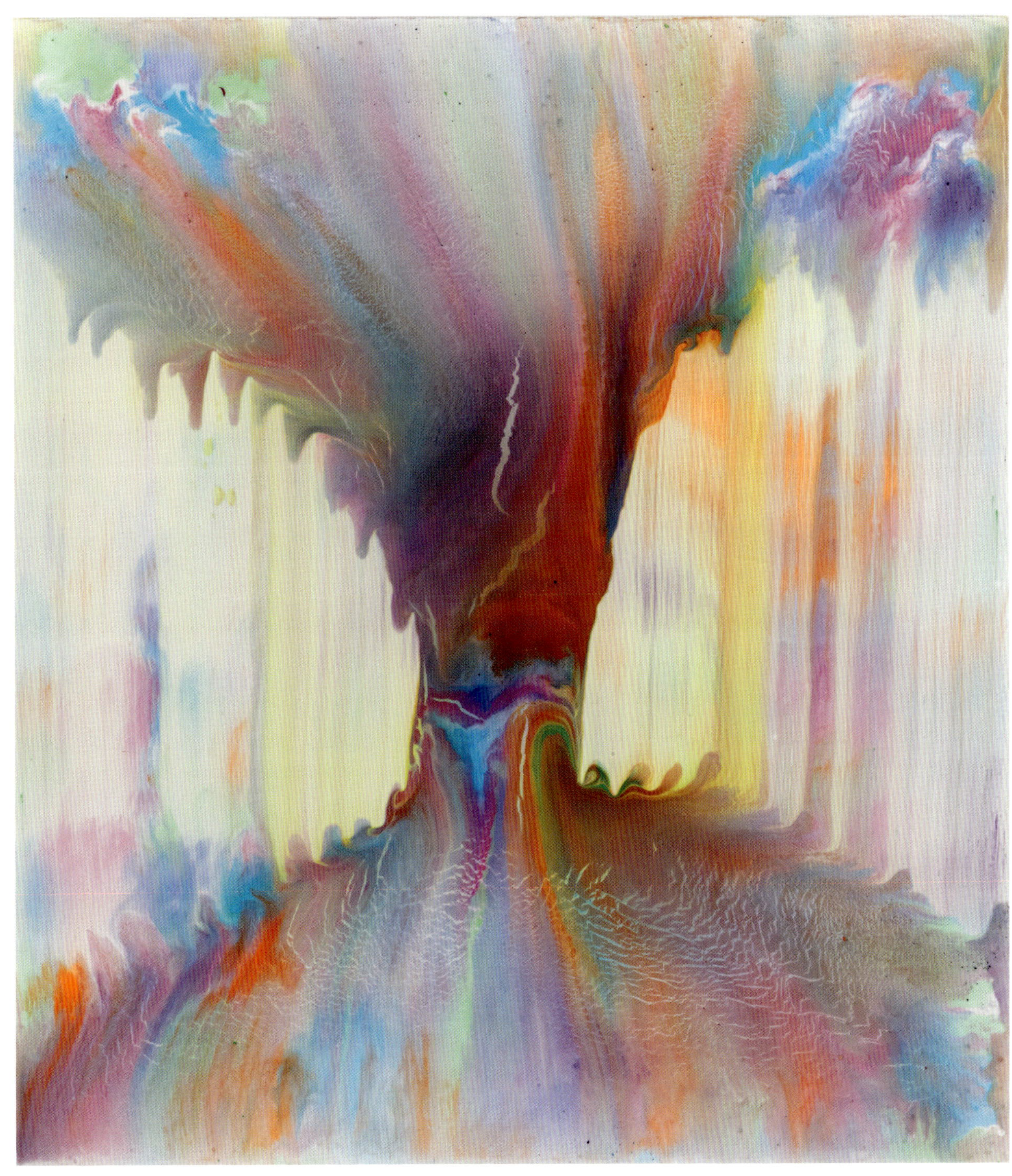

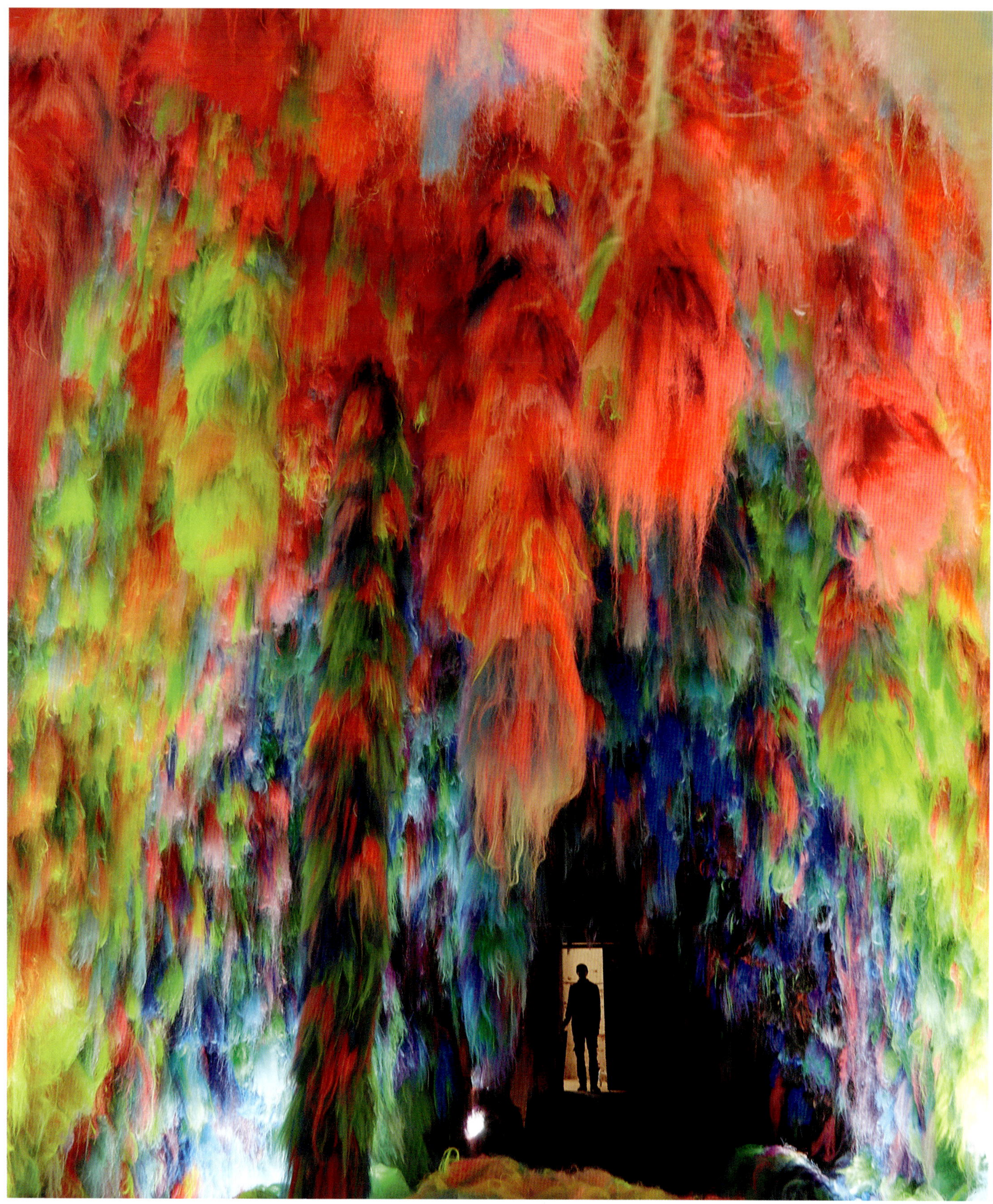

Hyperweb 2023

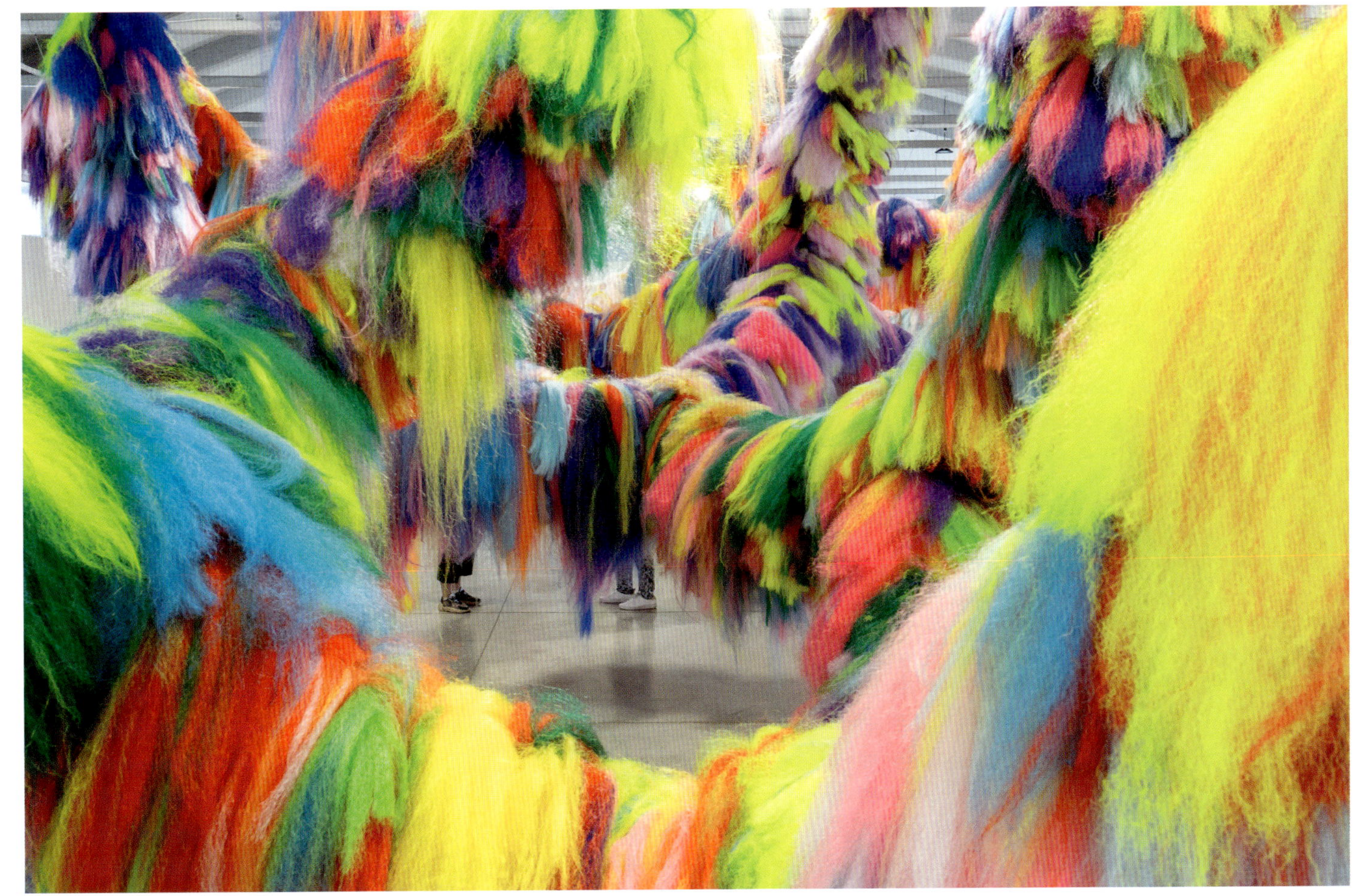

Derrick Adams

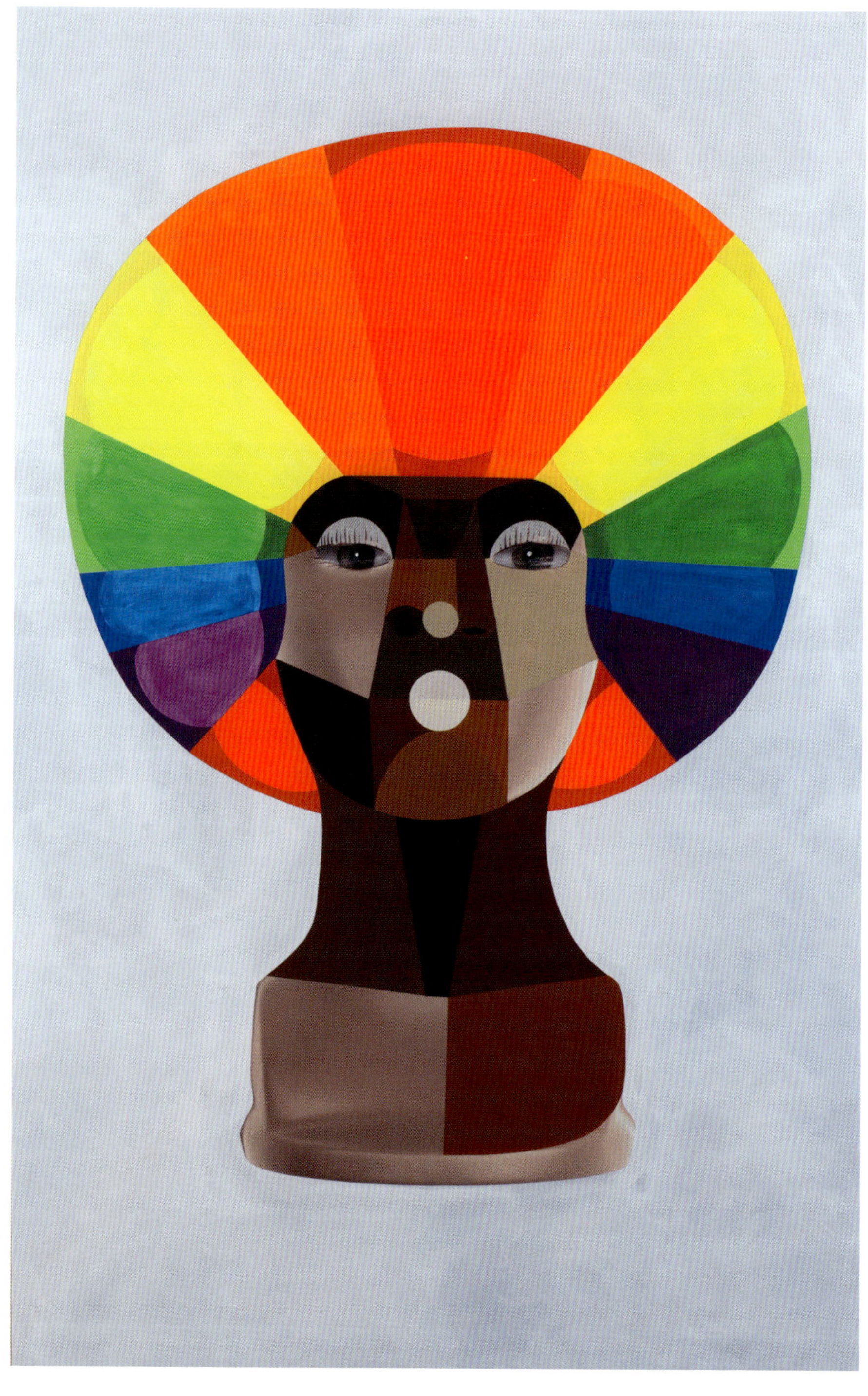

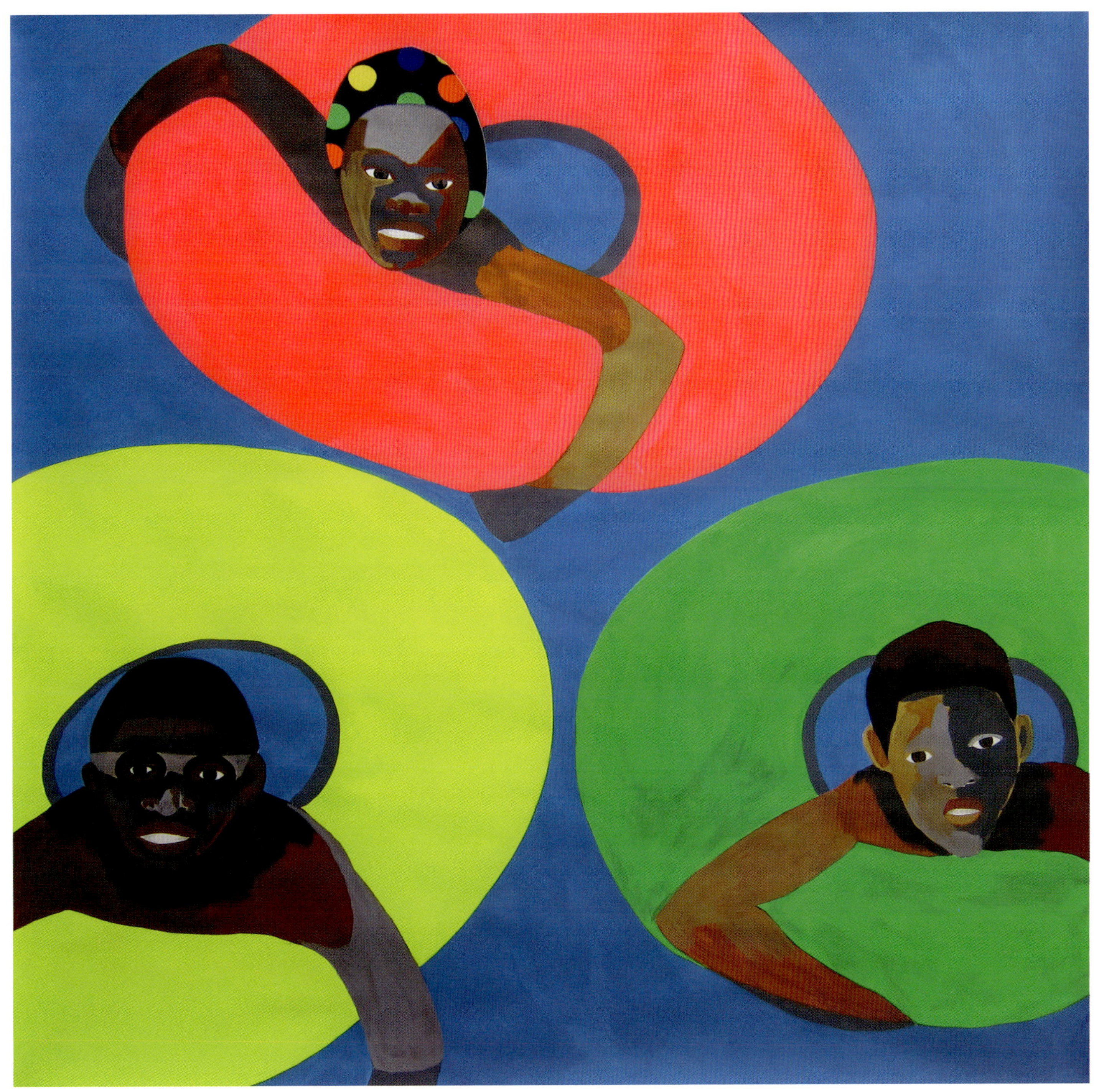

Floater 15   2016

Daniel Buren

Catch as catch can   2014

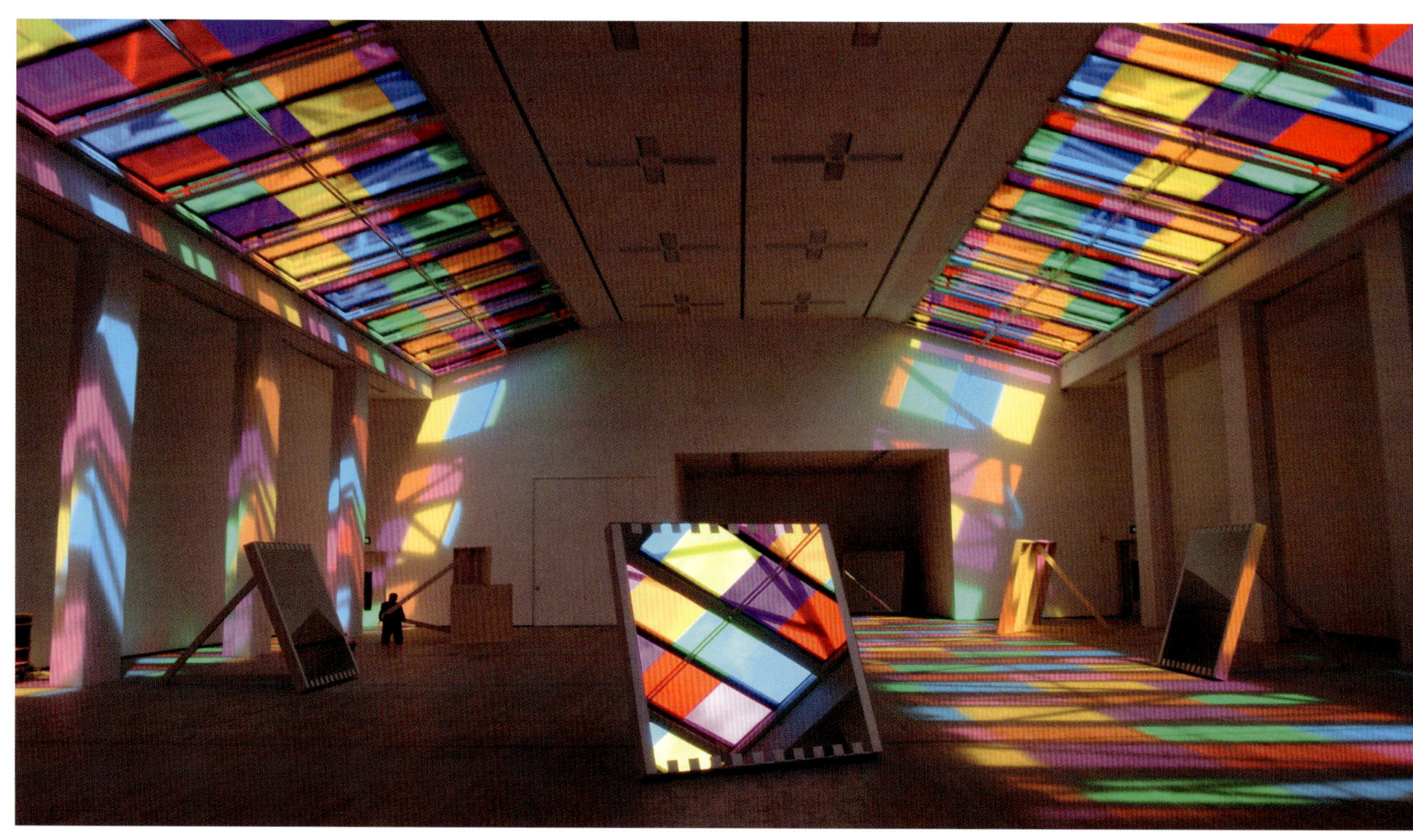

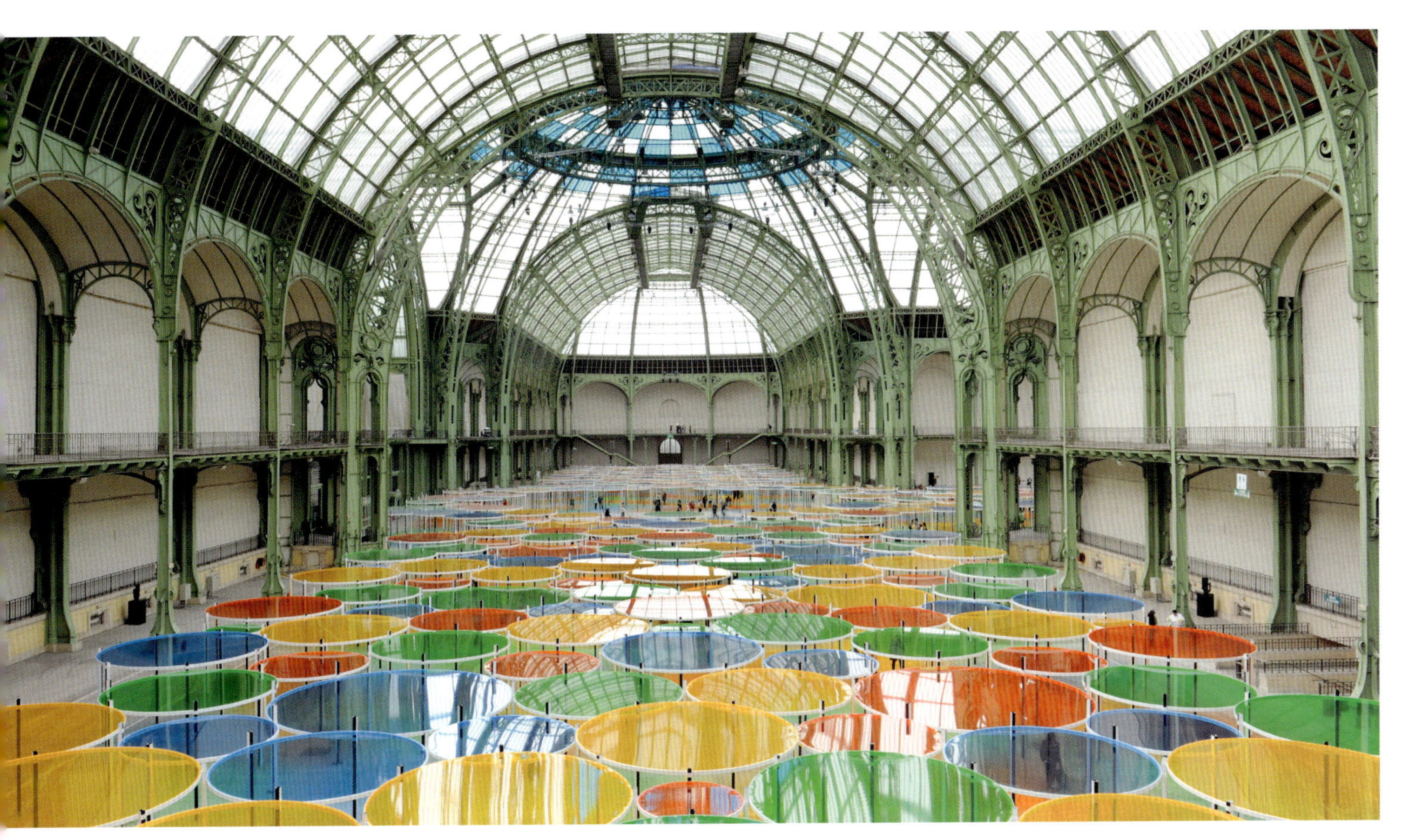

Excentrique(s) 2012

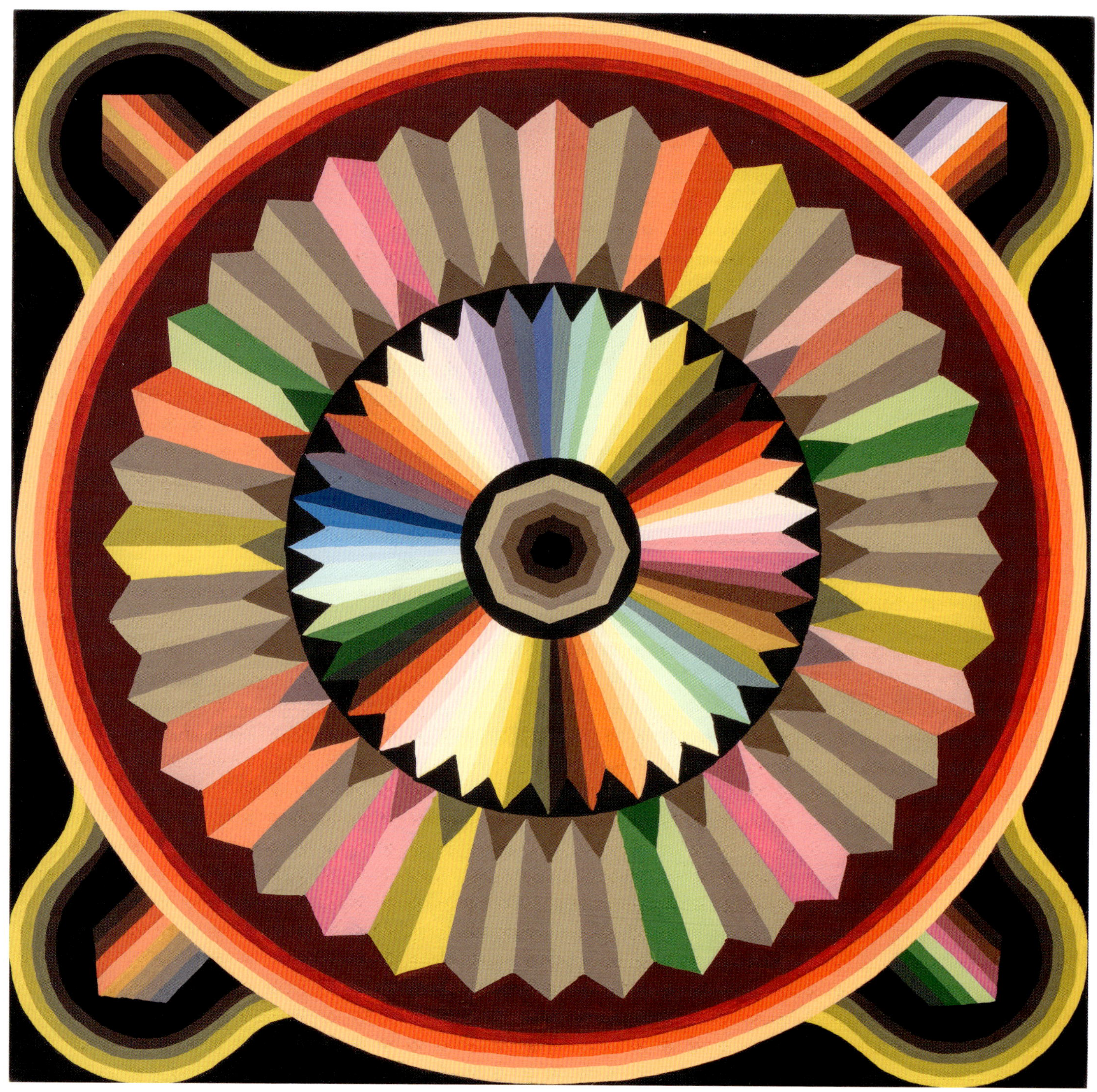

Lost Path   2024

Edie Fake

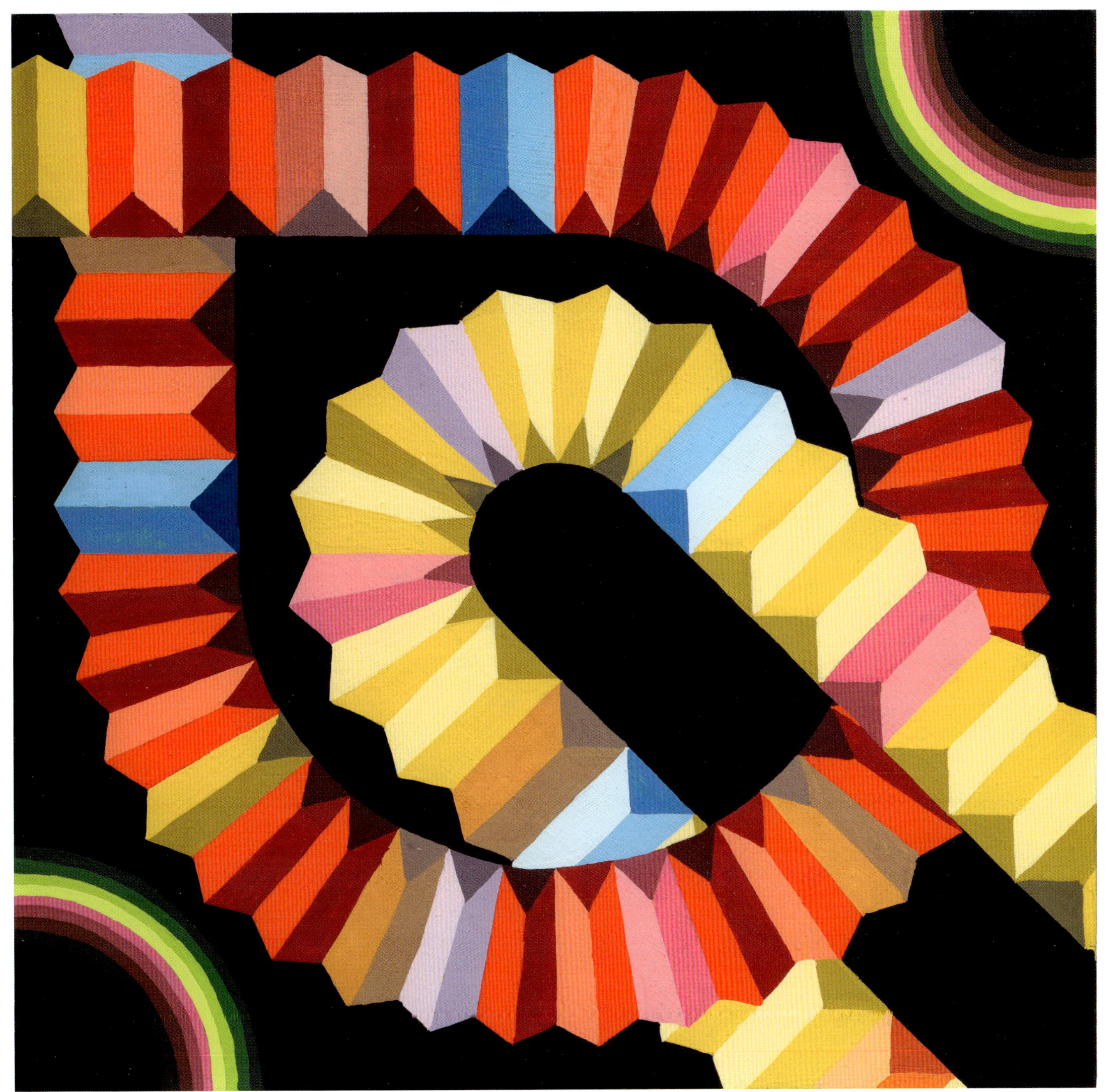

Twist 2024

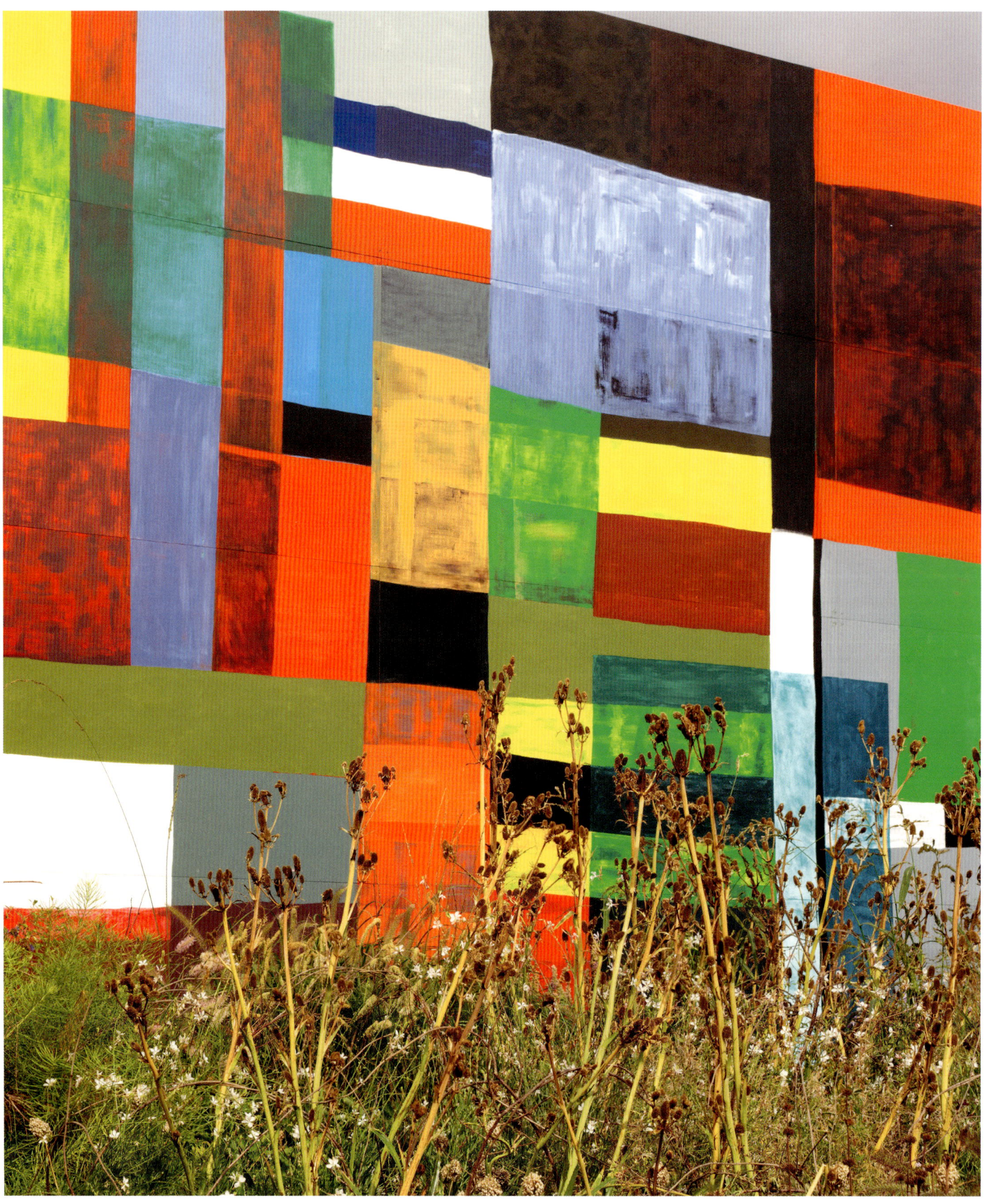

Atta Kwami

Another Moment   2019

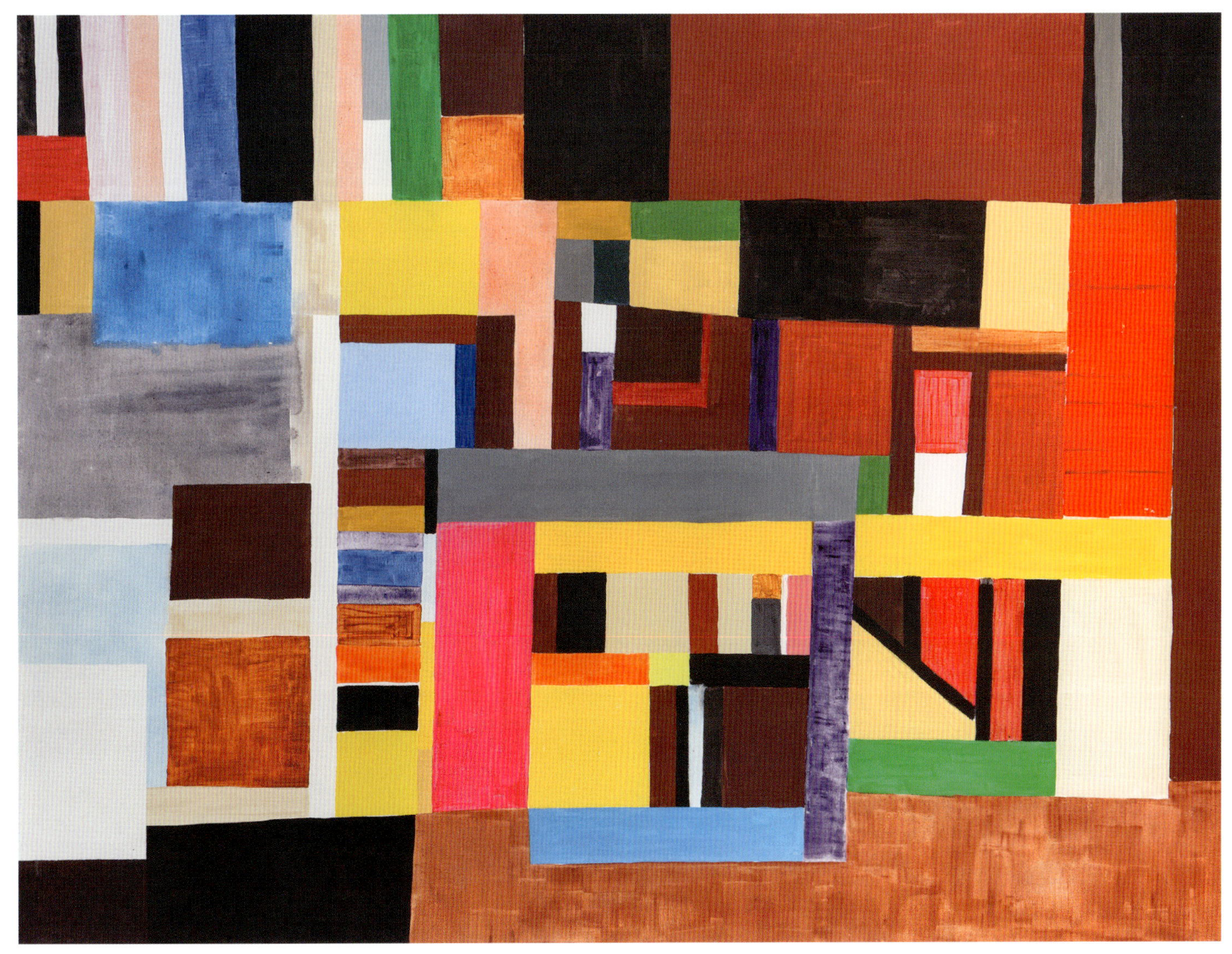

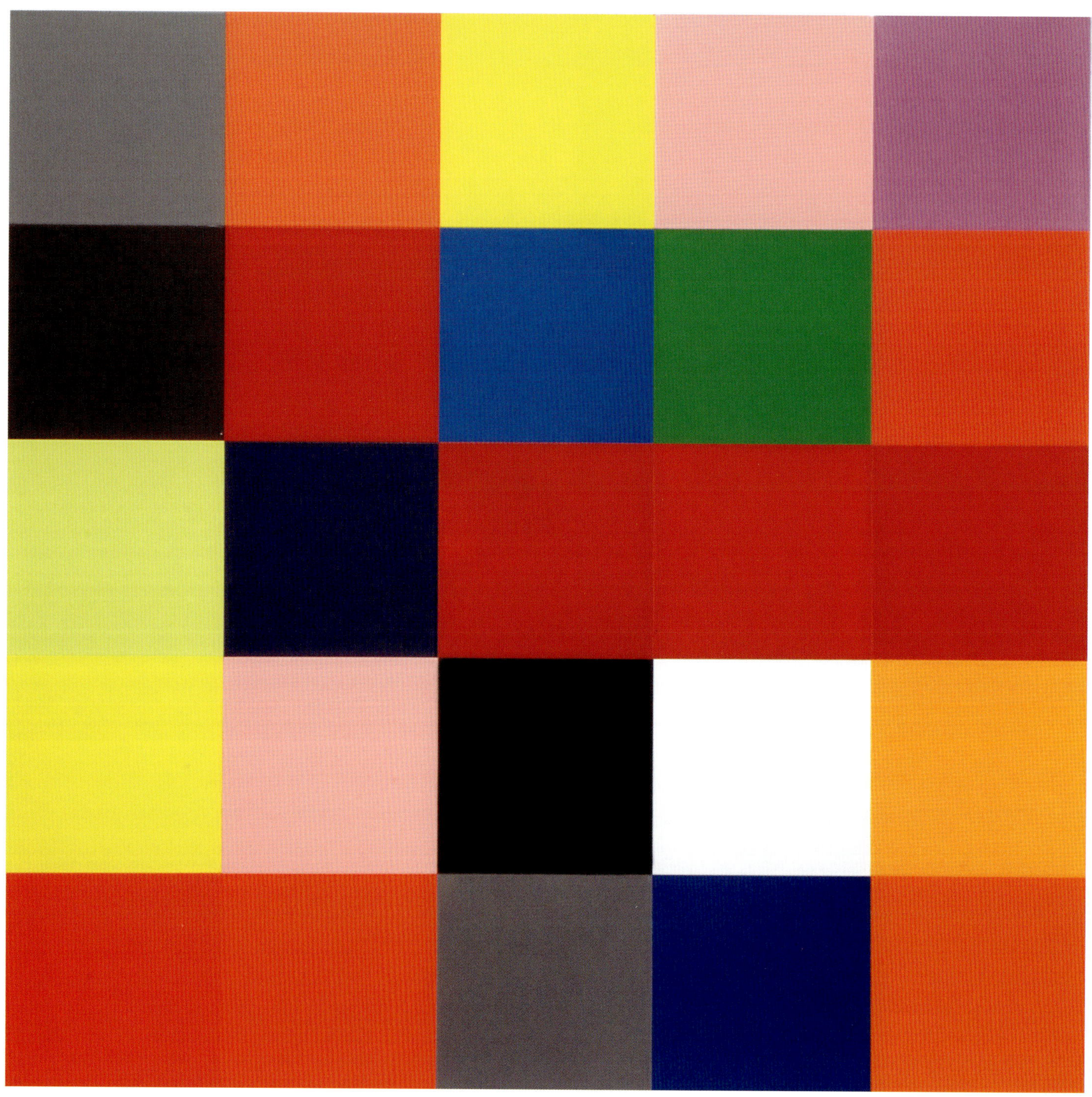

25 Colors   2007

Gerhard Richter

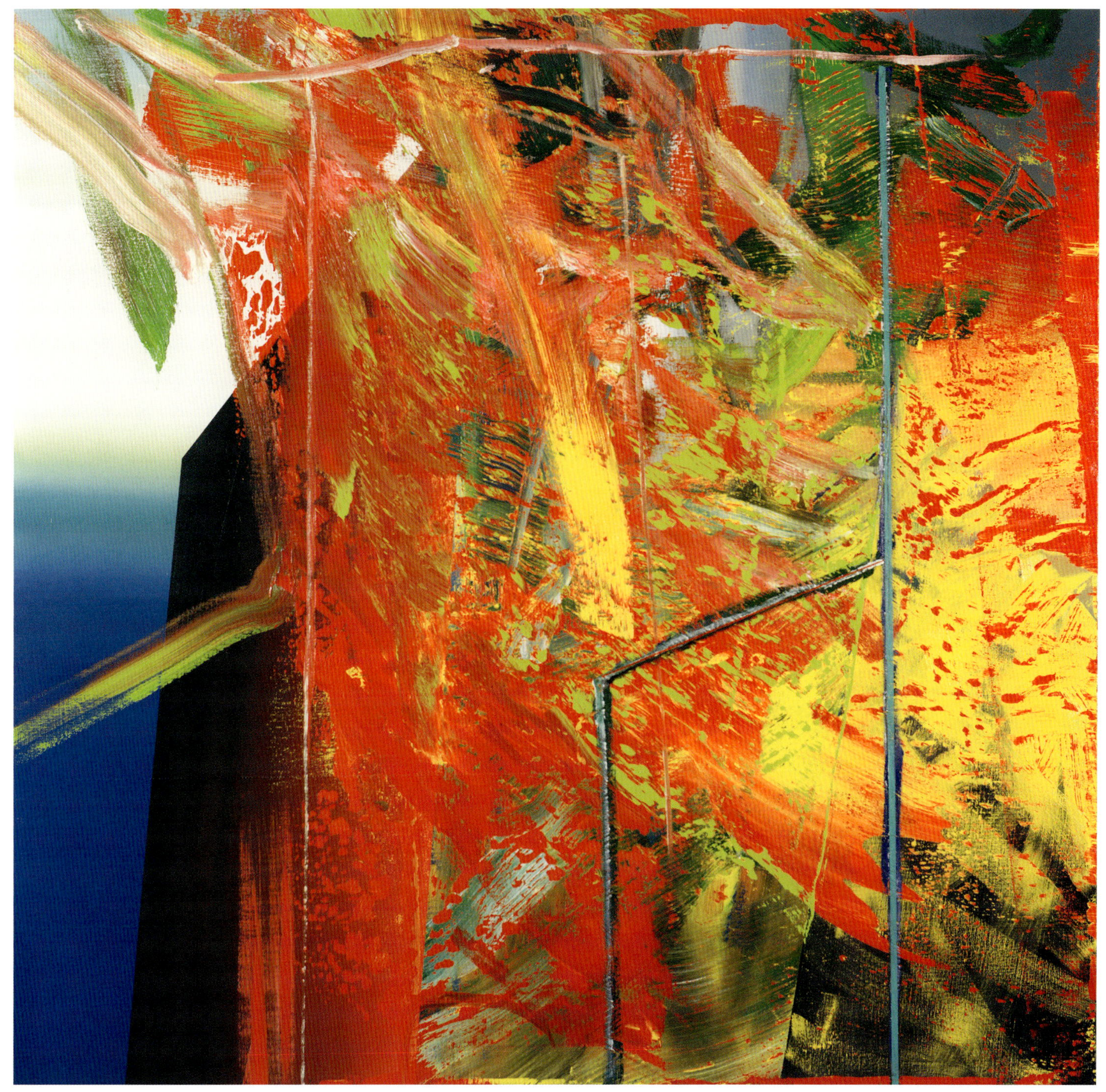

Chair 1985

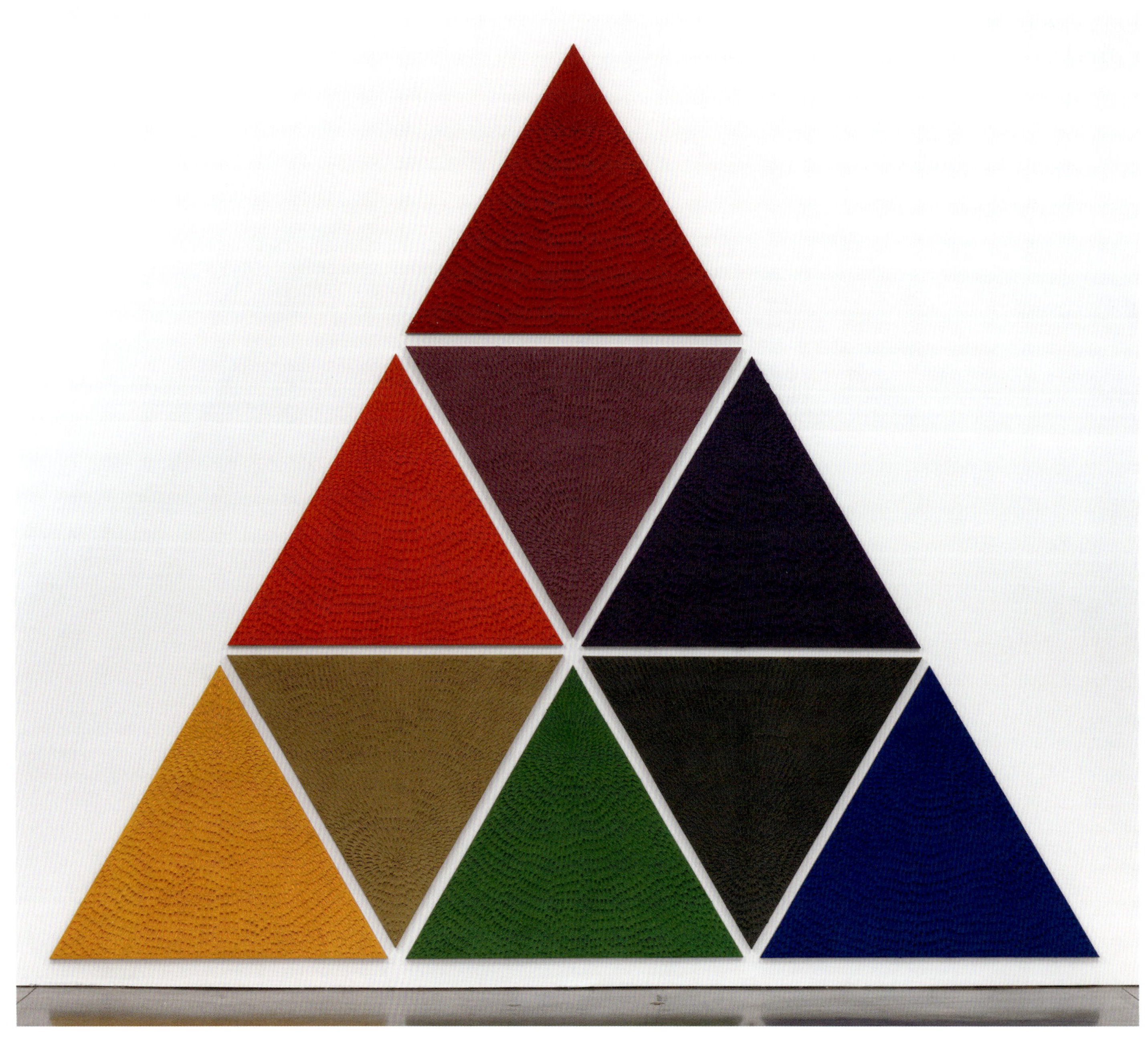

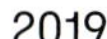

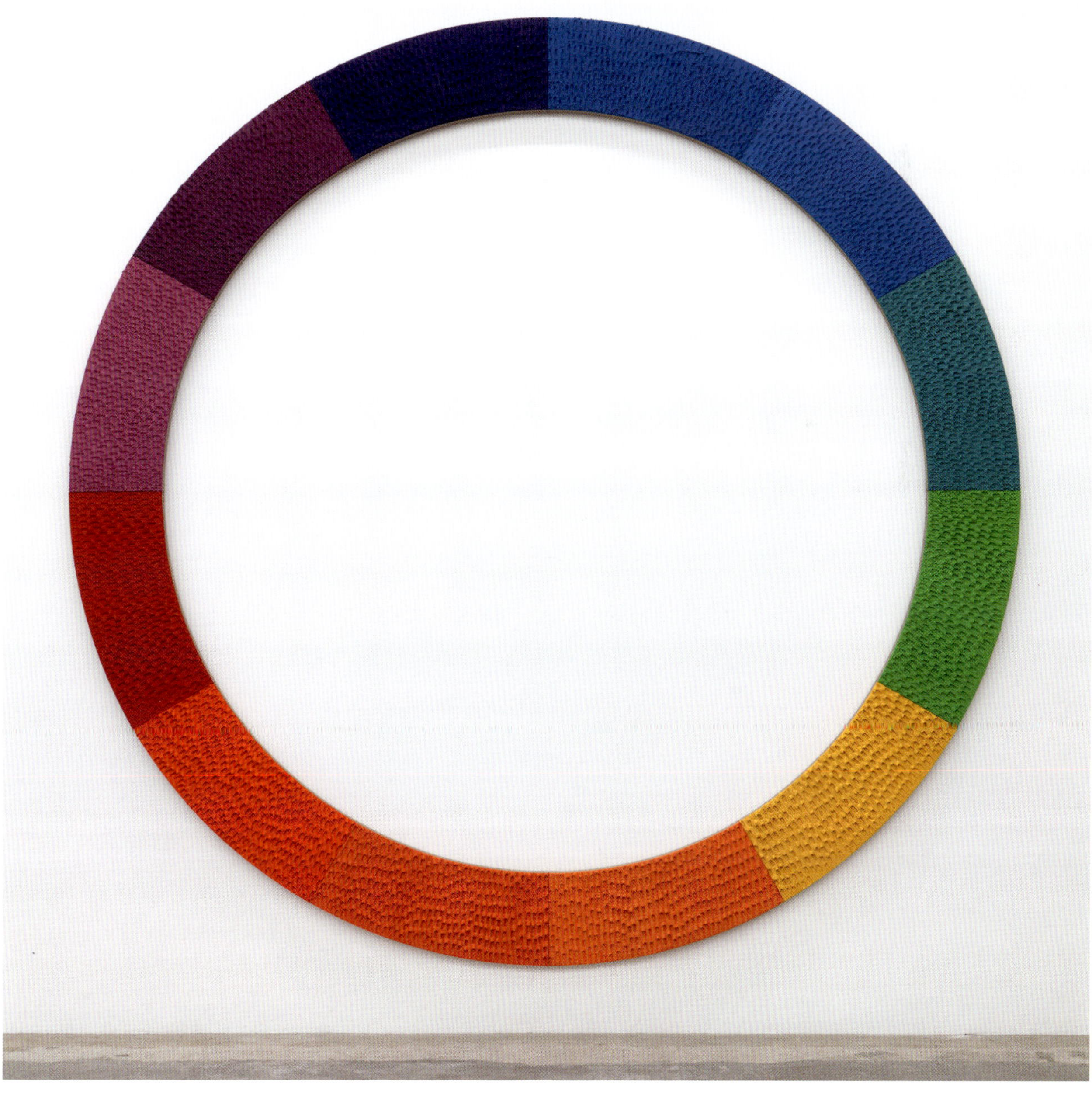

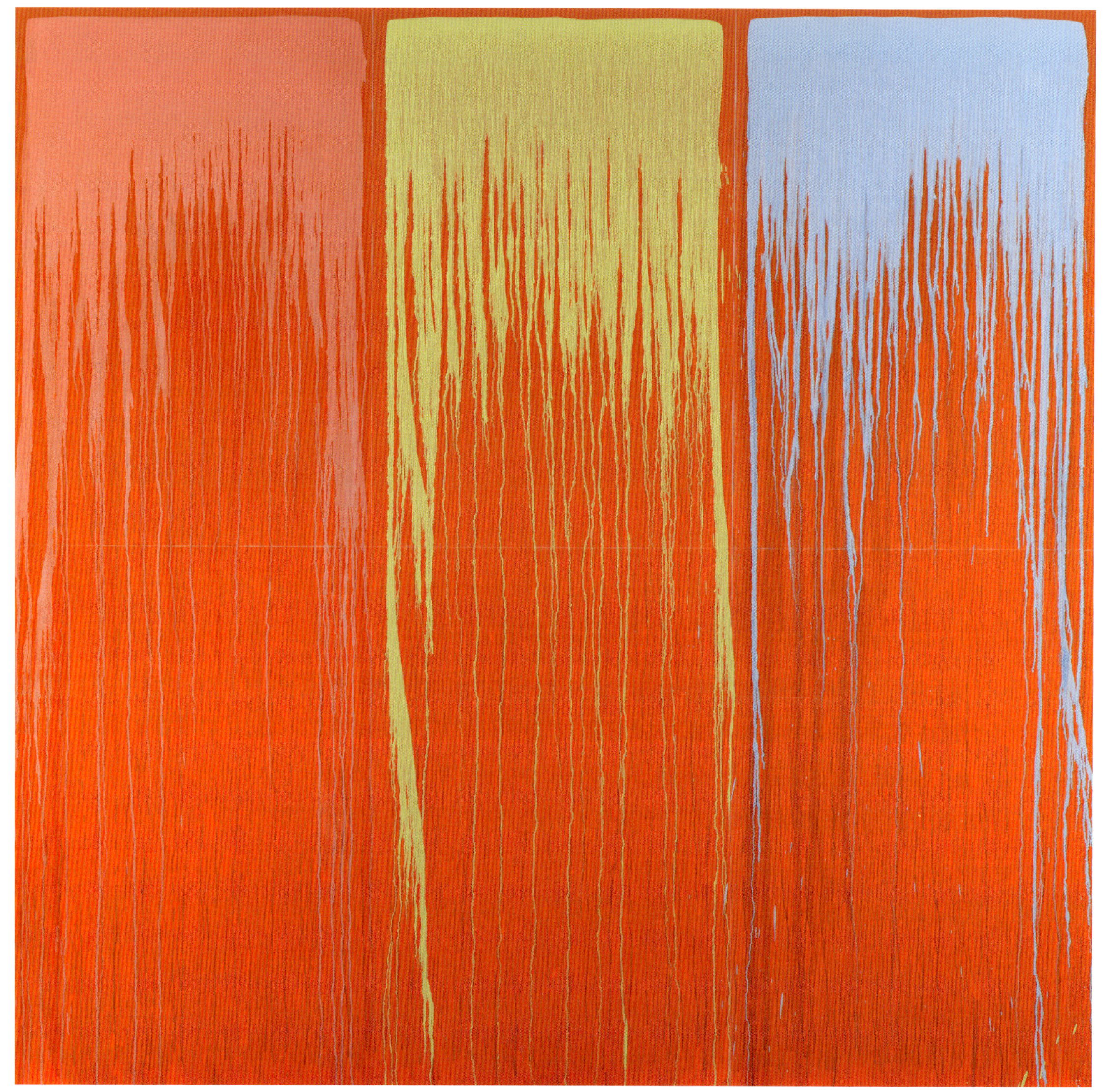

Rainbow Waterfall #5   2022

Pat Steir

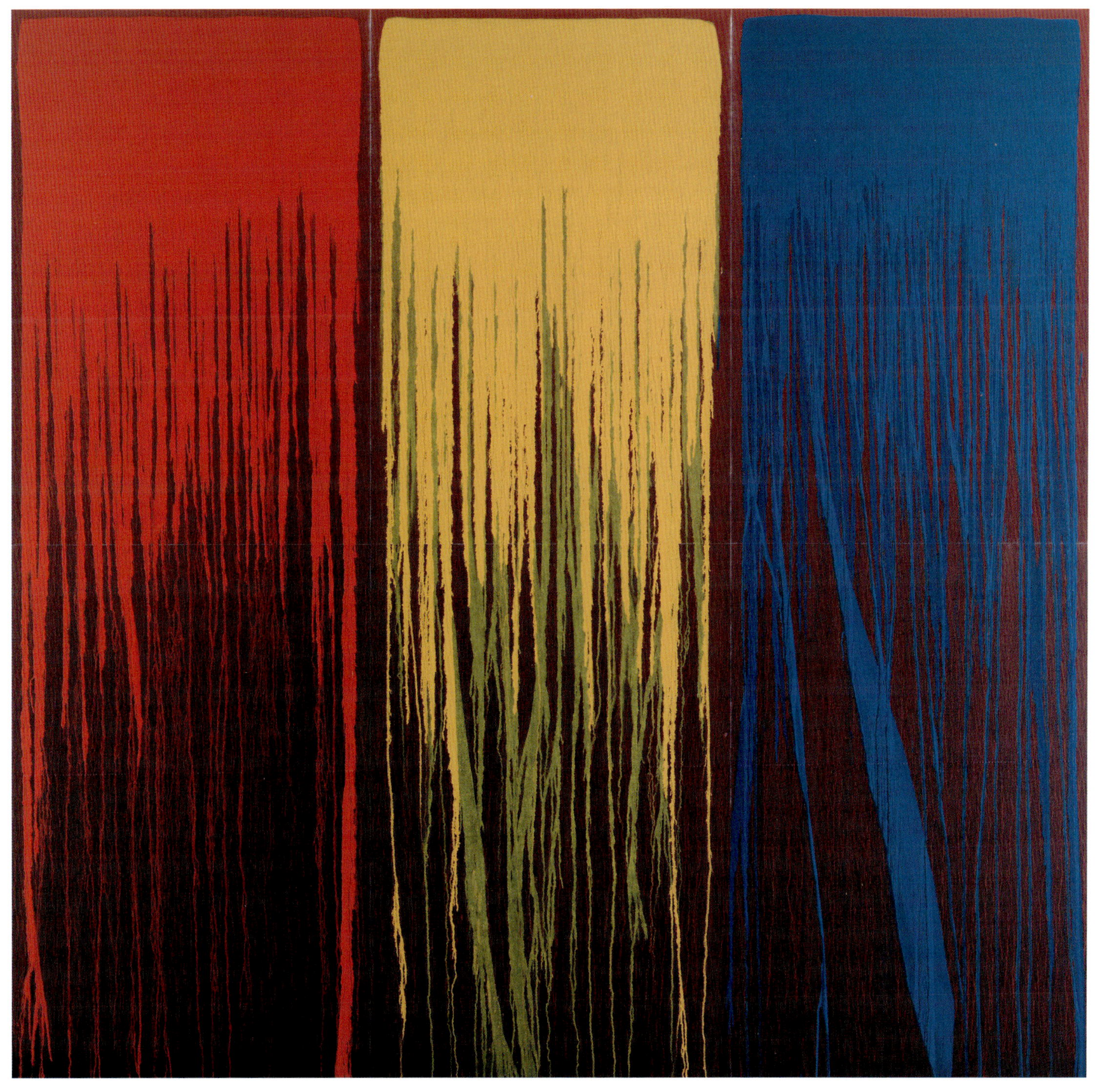

Rainbow Waterfall #1 2022

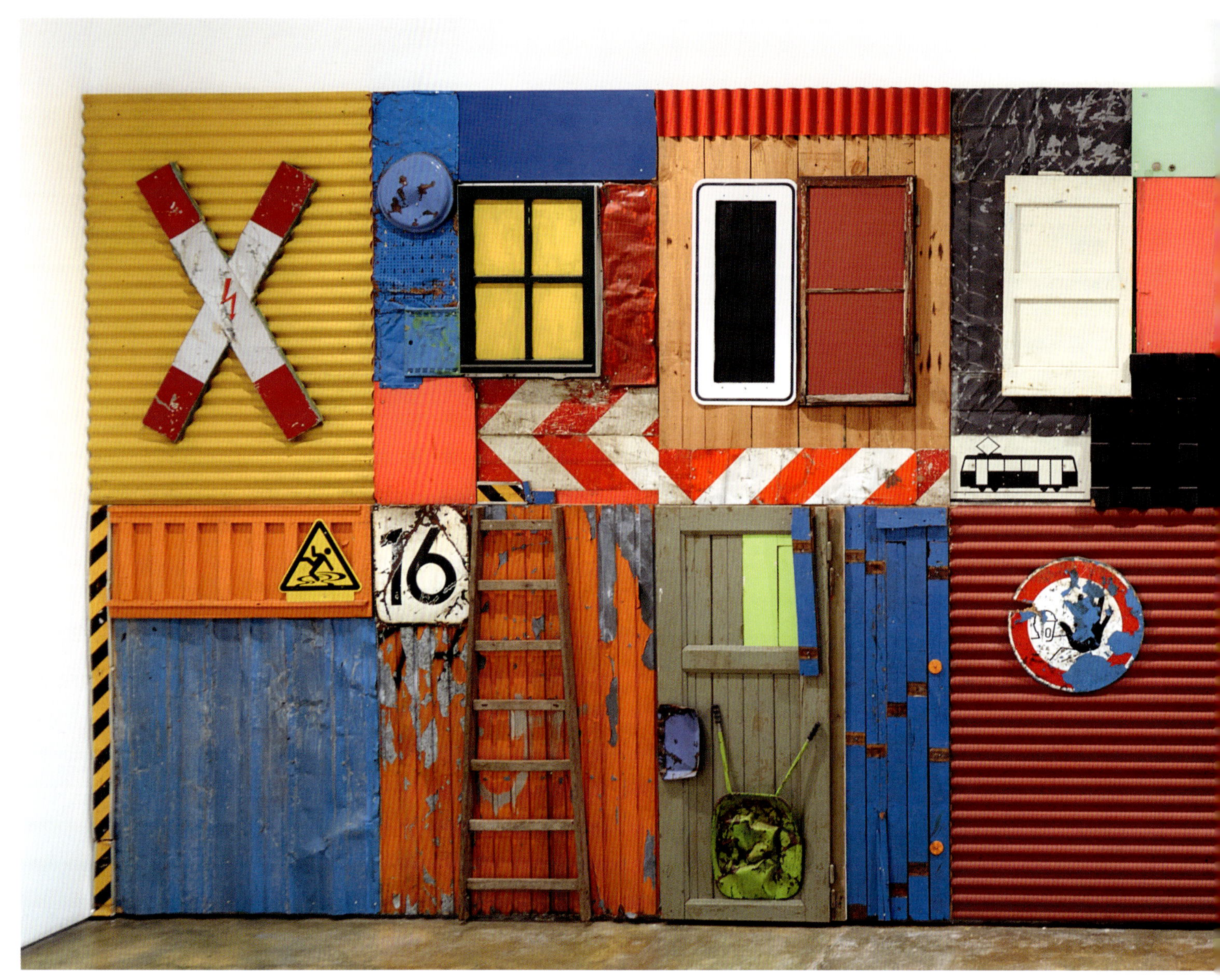

António Ole

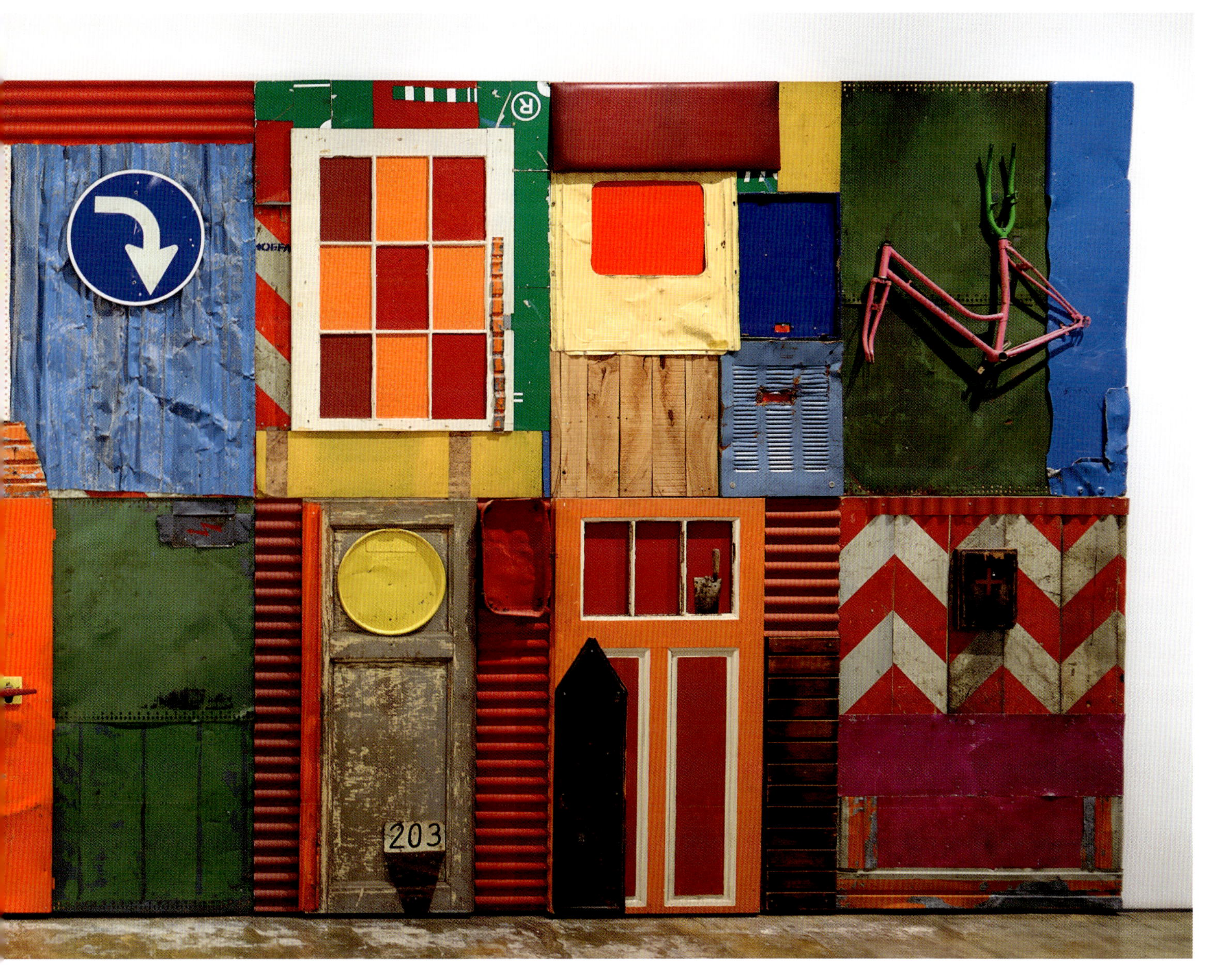

Township Wall (nº10), Düsseldorf   2004

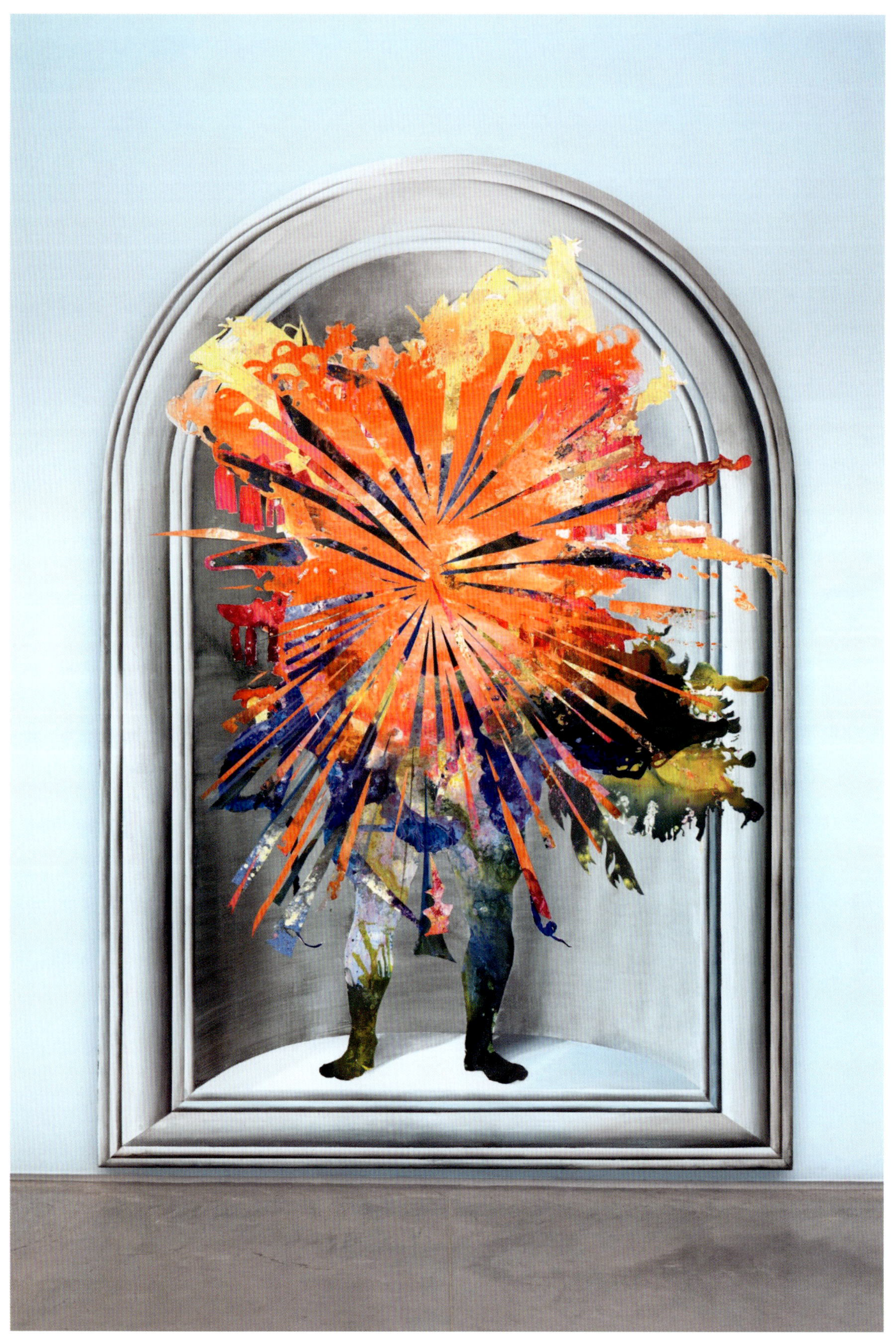

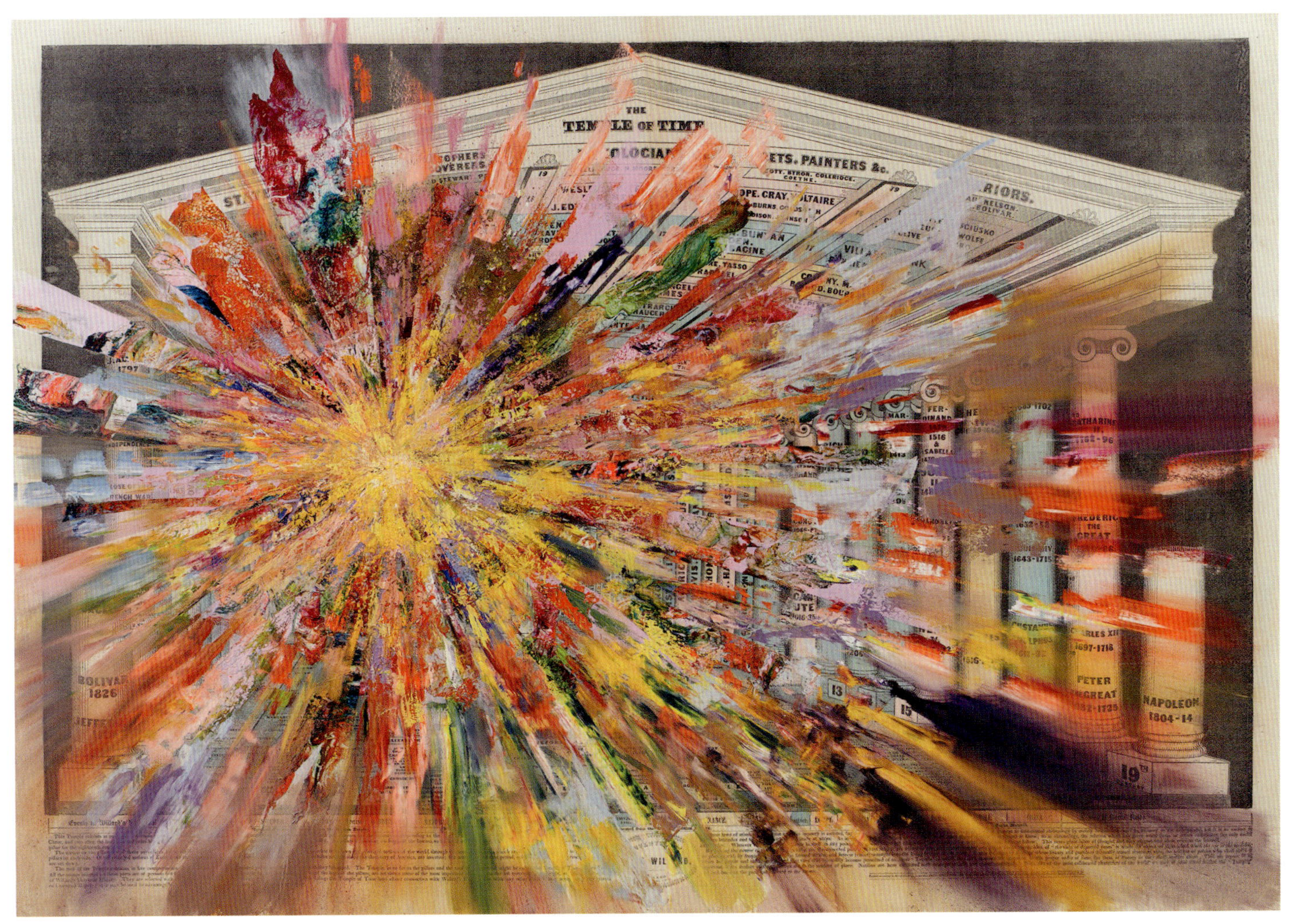

Untitled (Temple of Time)   2020

Firelei Báez

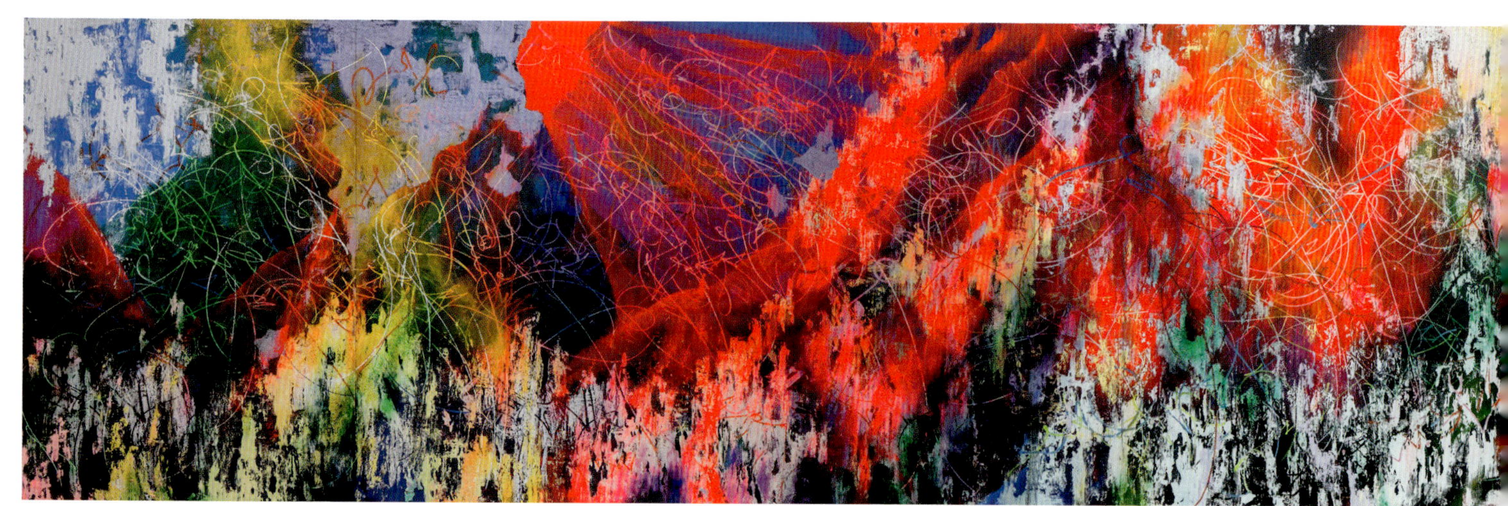

ONE Union of the Senses   2014

José Parlá

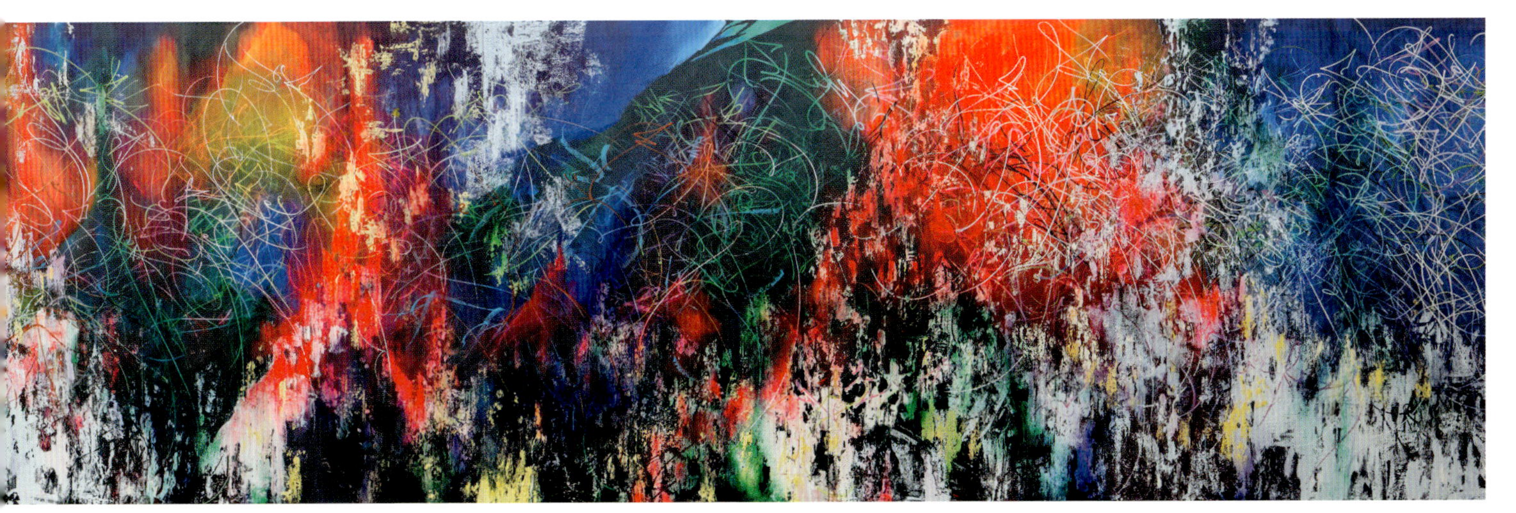

Kevin Beasley

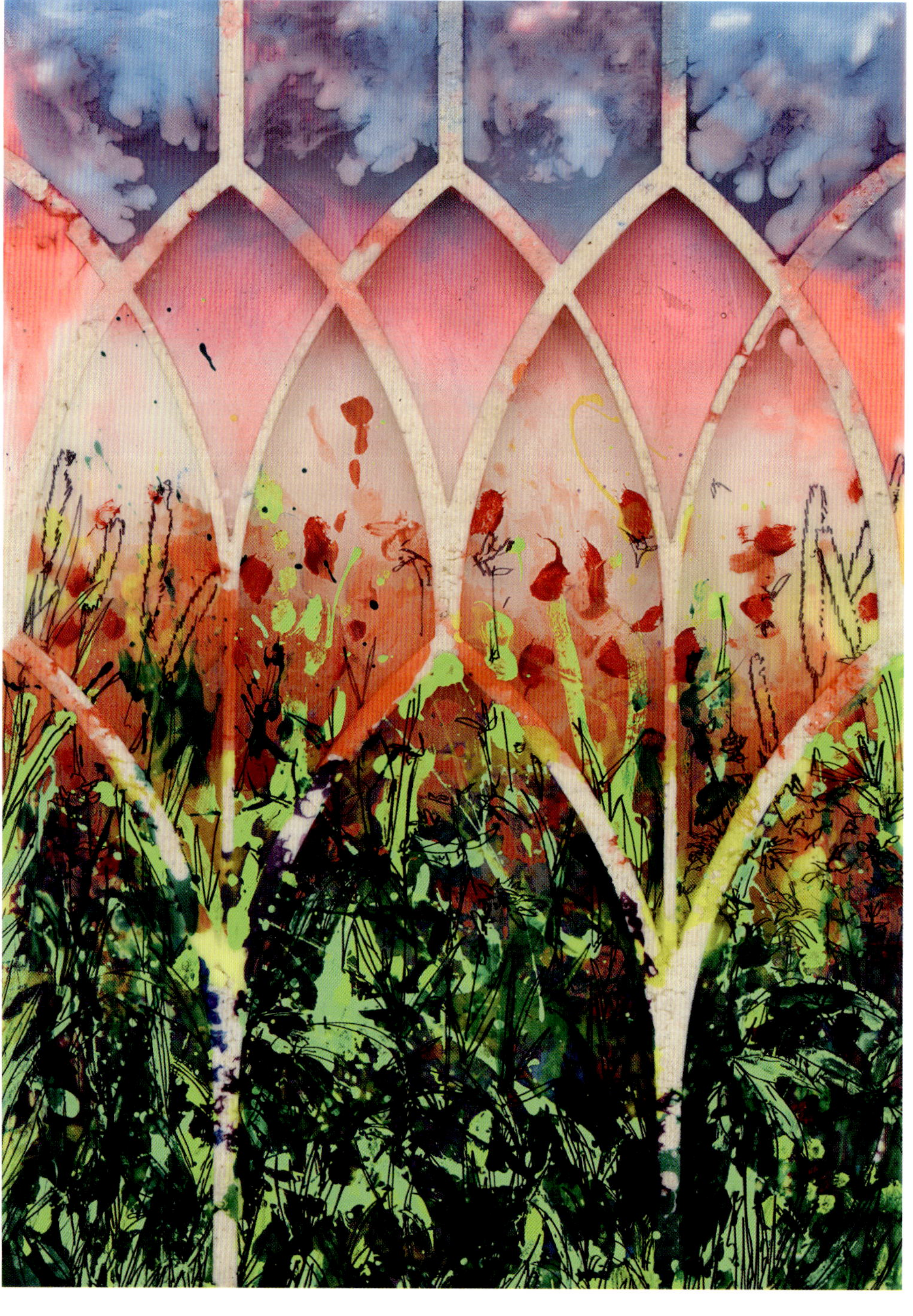

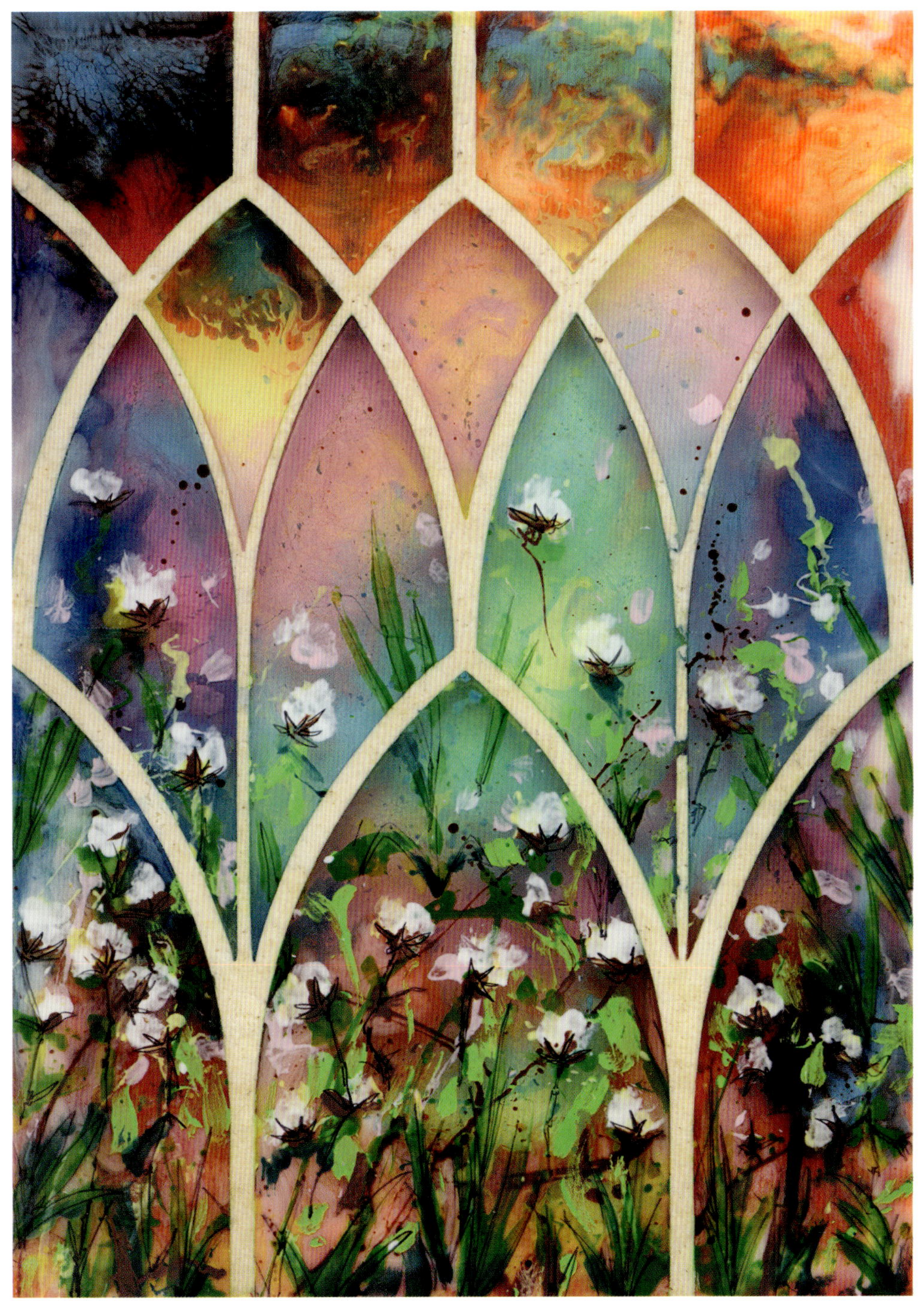

The child (Gift)   2009–20

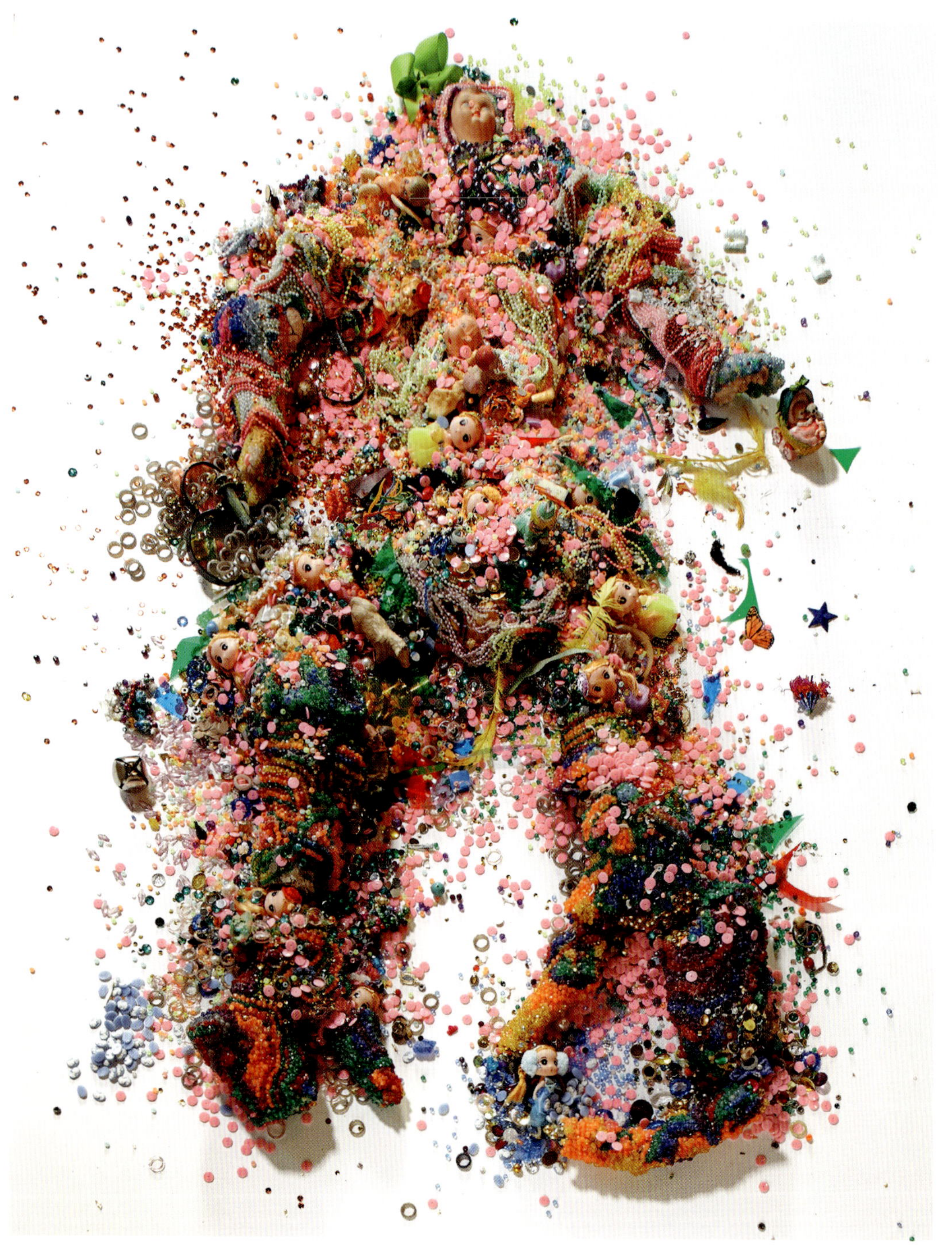

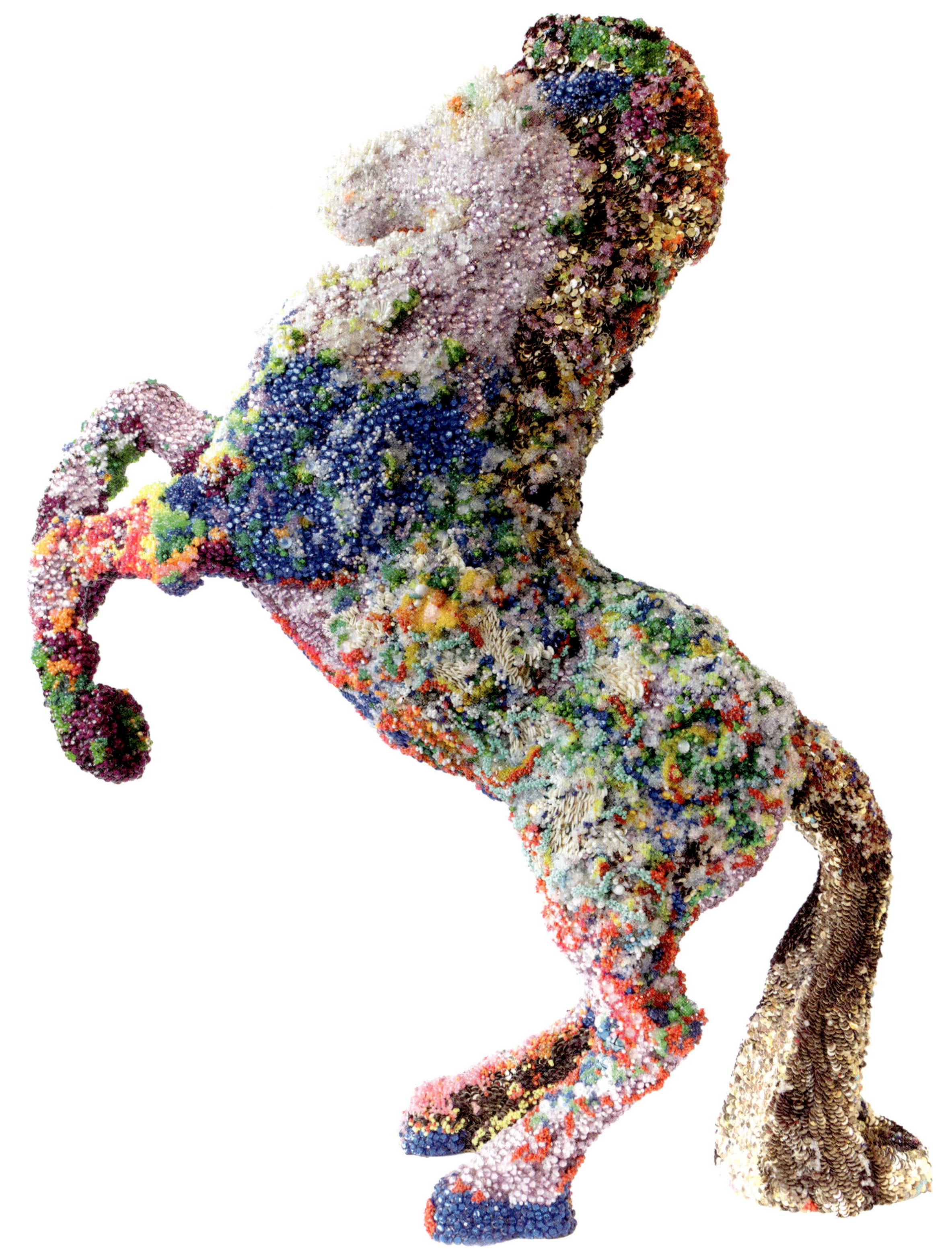

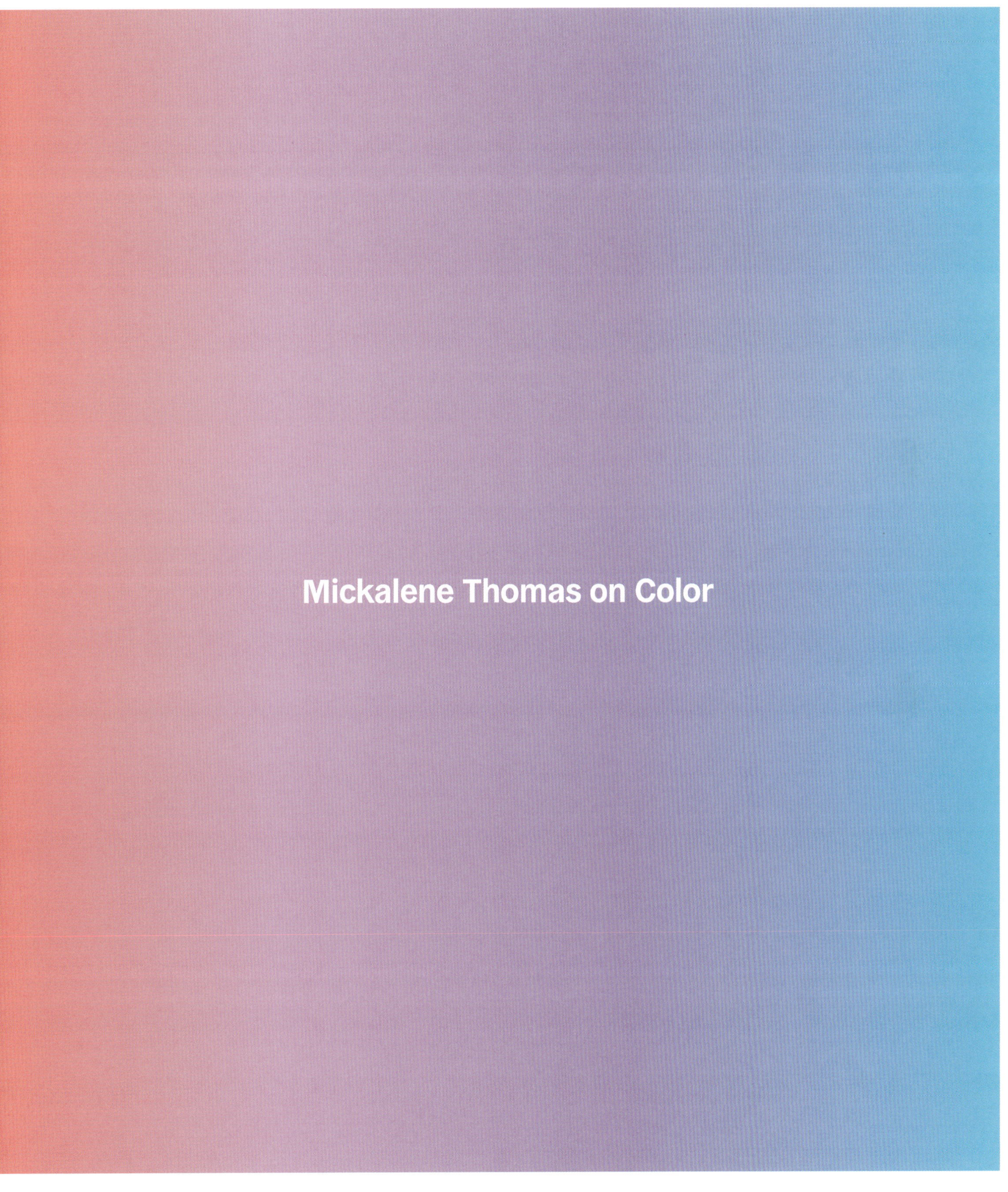

Mickalene Thomas on Color

When you see a rainbow, what do you feel?

Rainbows feel like imagination brought to life—they are surreal. Every time I see one, I'm filled with excitement. They bring a sense of peace and quiet reassurance, a gentle reminder that calm follows every storm. In their fleeting beauty, I find the strength to believe I'm on the right path.

What was your first pivotal color moment in your childhood?

Many aspects of my work are shaped by the domestic environments I experienced as a child in my family's homes, particularly my grandmother's living room. This is where I first encountered bold colors and wallpapers that continue to impact my work. Everything from the placement of lamps to the textures on the sofas that my models lounge on are meant to evoke a narrative of a shared womanly experience that I recall in those living rooms. The scenes pay homage to the past where women would gather, sit in the parlor after church, and aunties would gather late in the evening after coming in from an event and just laugh together.

How important is hope in art right now?

Having hope is immensely important, especially right now. Although the world has advanced in many ways, it has been turned upside down as of late, and it feels as if we have moved slightly backward. There remains significant room for progress, particularly in the areas of identity freedom, representation, and social justice. As a Black queer woman, I know what systemic barriers exist in the world, and it's my commitment as an artist to help break them down, create impact, uplift, and amplify Black identity and power through my work.

Do you think other contemporary artists who use color are trying to tell us something specific about our world today … about society, politics, or the environment?

I can't speak on behalf of other artists about why they choose to use specific colors or not, but for me, color choice is inherent in my pieces. My work centers on Black women claiming their rightful space in the world, and I use vibrant colors and patterned textiles to help express their radical power and celebrate their beauty, femininity, and desire as acts of liberation from cultural oppression and marginalization.

Your work is immediately recognizable for its intense and rich color palettes. Could you describe your process for selecting the colors you use in a piece? Is it intuitive, planned, or a combination?

My signature technique is layered and complicated. From experience, I've figured out how to select the right process and materials that best execute my ideas. Color selection is an integral step as it helps reinforce my narratives. Everything works in harmony, though. My main techniques of silkscreen and collage allow for the disruptive and playful integration of painting and photography. The use of rhinestones is the seductive element that is an additive ingredient of pleasure. Collage is an essential means of discovery for me as I work. It allows me to learn and unlearn within my own process and helps me make sense of my compositions.

Are there certain colors you find yourself consistently drawn to, and if so, why do you think that is?

I'm attracted to colors that command attention, enhance my chosen narrative, and challenge the traditional standards of beauty. Gem-inspired hues such as bright pink, electric blue, deep green, mustard yellow, gold, and royal purple are consistent in my repertoire. I integrate layers of complexity to amplify these stories with photographic collages, painting, rhinestones, and glitter.

Do you ever start a piece with a particular color in mind, or does the color scheme emerge as the work progresses?

Sometimes I start with a particular color in mind, but not always. I would say my color is blue! Blue is representative to me of the water that surrounds us above and below. My color choices are highly intentional, and if I want to make a direct historical reference or recreate an image, color is top of mind before I start working. Other times, color emerges organically through experimentation. As I develop a composition, a dialogue between different colors, textures, and materials emerges. Based on this, I decide what combination of the three best fits the emotions, memories, or feelings I want viewers to experience.

The vibrancy of your colors often evokes a sense of joy and celebration. Is this an intentional emotional response you aim to elicit from your audience?

I like to be provocative and bold with my use of color because it sets the tone for what I am trying to communicate. My work tends to be rather exuberant in color and material, even though it often carries important messages and new storylines— namely those where Black women can claim space and embrace their beauty, femininity, and power. By juxtaposing different elements in my work, I can spark new dialogues and challenge traditional representations of women and liberate cultural oppression and marginalization in memorable ways.

Do you use the reflective quality of rhinestones and glitter to manipulate light and create different color perceptions for the viewer?

The addition of rhinestones in my work creates a sense of pleasure, seduction, and shine. The sparkling rhinestones have become a signature of mine, and I love how they add a level of exuberance to my paintings and core narratives. The reflective and colorful gems bring more attention to the beauty, essence, and elegance of the Black bodies I'm portraying.

We don't encounter rainbows nearly as often as we should, which is perhaps what makes them feel so magical. Whether seen in nature or reflected in art, rainbows are a welcome surprise, and their rarity only enhances their impact. They offer us a sense of radical acceptance, fantasy, and optimism, no matter where—or how—we experience them.

These are the kinds of emotions I strive to evoke in my work. I want viewers to be completely absorbed and transfixed—stopped in their tracks, much like they are by a rainbow, and filled with a sense of wonder and quiet awe.

Interview by Valentine Uhovski

Do Ho Suh

Jet Lag (detail)   2022

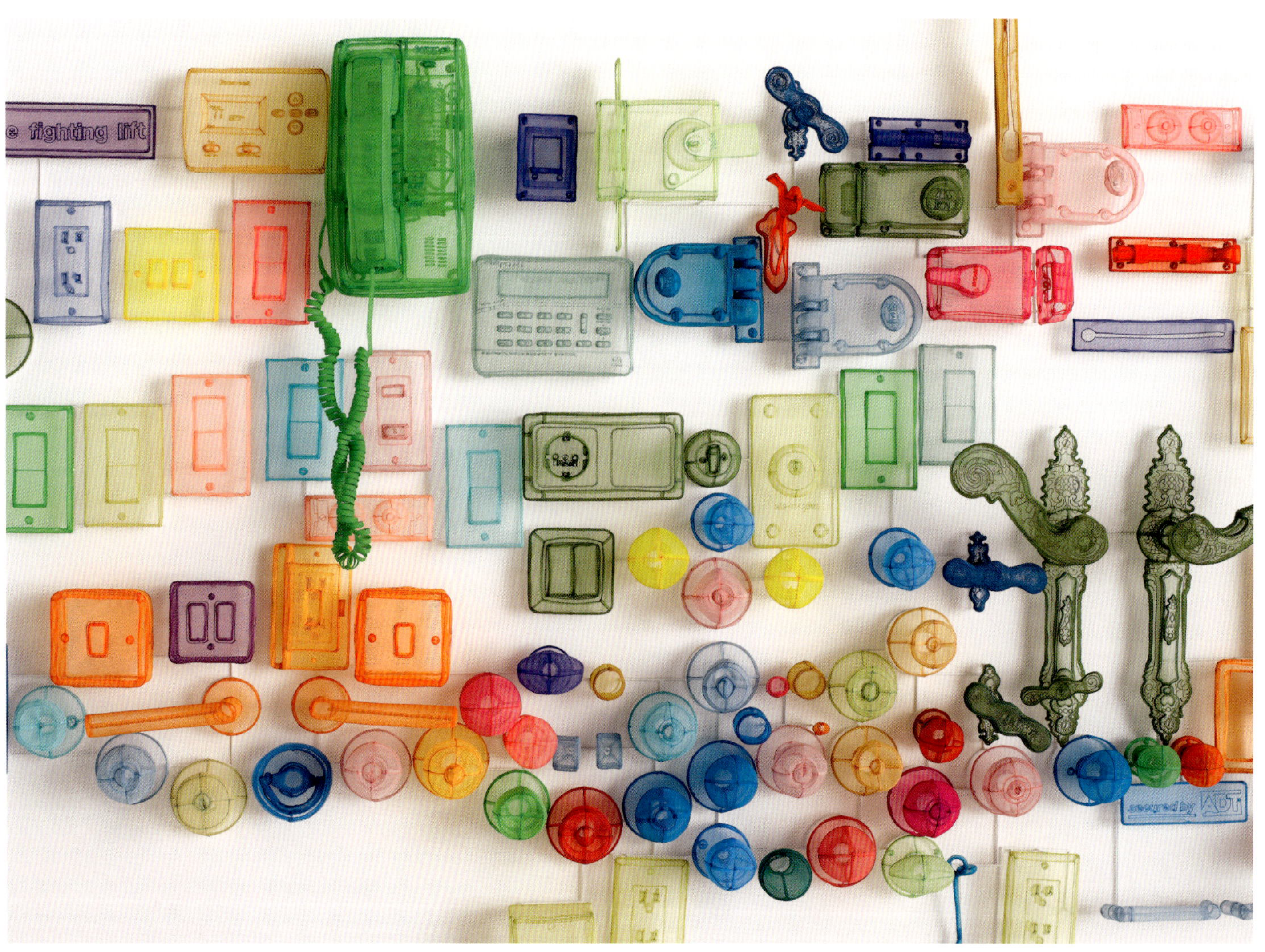

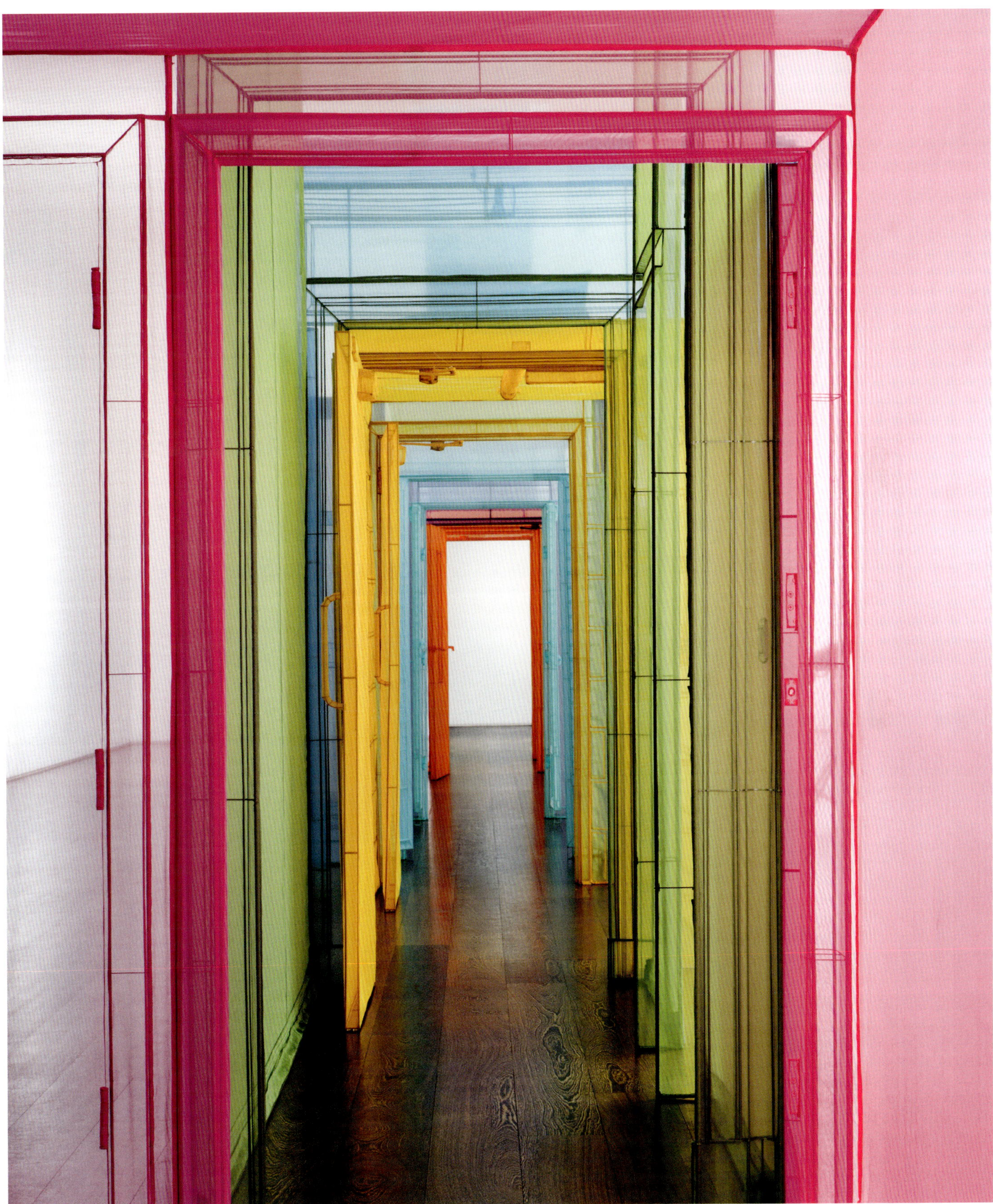

Lauren Halsey

auntie fawn on tha 6   2021

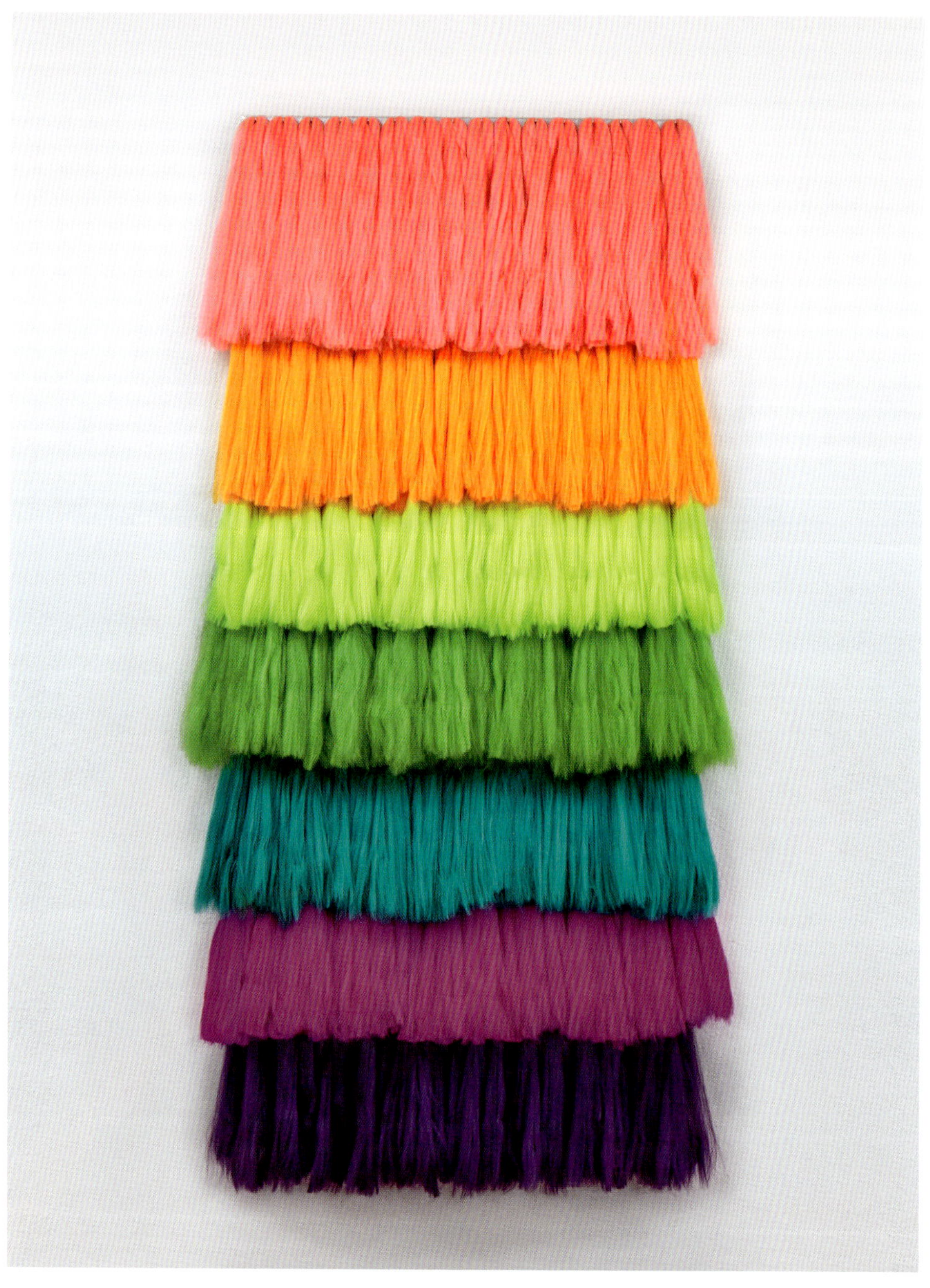

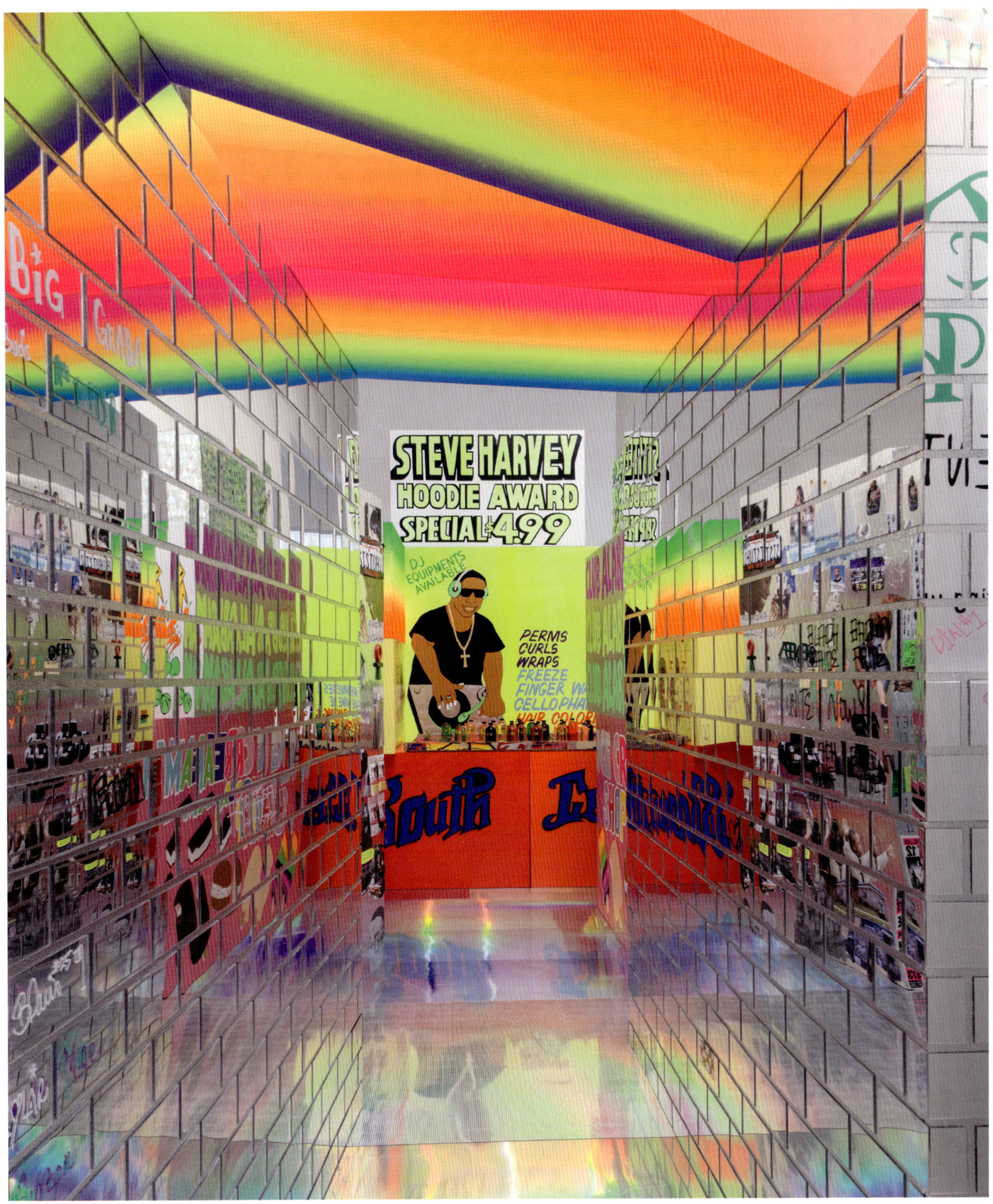
BiG
GRAND
STEVE HARVEY
HOODIE AWARD
SPECIAL $4.99
DJ EQUIPMENTS AVAILABLE
PERMS
CURLS
WRAPS
FREEZE
FINGER WA
CELLOPHA
HAIR COLOR
South

Jeffrey Gibson

Installation view: *Jeffrey Gibson: the space in which to place me*   2024

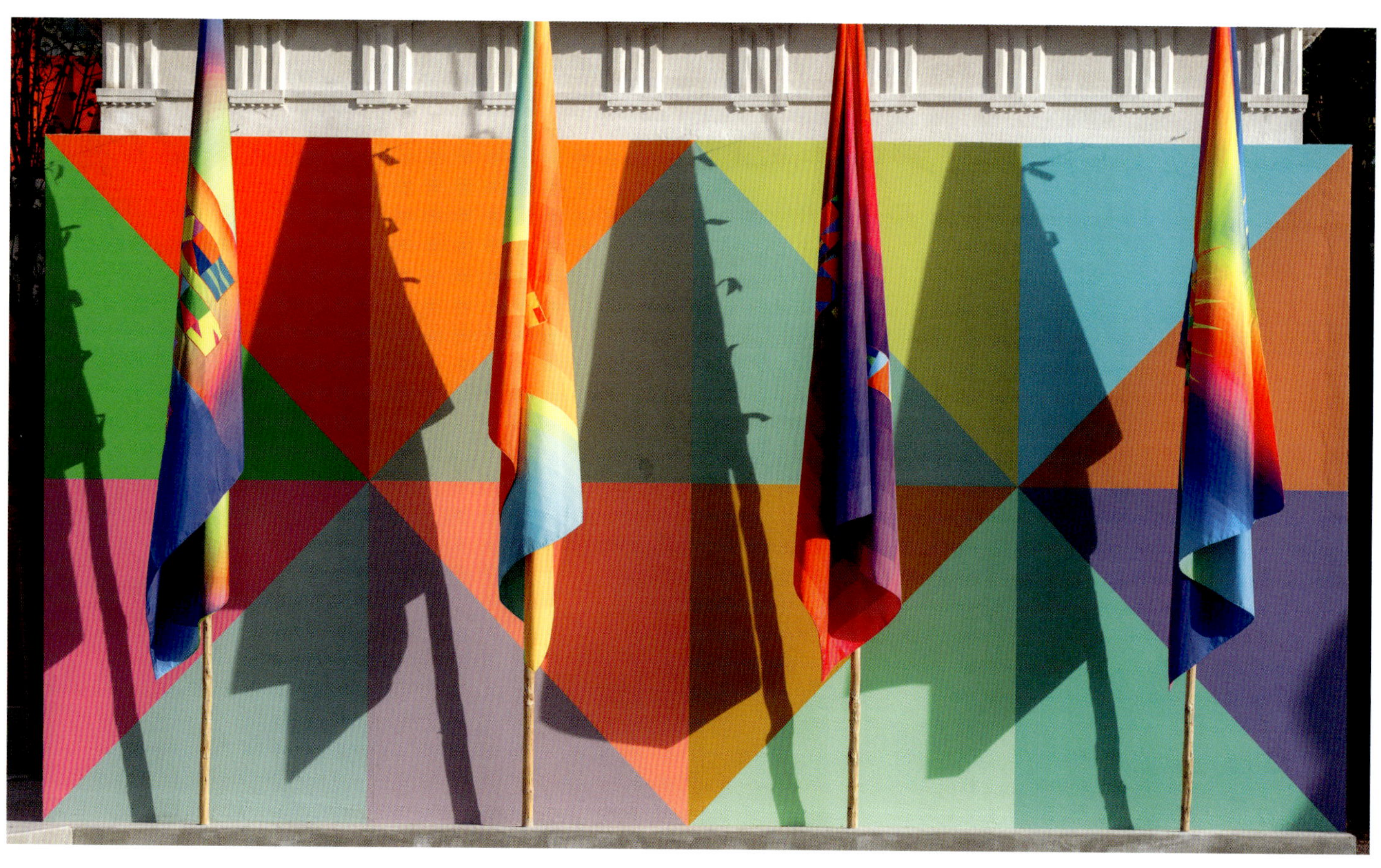

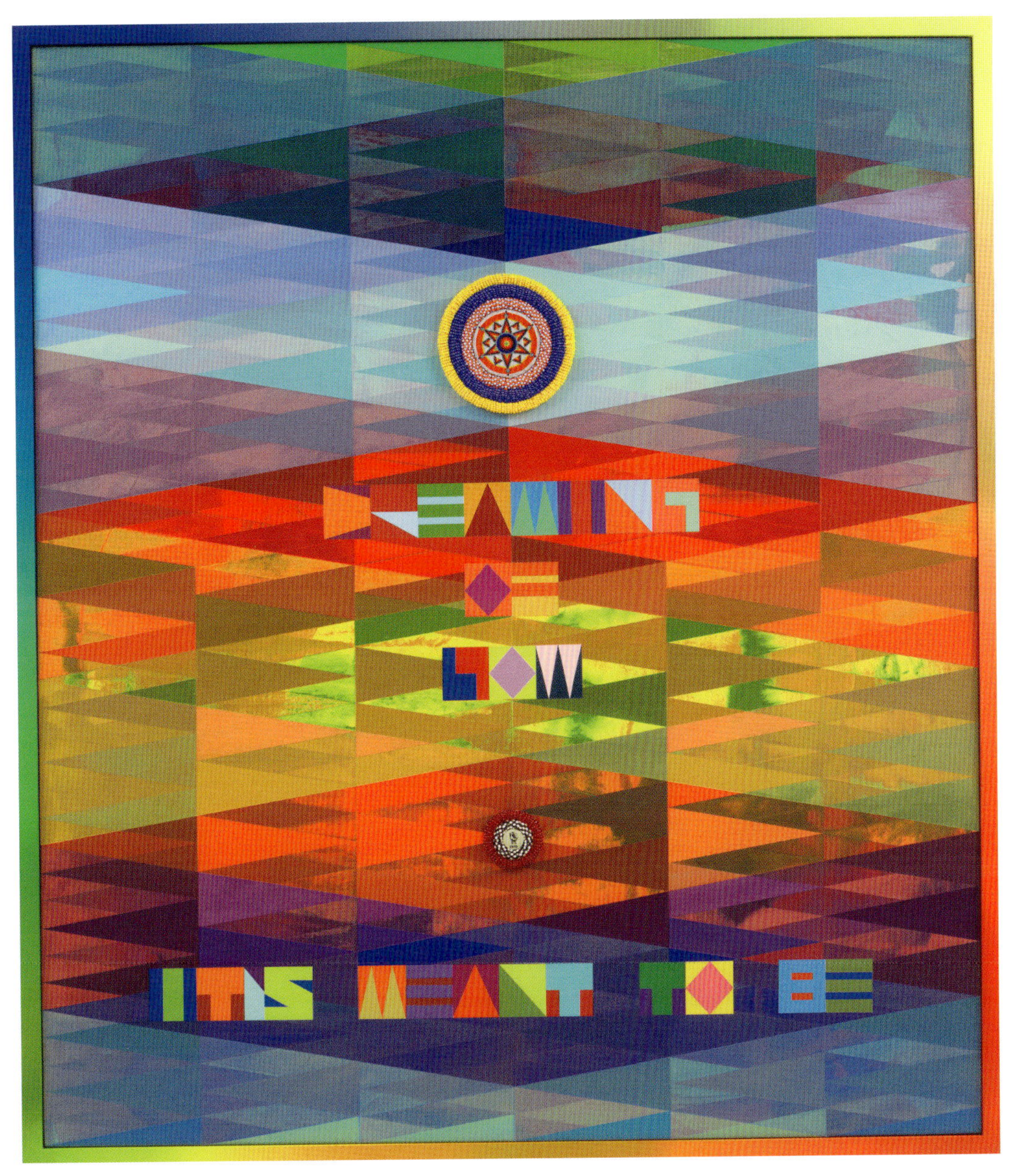

DREAMING OF HOW IT'S MEANT TO BE   2023

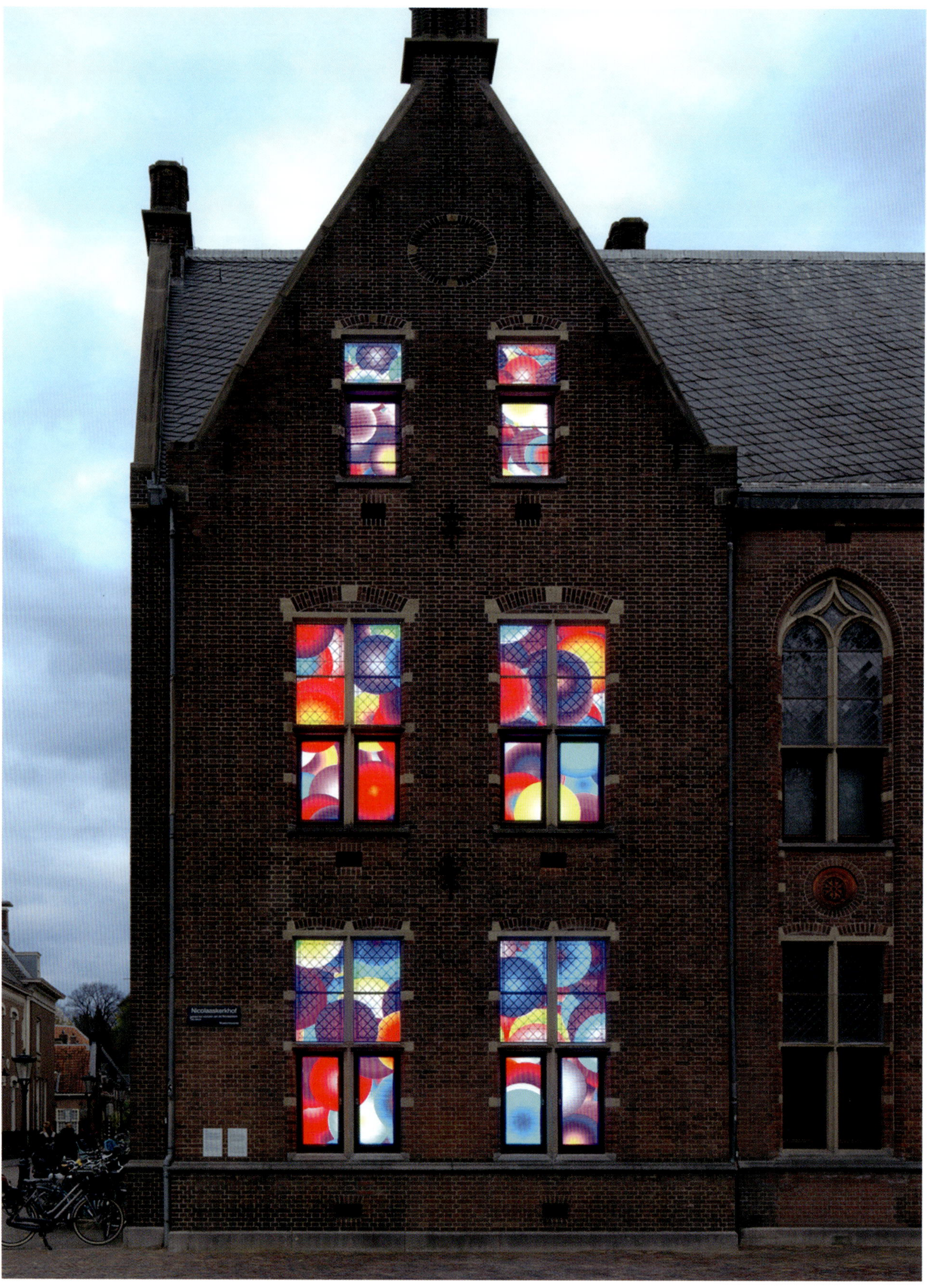

Rafaël Rozendaal

Random Fear (with Mirrors) 2019

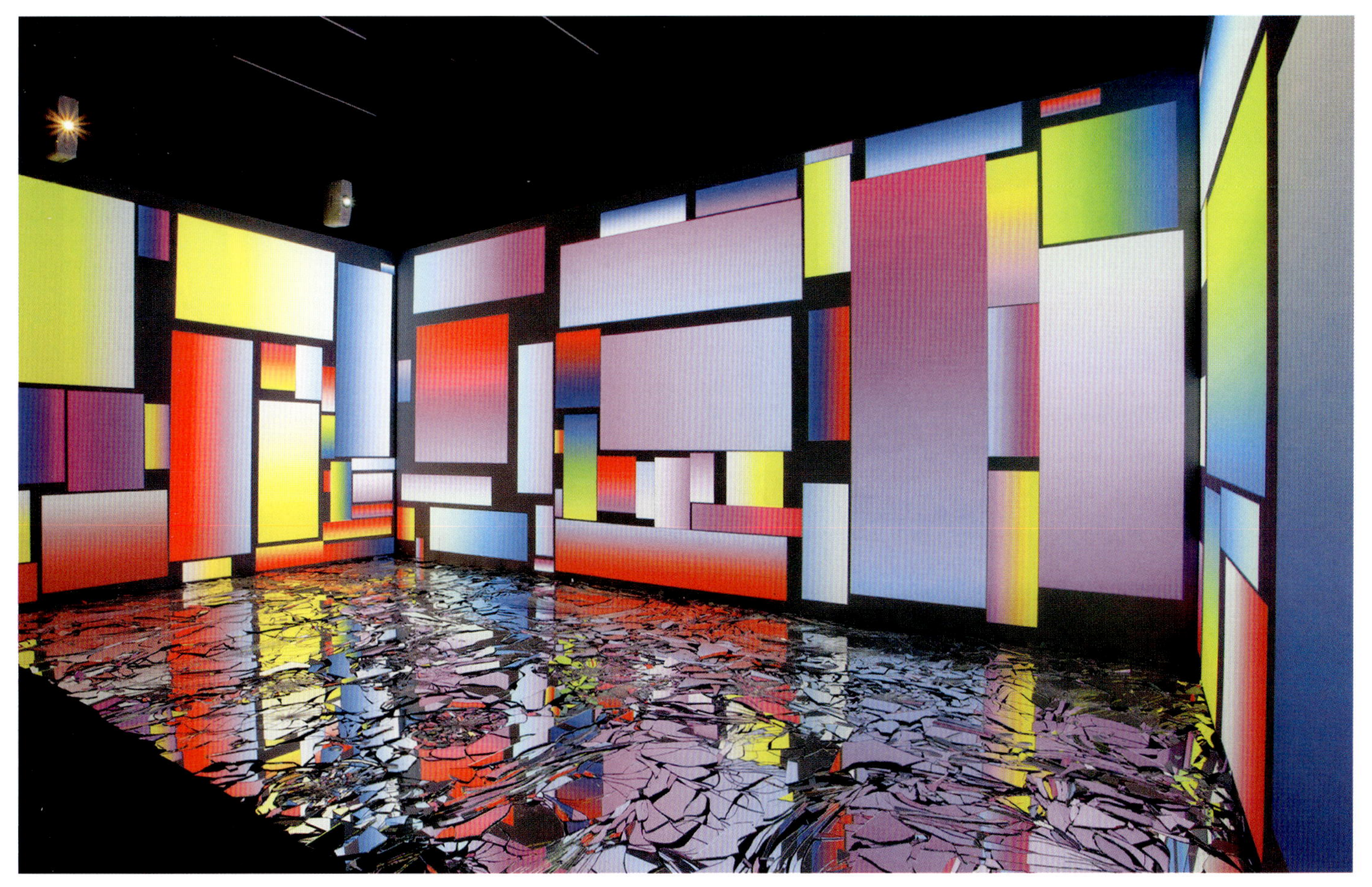

Hiva Alizadeh

Untitled (light curls) (detail)   2021

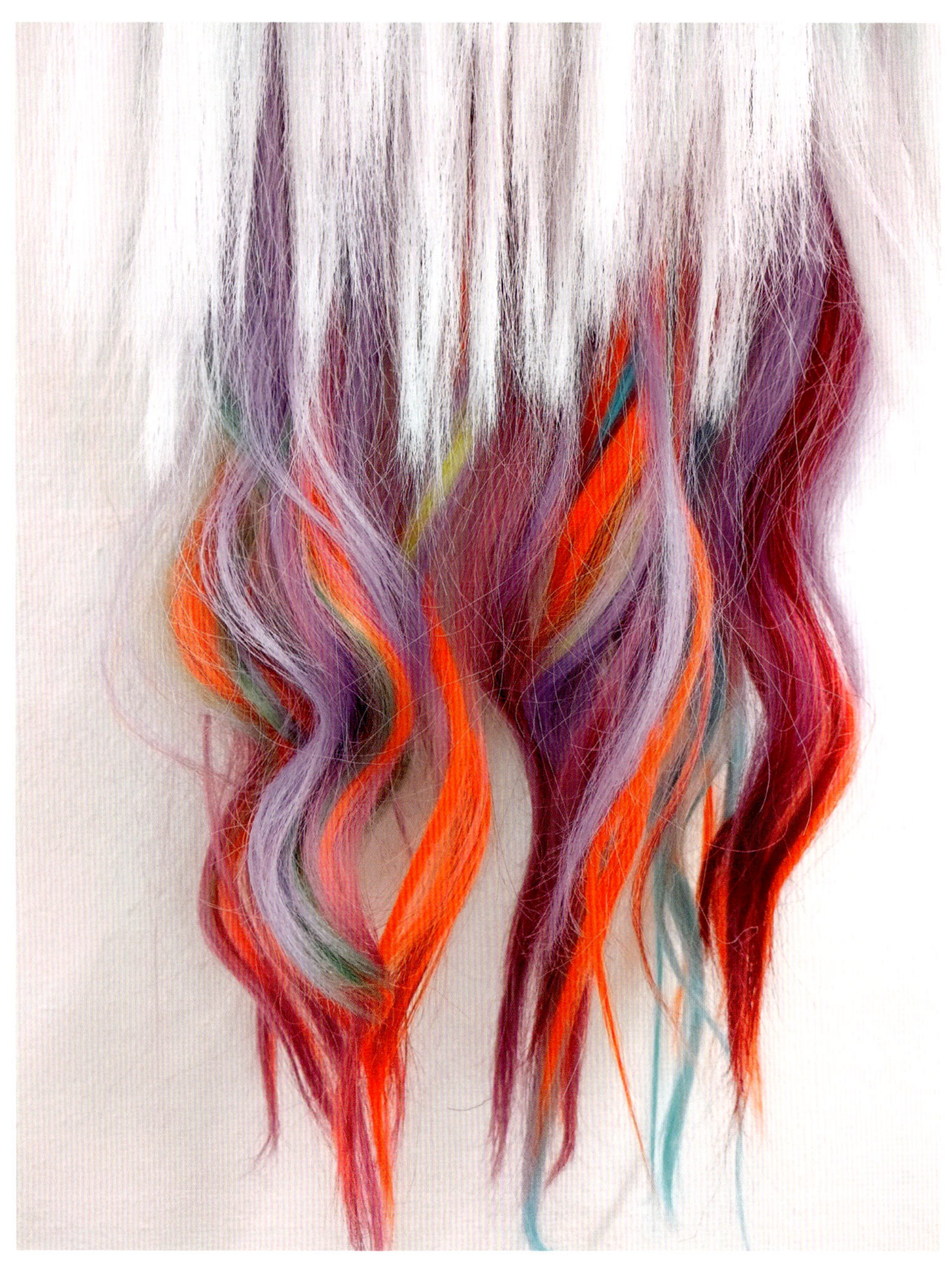

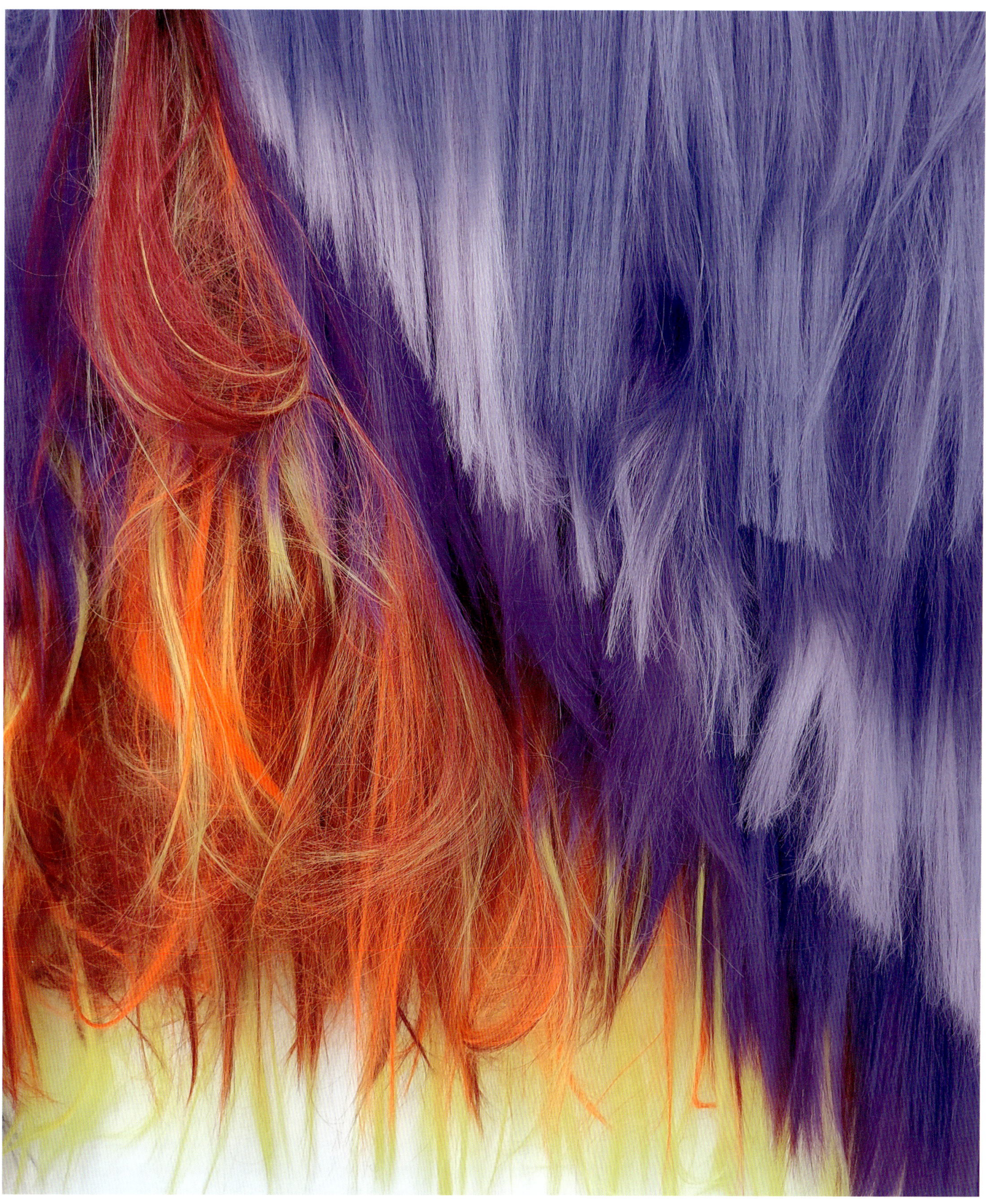

Alex Israel

Wave   2018

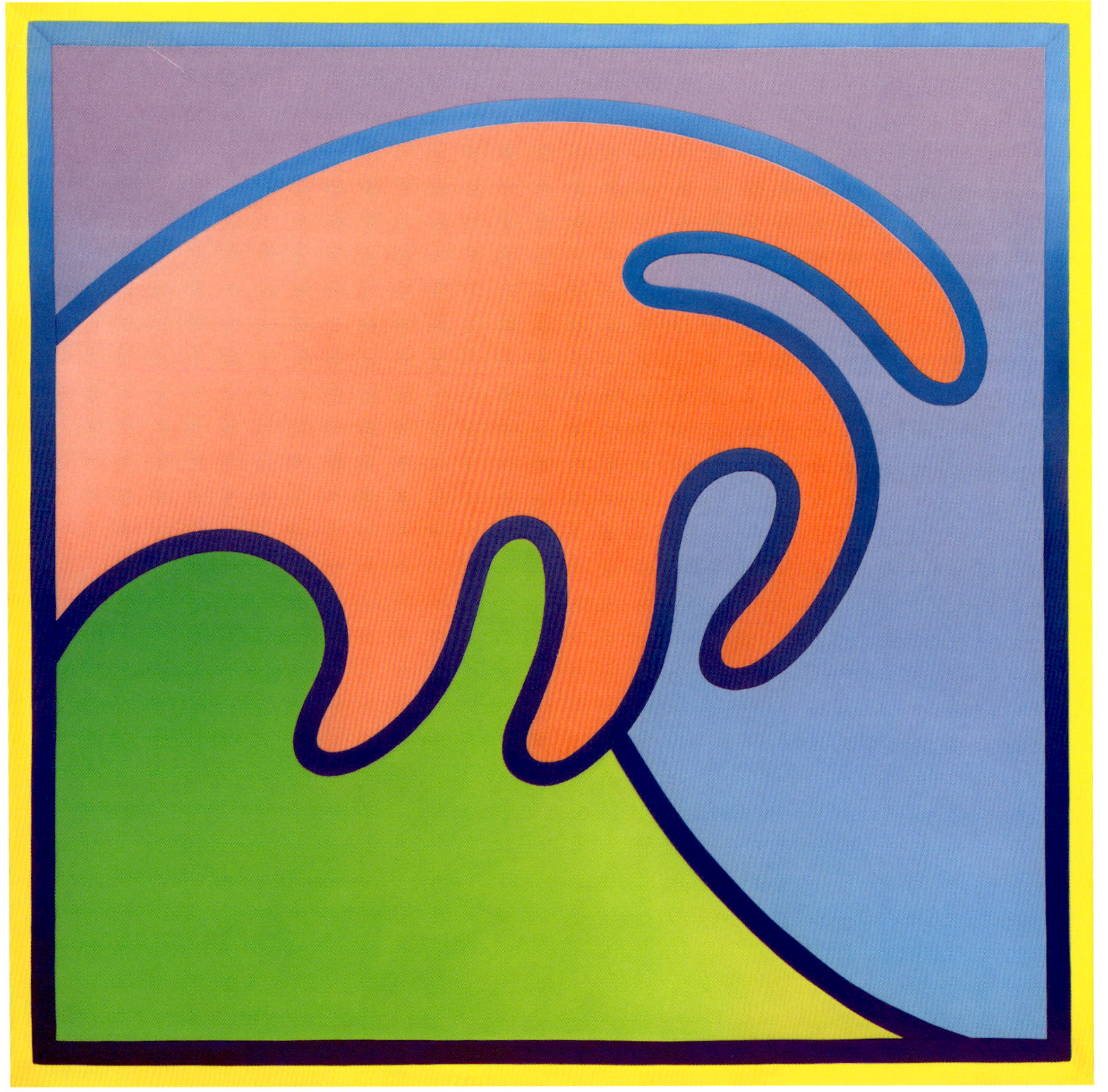

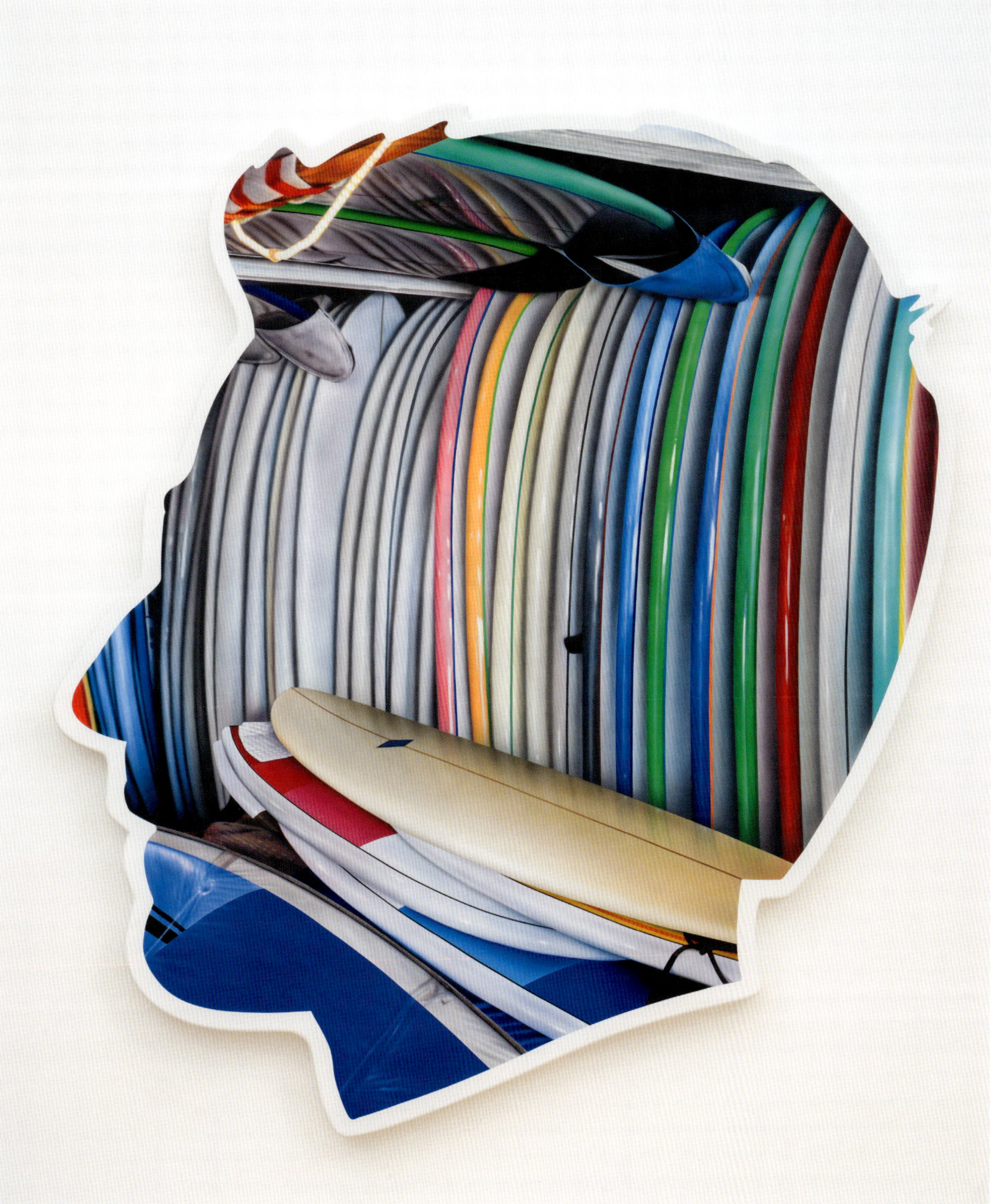

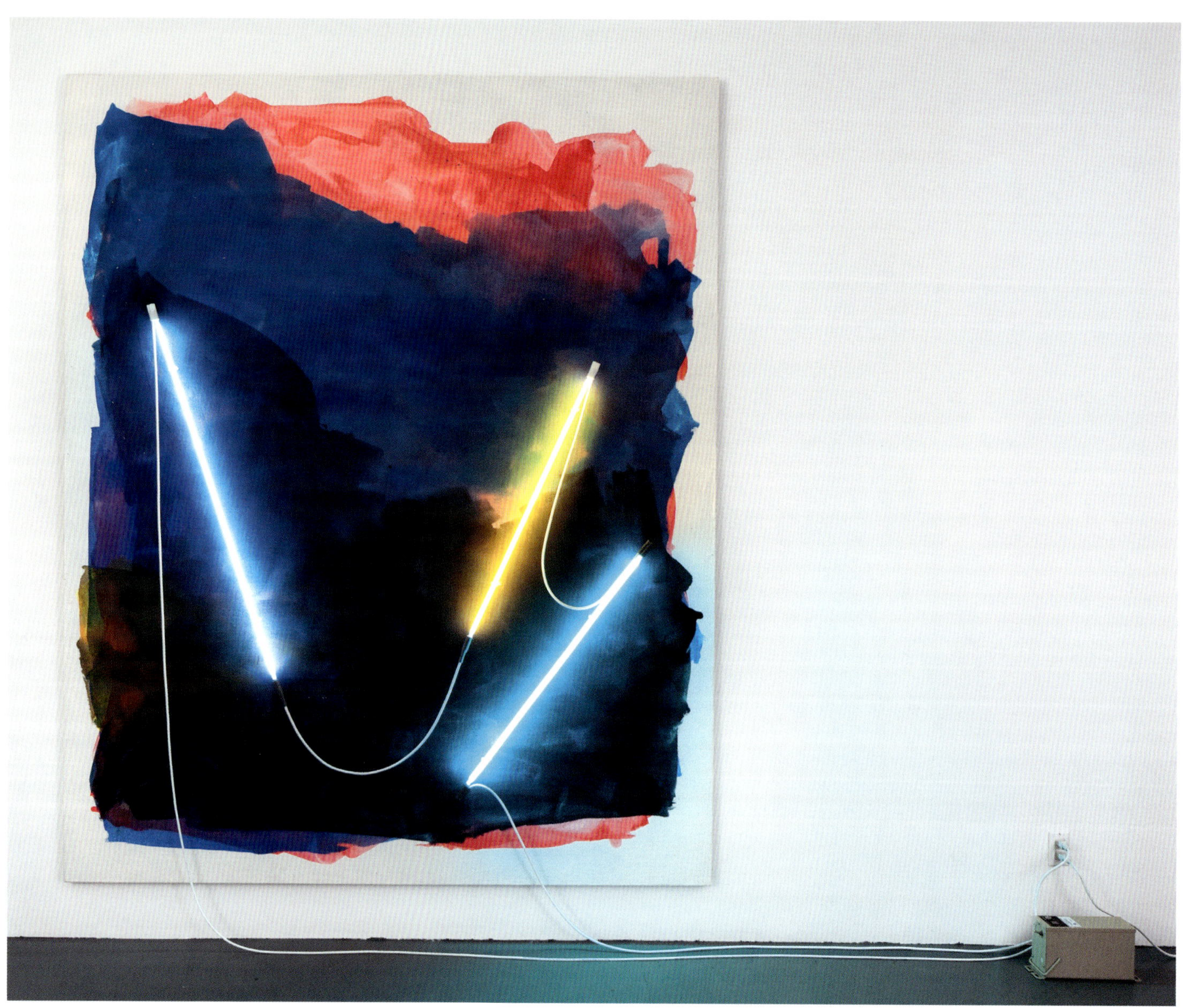

Coney Island 2012

Mary Weatherford

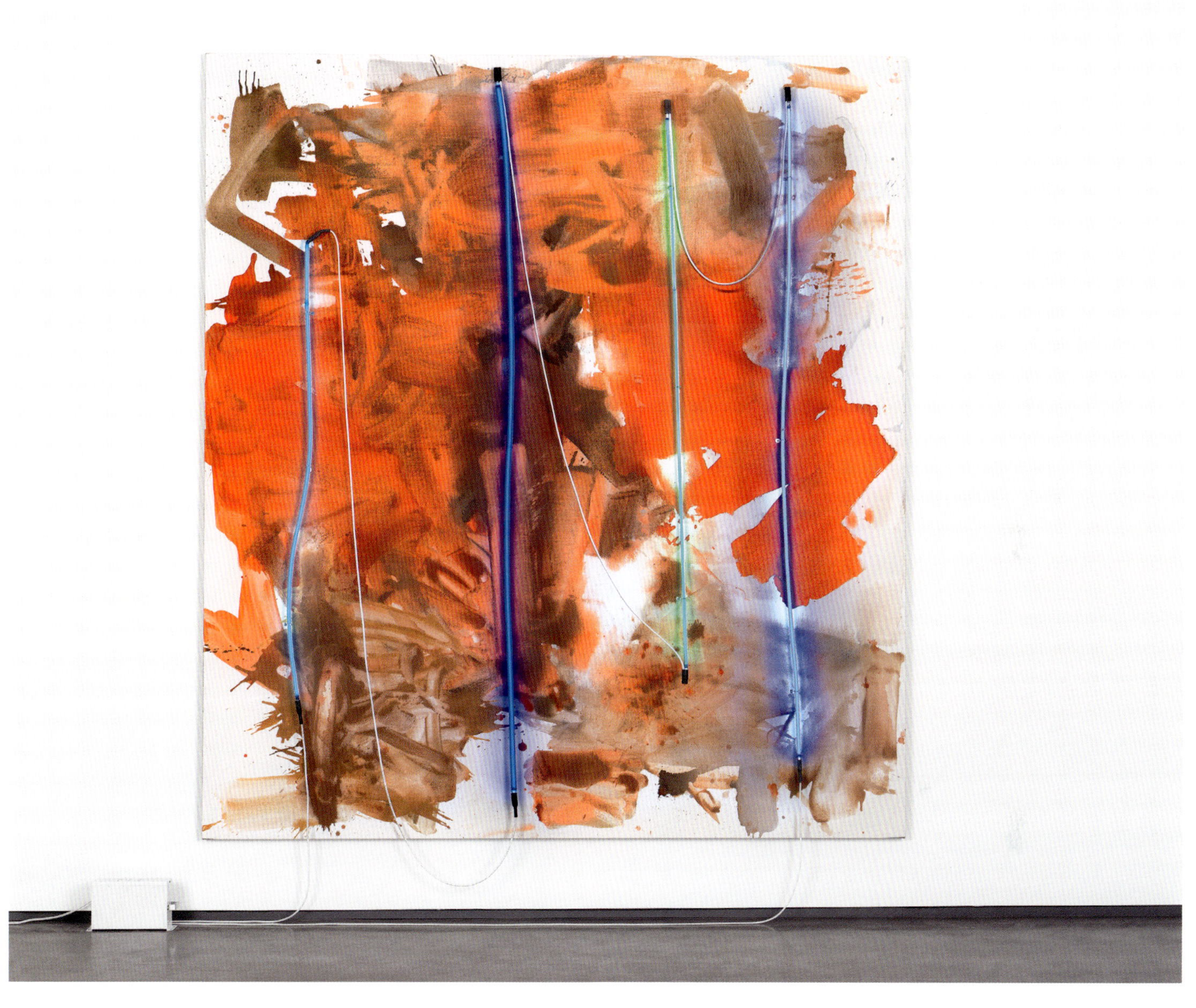

Blue Cut Fire   2017

Sho Shibuya

Sunrise from a small window   May 2020–ongoing

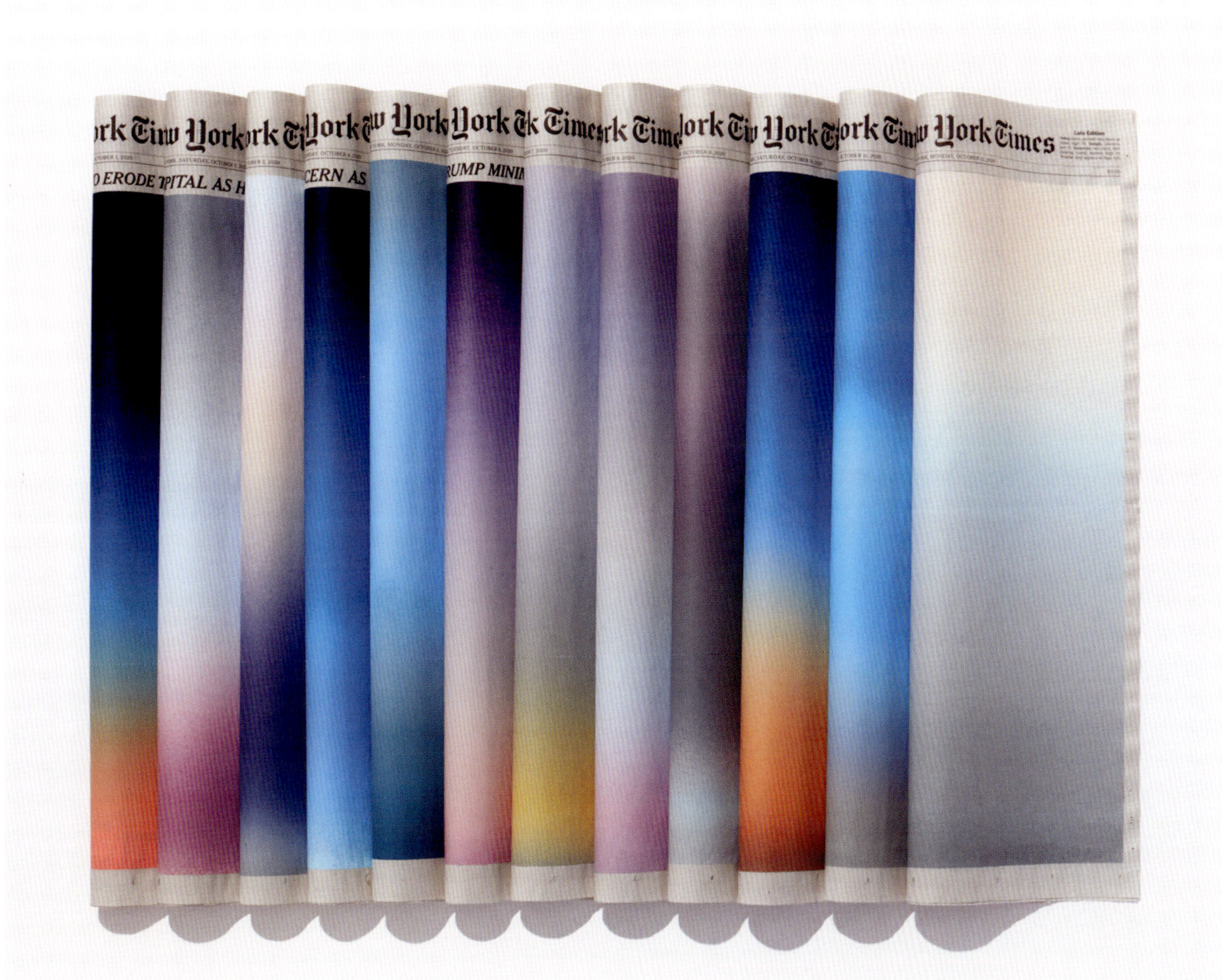

Sunrise from a small window   May 2020–ongoing

Justin Morin

How to drape the sound of waves   2019

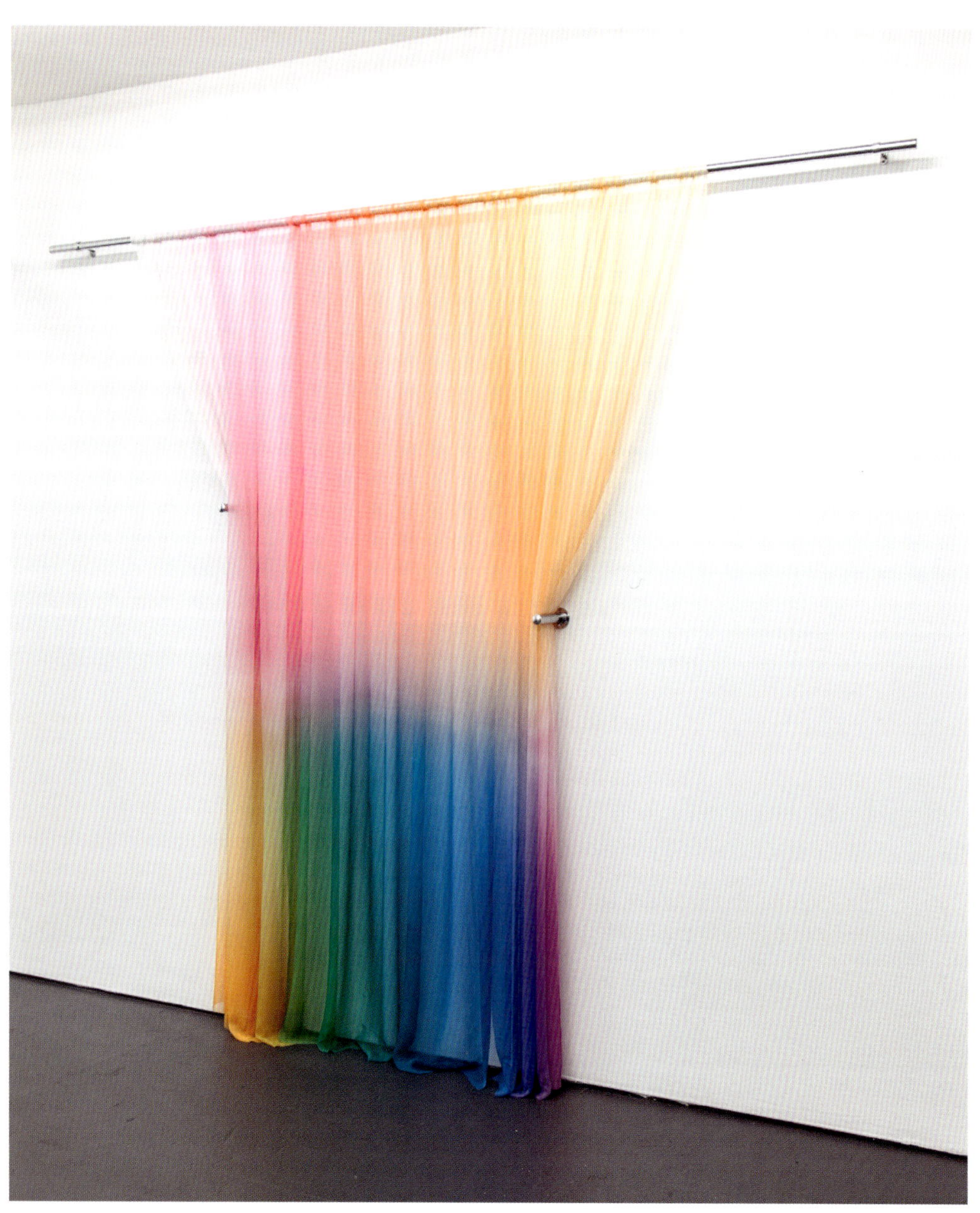

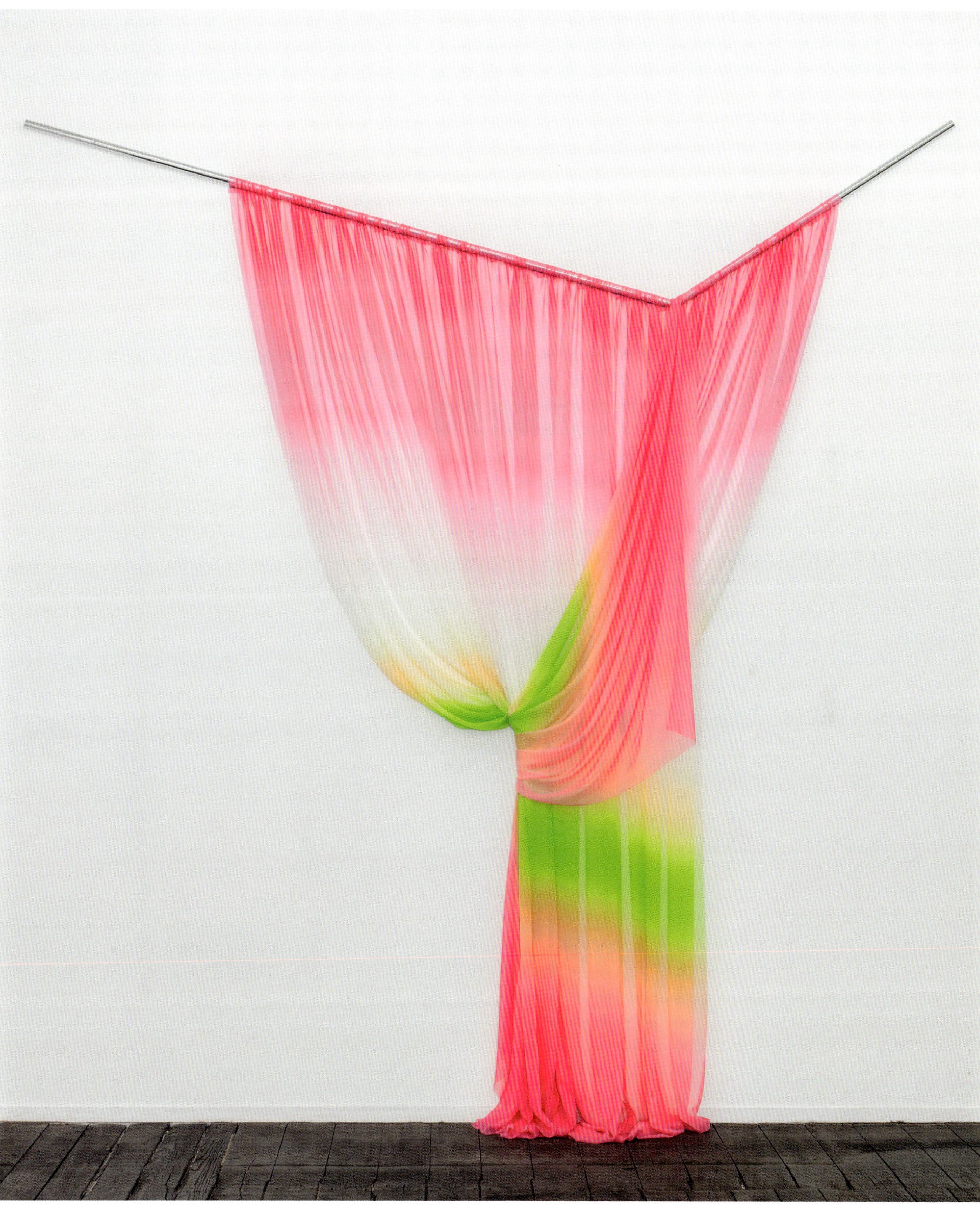

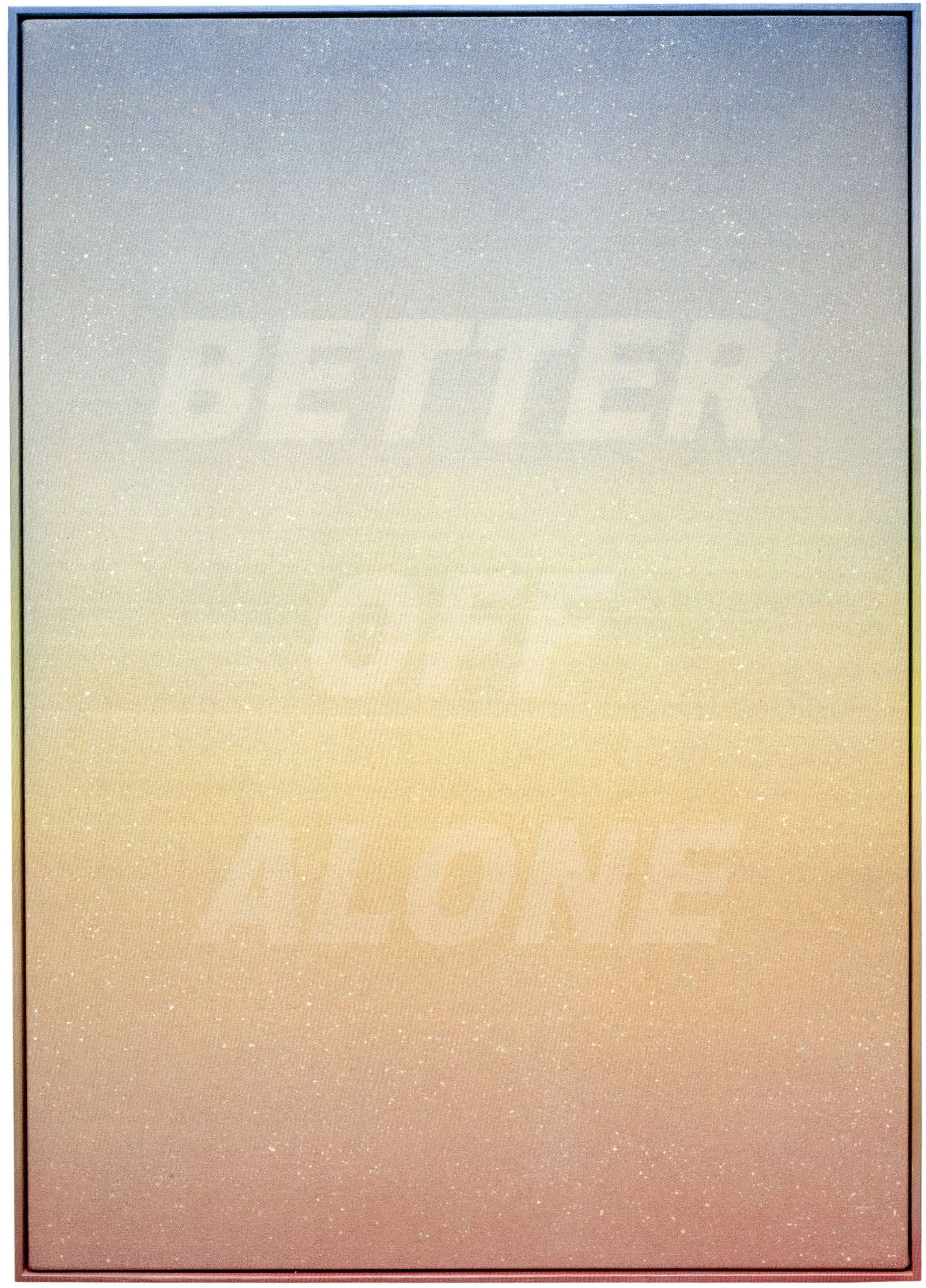

BETTER
OFF
ALONE

Better off alone, II   2022

Future Reflections, I   2024

Spencer Finch

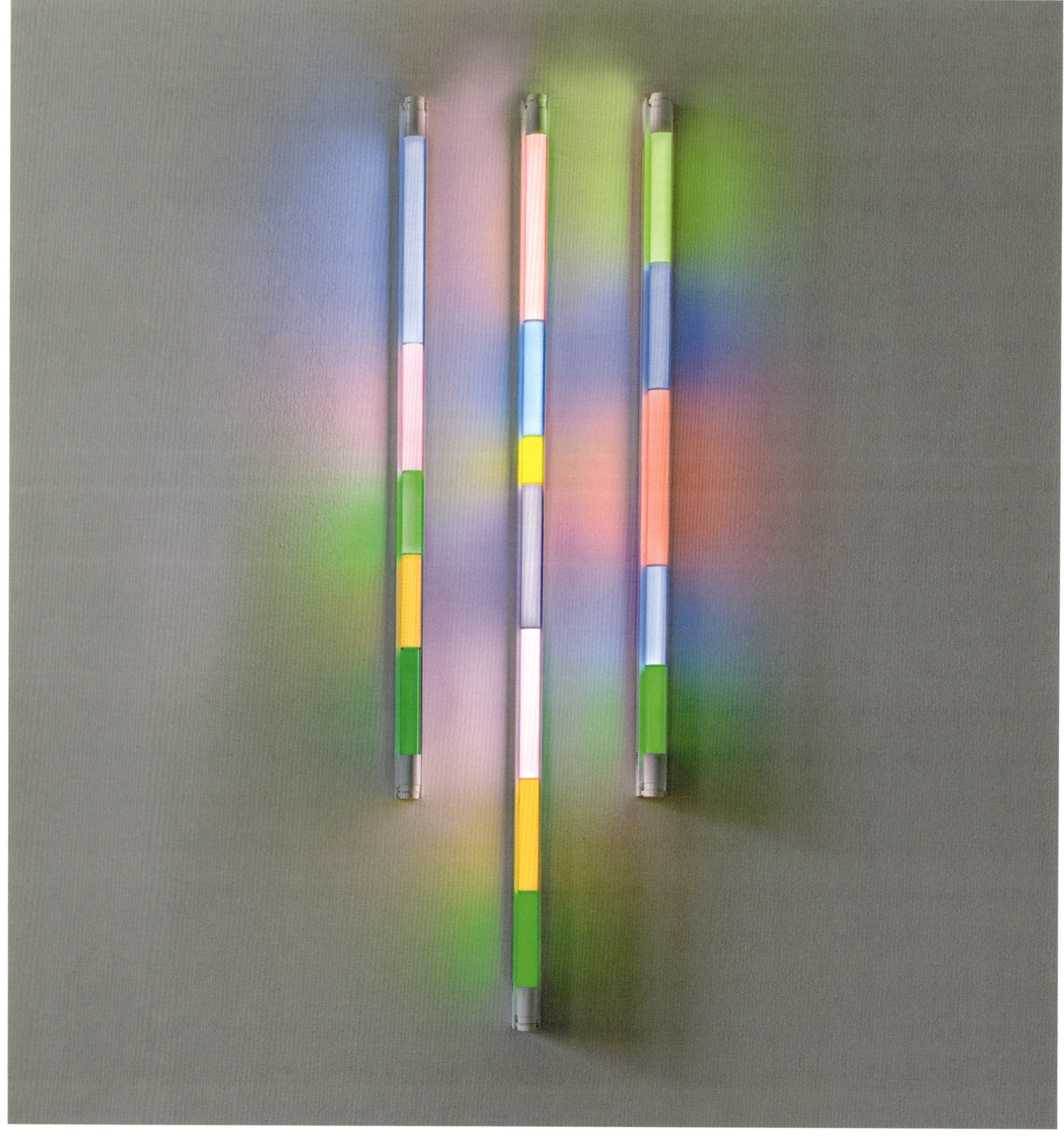

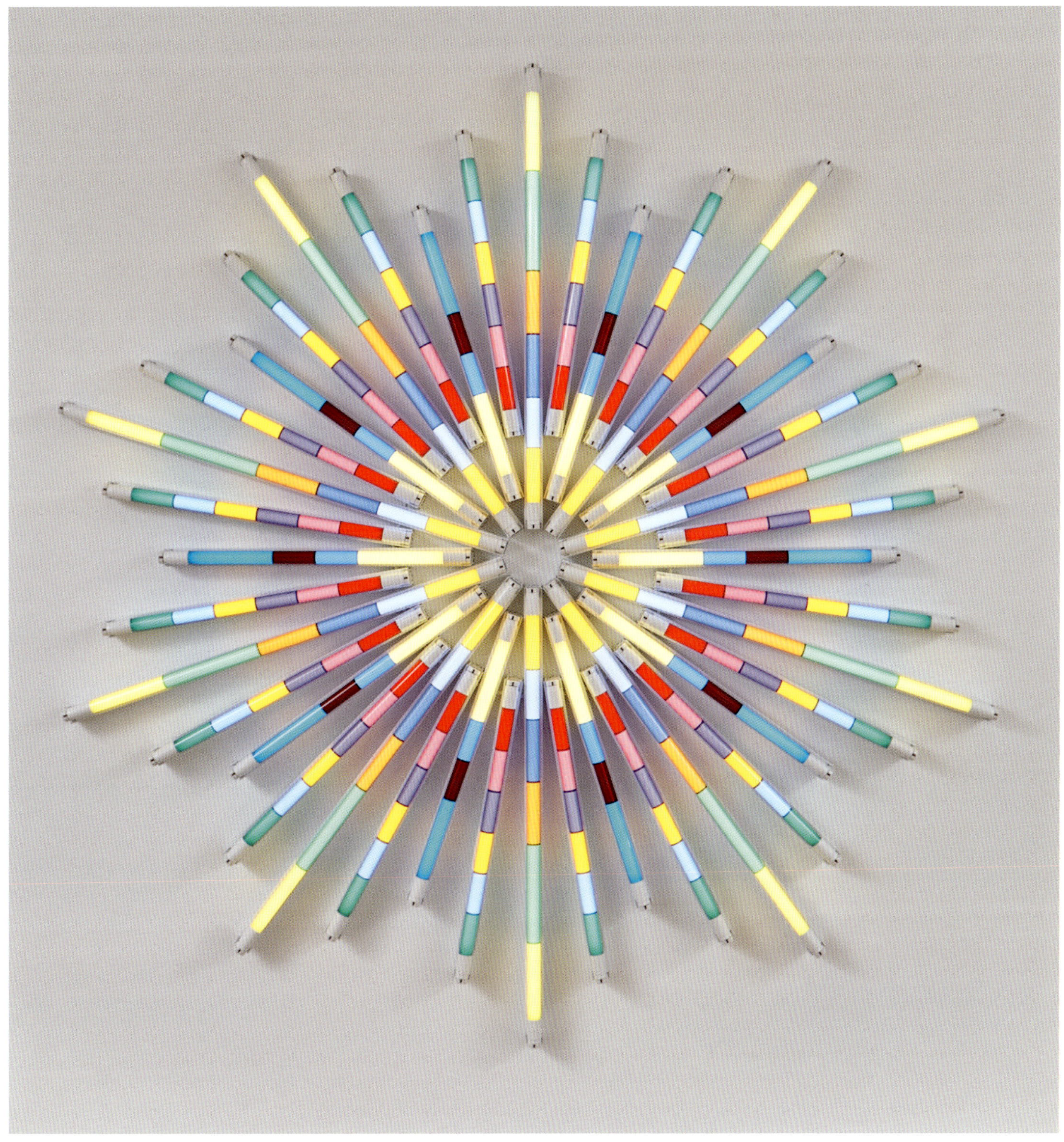

Judy Chicago

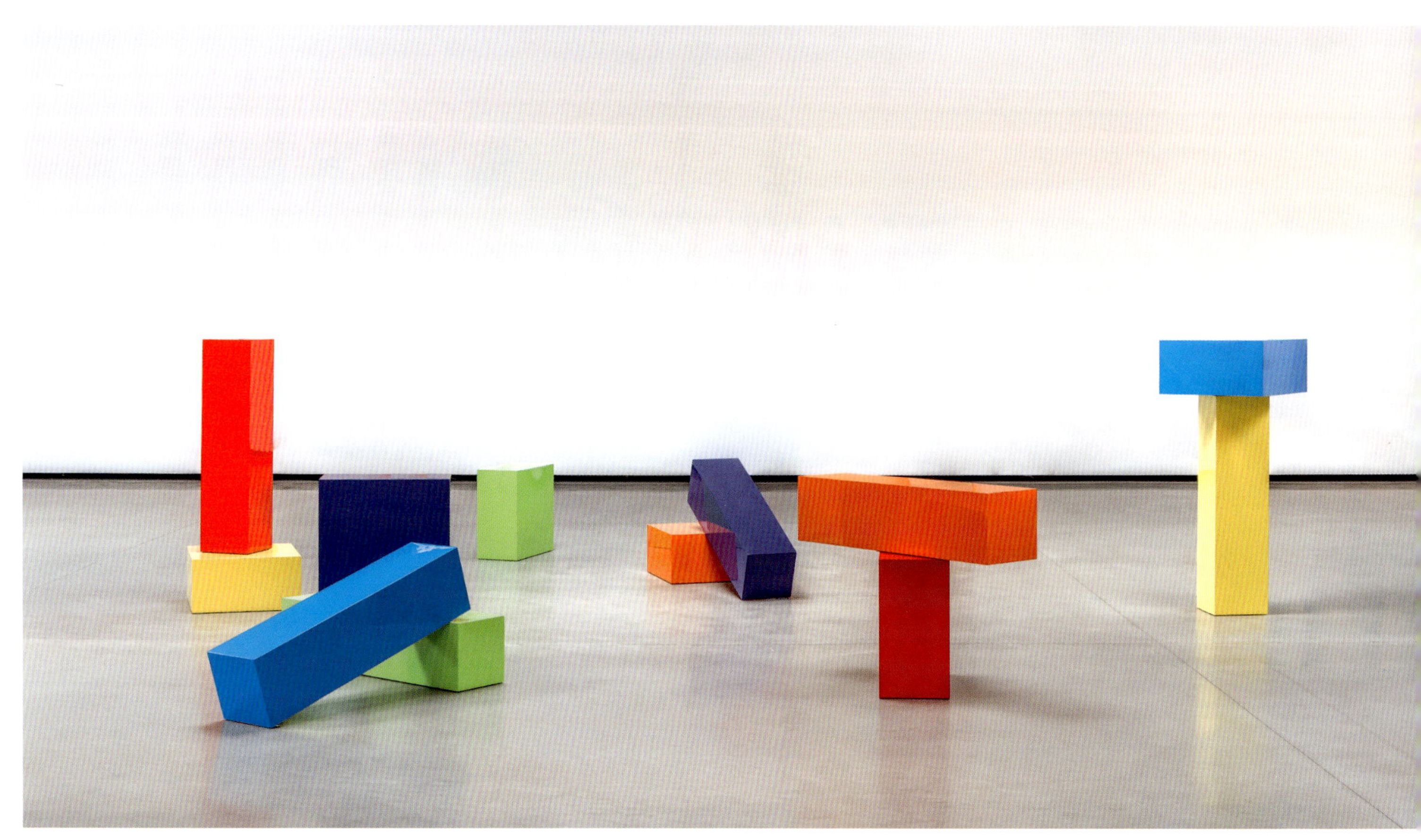

Rearrangeable Rainbow Blocks 1965/2022

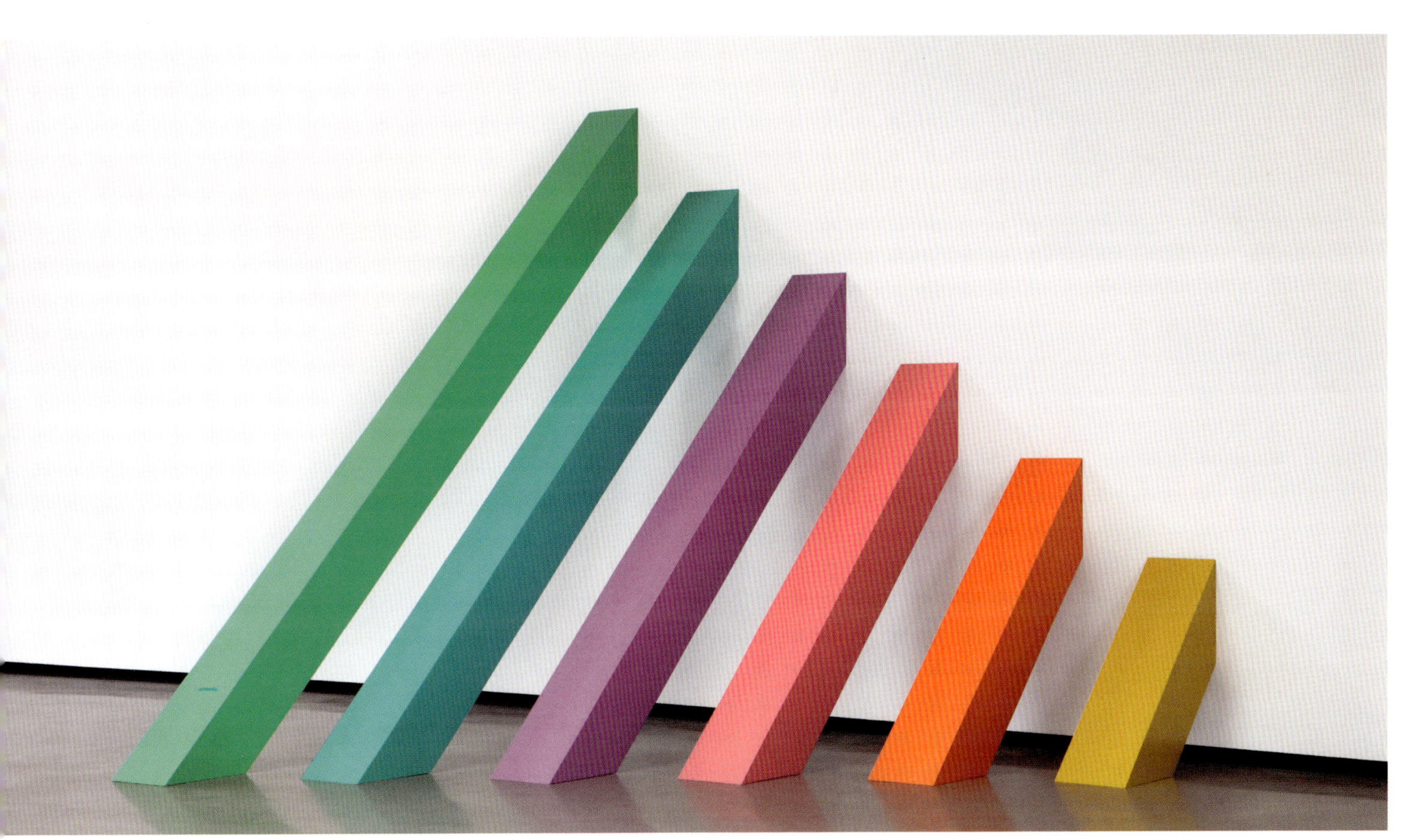

Rainbow Pickett 1965/2021

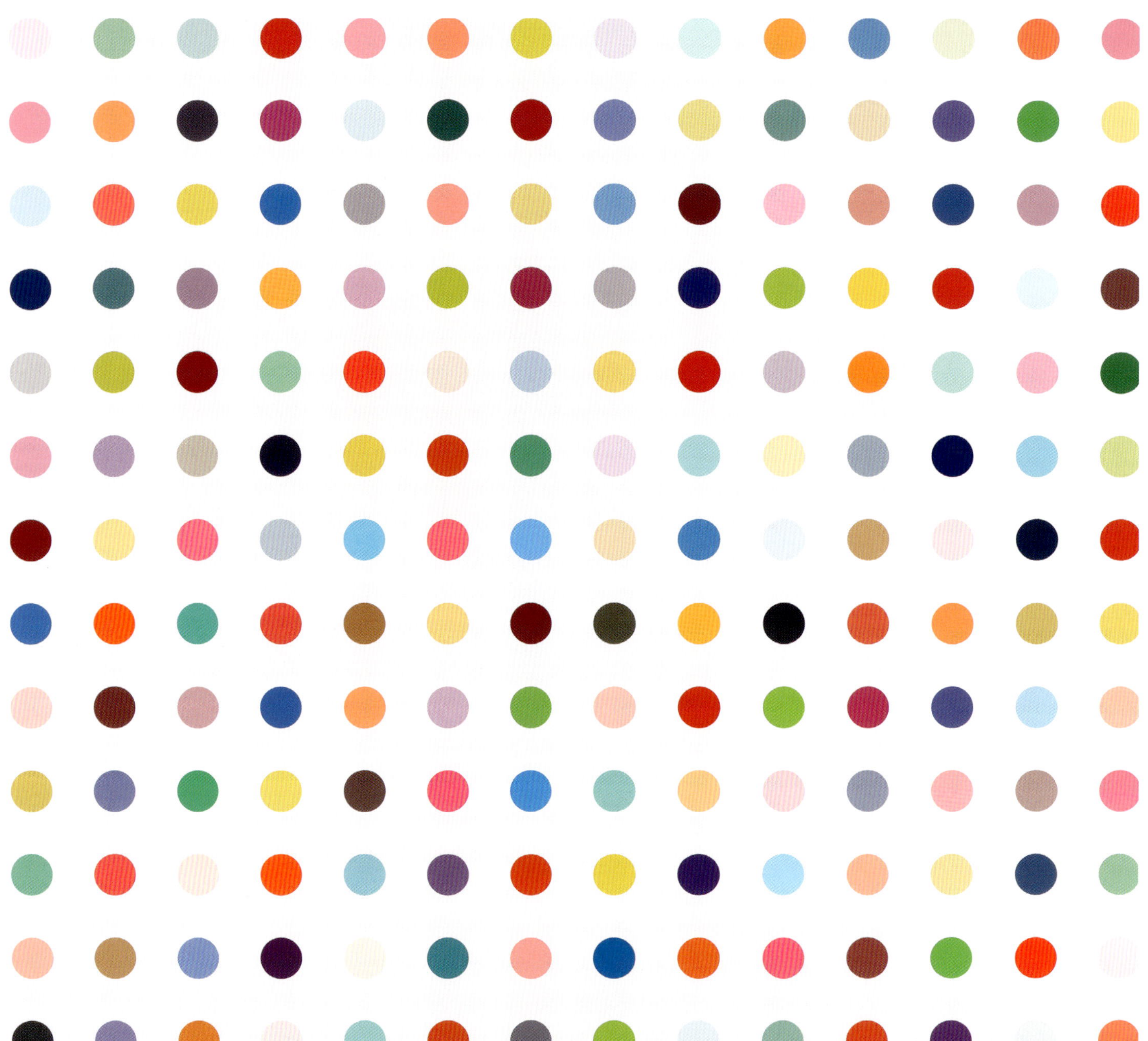

Cobalt Chloride   2021

Damien Hirst

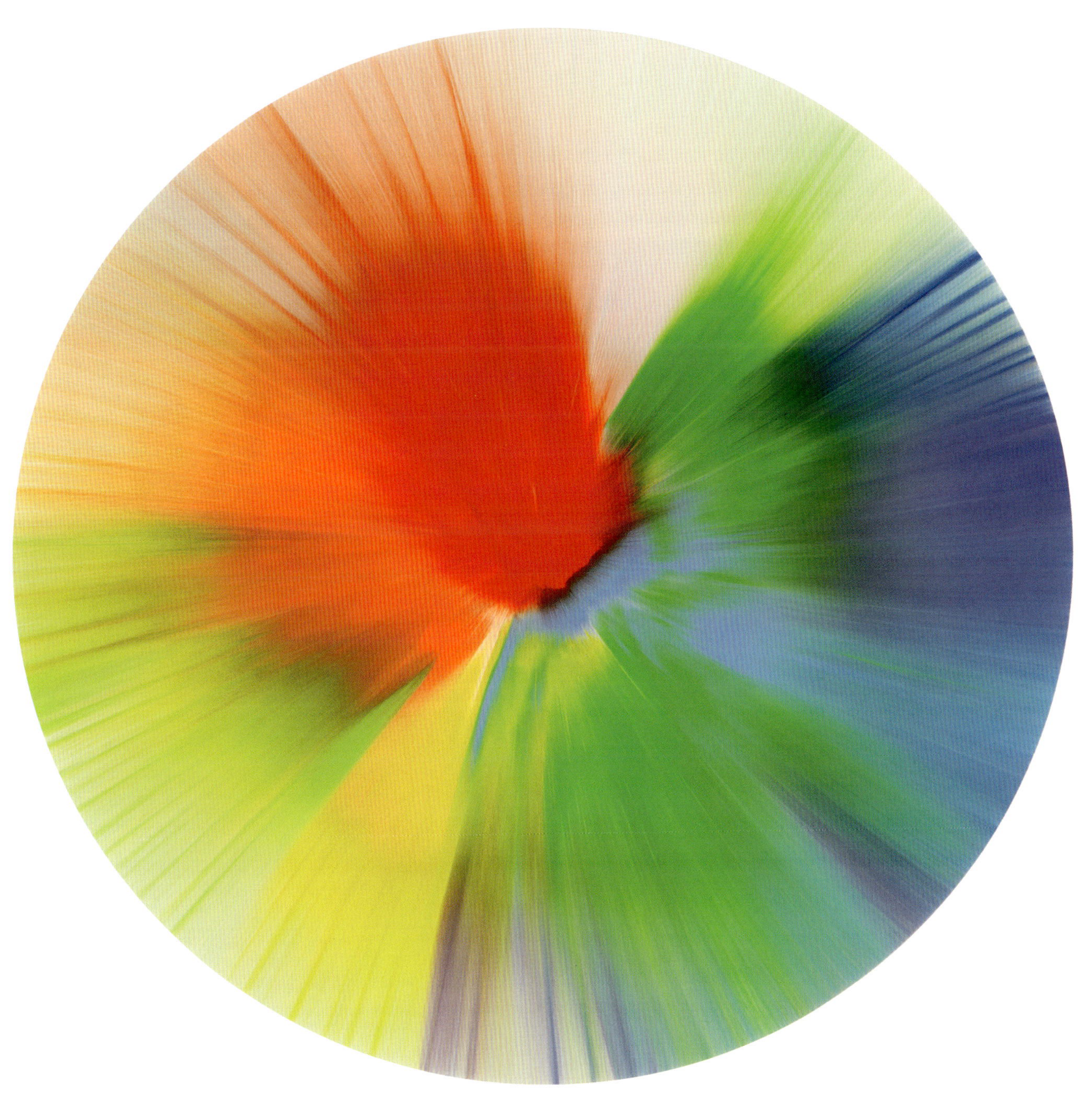

Beautiful Fart in a Japanese Garden Painting   2008

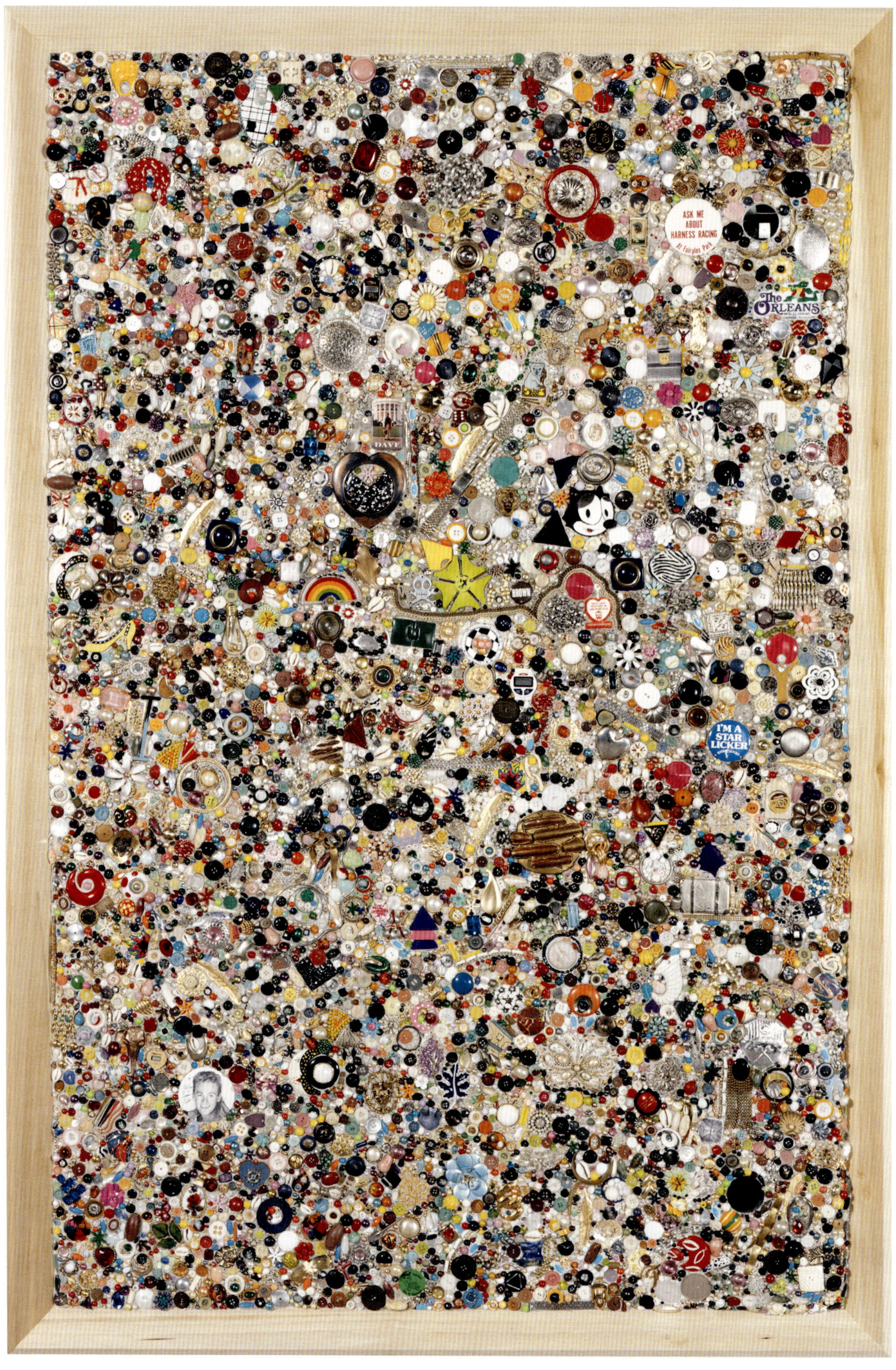

ASK ME
ABOUT
HARNESS RACING
The ORLEANS
I'M A
STAR
LICKER

Mike Kelley

Deodorized Central Mass with Satellites   1991/1999

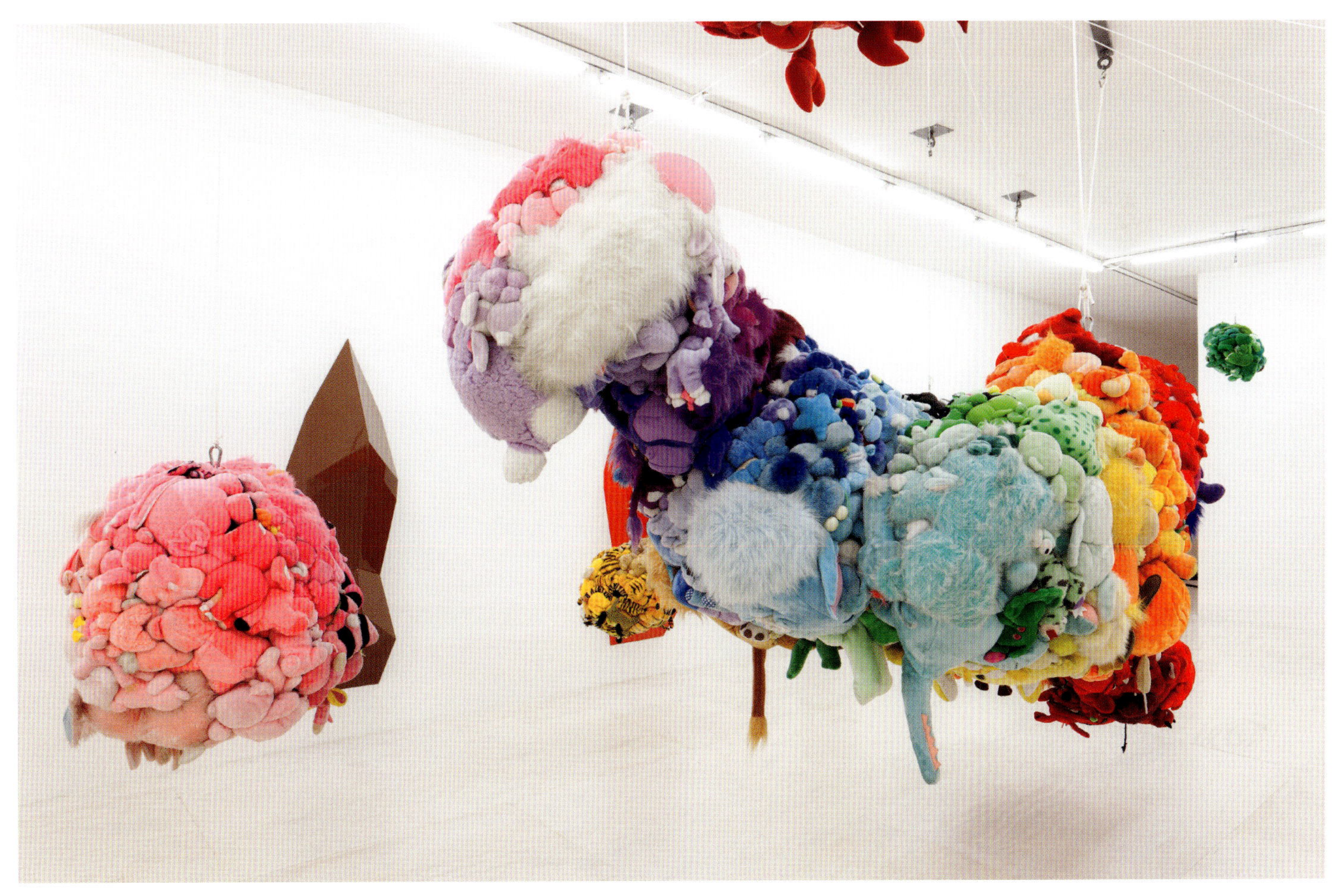

Sam Gilliam

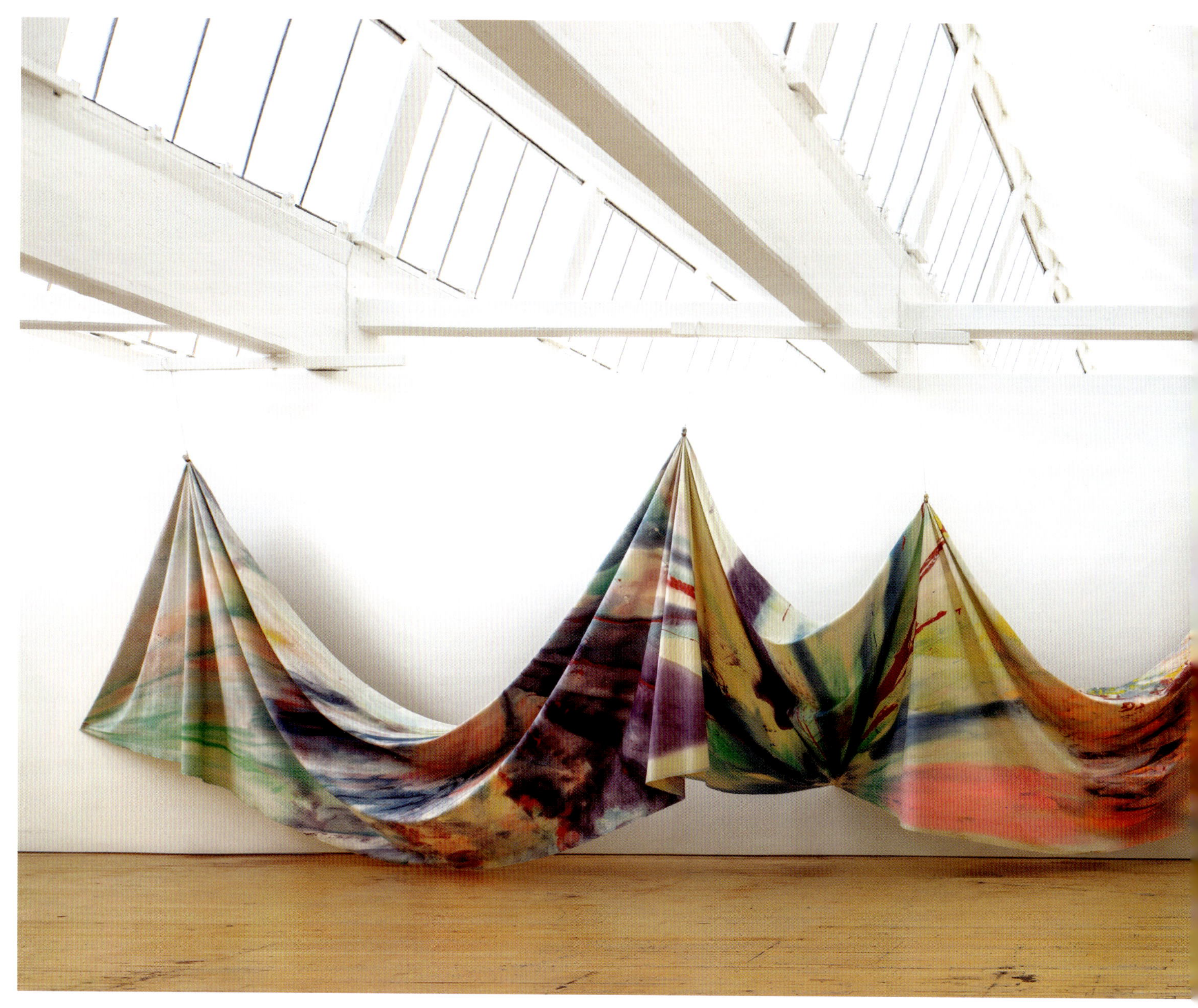

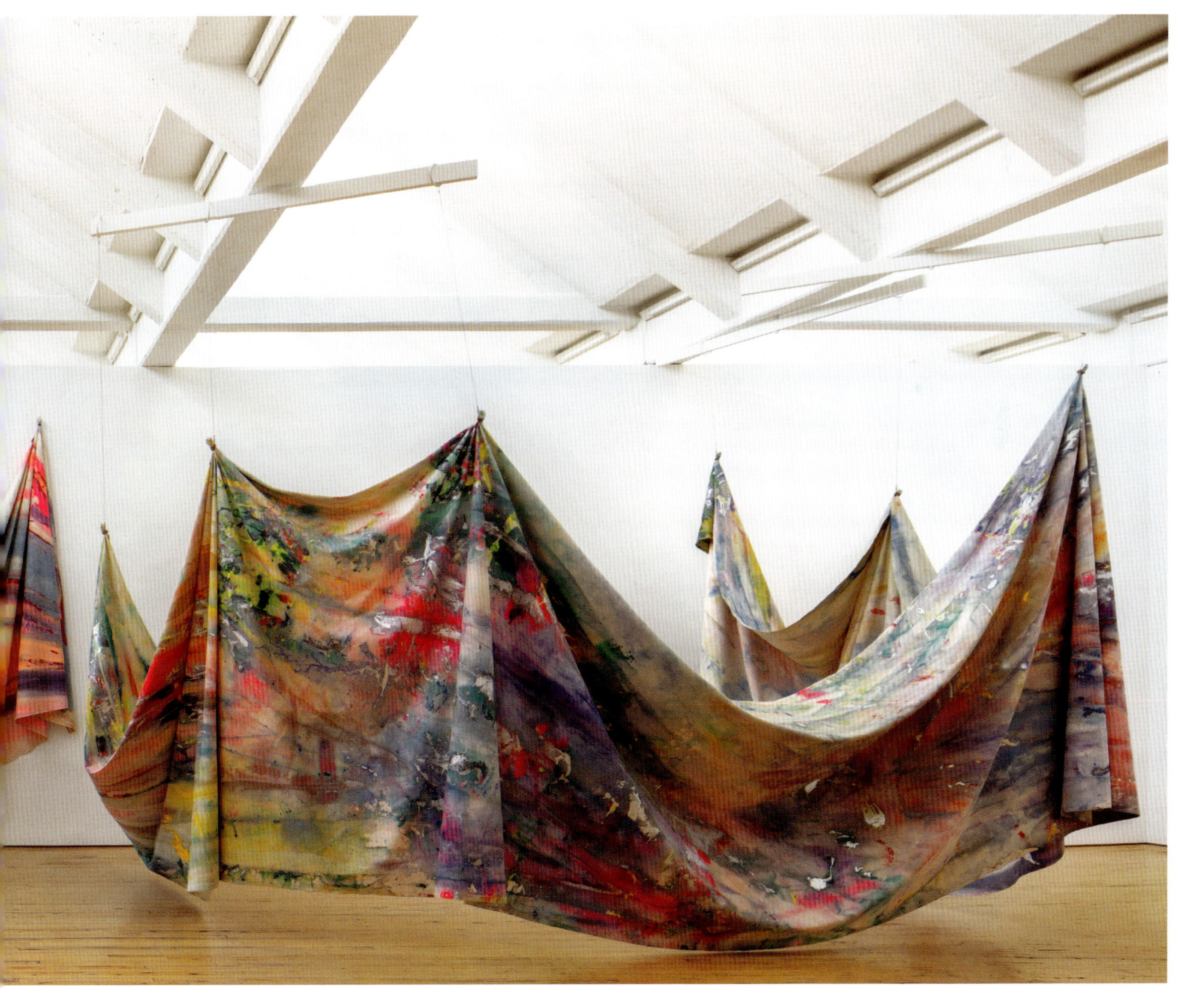

Leslie Martinez

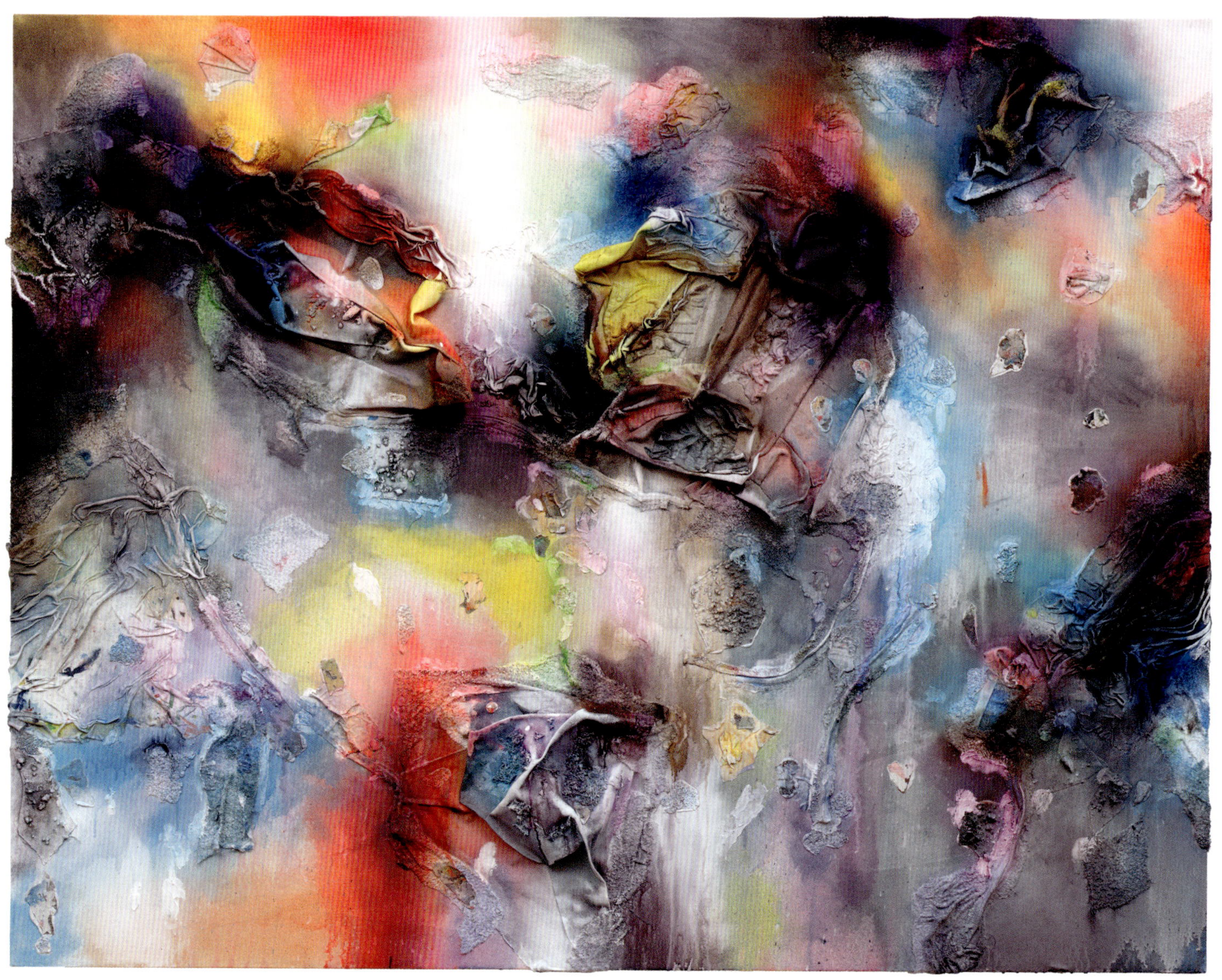

The Decorum of this Body 2023

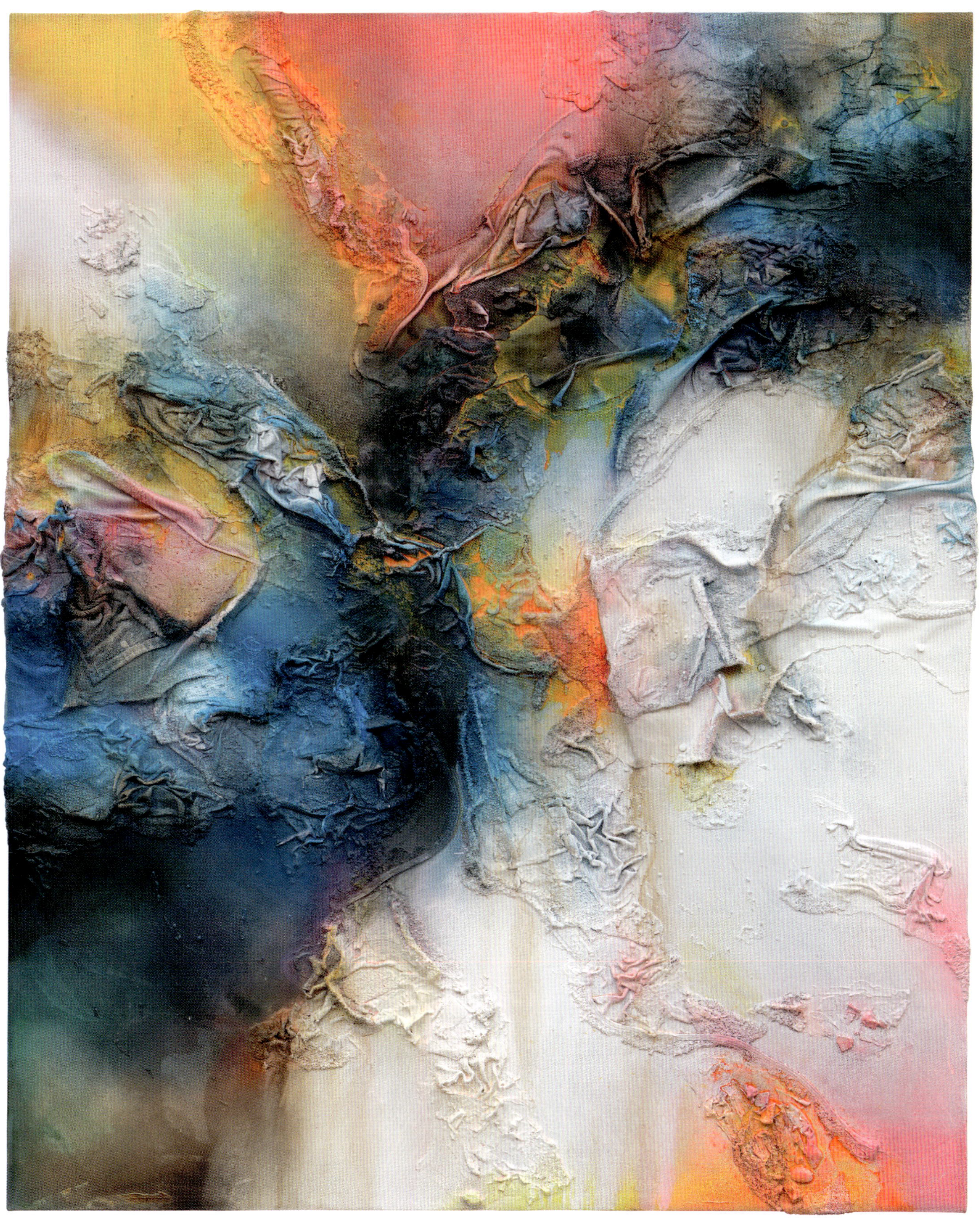

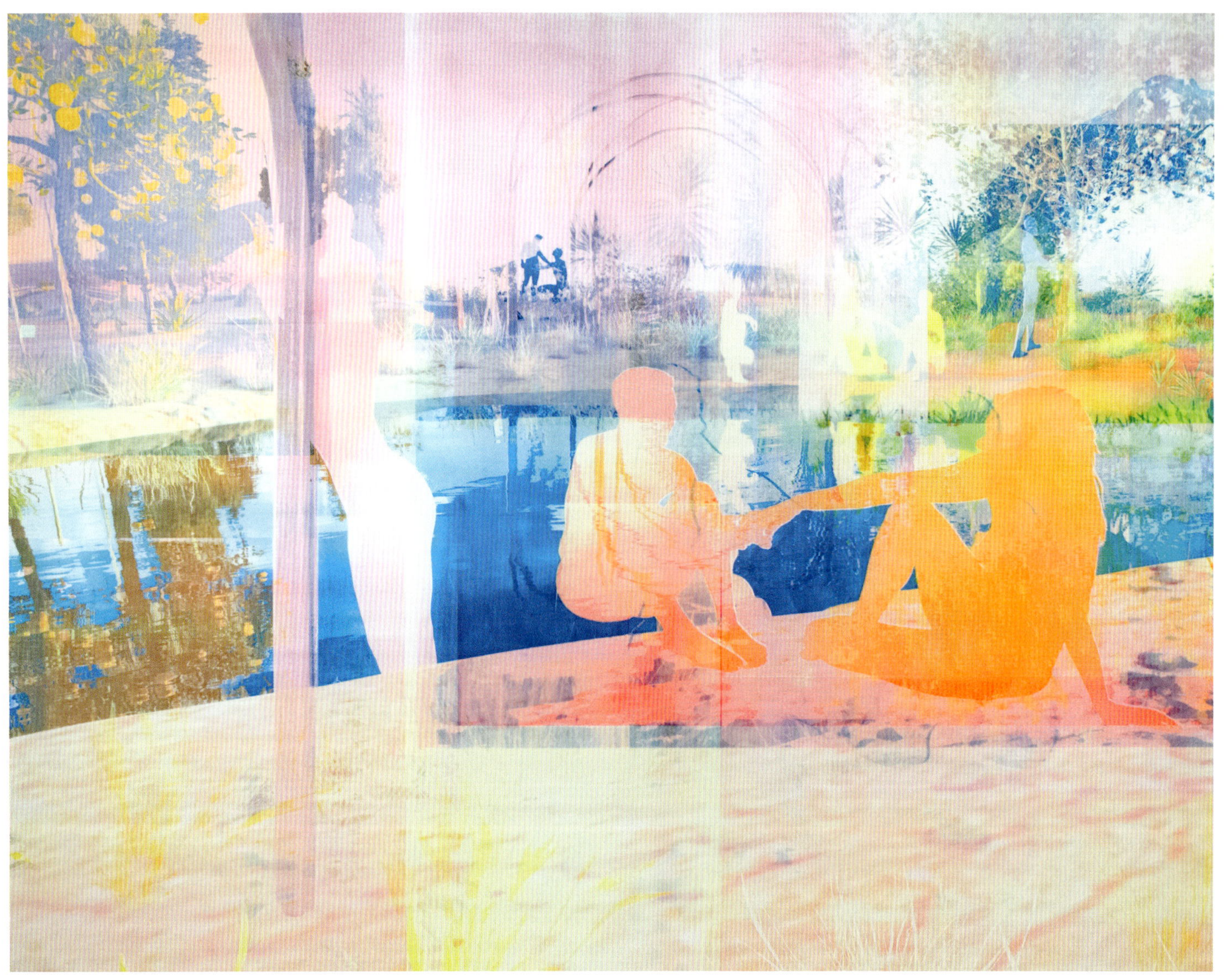

In the dust of summer   2023

Zoe Walsh

Drift and cling to shape   2023

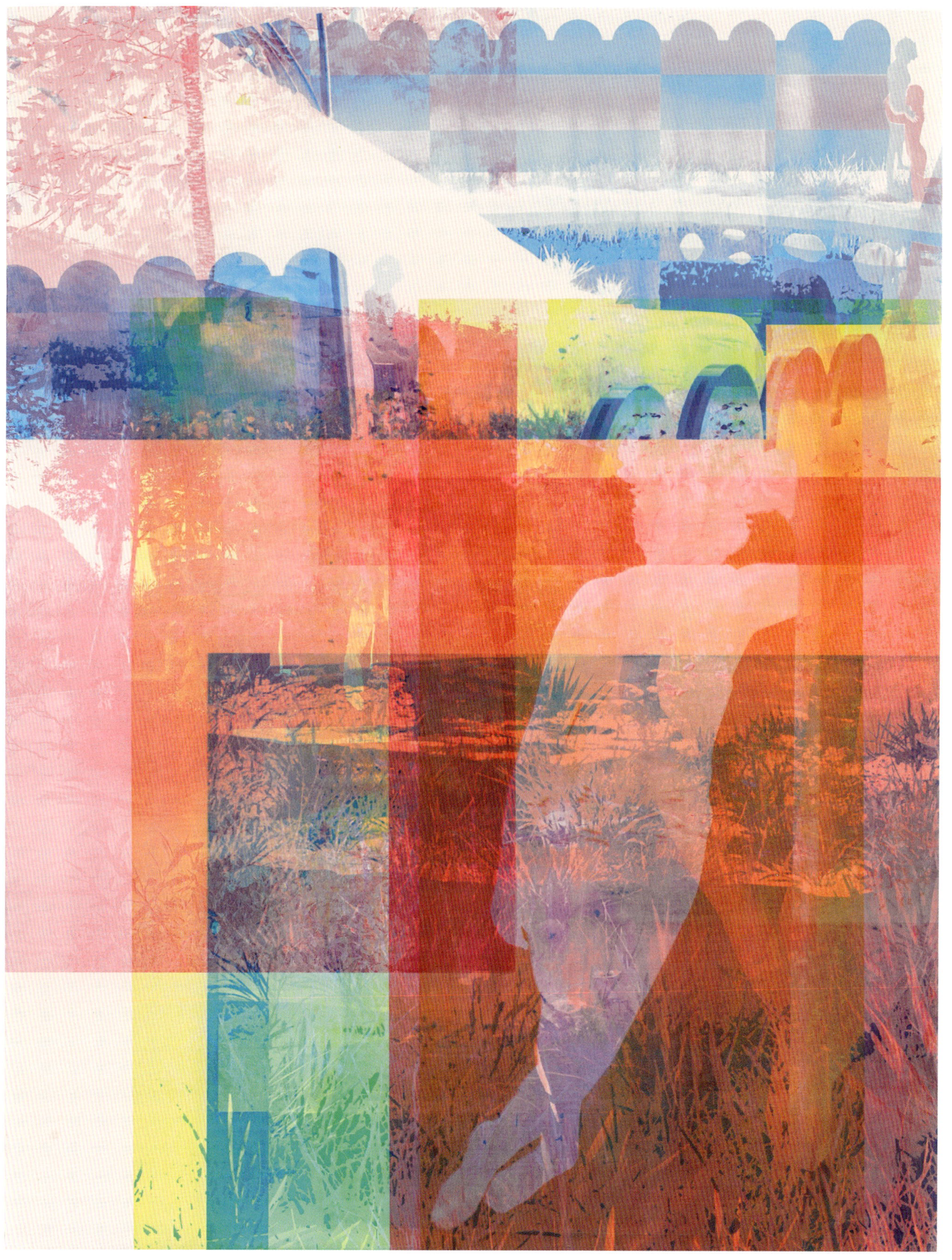

Matthew Stone

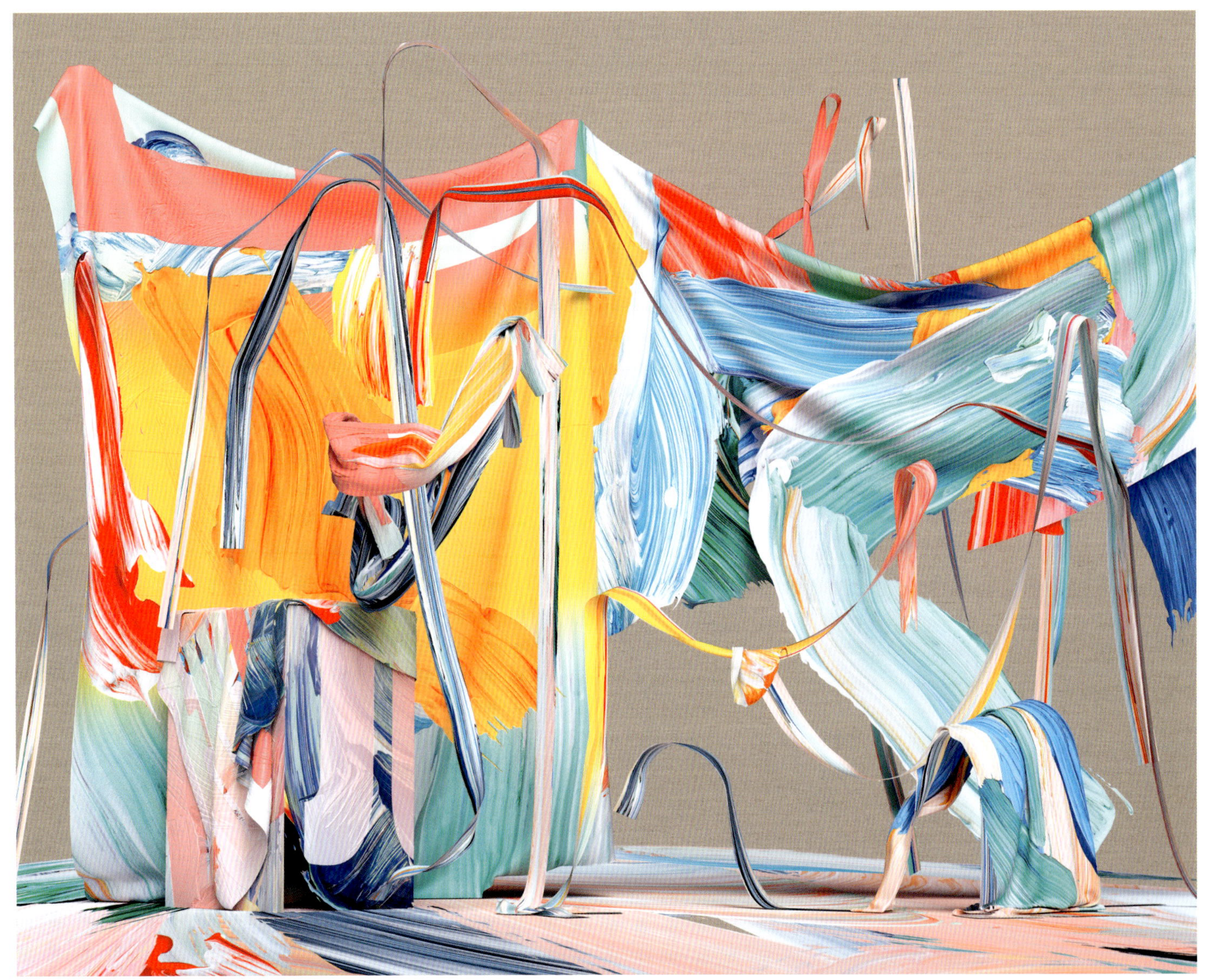

Holding (Removed) 2019

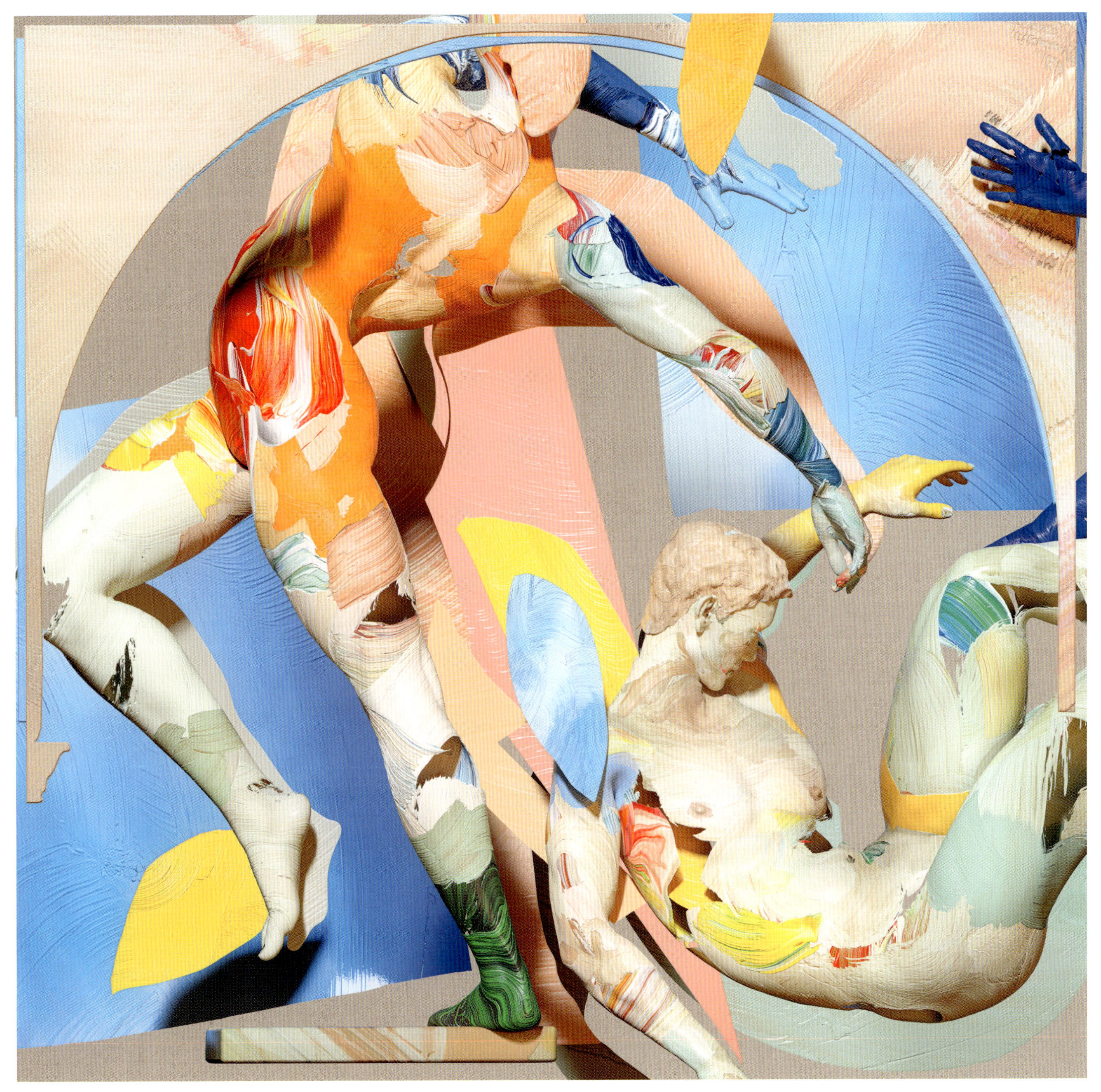

La Danse Inachevée (Virtual Mix) I (after Matisse) 2024

117

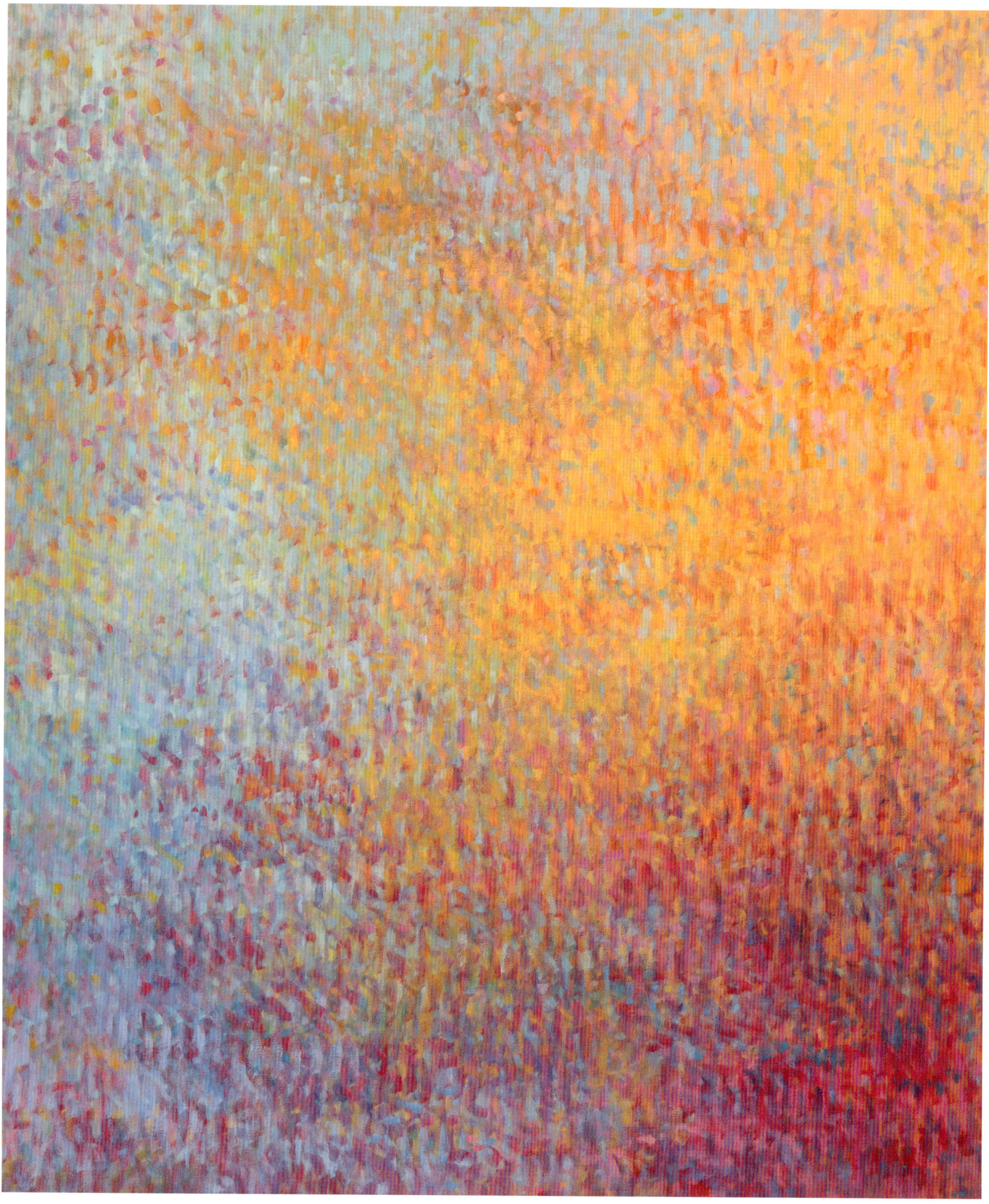

Jean-Baptiste Bernadet

Untitled (Vetiver XVIII) 2015

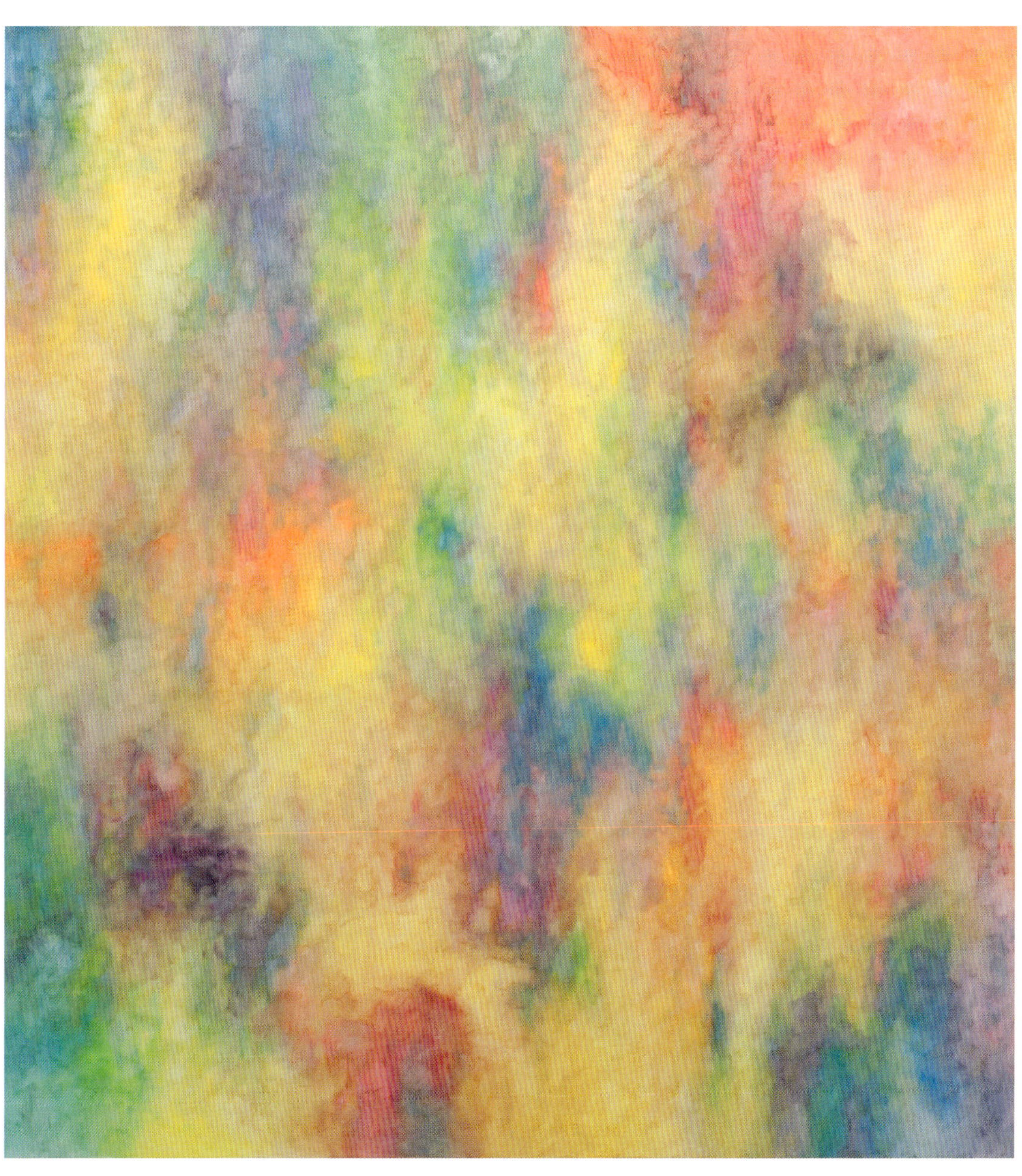

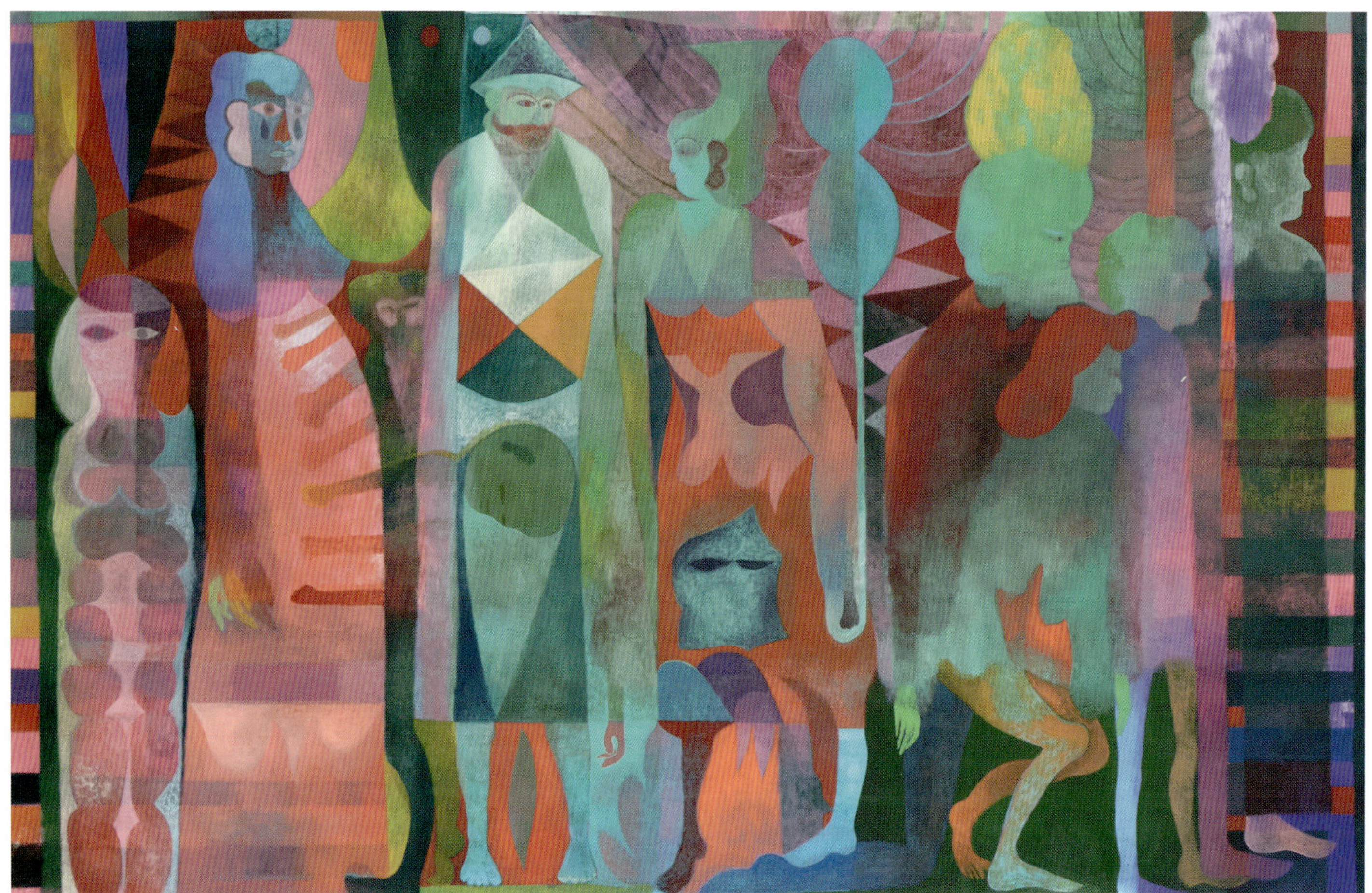

The Past Awaiting the Future/Arrival of Drummers   2023

Maja Ruznic

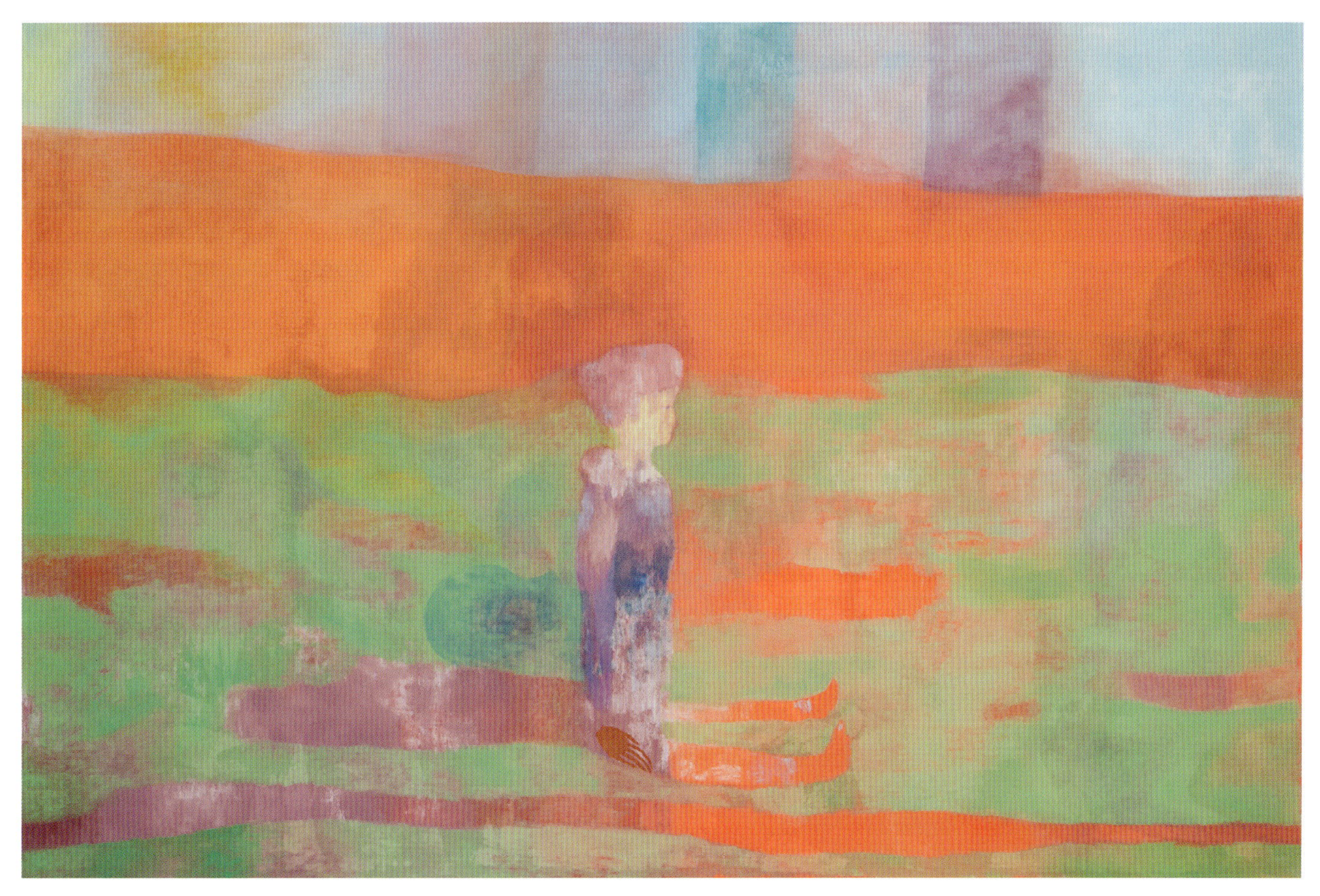

Deep Calls to Deep   2023

Zach Harris

Study for 20/20   2016–17

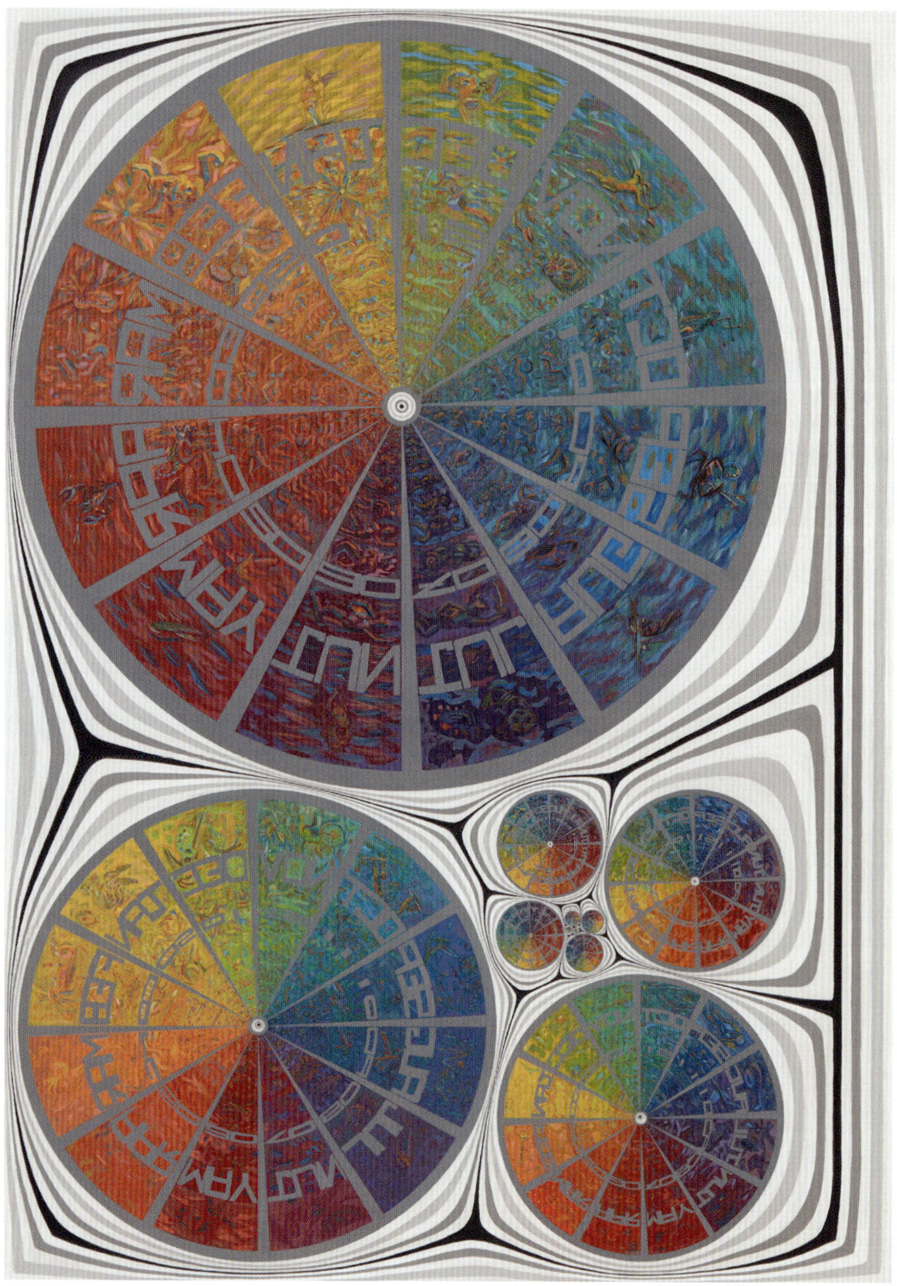

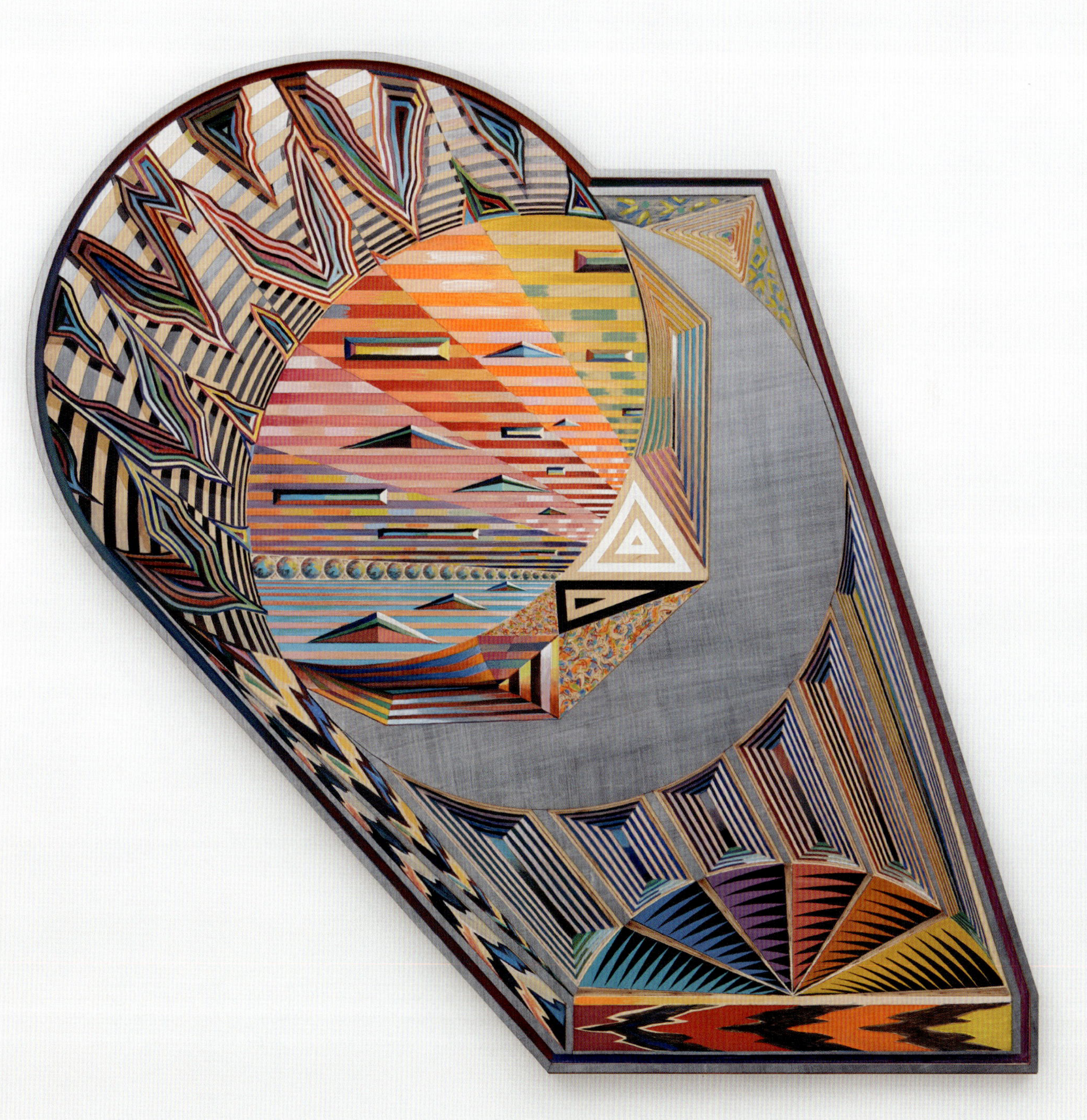

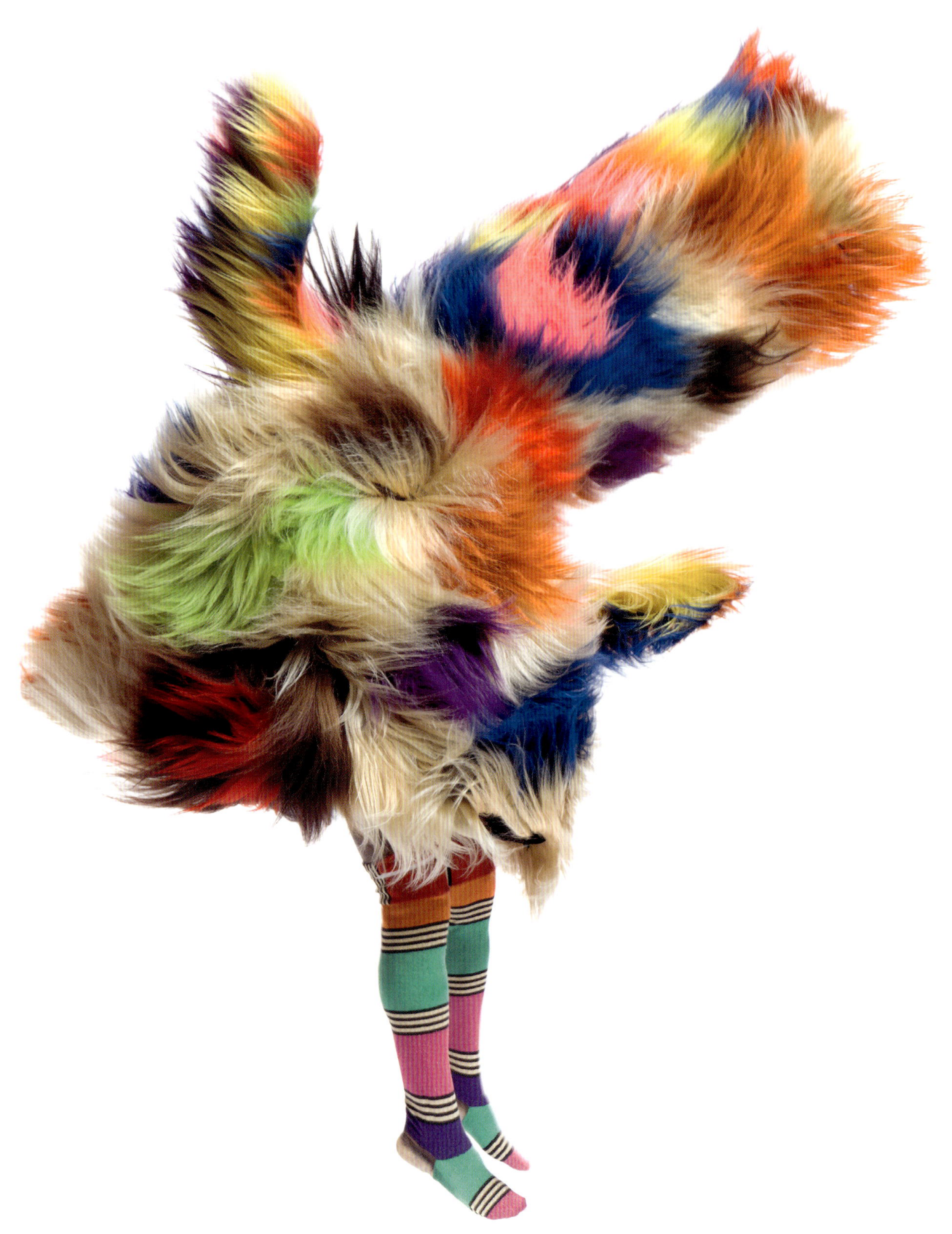

Nick Cave

Installation view: *The Let Go*   2018

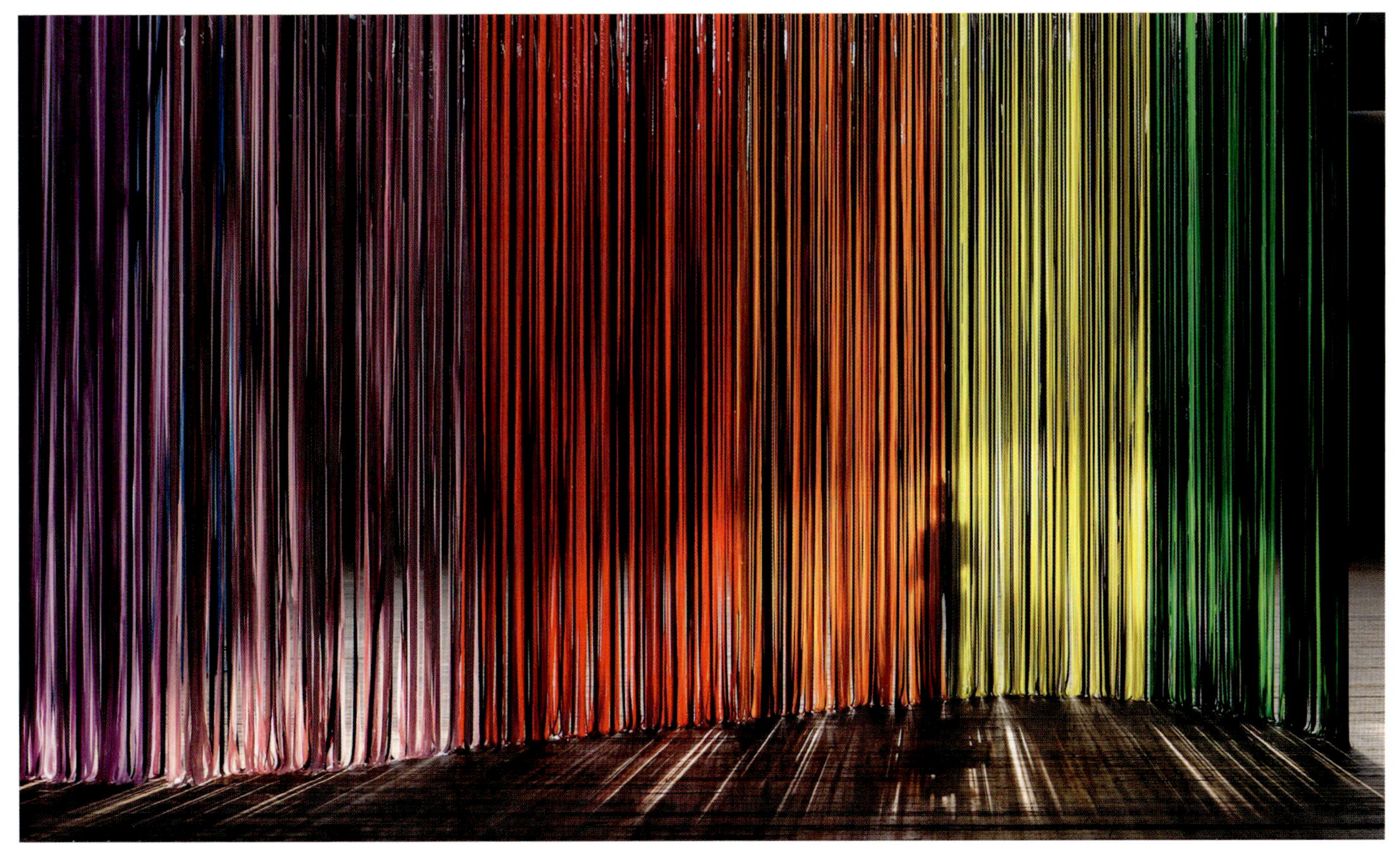

Sarah Anne Johnson

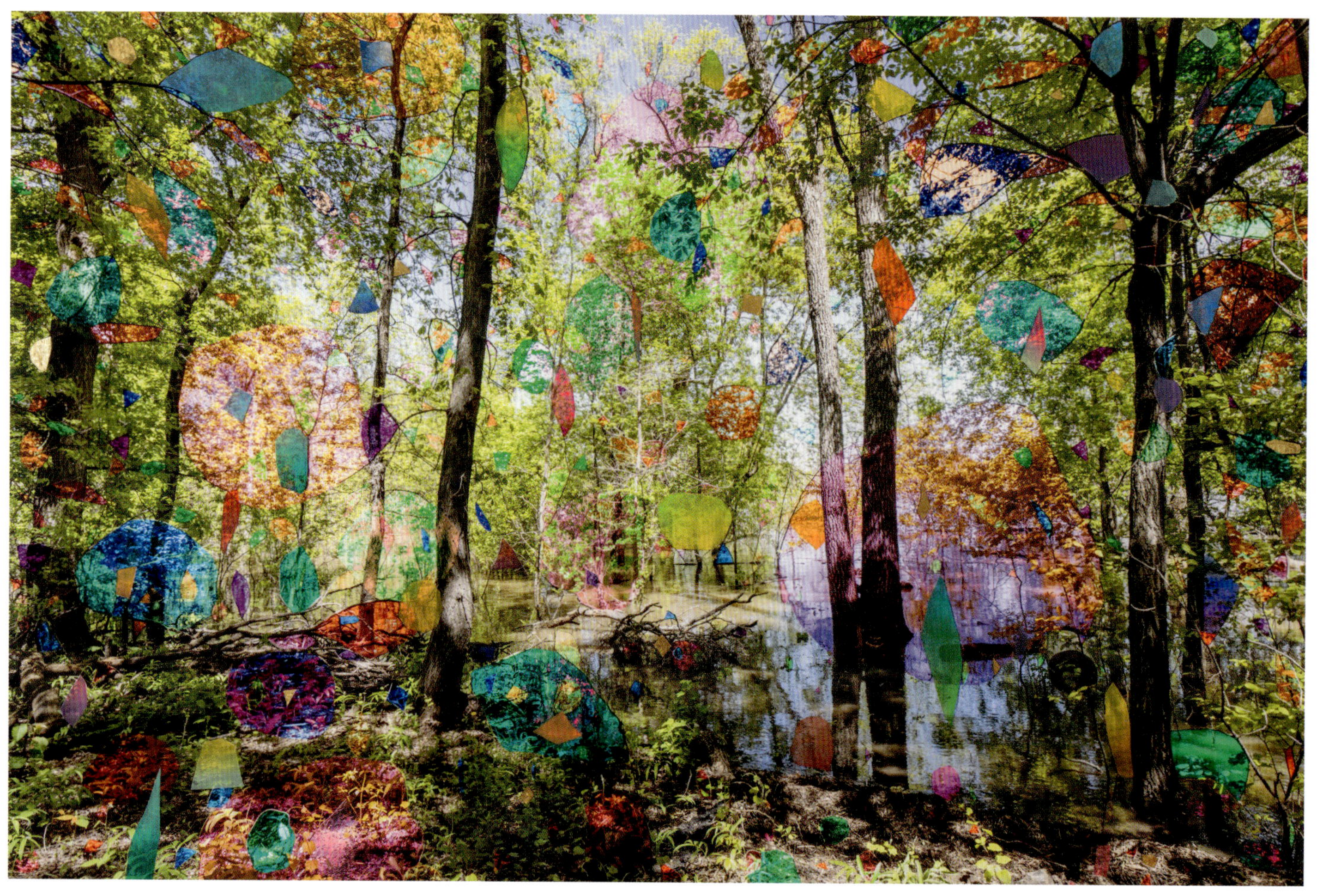

FMMTY 2023

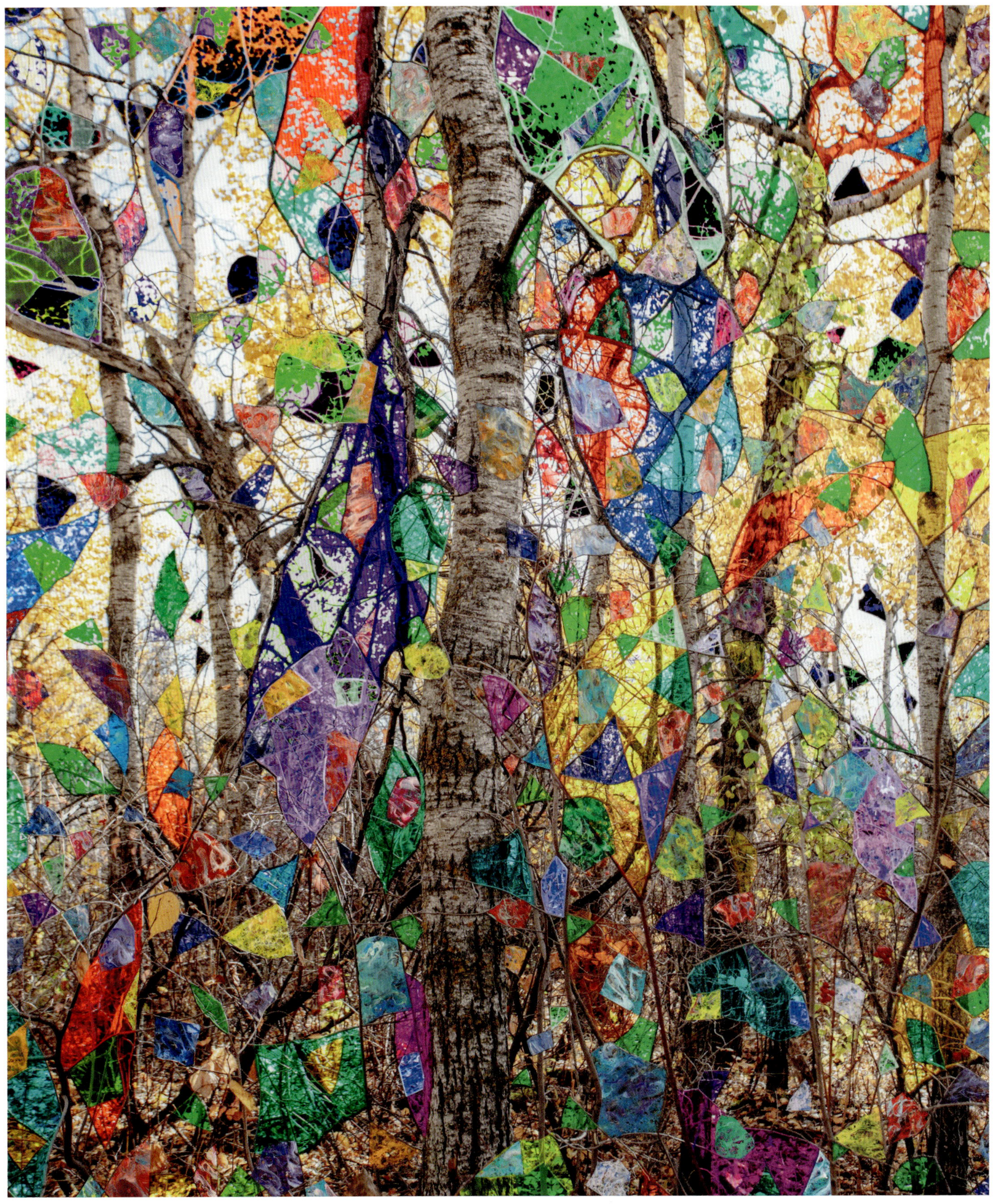

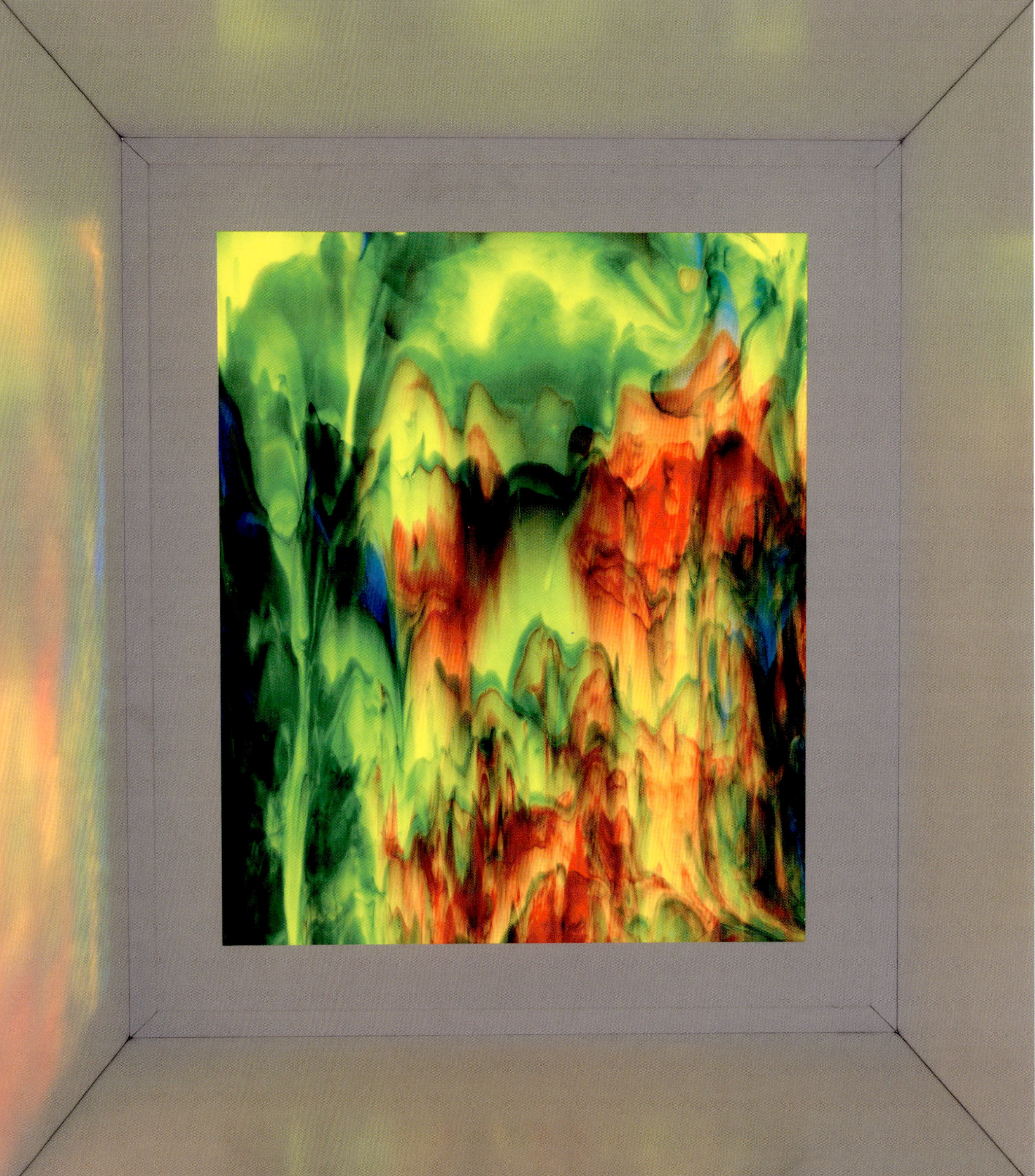

Untitled (Hartland, VT, Ferns 4H) 2013

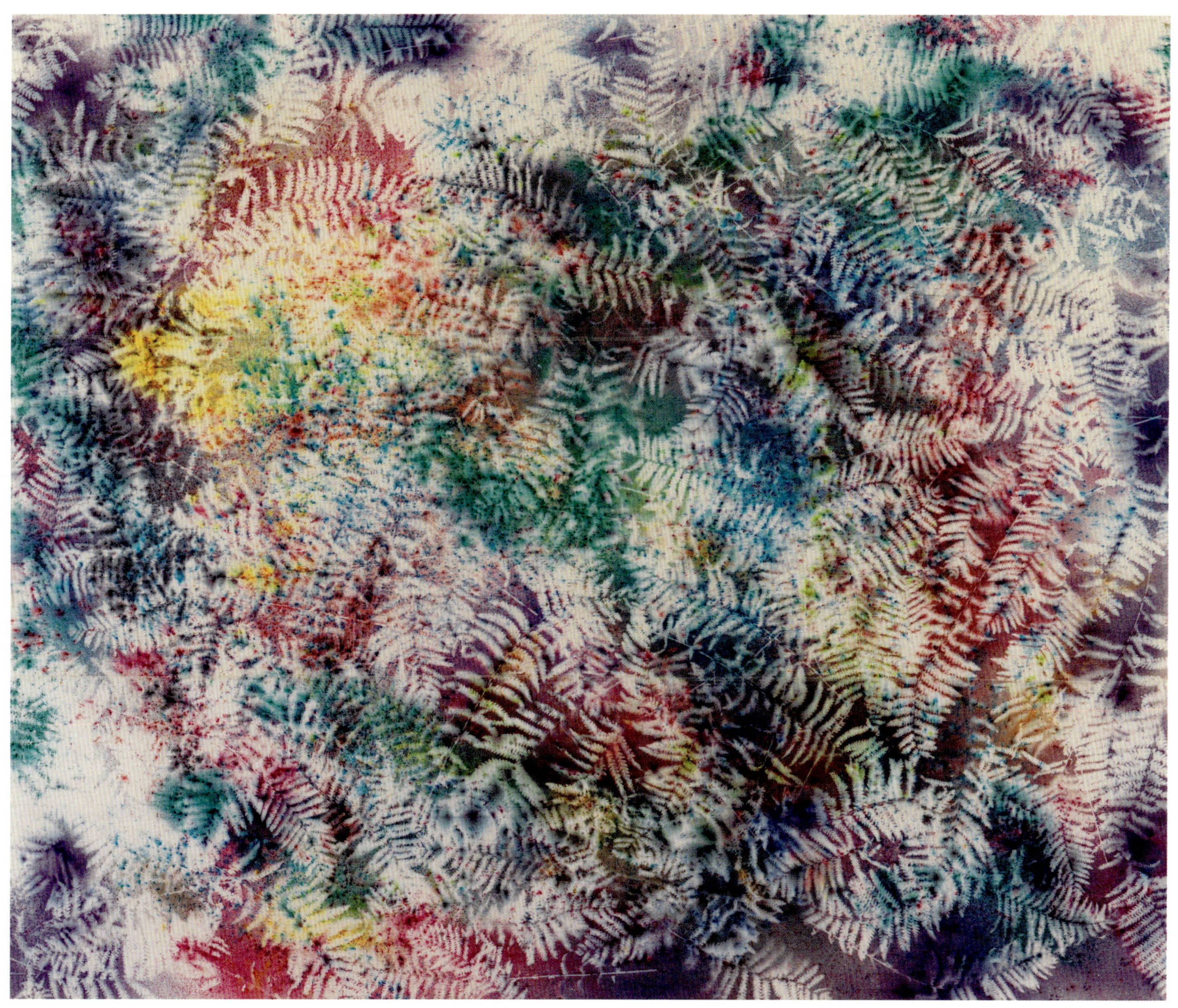

Sumo 2024

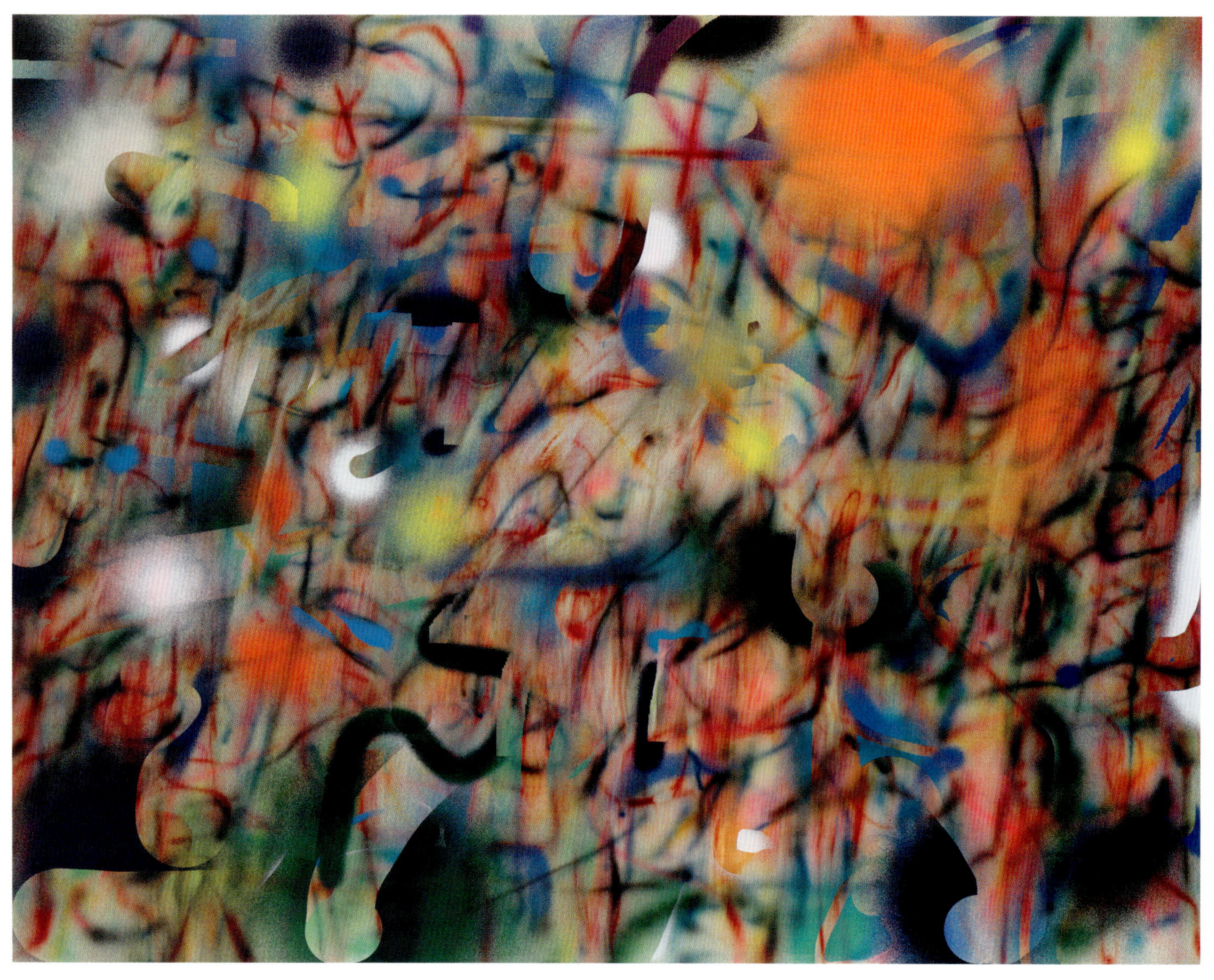

Julie Mehretu

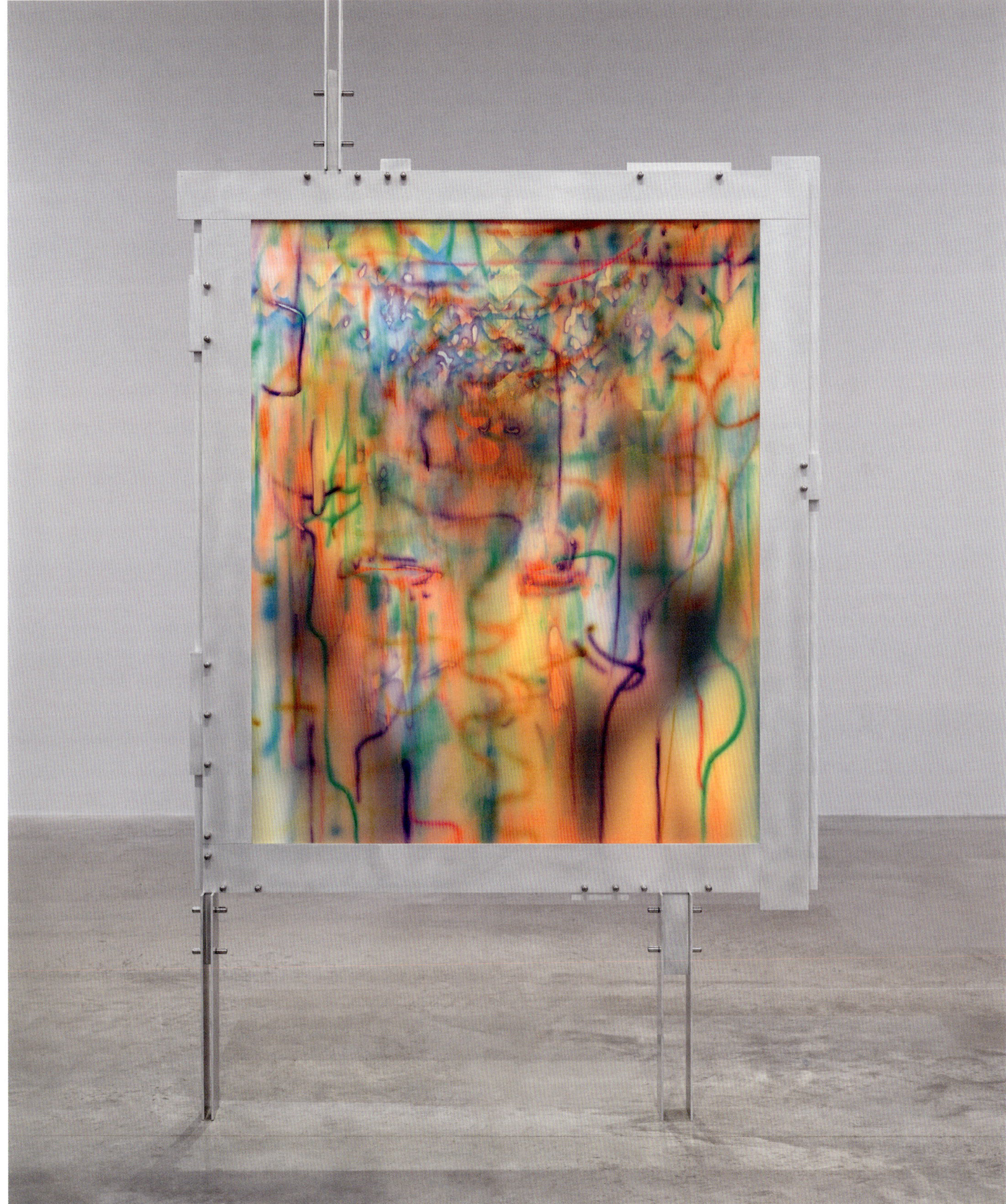

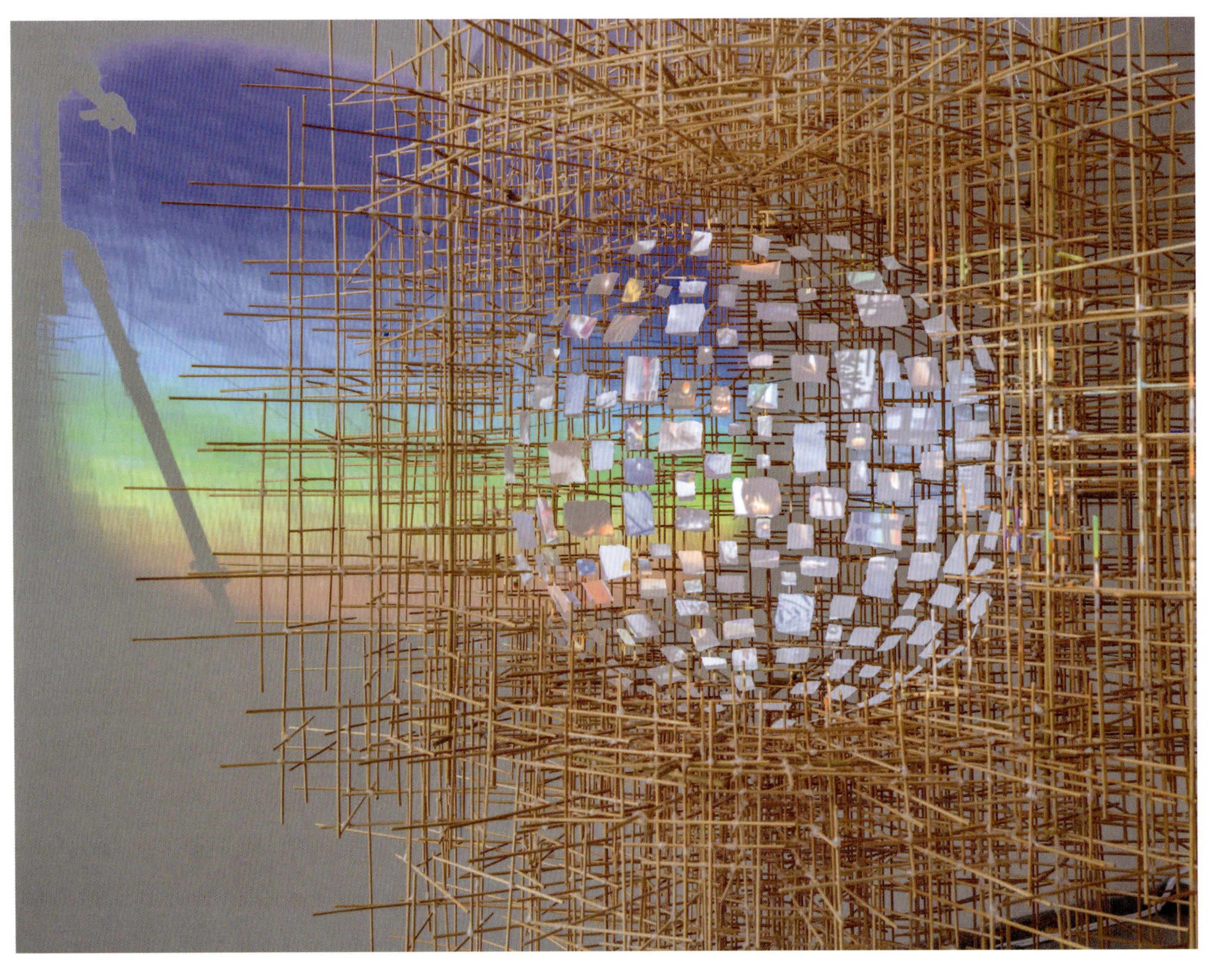

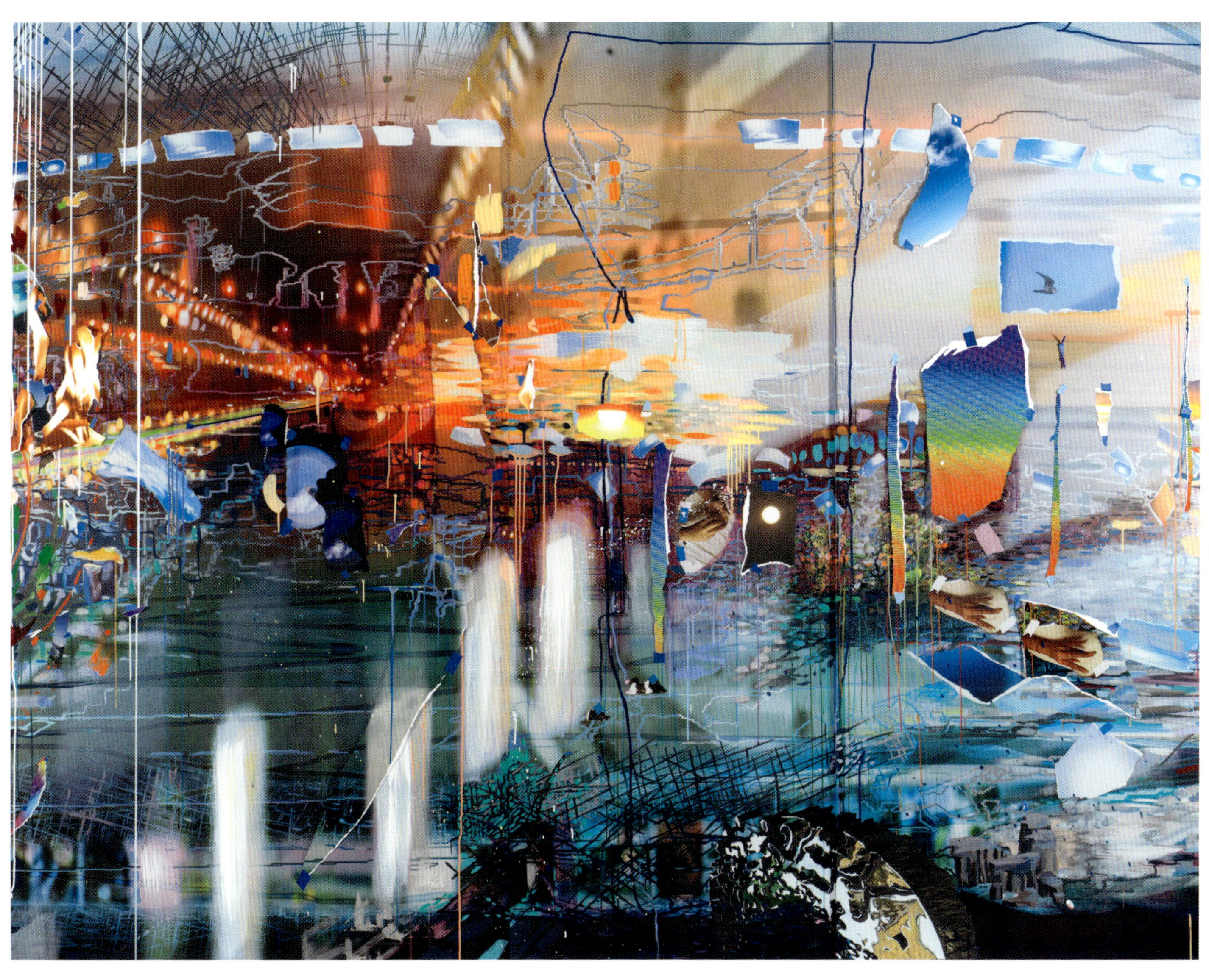

Jennifer Steinkamp

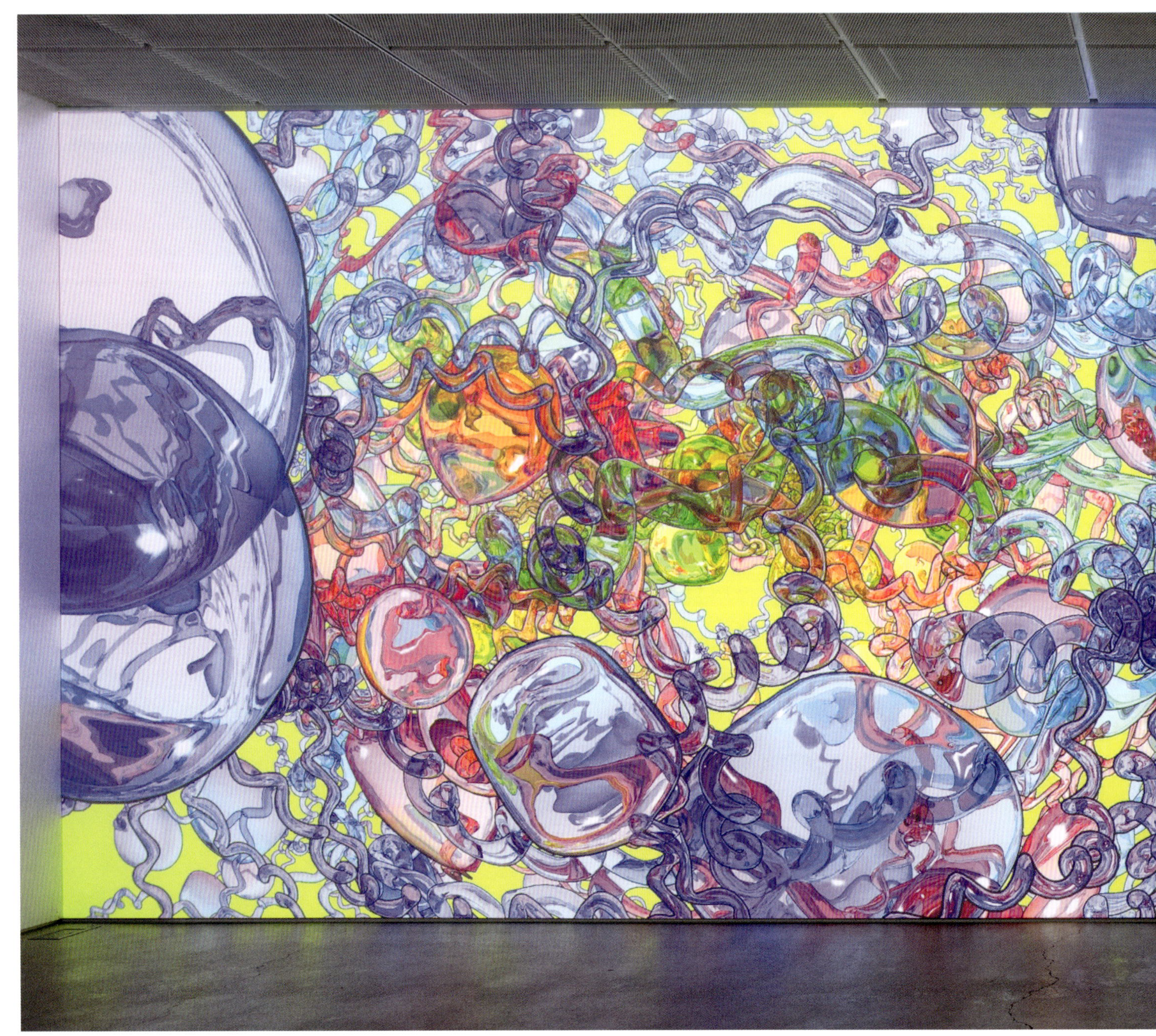

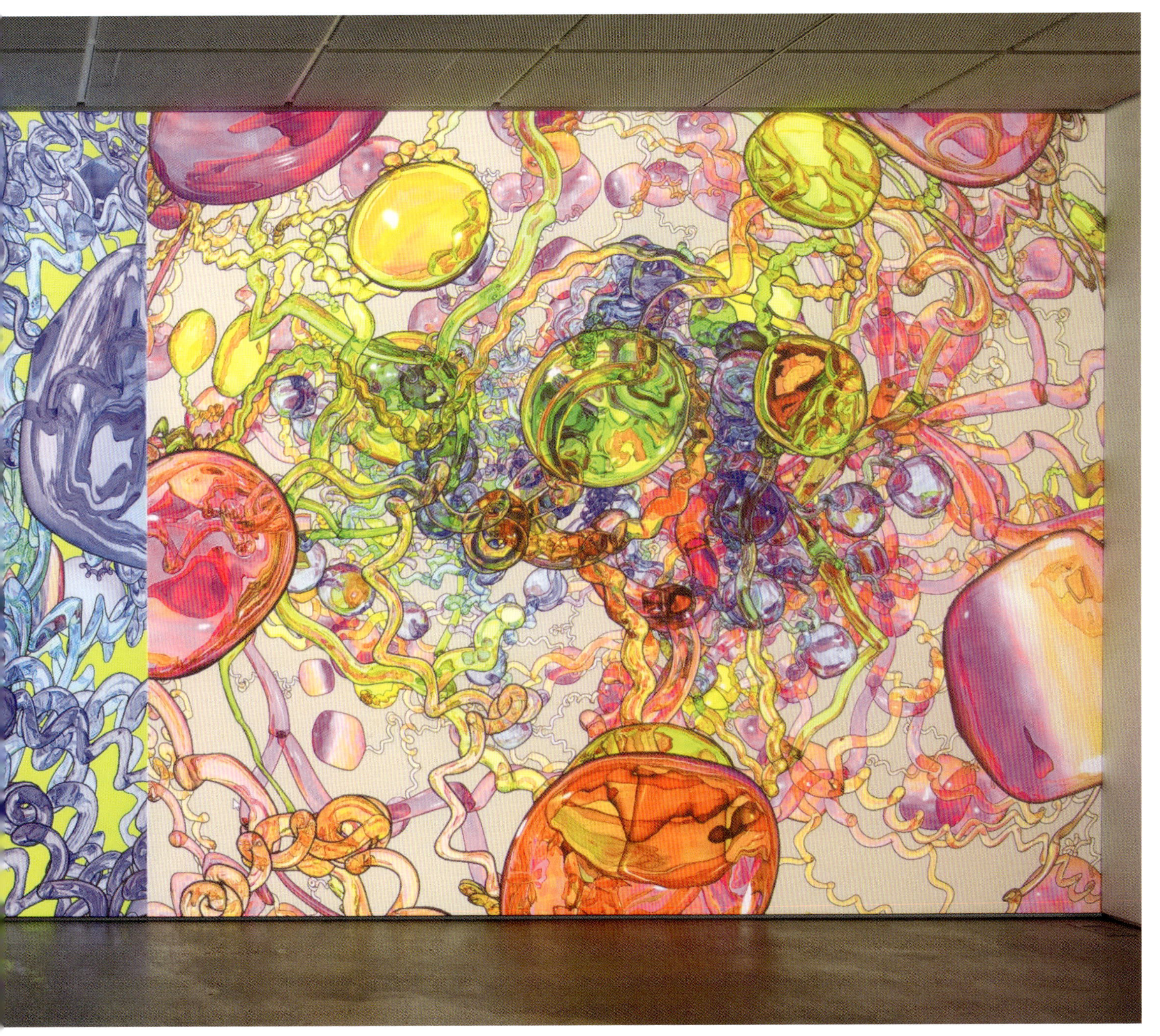

Krista Kim

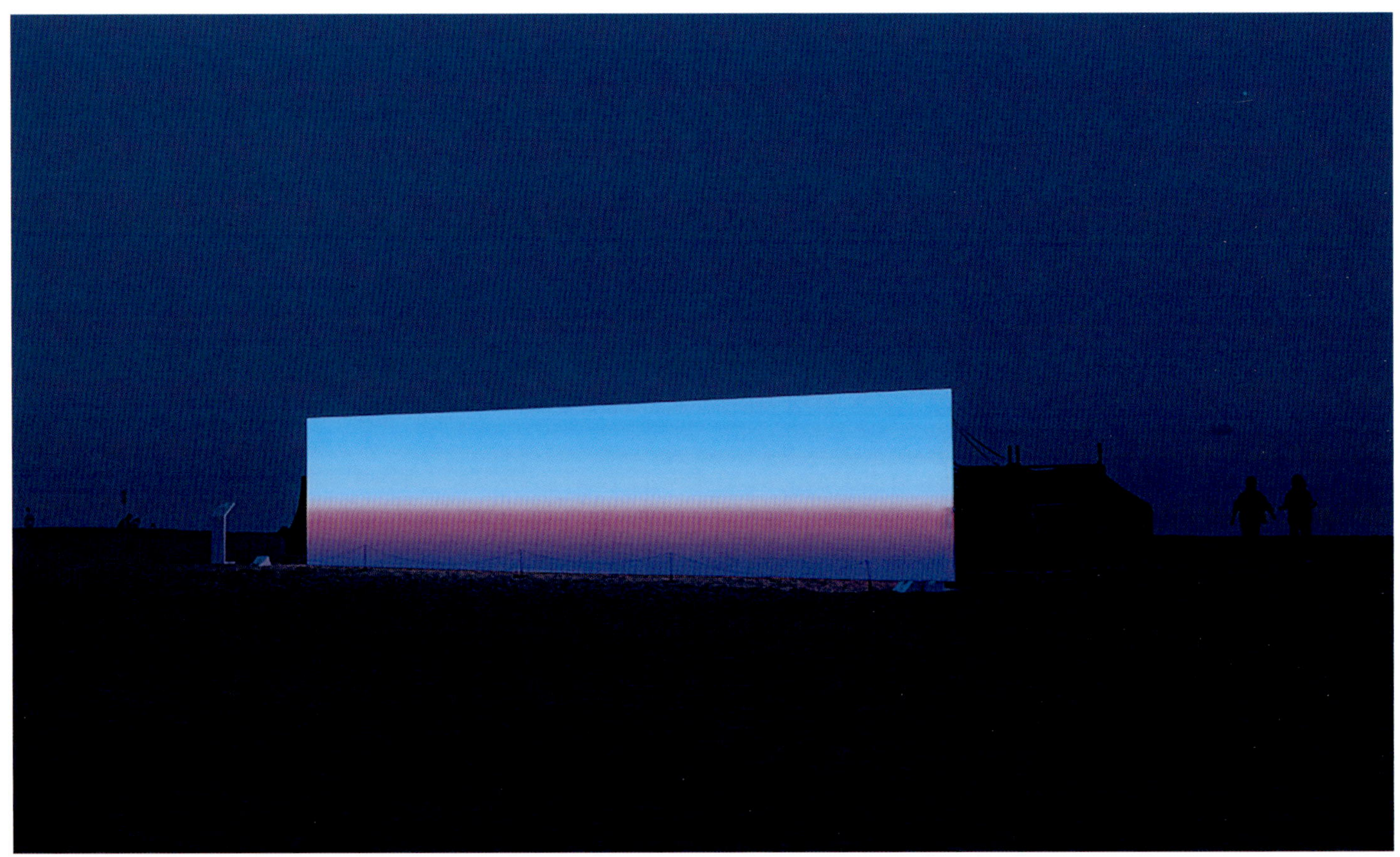

Continuum 2022

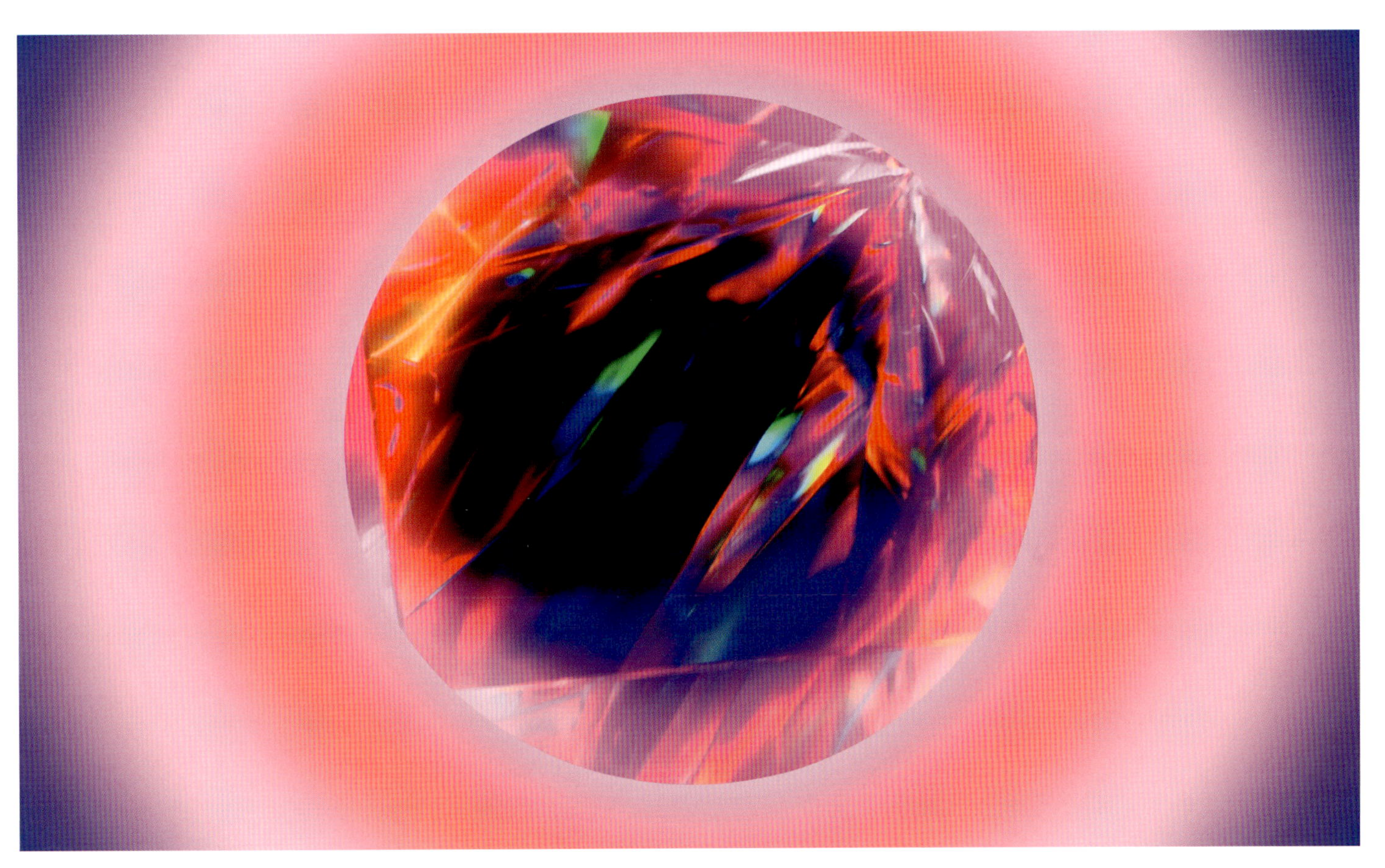

Mirror of the Mind, v. 9   2022

Phillip K. Smith III

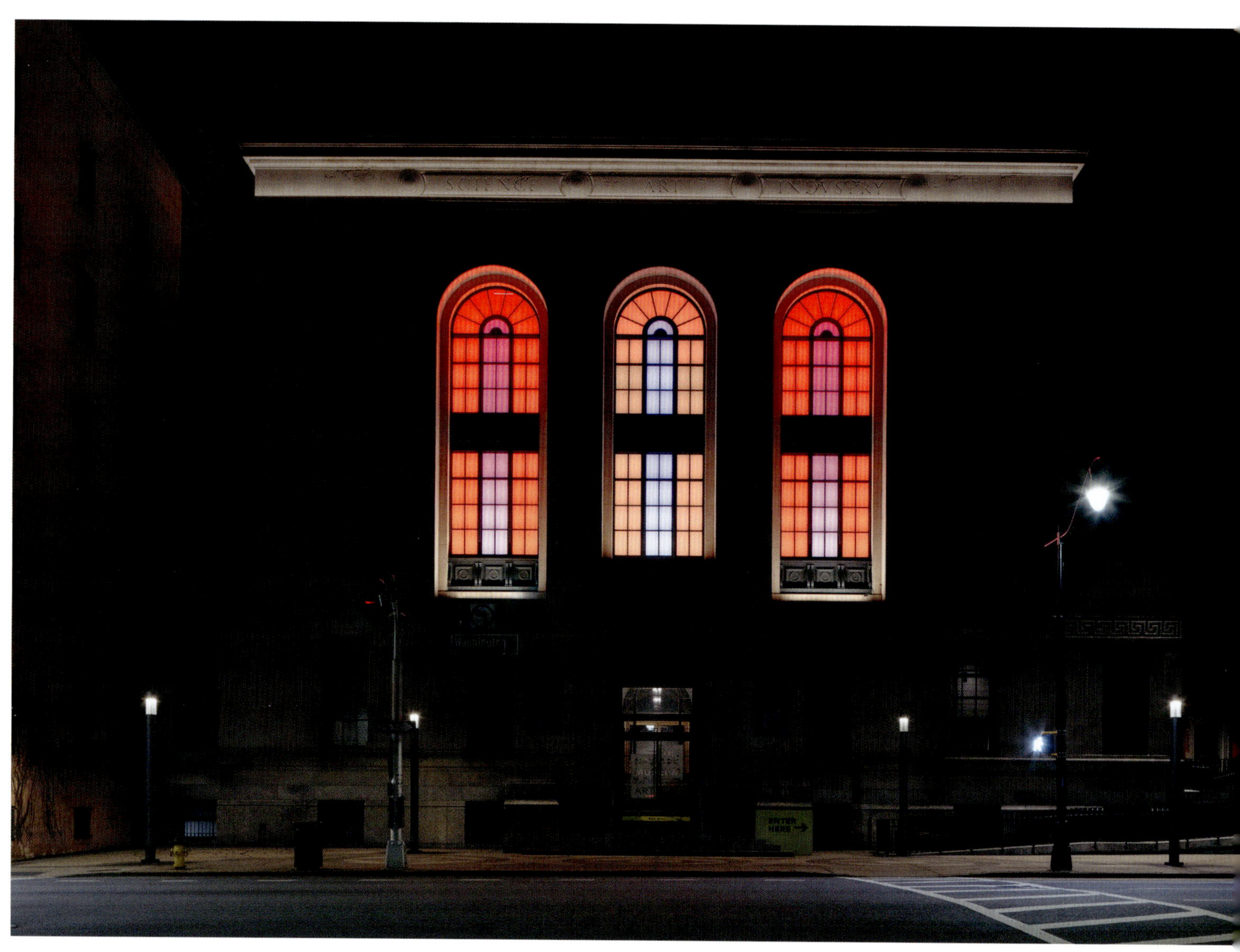

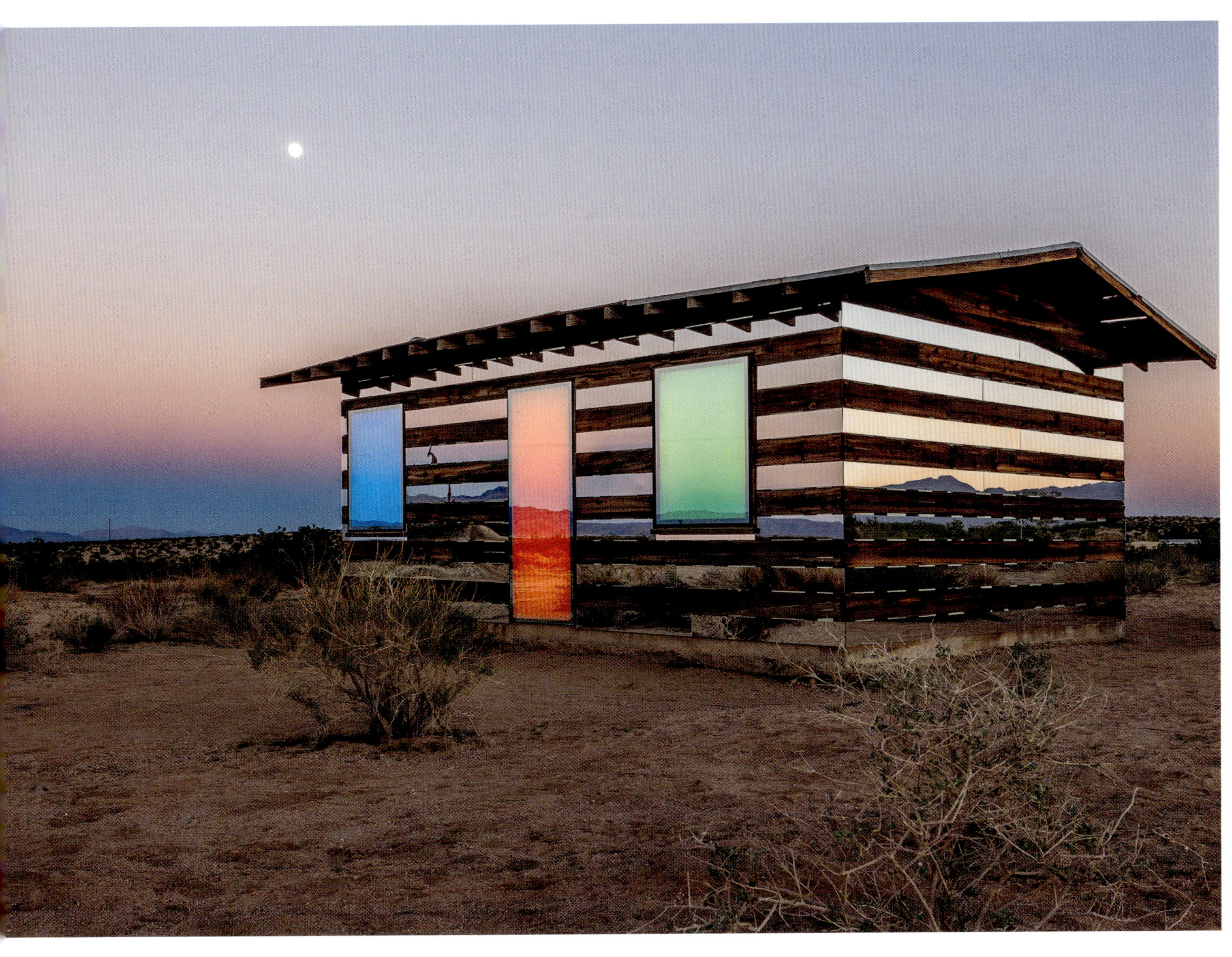

Alteronce Gumby

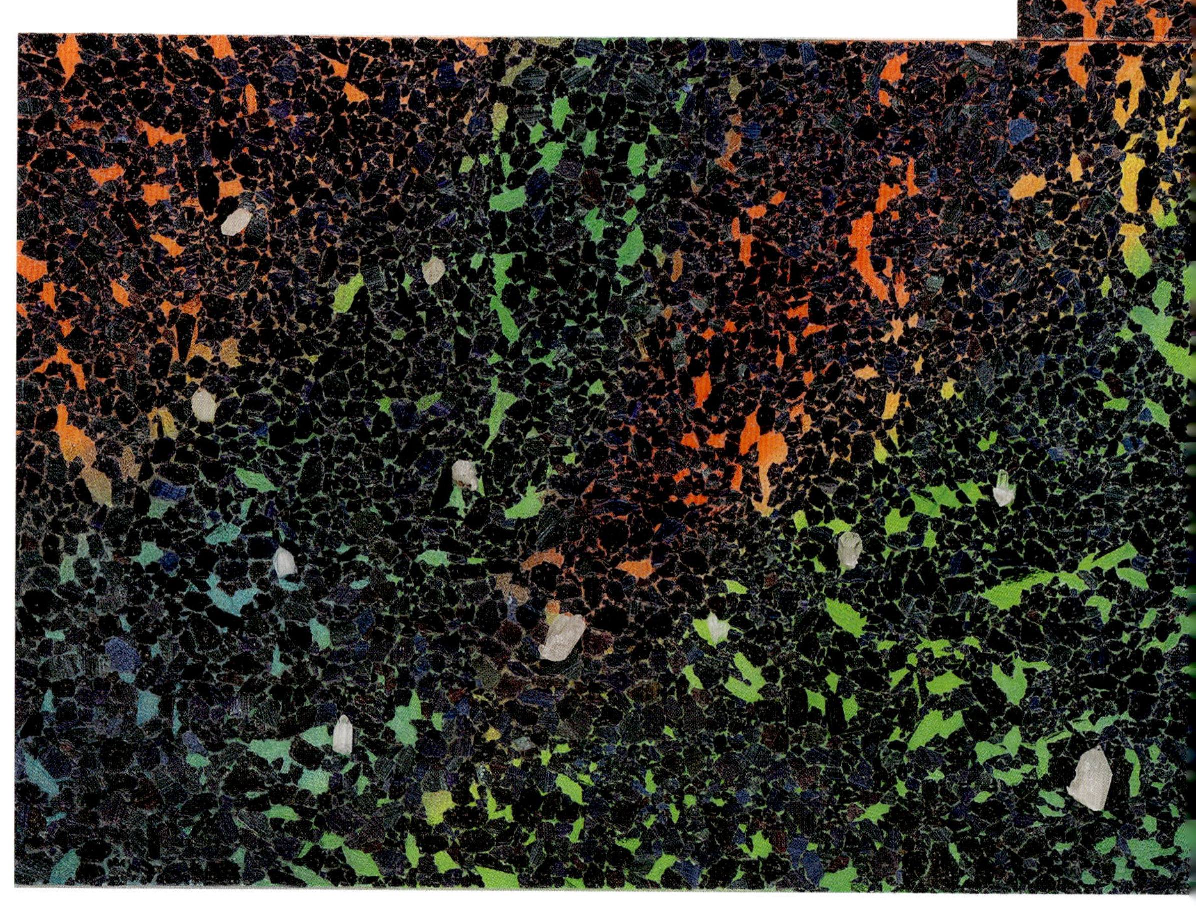

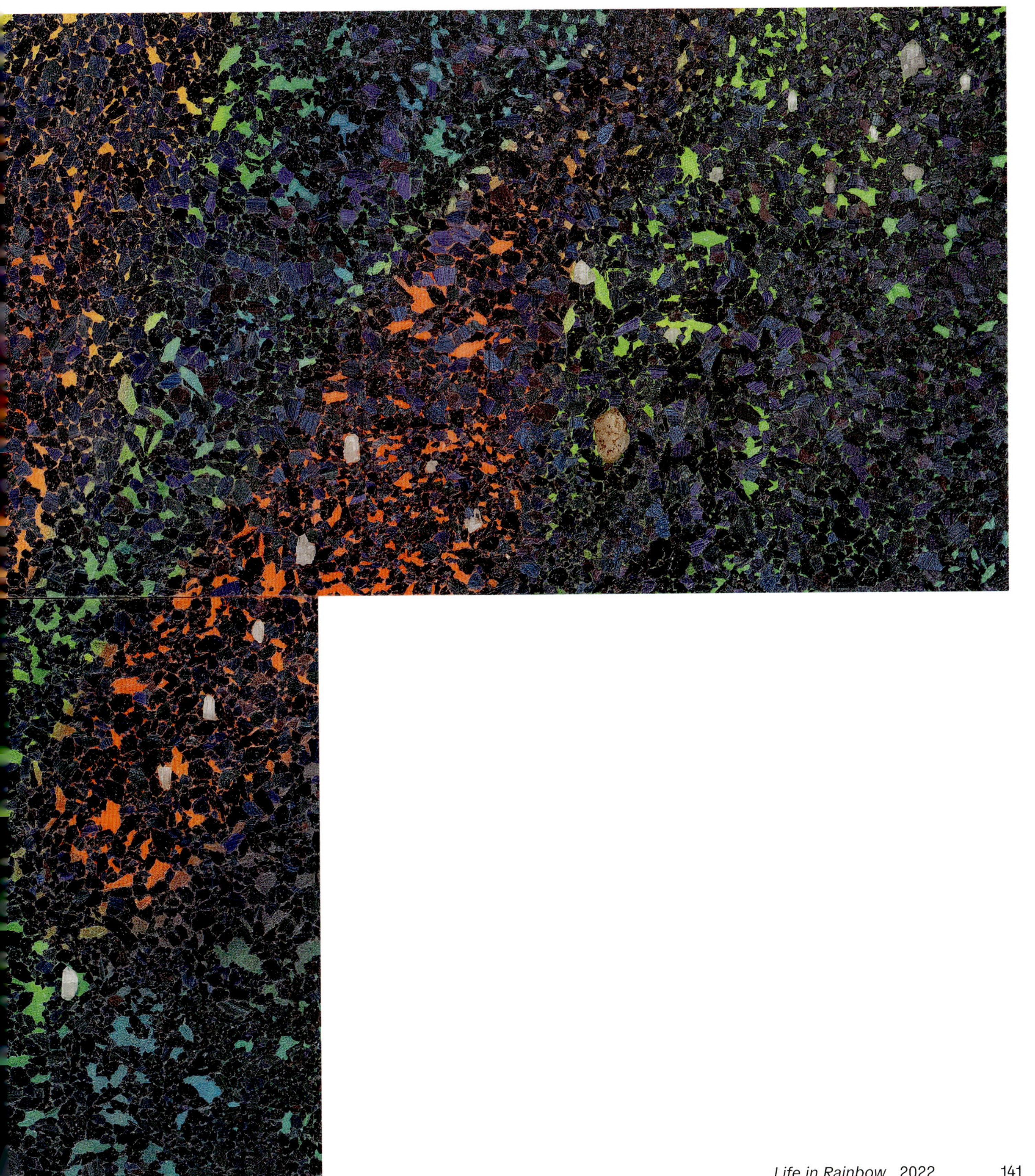

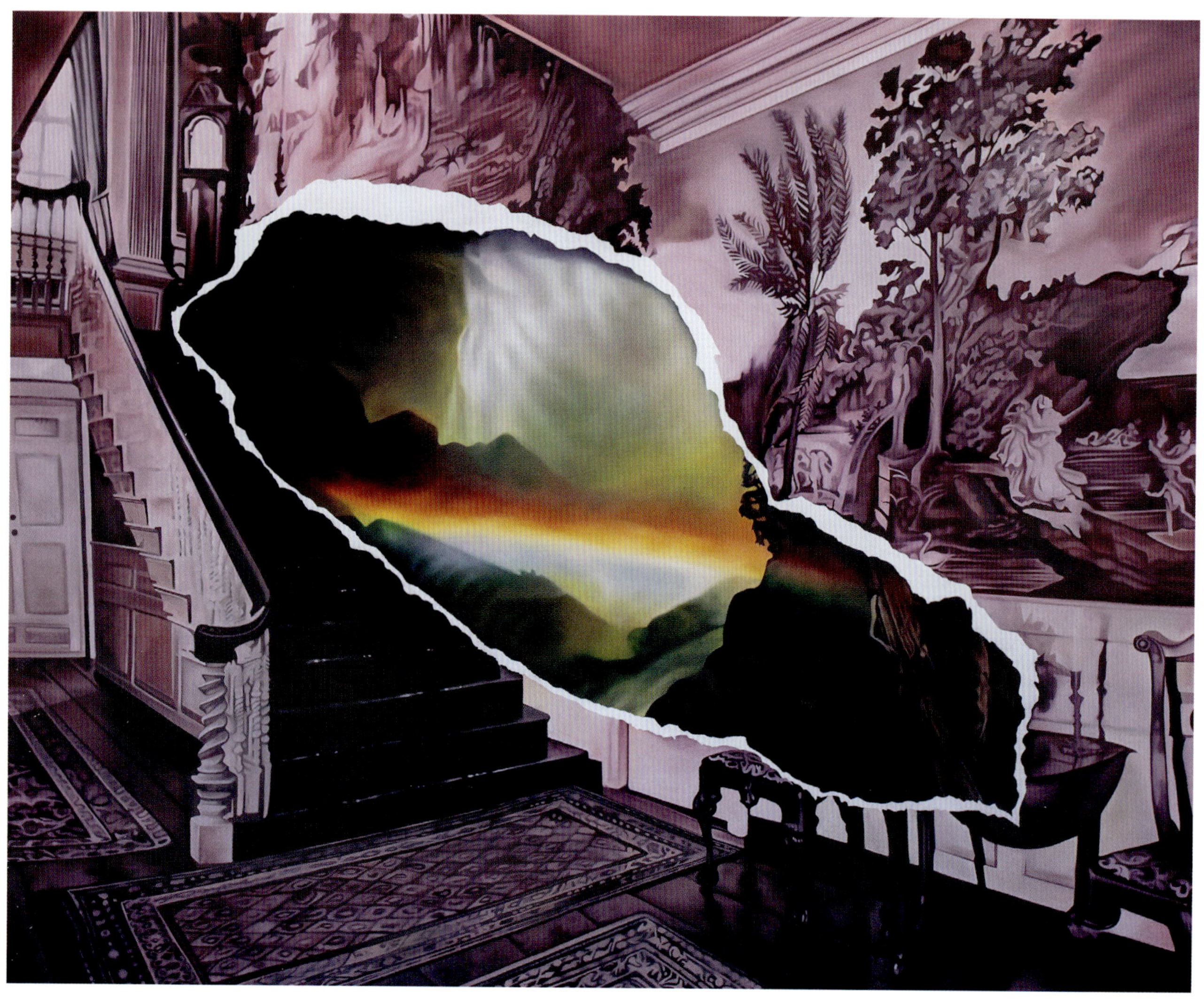

Echoes of Nature Boy   2019

Ariana Papademetropoulos

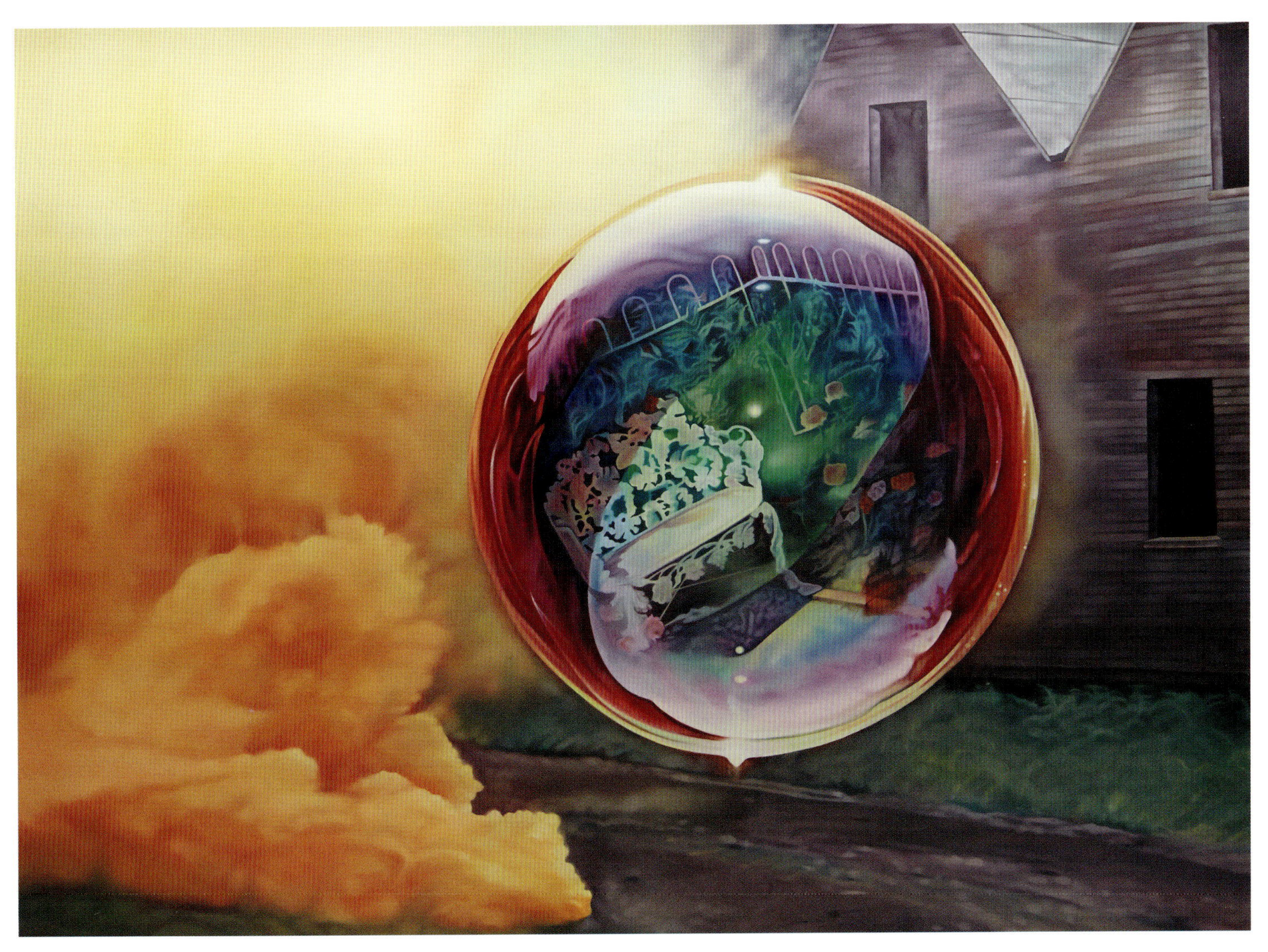

Espulsione dalla discoteca 2020

Monira Al Qadiri

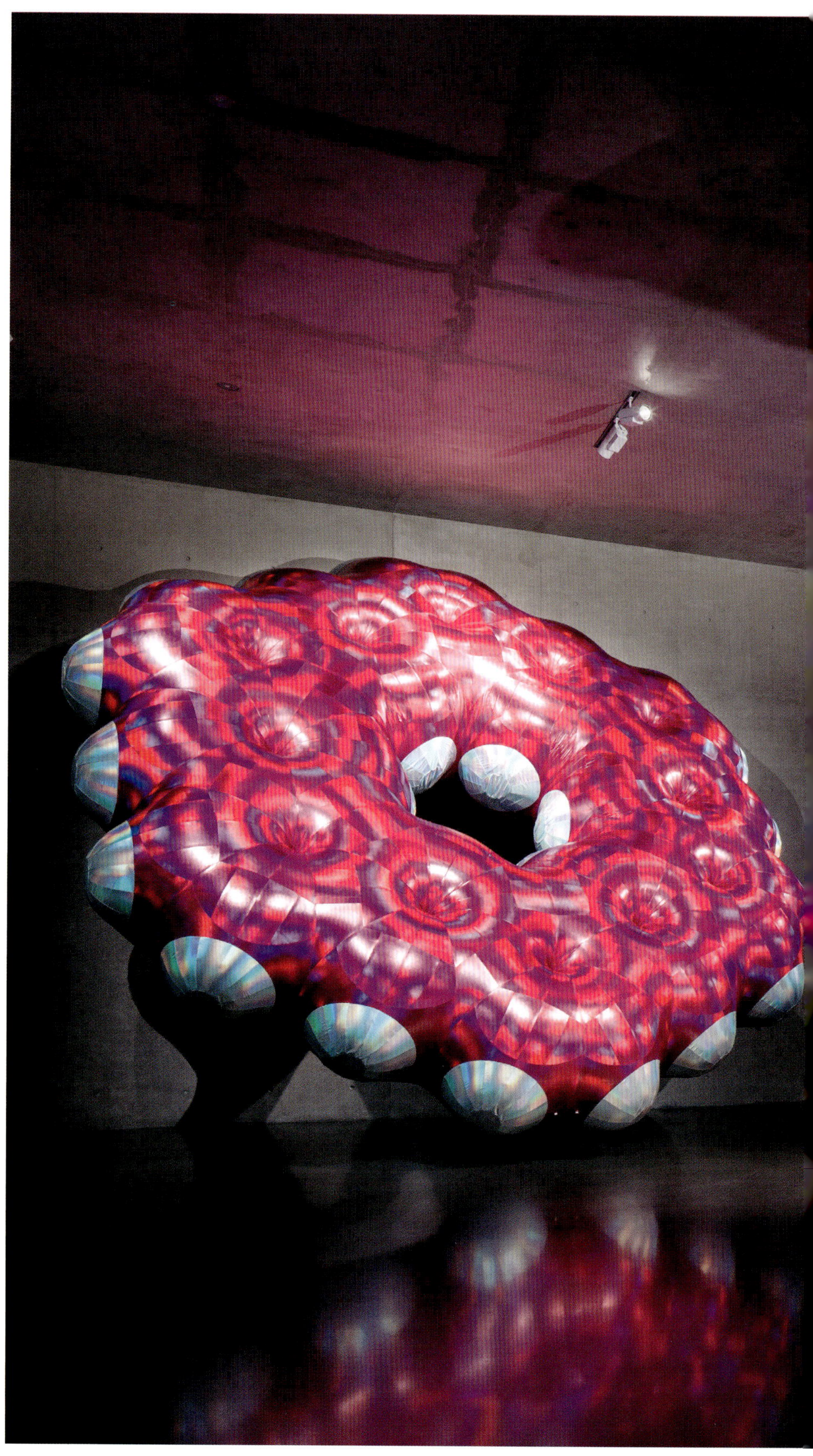

BENZENE FLOAT 2023

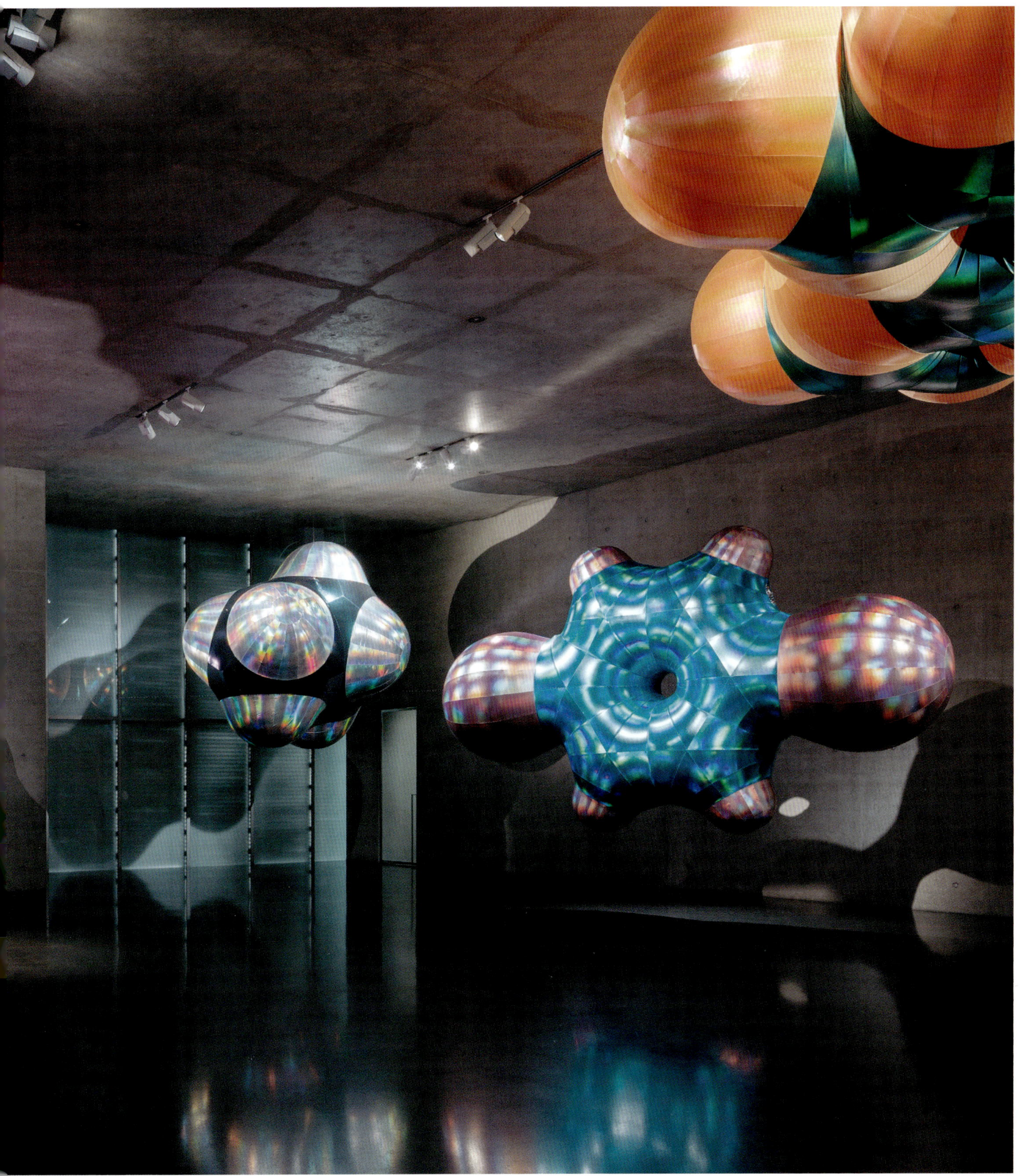

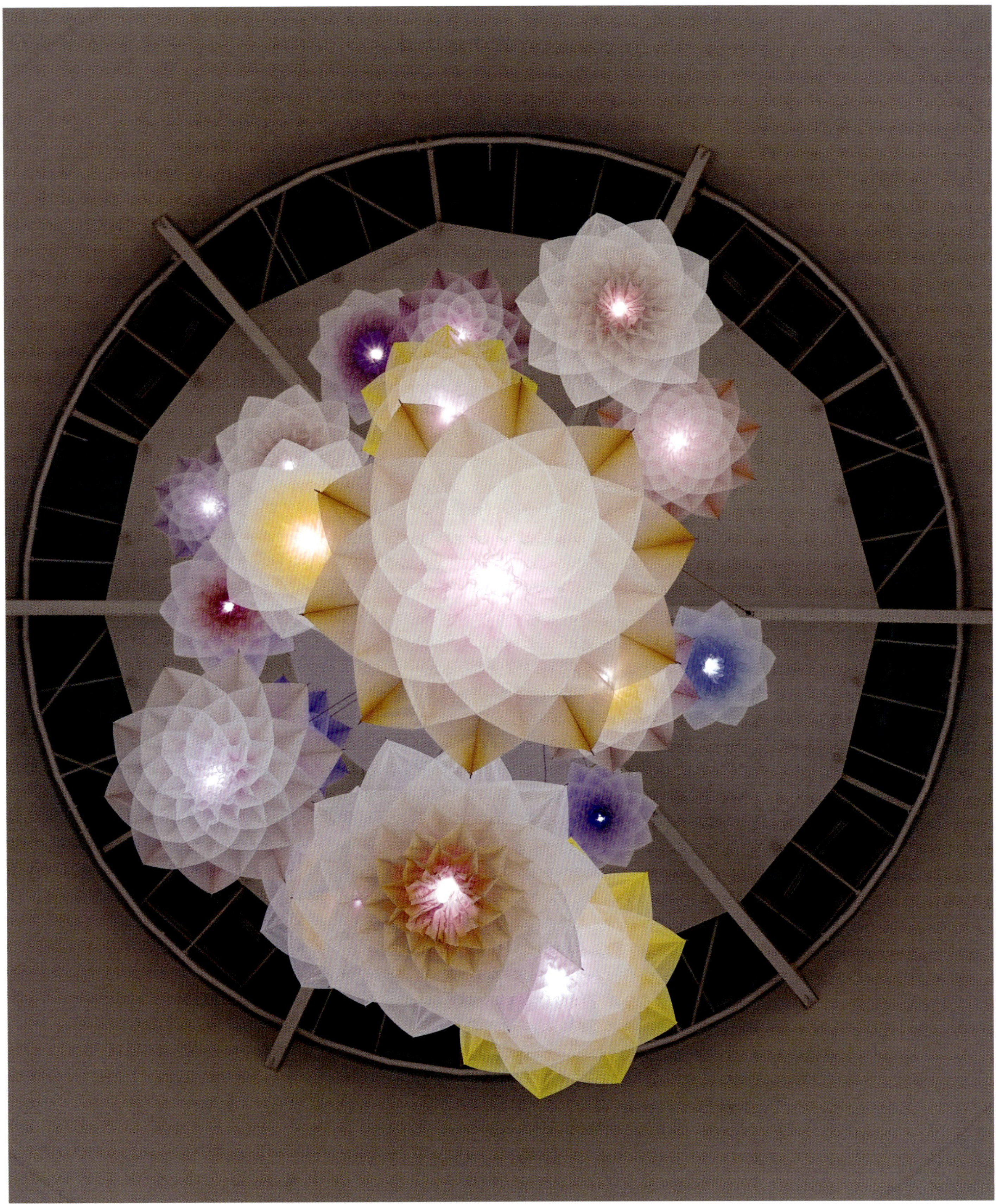

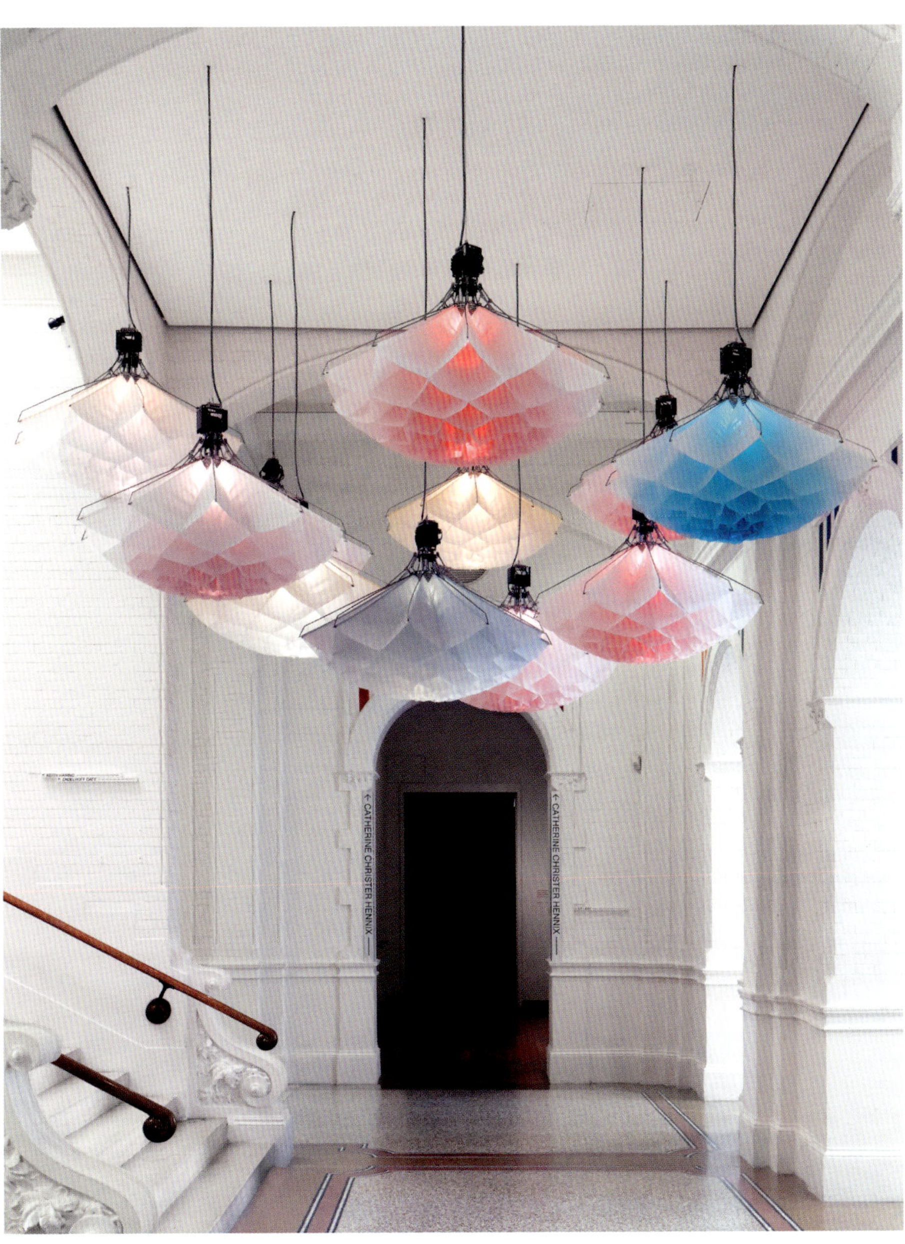

Meadow   2017

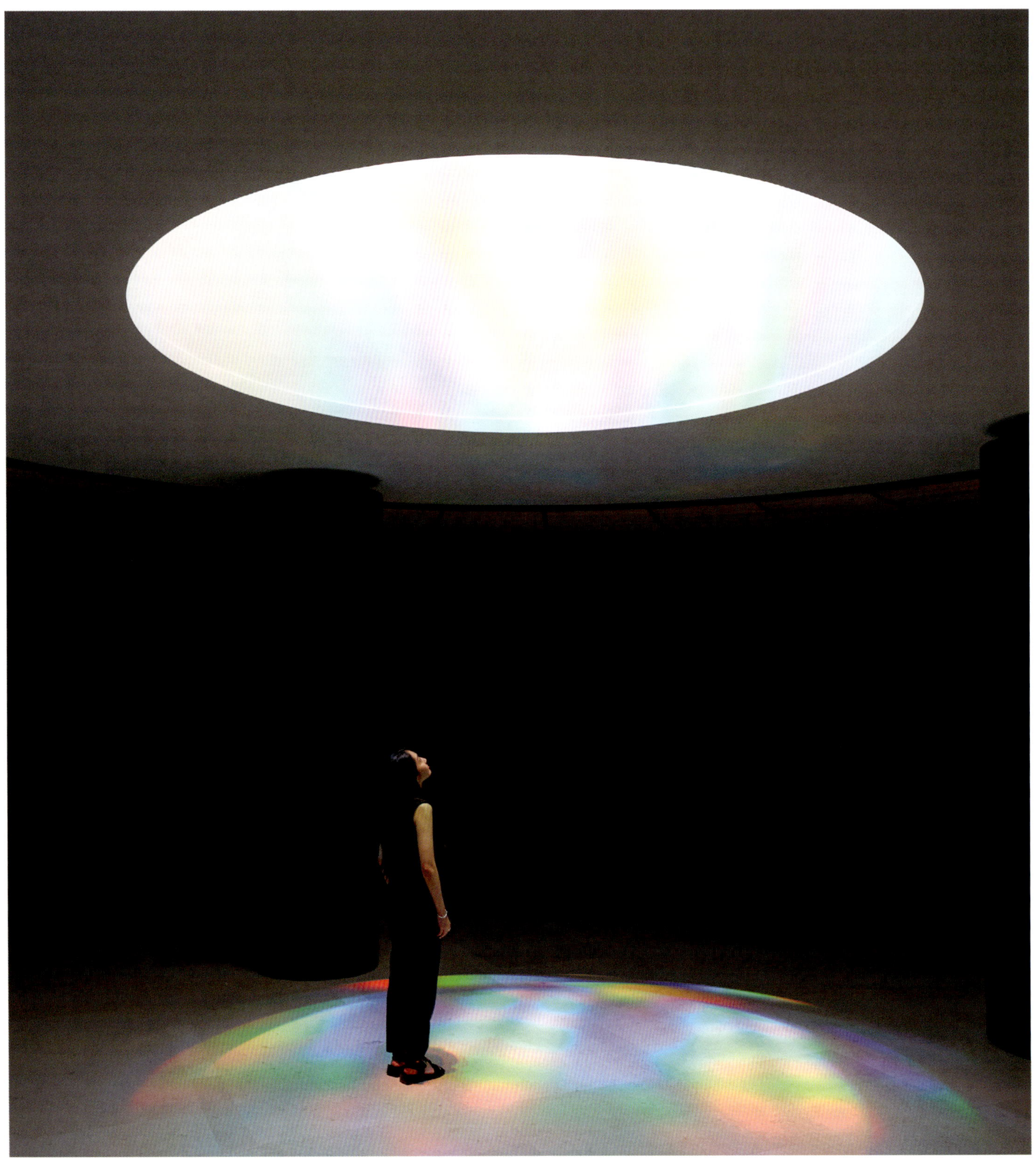

Kimsooja

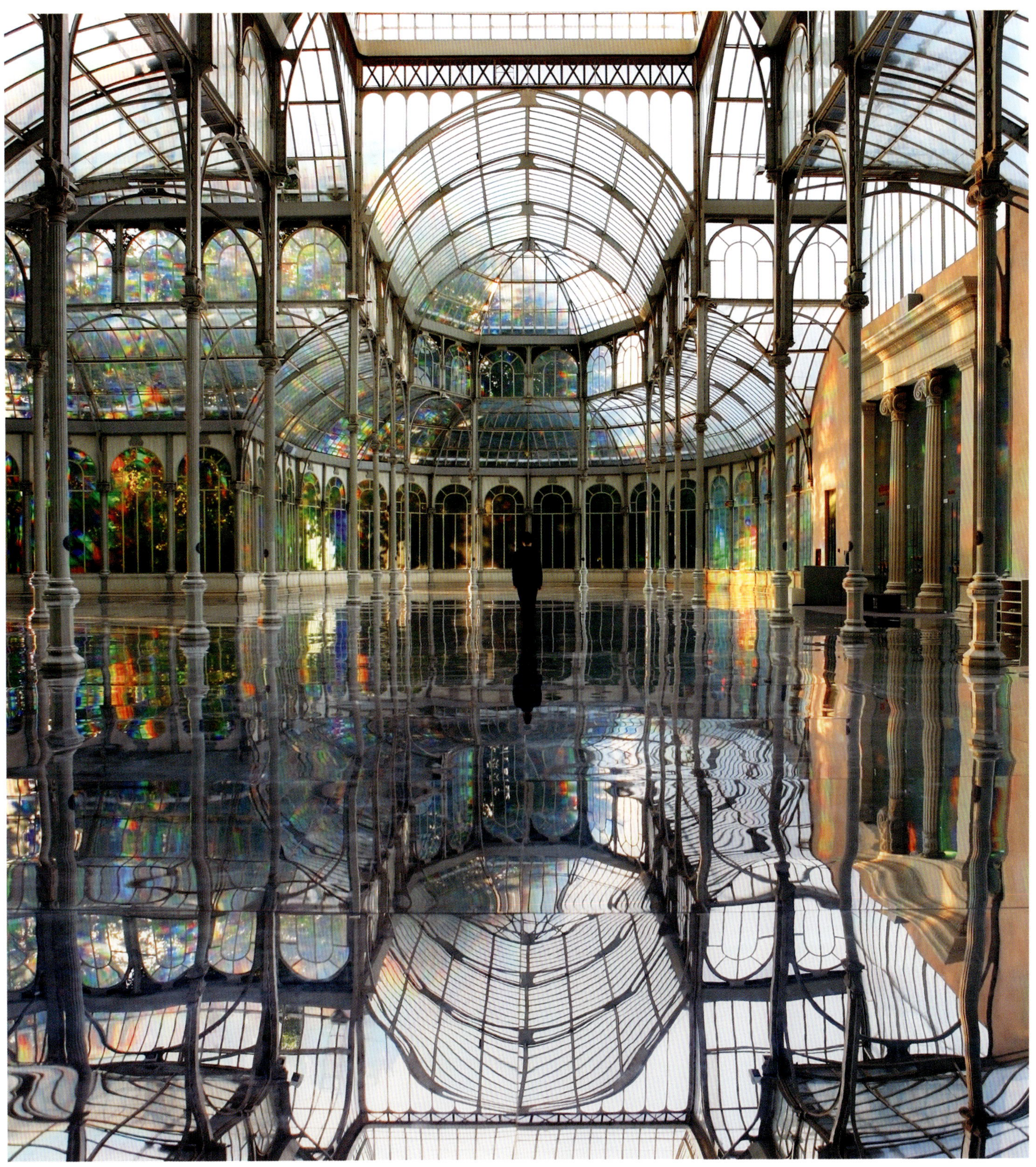

Spectrum 2017

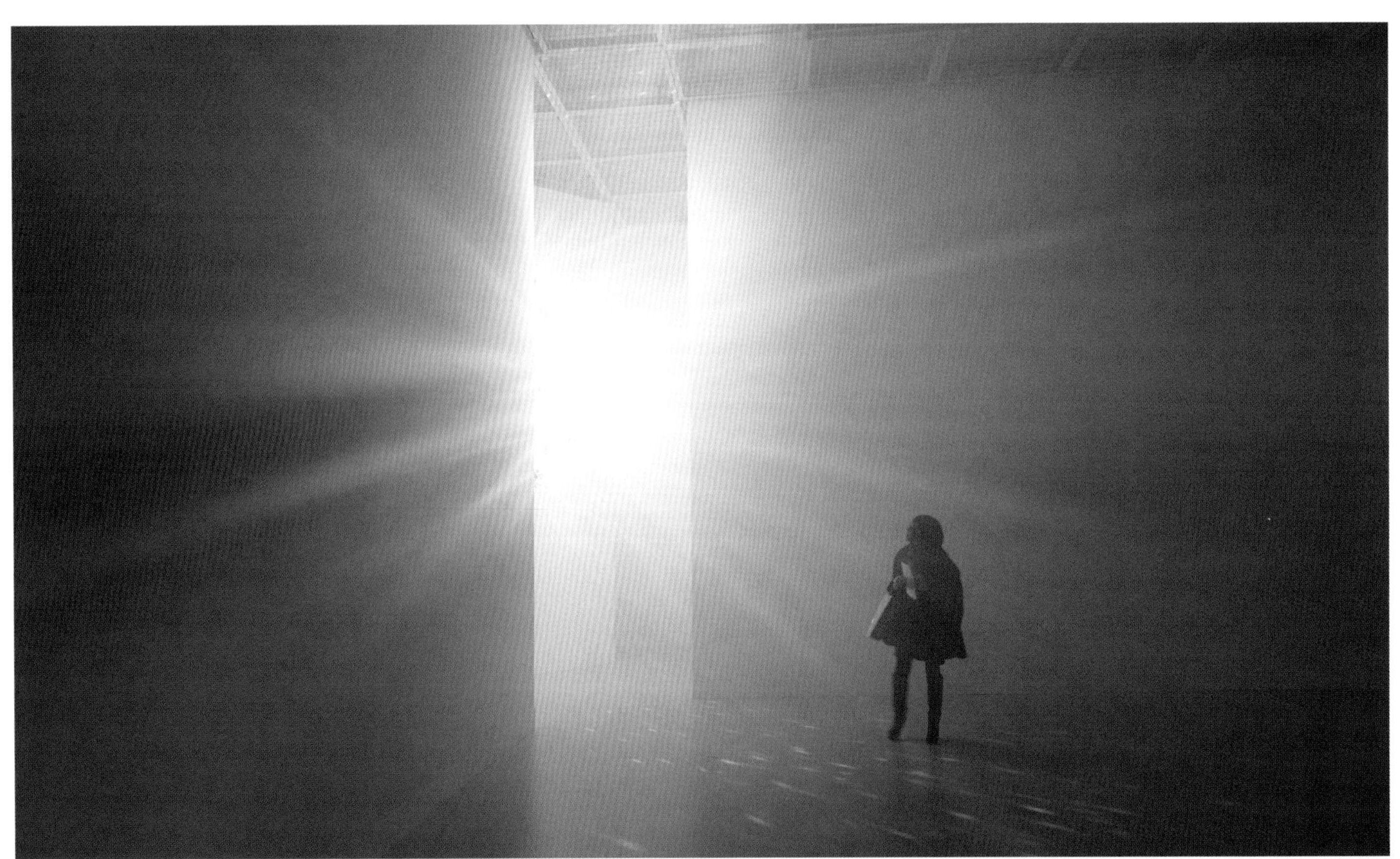

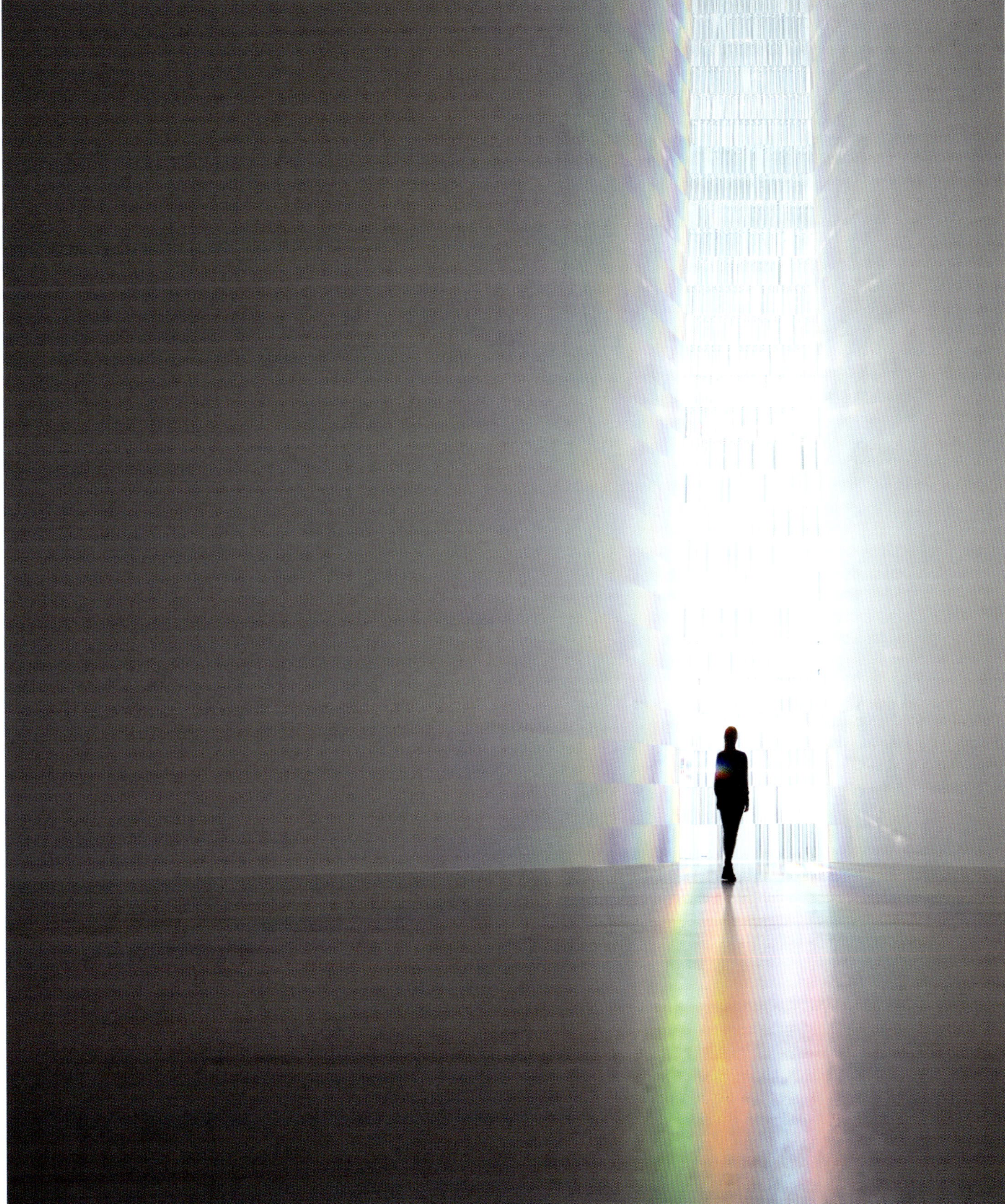

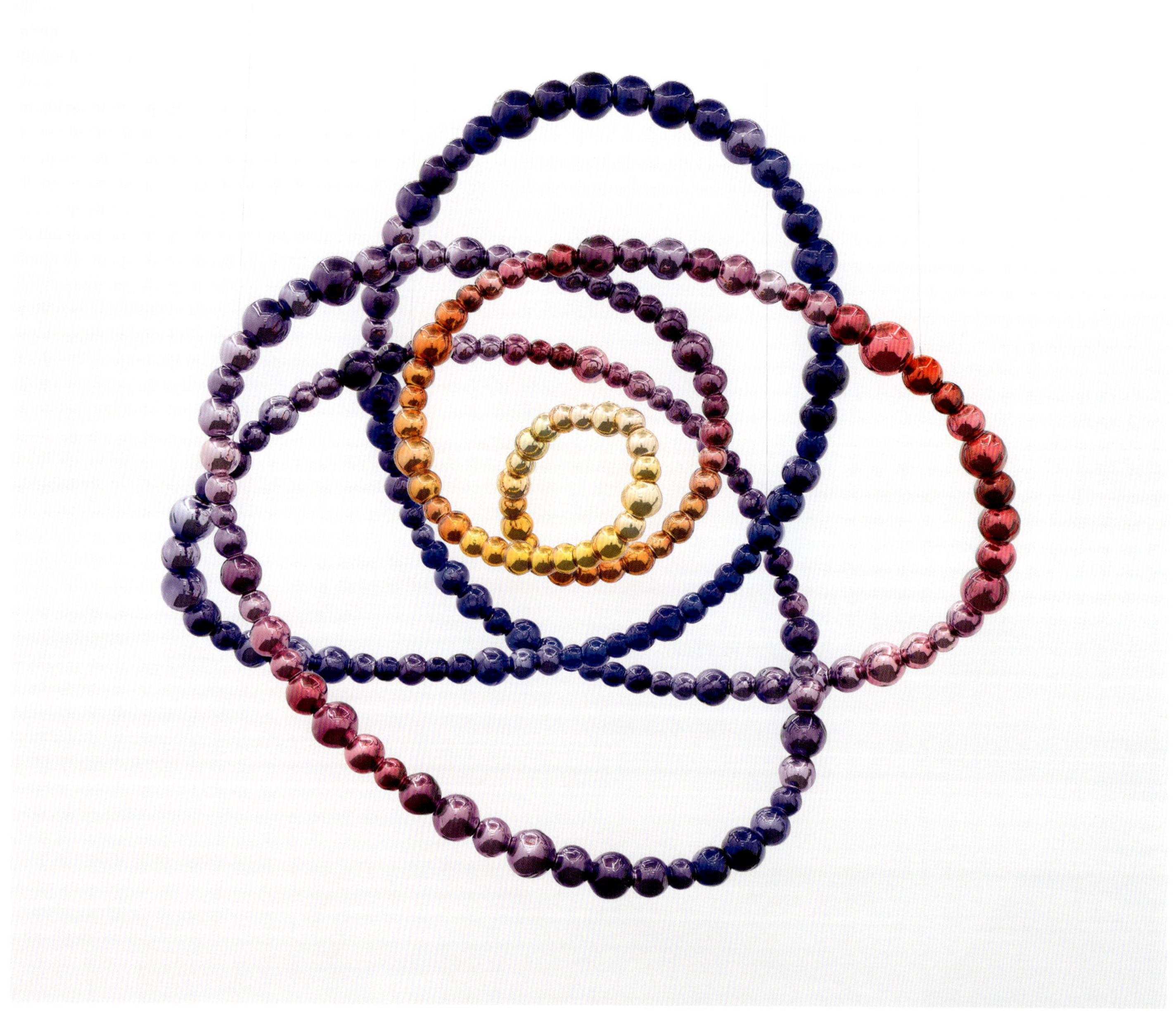

Wild Pansy   2017

Jean-Michel Othoniel

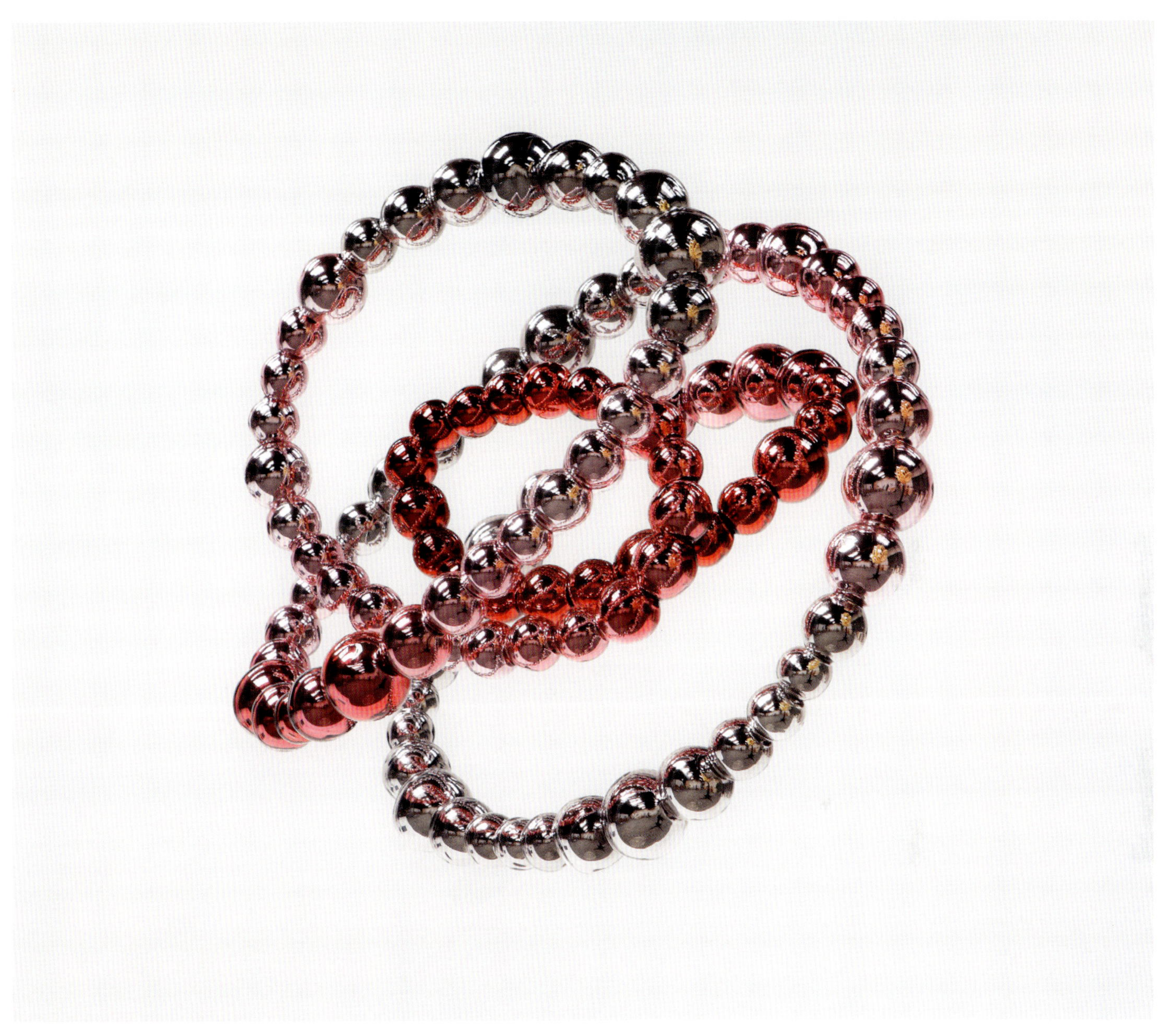

Pink Lotus 2016

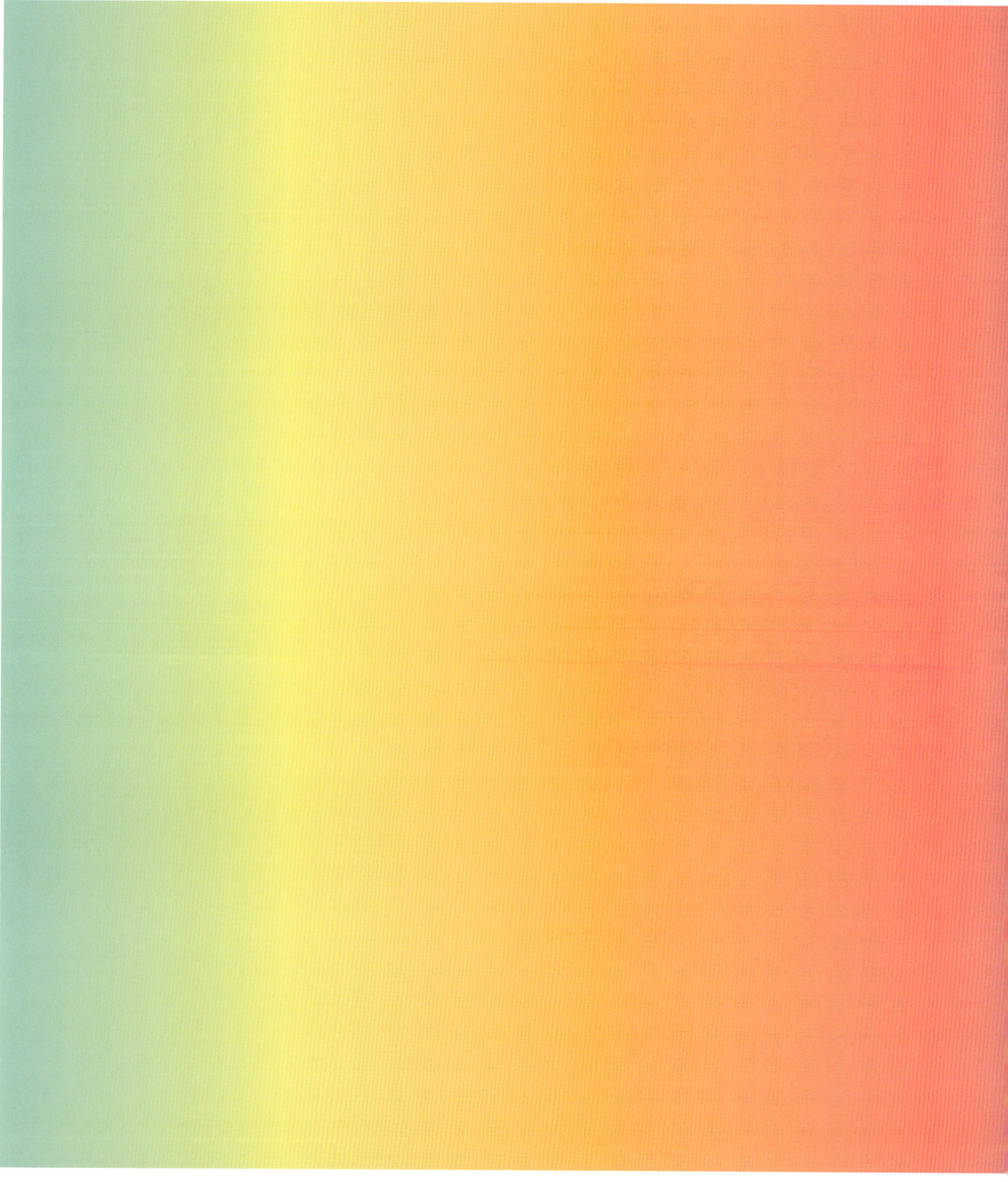

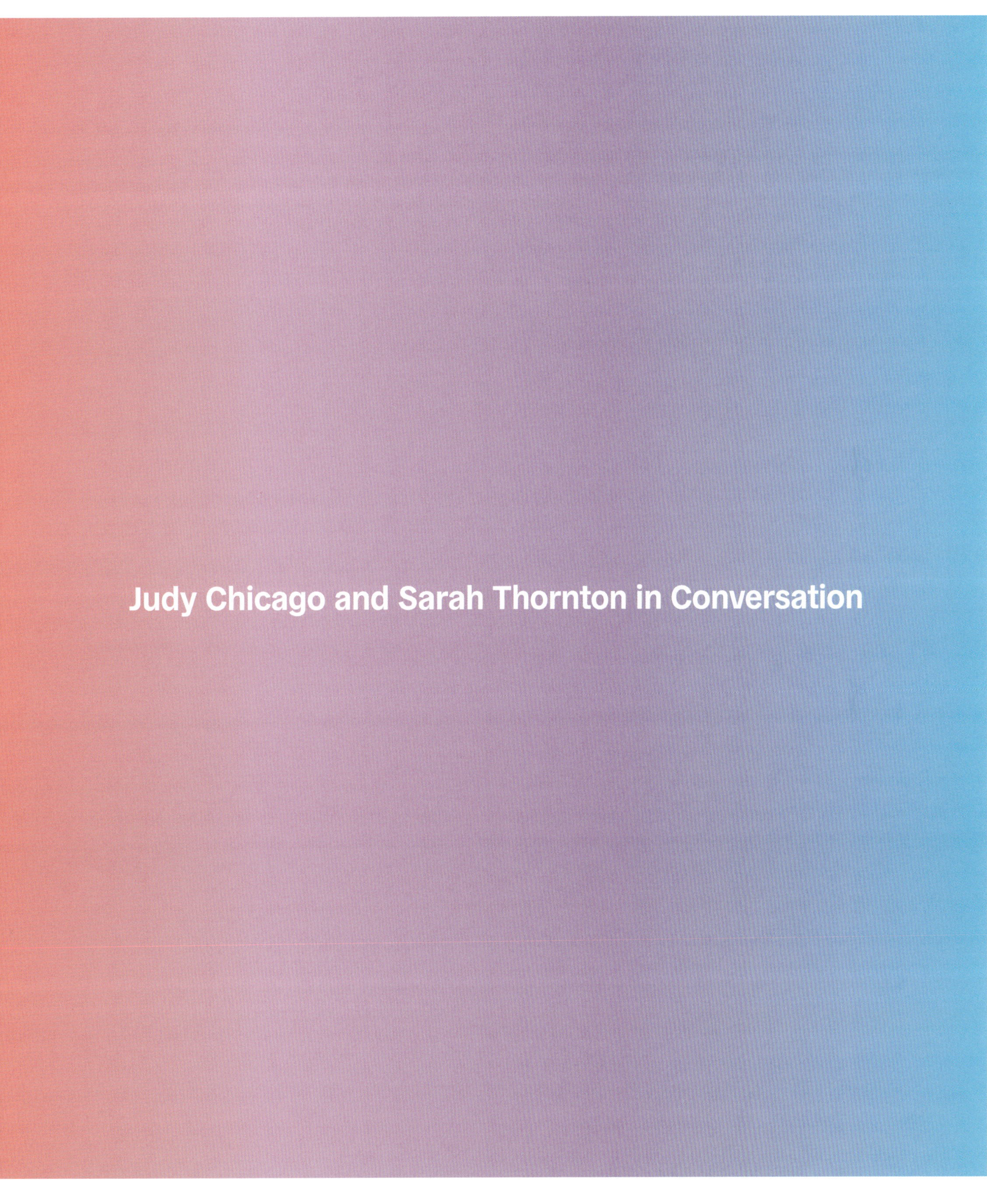

Judy Chicago and Sarah Thornton in Conversation

SARAH THORNTON: Let's discuss color. From your childhood, what do you recall about color? Were there any experiences that significantly influenced your appreciation of color?

JUDY CHICAGO: When I was five years old, I started going to the Art Institute of Chicago every Saturday. They had big classes for members' kids. We had no money, so my mother borrowed a membership card from a friend.

I spent most of my time upstairs in the Impressionist galleries. Someday, hopefully, an art historian will do an analysis of my use of color in relation to Seurat's *La Grande Jatte*! I was fascinated by the way he used color opposites to make shimmering forms—also, Monet's haystacks. I'd stare at them and study the changing light. And Toulouse-Lautrec: he used red to move your eye around the canvas. Luminosity and the idea that color could influence the viewer—these ideas were pivotal to my development as an artist.

THORNTON: The Impressionists were heavily influenced by the science of light and sight; rainbows are phenomena of light and moisture.

CHICAGO: I have always had this very personal sense of color. When I was at UCLA, the art faculty favored ochers and olive greens. Hideous. From the beginning, I liked creams, pinks, lavenders, and turquoises. Of course, they *hated* my colors. They recoiled from them. My colors were too bright and emotional.

THORNTON: And feminine!

CHICAGO: Absolutely, sexism was ingrained in the curriculum.

THORNTON: Sexist color theory!

CHICAGO: That's funny *and* true.

THORNTON: Was it your interest in femininity as a subject matter that led you to that palette? Or were you being a contrarian?

CHICAGO: No, I wasn't so much a contrarian. I was just out of the loop—completely oblivious to all the etiquette and social expectations of women then. I was in a whole other place. I had a vision, and I knew I had a destiny. My gender consciousness came from my father's political activism and his belief in equal rights for women. But I never thought about it in terms of art at that time.

THORNTON: So, in 1964, you graduated from UCLA. What then?

CHICAGO: I spent my first decade as a professional artist trying to be one of the boys in the LA art scene. The Finish Fetish guys loved candy colors. Candy apple is one of the great car colors of all time, which I learned about when I went to auto body school to learn spray-painting. There was no prohibition against color among those guys. My colors fit right in. But it was still the heyday of Minimalism.

THORNTON: Do you remember the first piece in which you used a rainbow spectrum?

CHICAGO: *Rainbow Pickett* might have been the first. It was shown in the *Primary Structures* show in New York in 1966. I was one of three women in an exhibition of forty-two artists.

THORNTON: That exhibition was the defining moment in Minimalism. But *Rainbow Pickett* is not actually the seven colors of the rainbow …

CHICAGO: Right. It just feels like a rainbow. Graded color is spectral; it's rainbowlike. The first smoke piece I ever made was rainbowlike: *Raymond Rose Ritual Environment*, which we did for New Year's Eve in 1967. I fogged the street with smoke, then shone lights through two rotating color wheels that I'd built. As the smoke rose, we created swirling rainbows of colors in the sky. At that point, I thought, "I'm going to do fireworks," and my *Atmospheres* were born.

THORNTON: It is at about this time that you made your book of color studies, which is in the collection of the Getty Research Institute. Tell us about the book.

CHICAGO: The book consists of a series of more than seventy Prismacolor drawings, through which I explored how to convey emotion and movement through color. At that time—I guess it was 1967–68—I couldn't work through ideas in my head; I had to see *everything* on paper. If I did a drawing with eight colors, I'd wonder what would happen if I changed one of the colors from warm to cold (or vice versa), so I would draw it to find out. It educated me in the subtlety of colors—the impact of their hues, temperatures, and positions in relation to each other.

THORNTON: You were working with rainbows a decade before the advent of the gay pride flag, which artist Gilbert Baker designed at the request of Harvey Milk. The flag debuted at the San Francisco Gay Freedom Day Parade in 1978.

CHICAGO: There are a gazillion versions of the pride flag, but the original had eight colors, each with a symbolic meaning. Harvey Milk was Jewish. The original flag started with pink. Guess what the pink stood for? The pink triangles that homosexuals had to wear in the Nazi concentration camps during the Holocaust. But then, the pink was dropped, ostensibly because they couldn't get pink dye. I think it's an erasure, probably related to incipient antisemitism.

THORNTON: Or, maybe, it's an erasure of something too horrific for a flag that is meant to be celebratory? How bizarre is it that you created many bodies of work around rainbows, and then a decade later, the form gets picked up as an emblem of nonconforming gender and sexuality? I would assume it was because you were trying to find an artistic language true to yourself.

CHICAGO: Yes, that's right. Also, shading and color gradation were big issues for me. It's why I liked spray-painting so much. It allowed me to fade or grade all my colors.

THORNTON: Does that ombré blending relate to the body? A kind of fluidity that is the opposite of the hard-edged borders and corners of machines.

CHICAGO: That's a good insight.

THORNTON: What do rainbows mean to you?

CHICAGO: I never chose to use rainbows because they meant such and such. I was attracted to spectral colors and used them for visual and expressive purposes. It's interesting that I ended up in New Mexico; after the summer monsoons here, we often see rainbows—sometimes double rainbows, which are considered a sign of good luck.

THORNTON: **Leprechauns keep their pot of gold at the end of the rainbow. In the Genesis story of the Deluge, which tells of Noah's Ark, the rainbow serves as a symbol of God's promise not to flood the earth again. Do you see rainbows as symbols of hope?**

CHICAGO: Yes, I've used the rainbow that way—definitely in the stained-glass window *Rainbow Shabbat* (1992). Donald Woodman, my husband, and I made a conscious decision to use a rainbow as a way to follow a Jewish mandate and choose hope. The inscription reads, "Heal those broken souls who have no peace and lead us all from darkness into light," which is based on a poem by a Theresienstadt survivor.

THORNTON: **How can rainbows help us at this time?**

CHICAGO: It goes back to hope: Choose hope. Seize joy and wonder in the face of darkness and stupidity. Embrace the rainbow.

SARAH THORNTON is a sociologist who writes about art, design, and people. Formerly the chief writer on art for the *Economist* and now a contributing editor to the *Financial Times*'s *HTSI* magazine, Thornton is the author of books, including the best-selling *Seven Days in the Art World*, which has been translated into twenty-two languages. Thornton lives in San Francisco and flies a rainbow flag outside her home all year round.

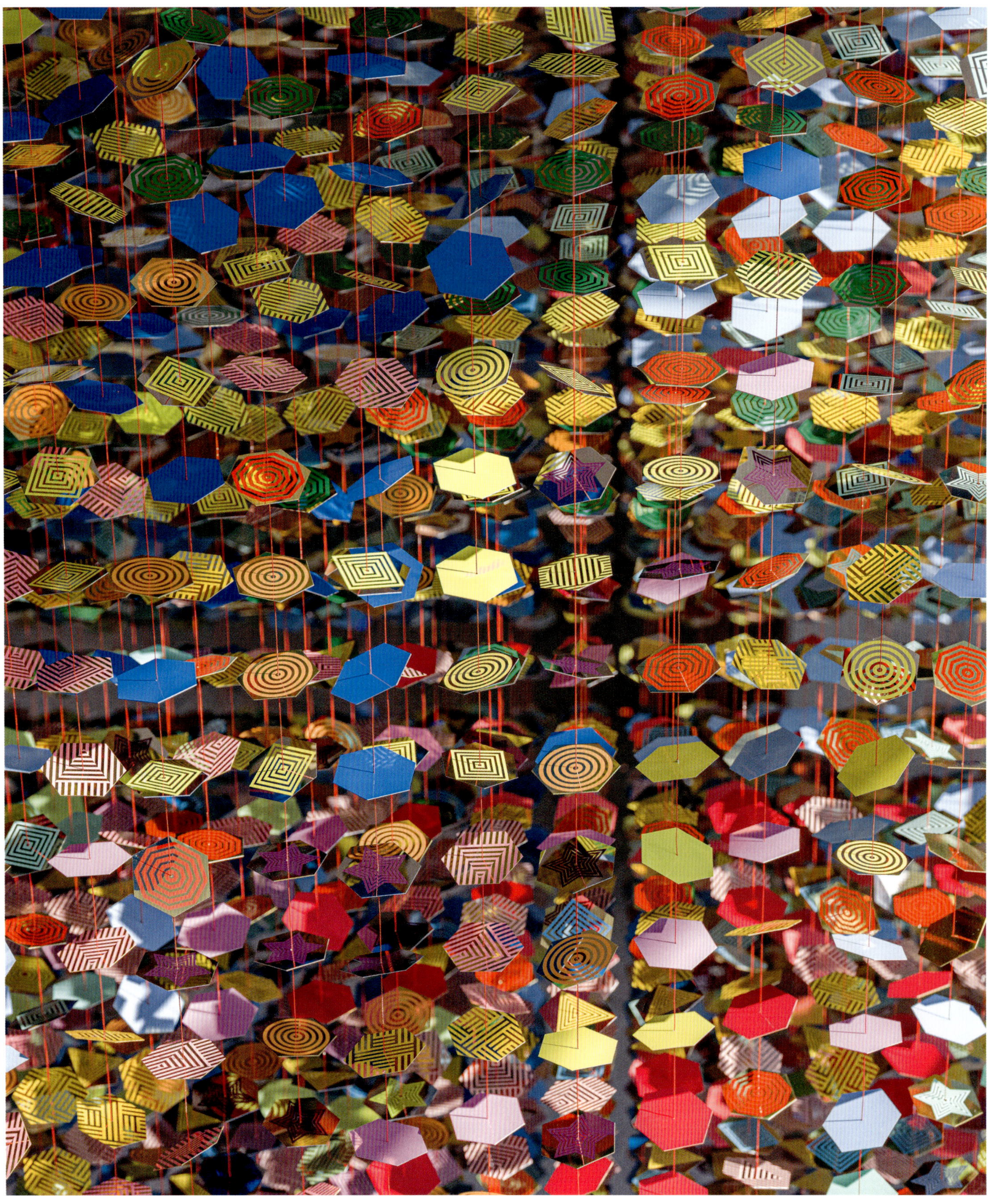

Pae White

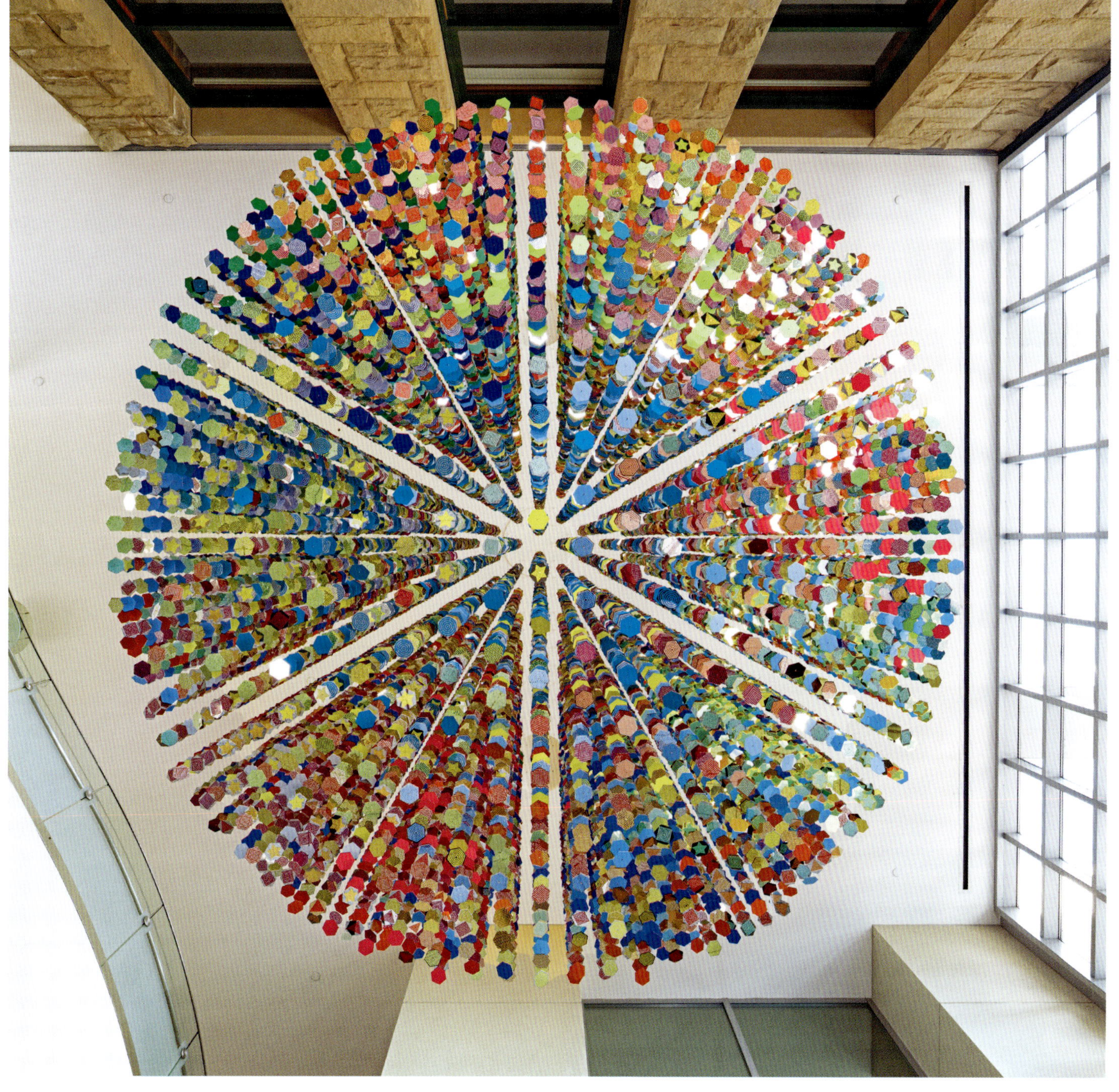

Mark Grotjahn

Untitled (Colored Butterfly White Background 10 Wings)   2004

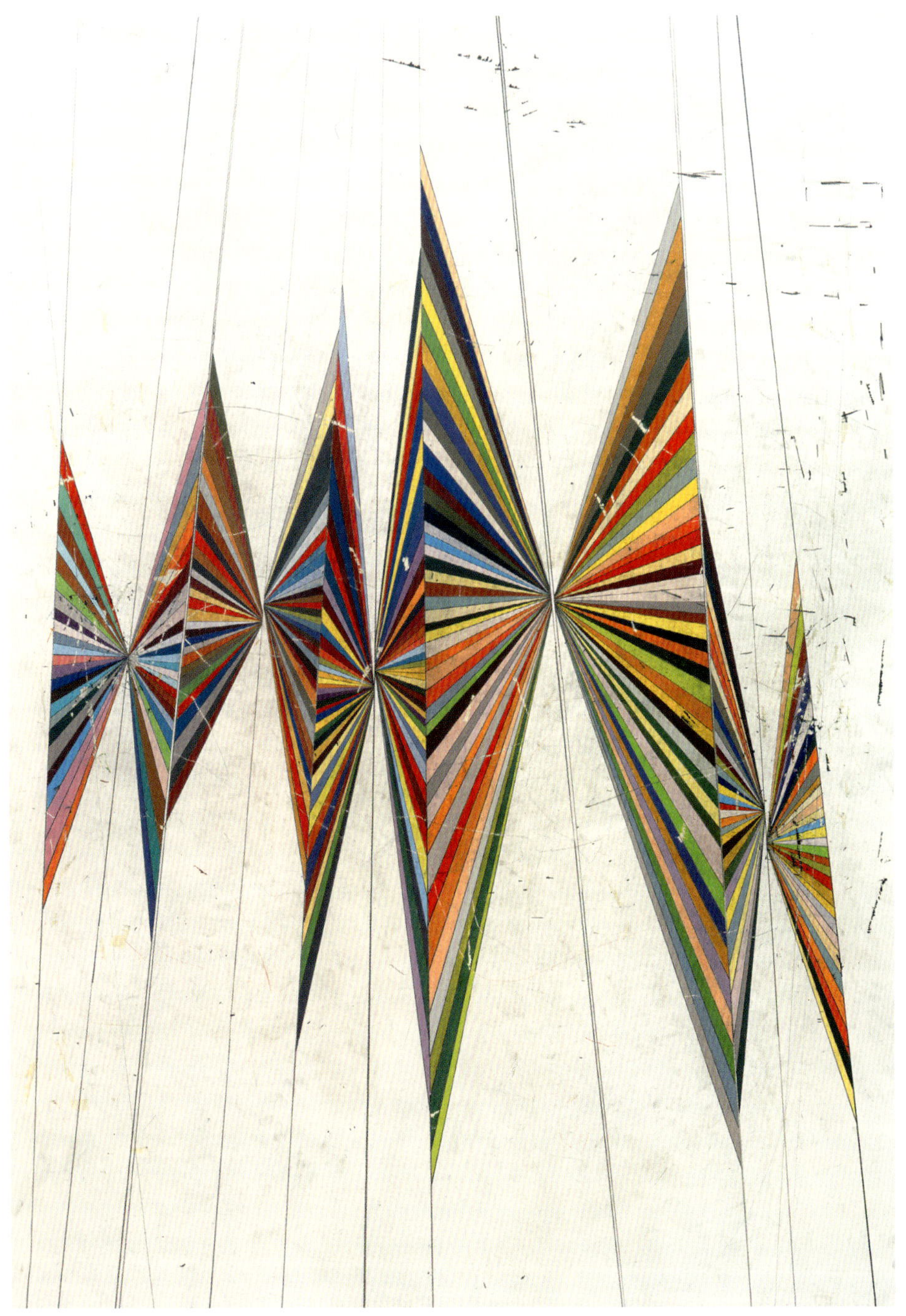

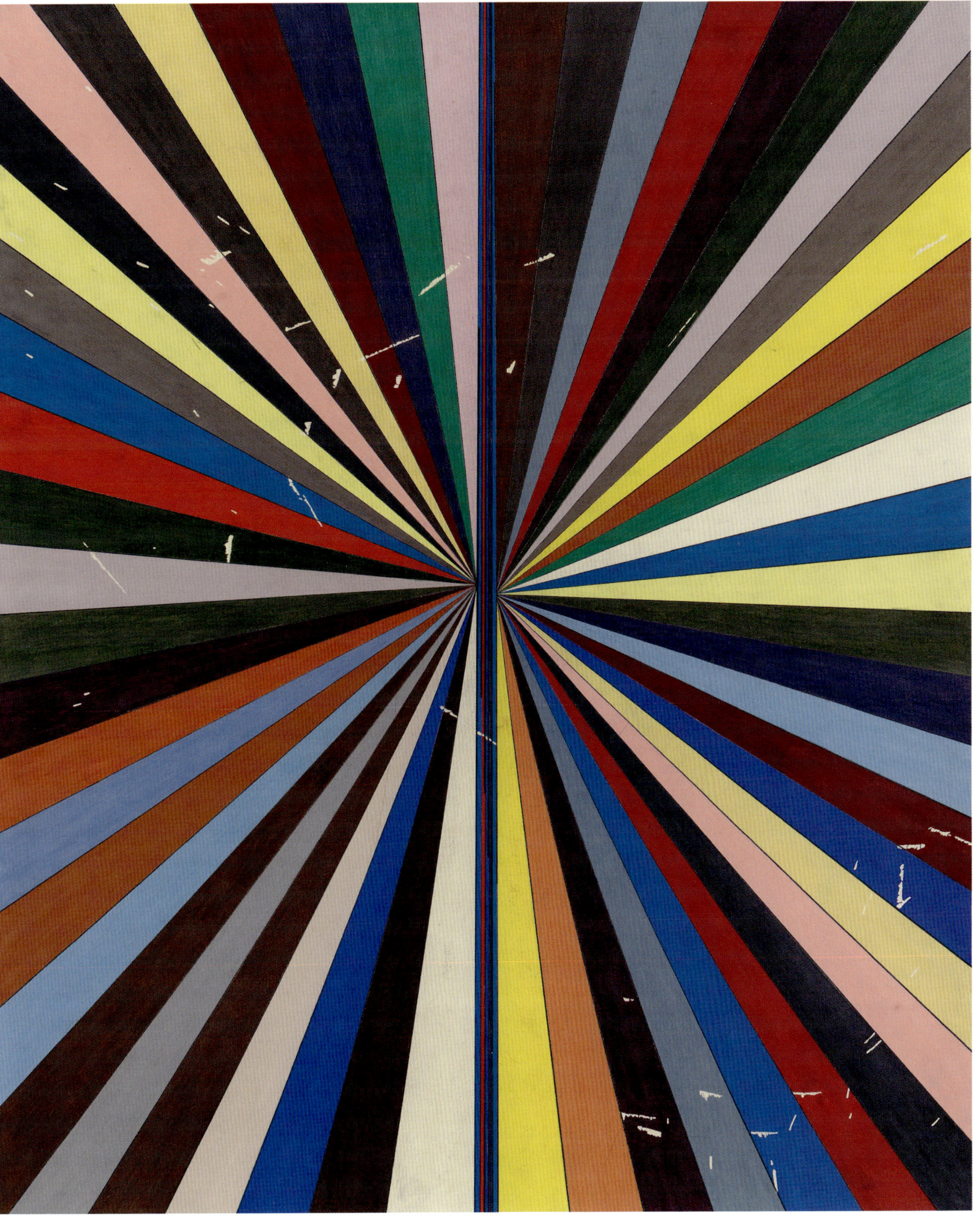

Polly Apfelbaum

For the Love of Gene Davis 2014

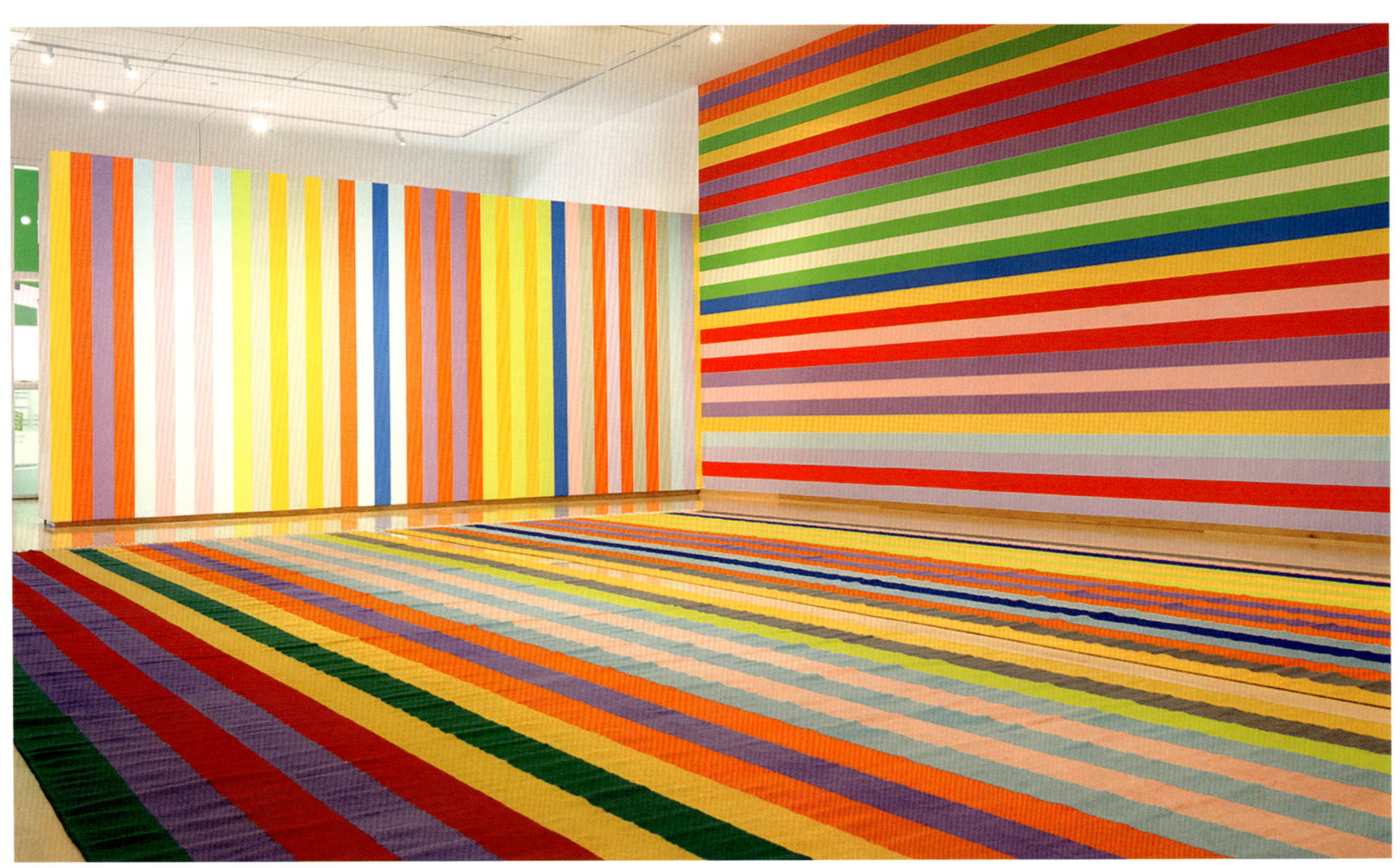

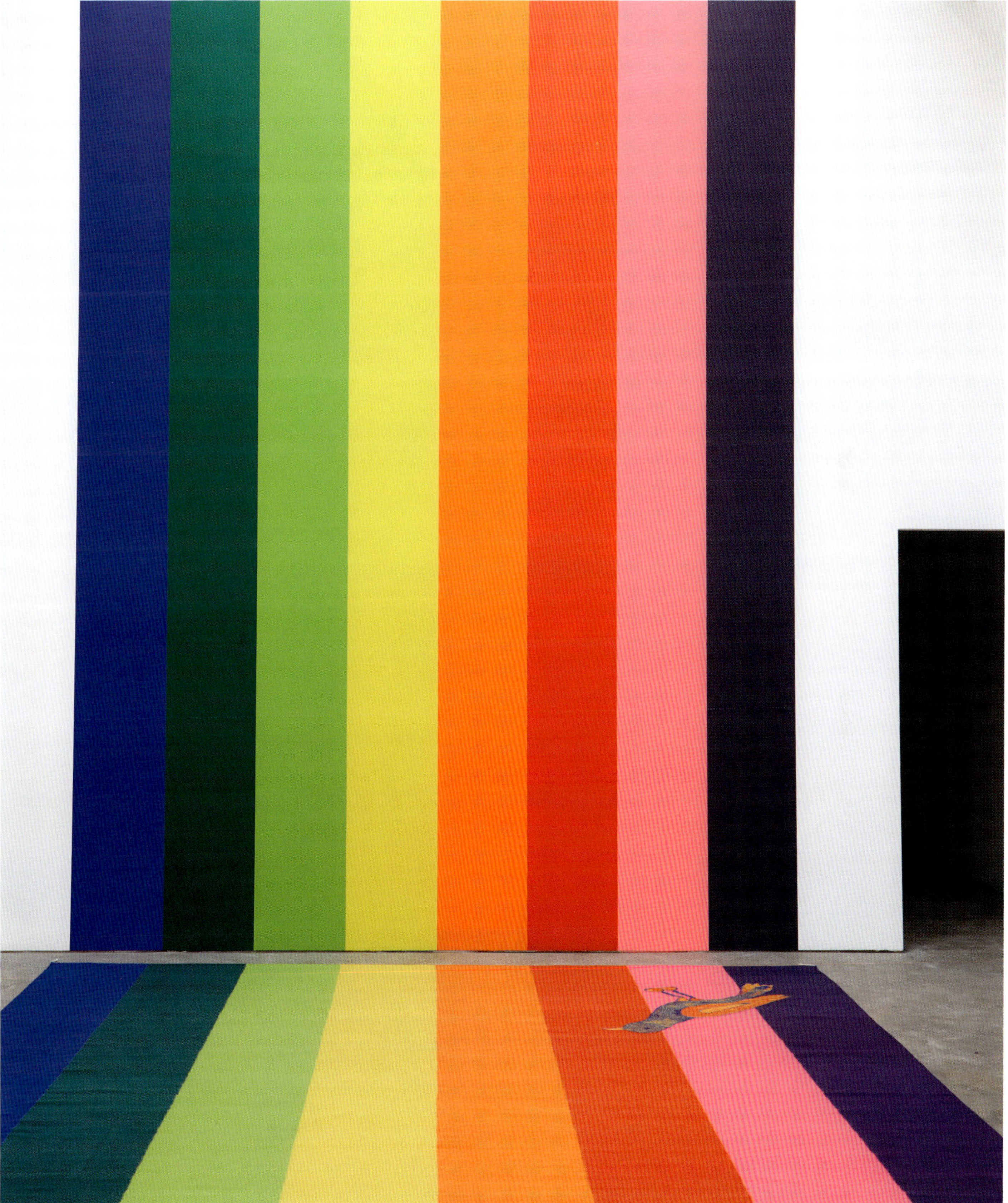

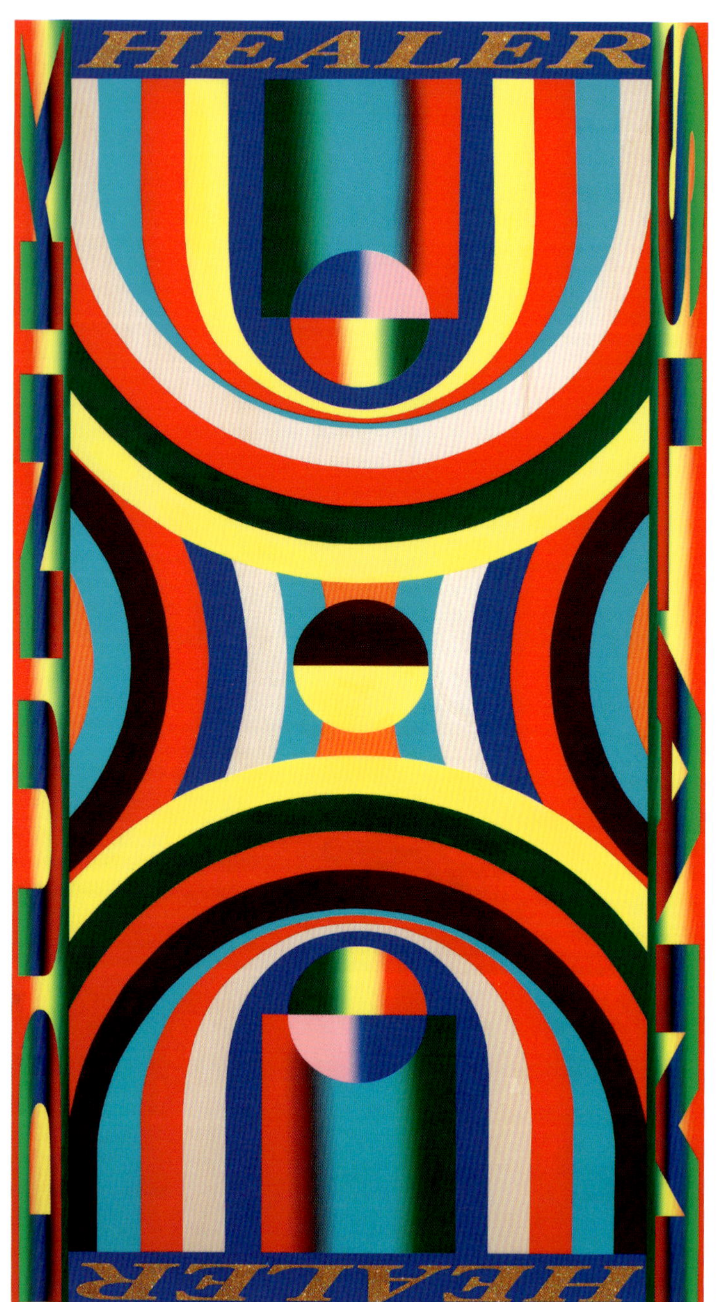

Julius Erving   2022

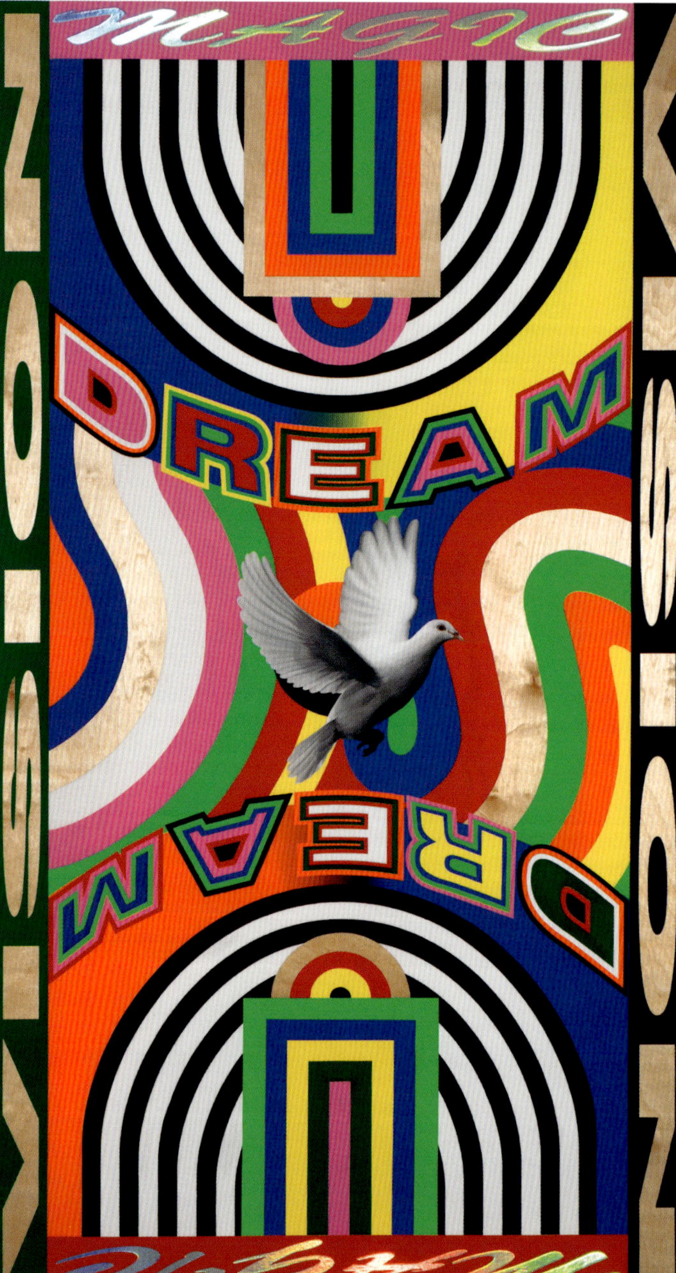

Larry Bird   2022

Lakwena Maciver

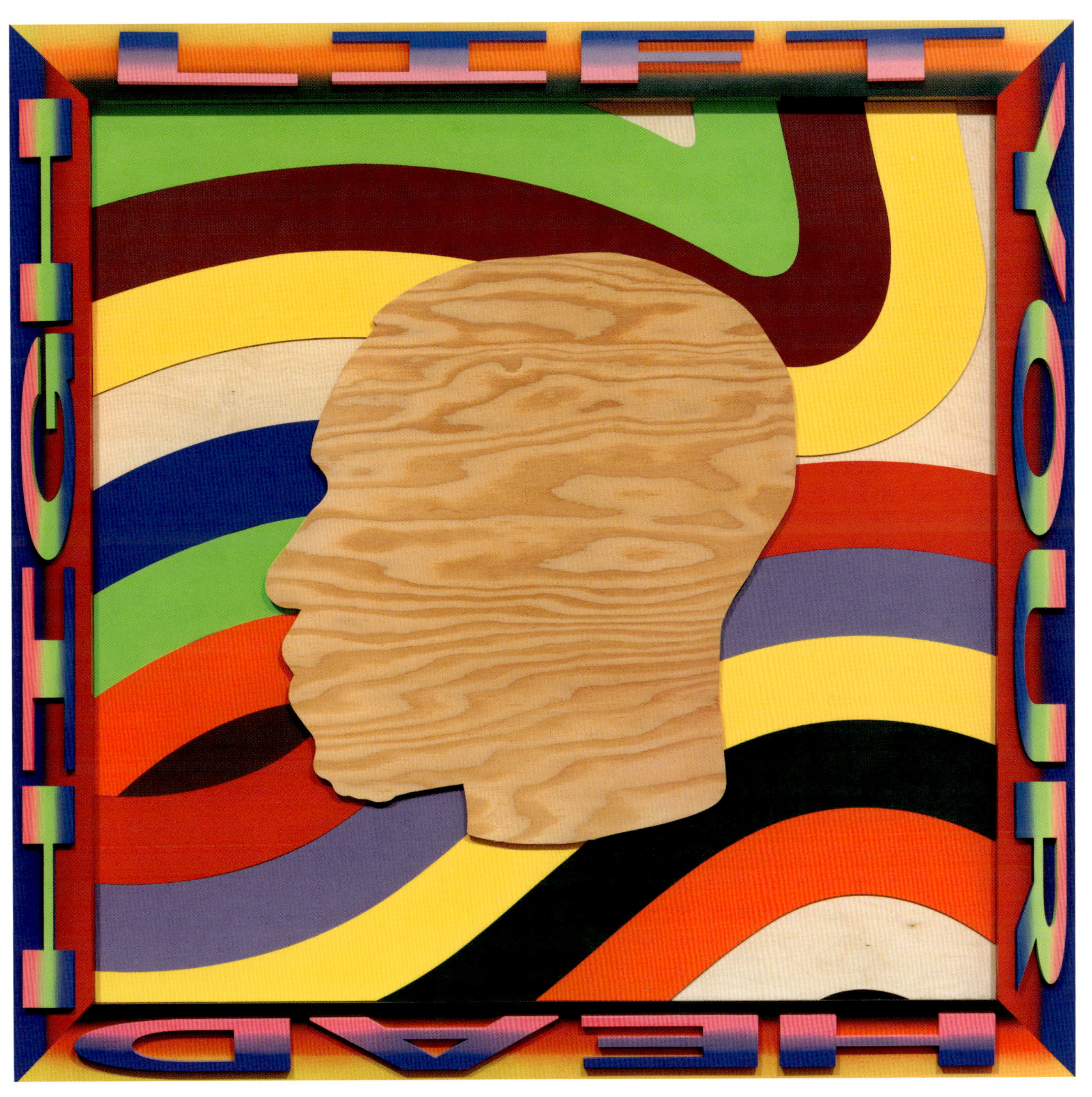

Lift Your Head High   2025

Melissa Cody

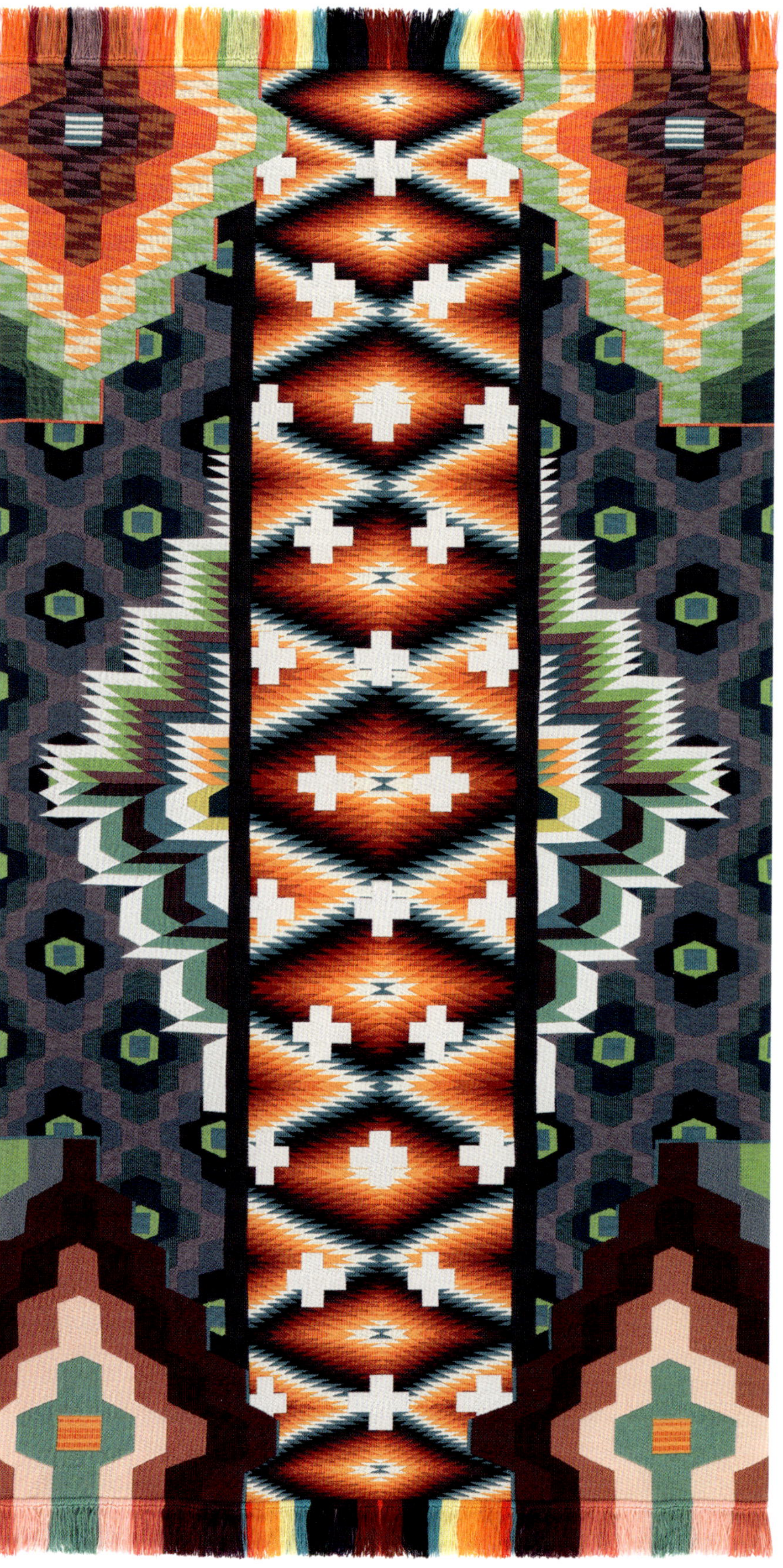

Scaling the Caverns   2023

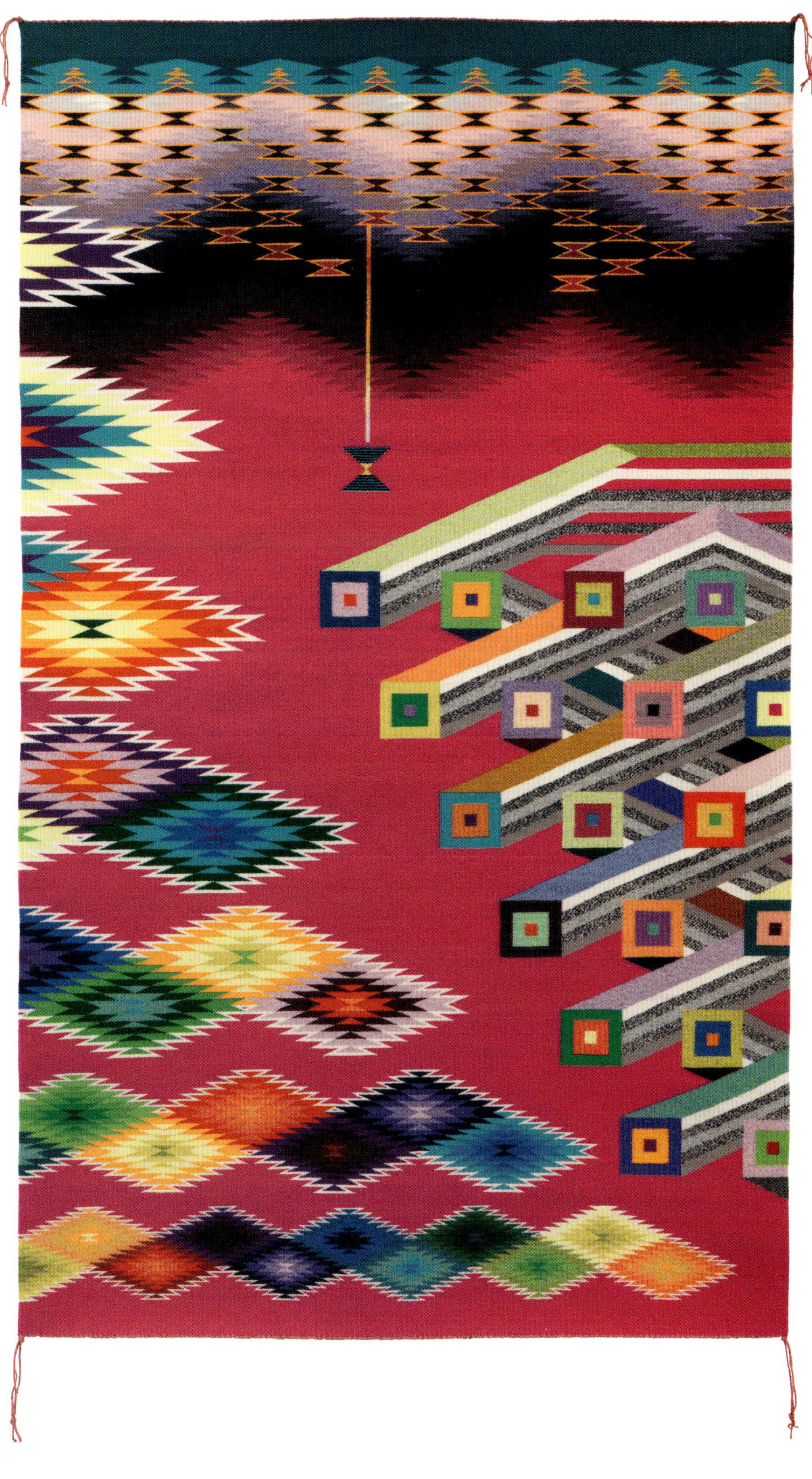

Into the Depths, She Rappels   2023

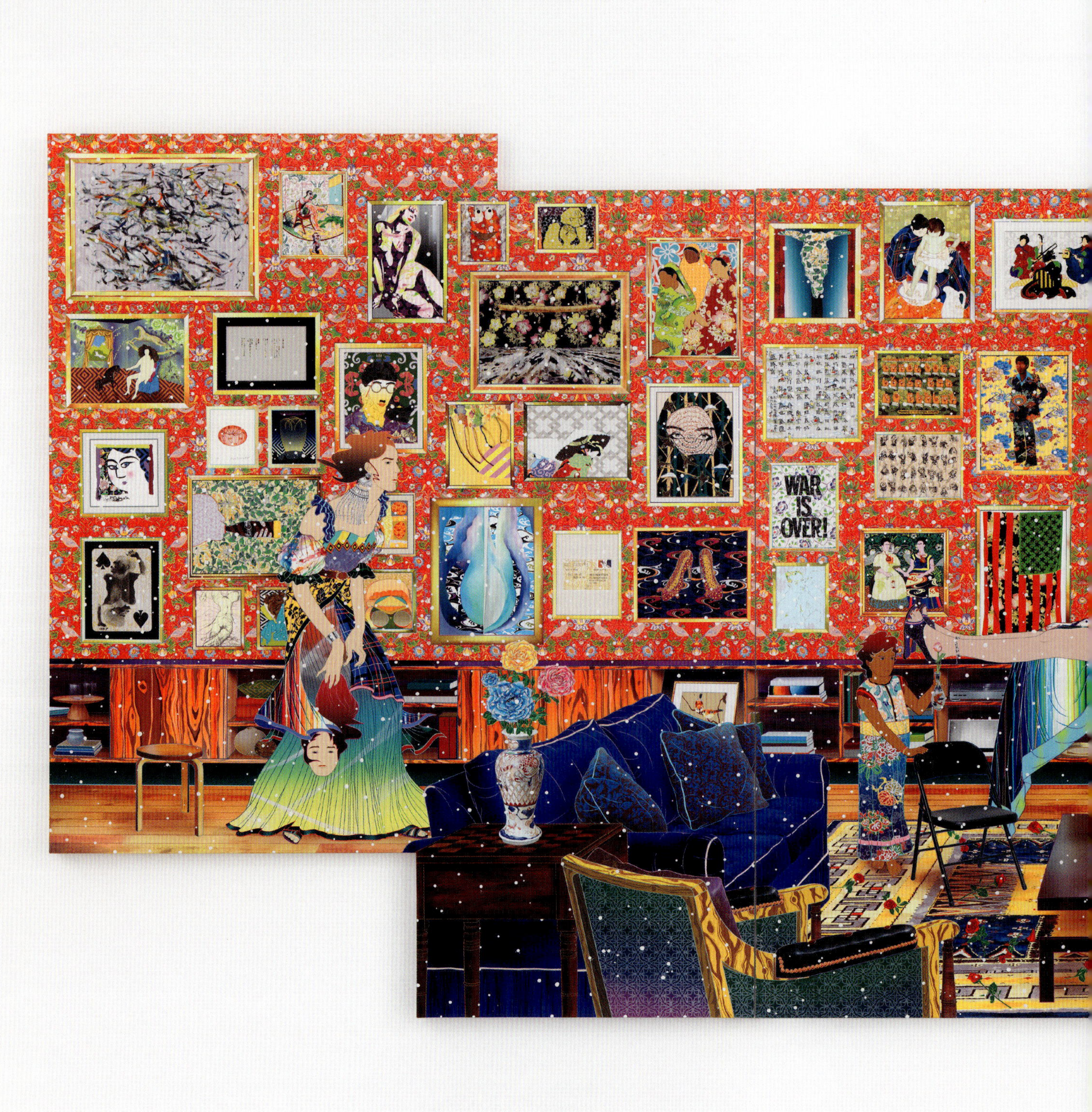

Tomokazu Matsuyama

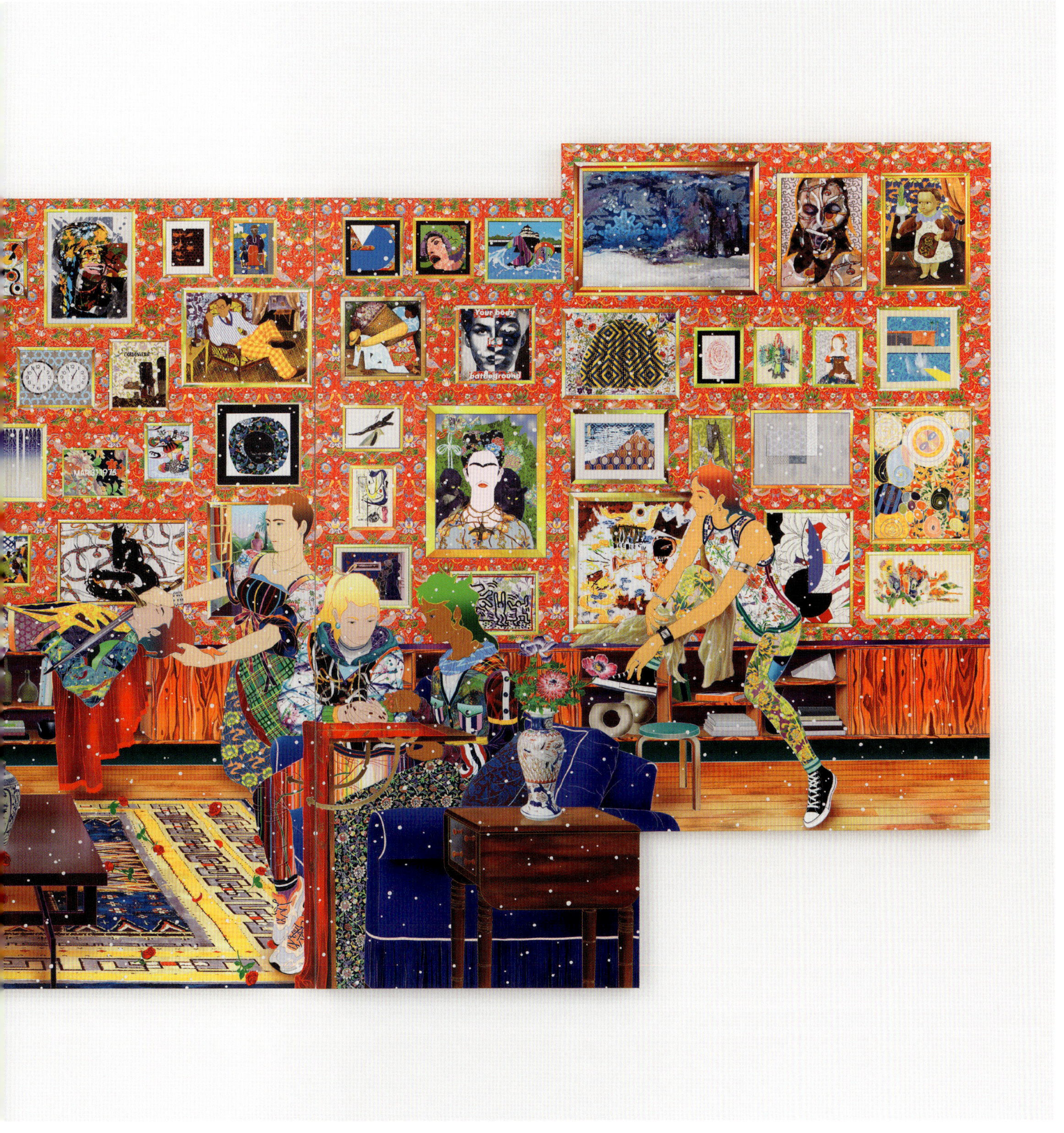

You, One Me Erase 2023

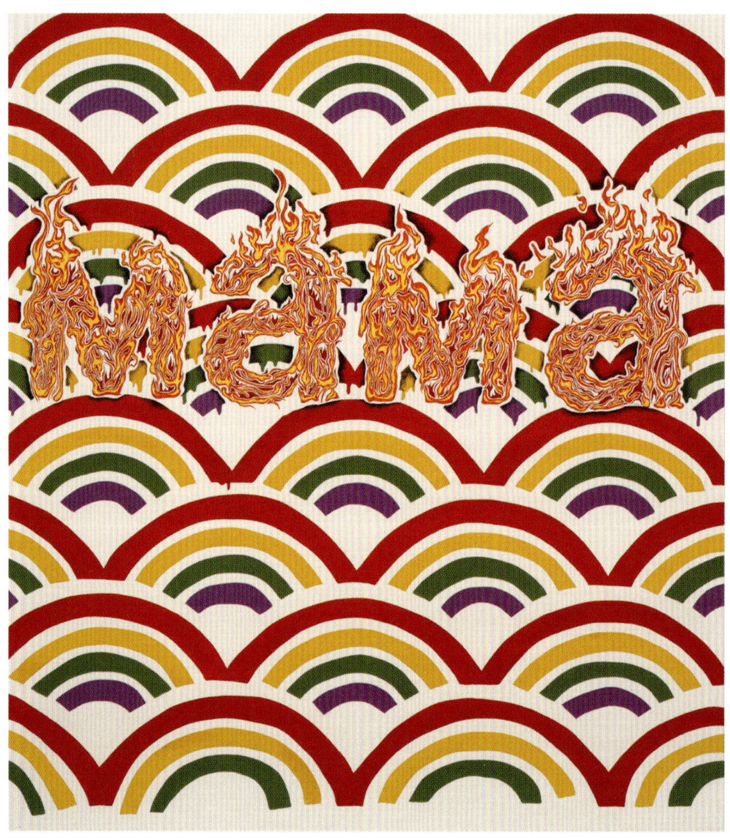

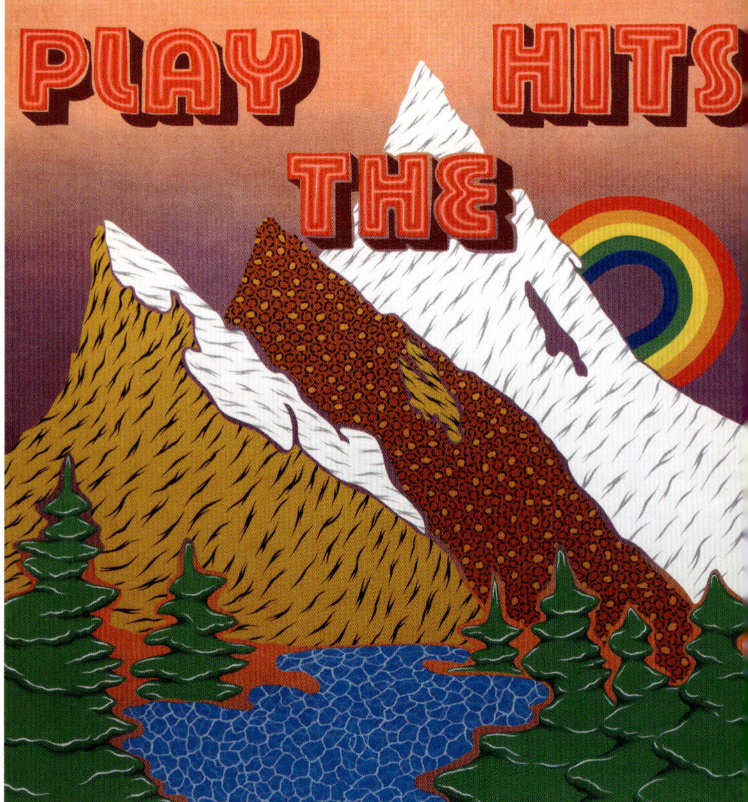

Joel Mesler

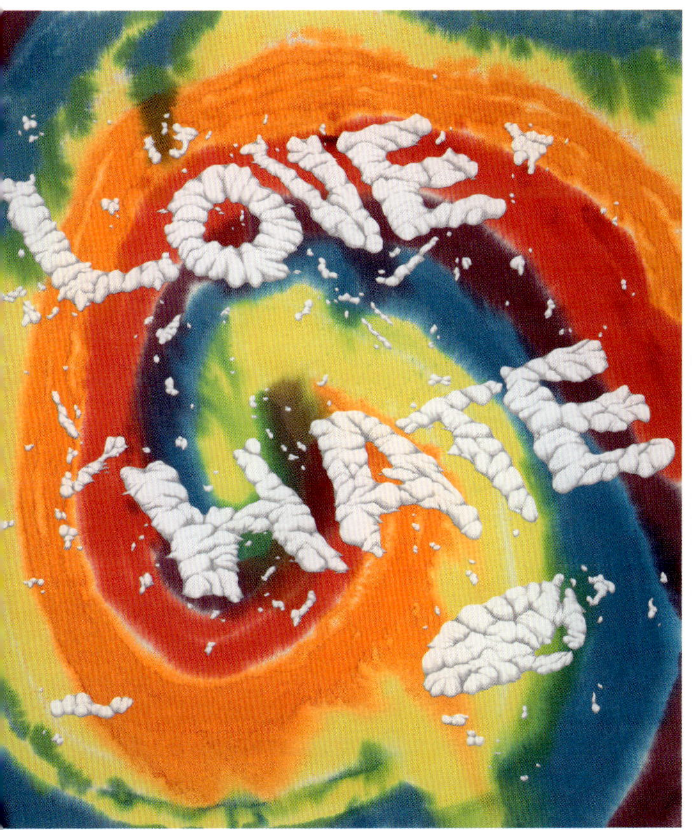
LOVE
HATE

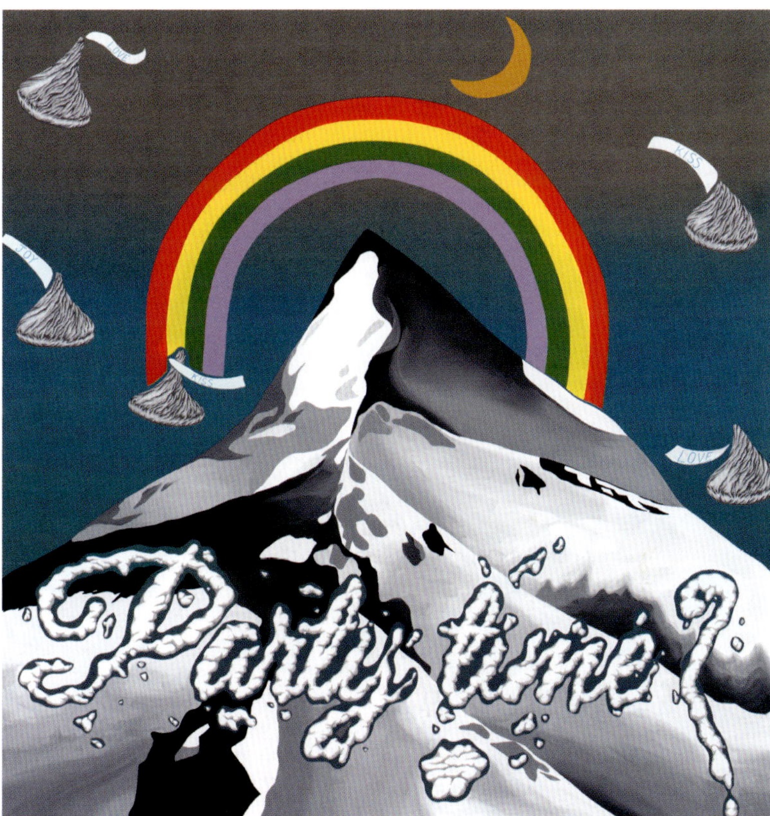
Party time

Art d'Ameublement (Catoodden)   2021

Mika Tajima

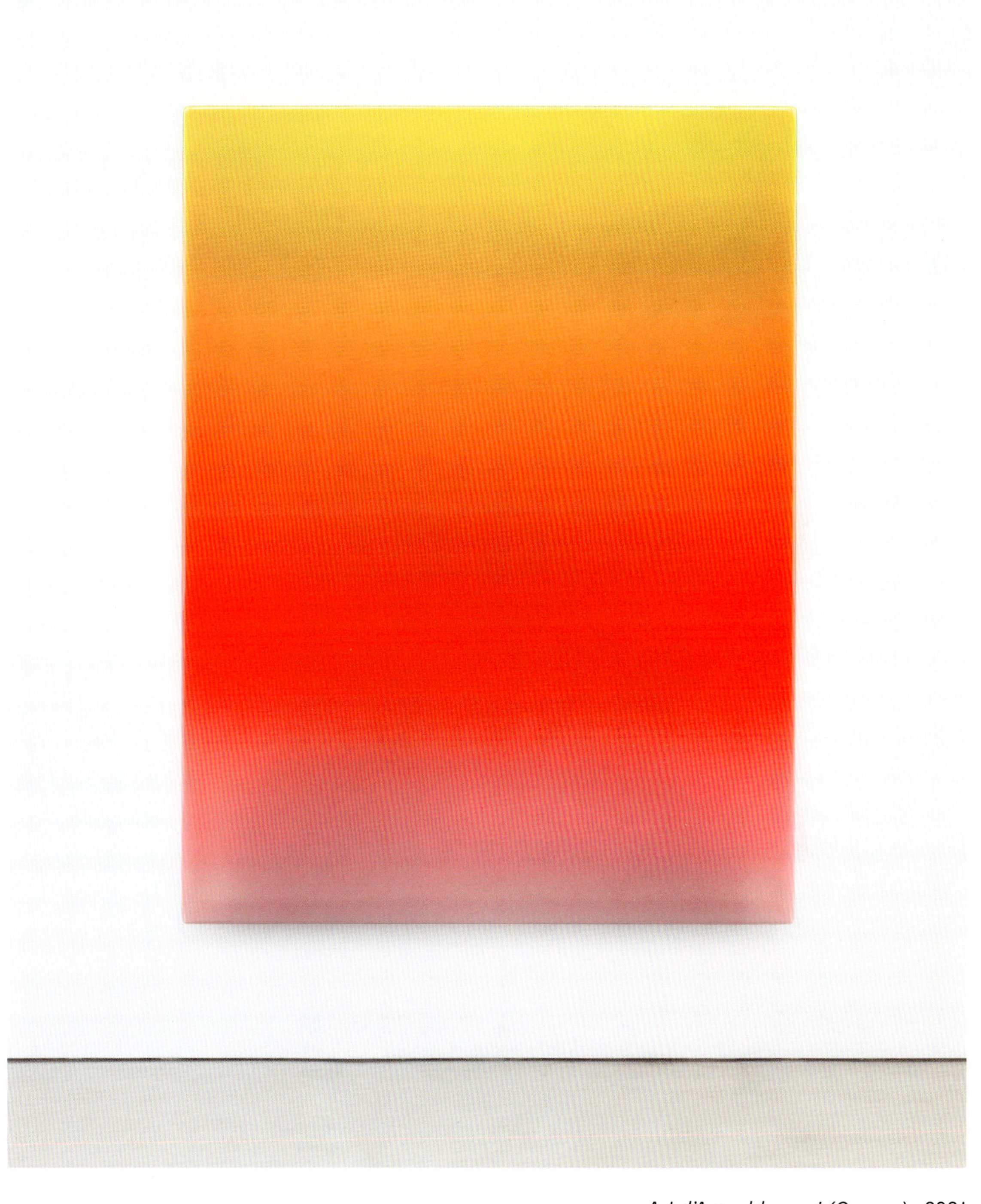

Art d'Ameublement (Onamu) 2021

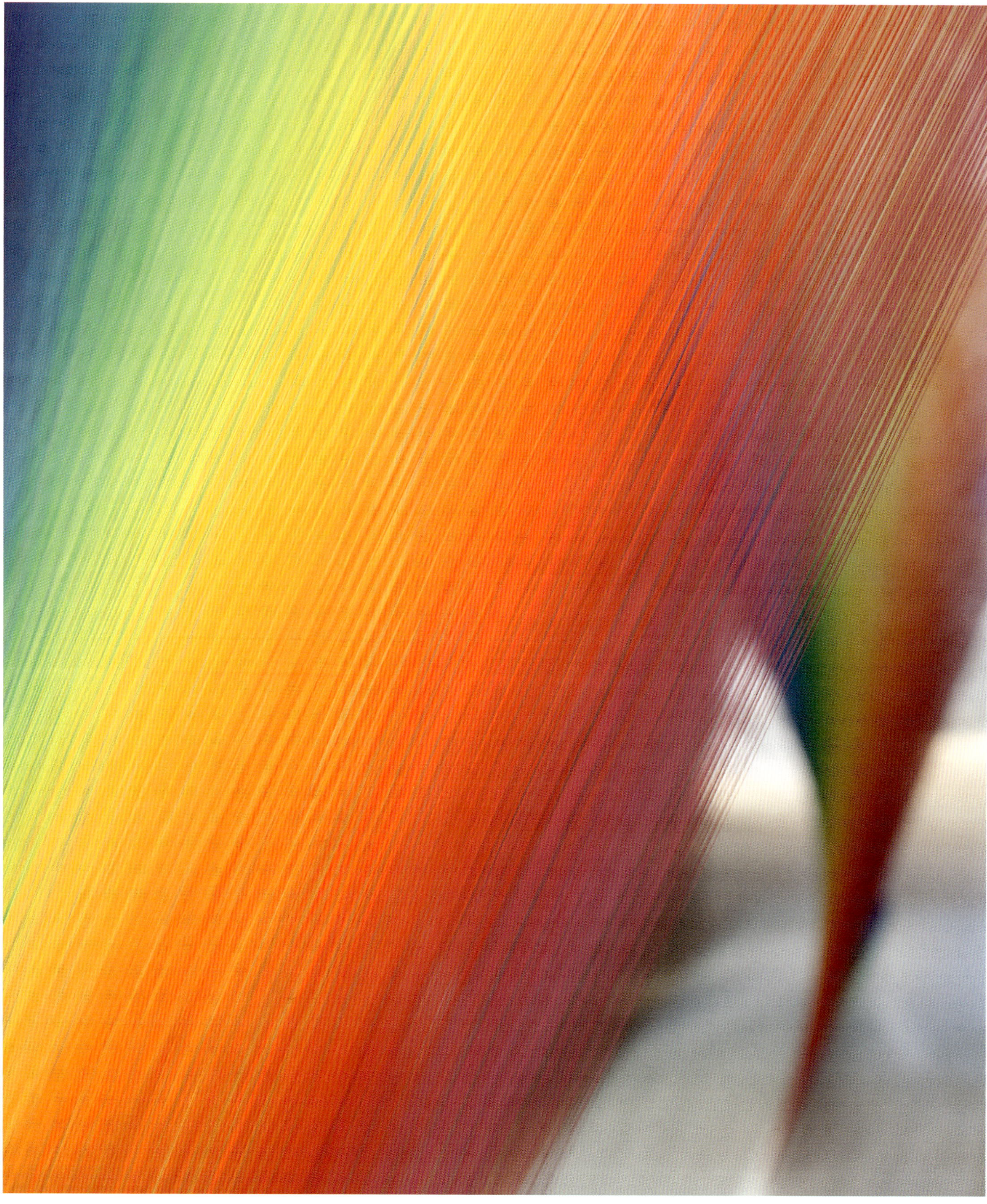

Gabriel Dawe

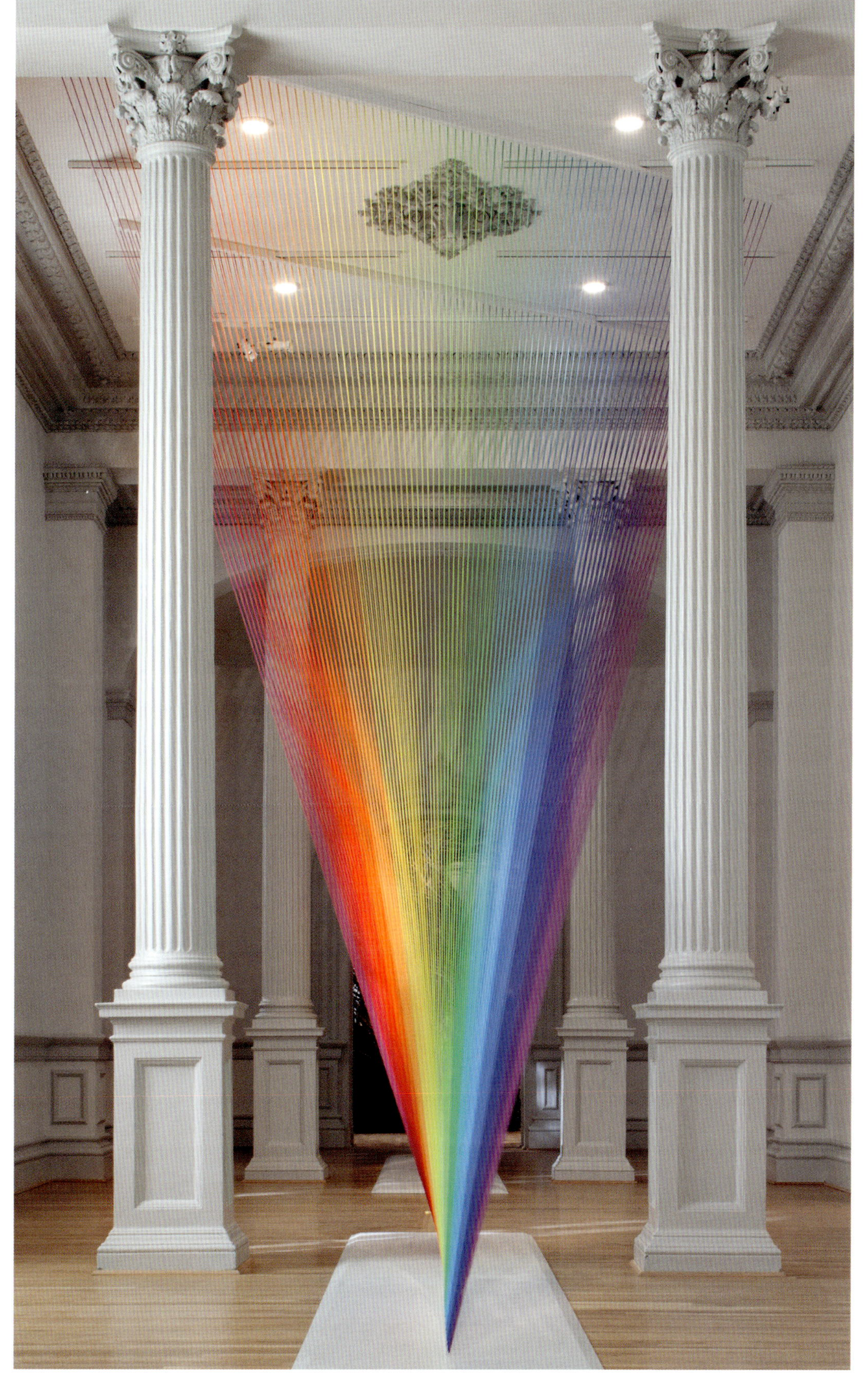

Plexus A1 2015   177

Sterling Ruby

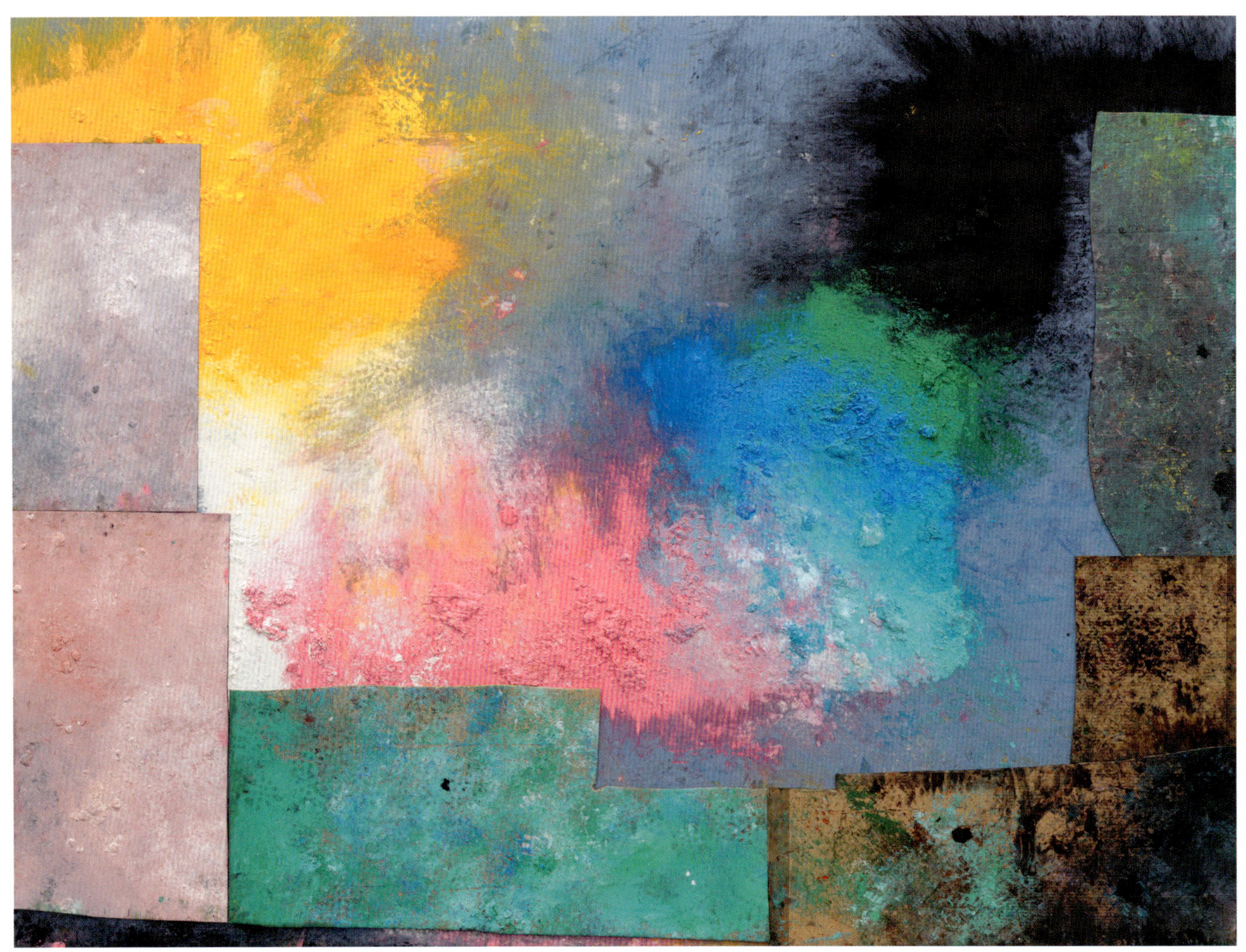

TURBINE. YOUR LIGHT GROWS DARK BY LOSING OF YOUR EYES. 2024

SP184 2011

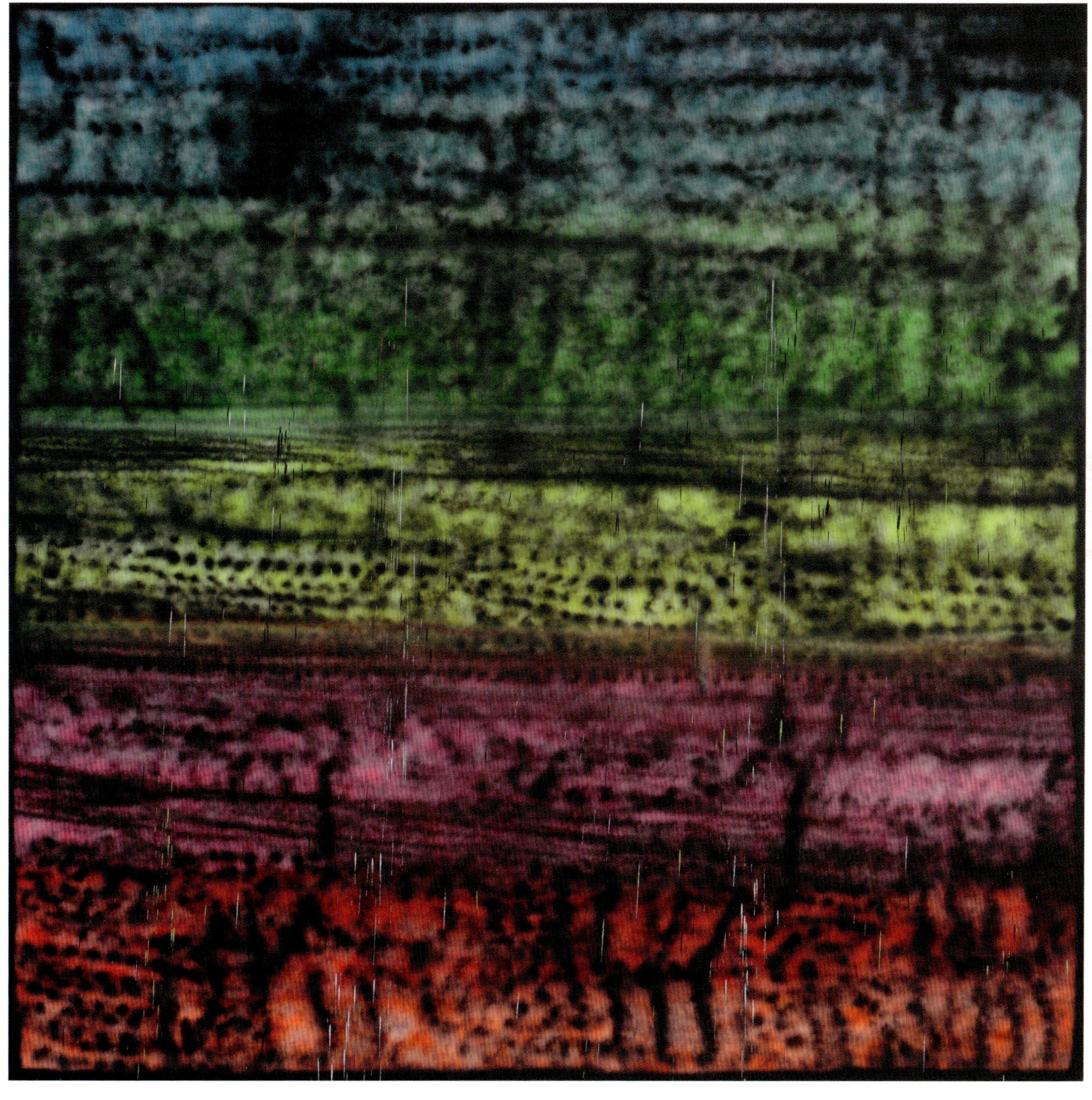

Hiroshi Sugimoto

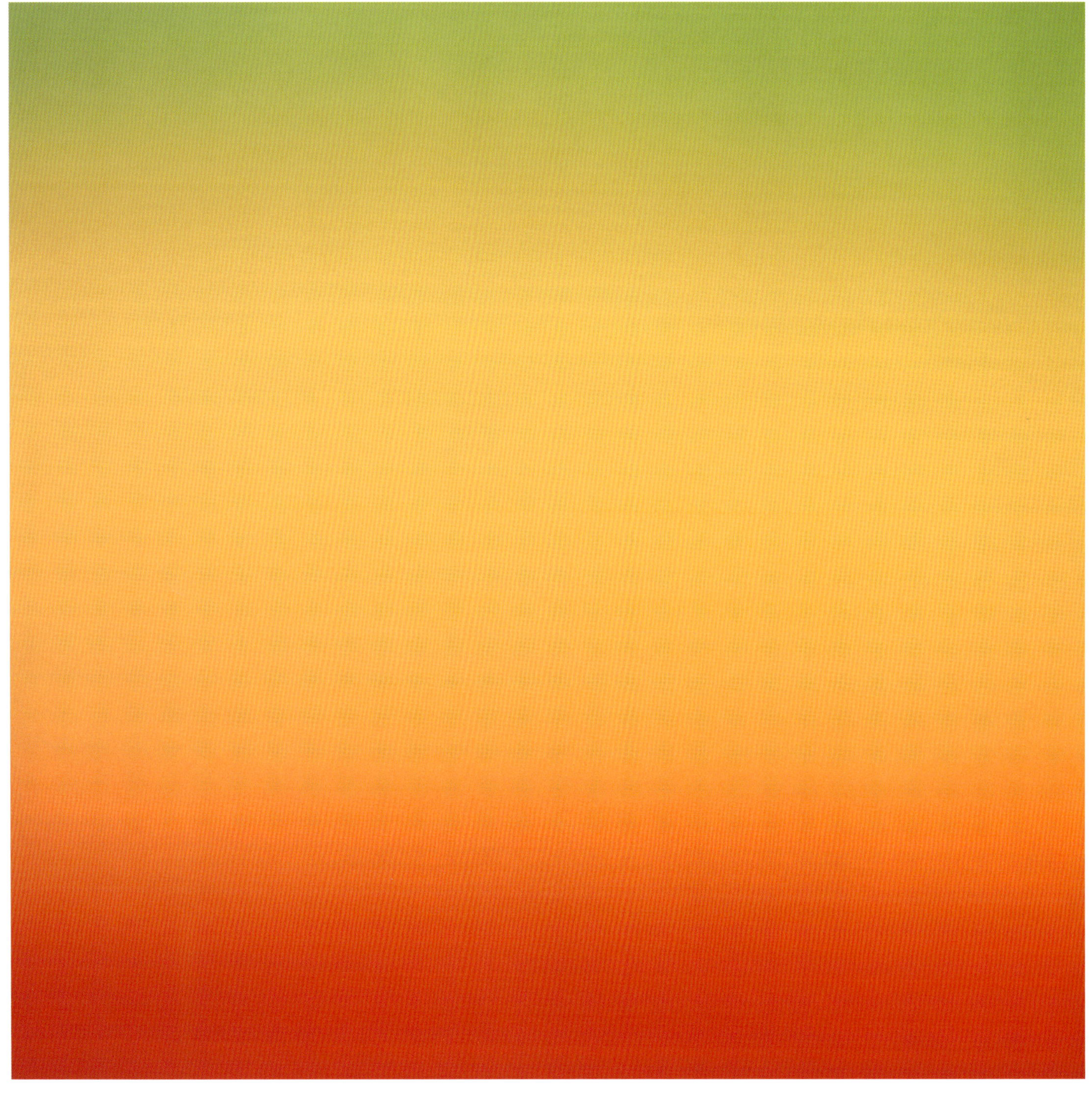

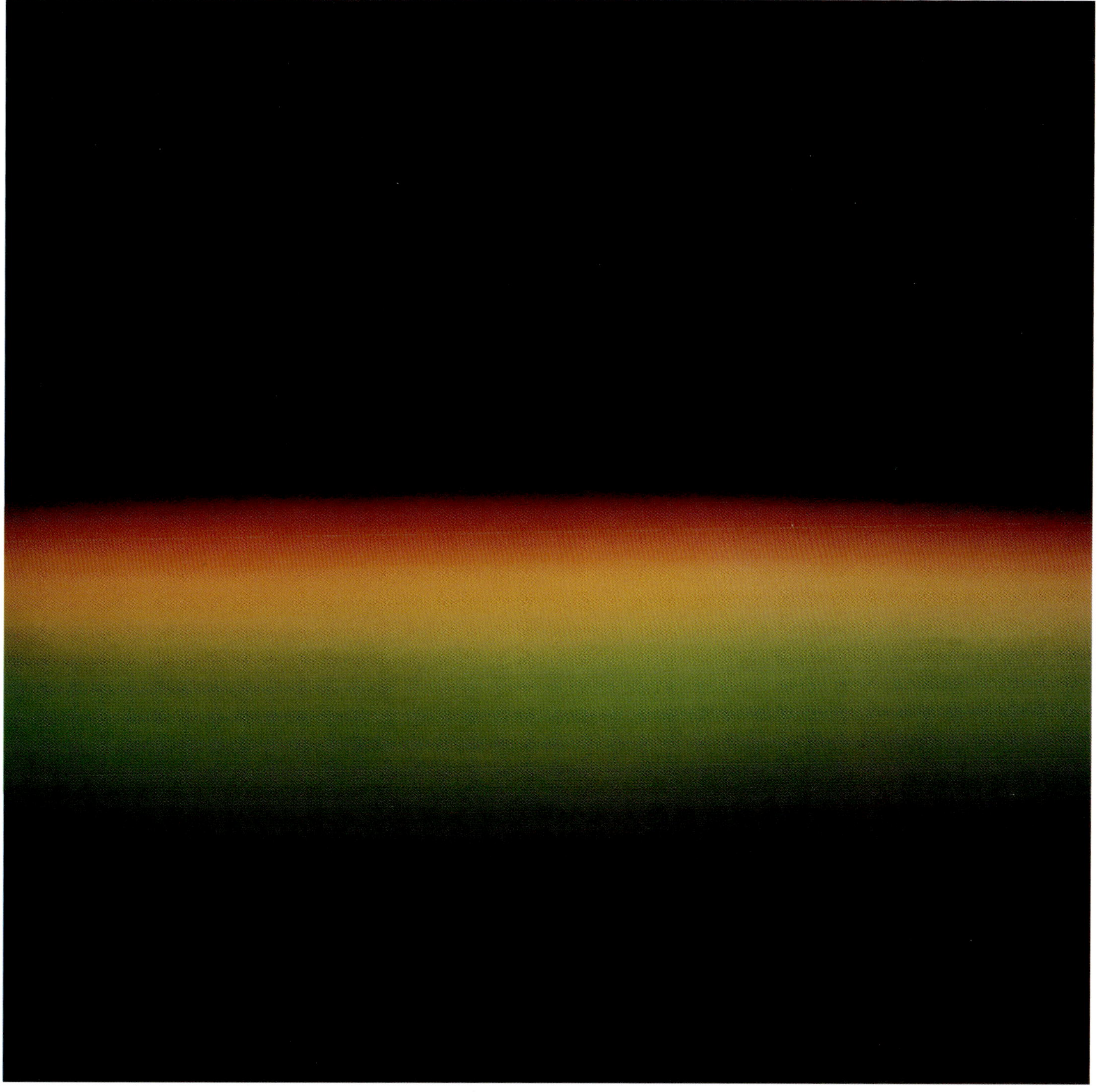

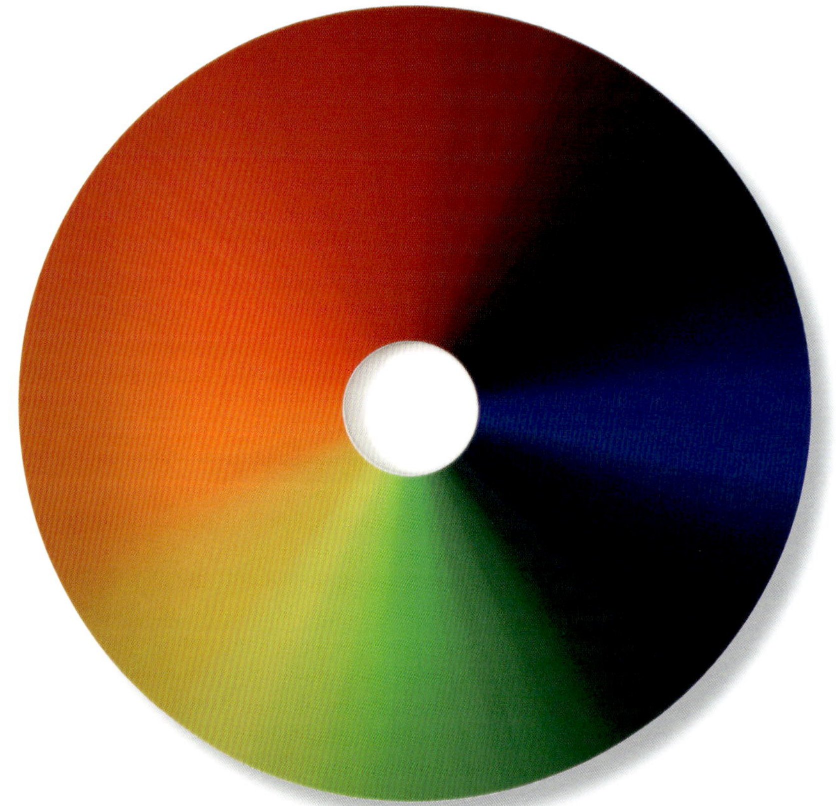

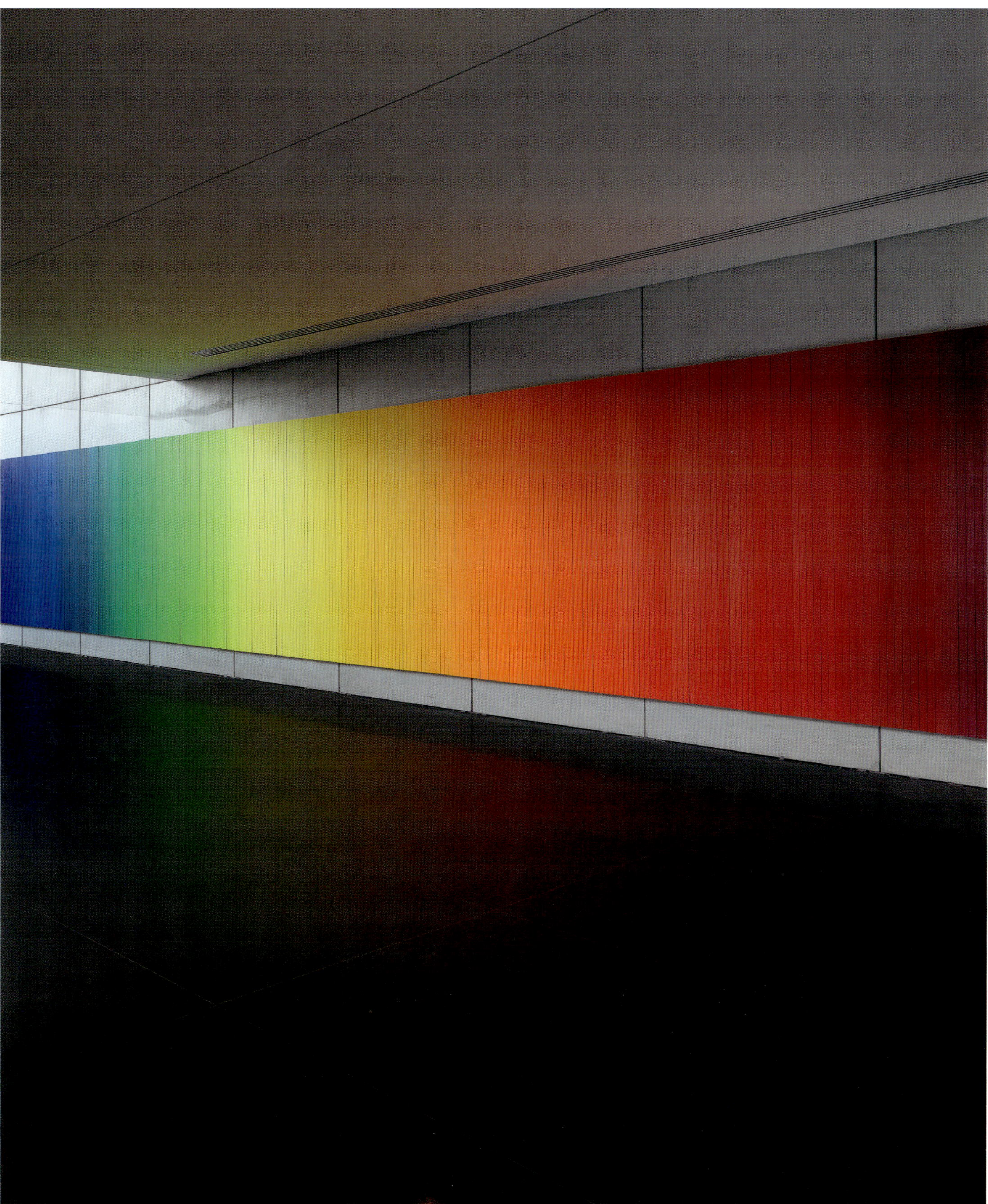

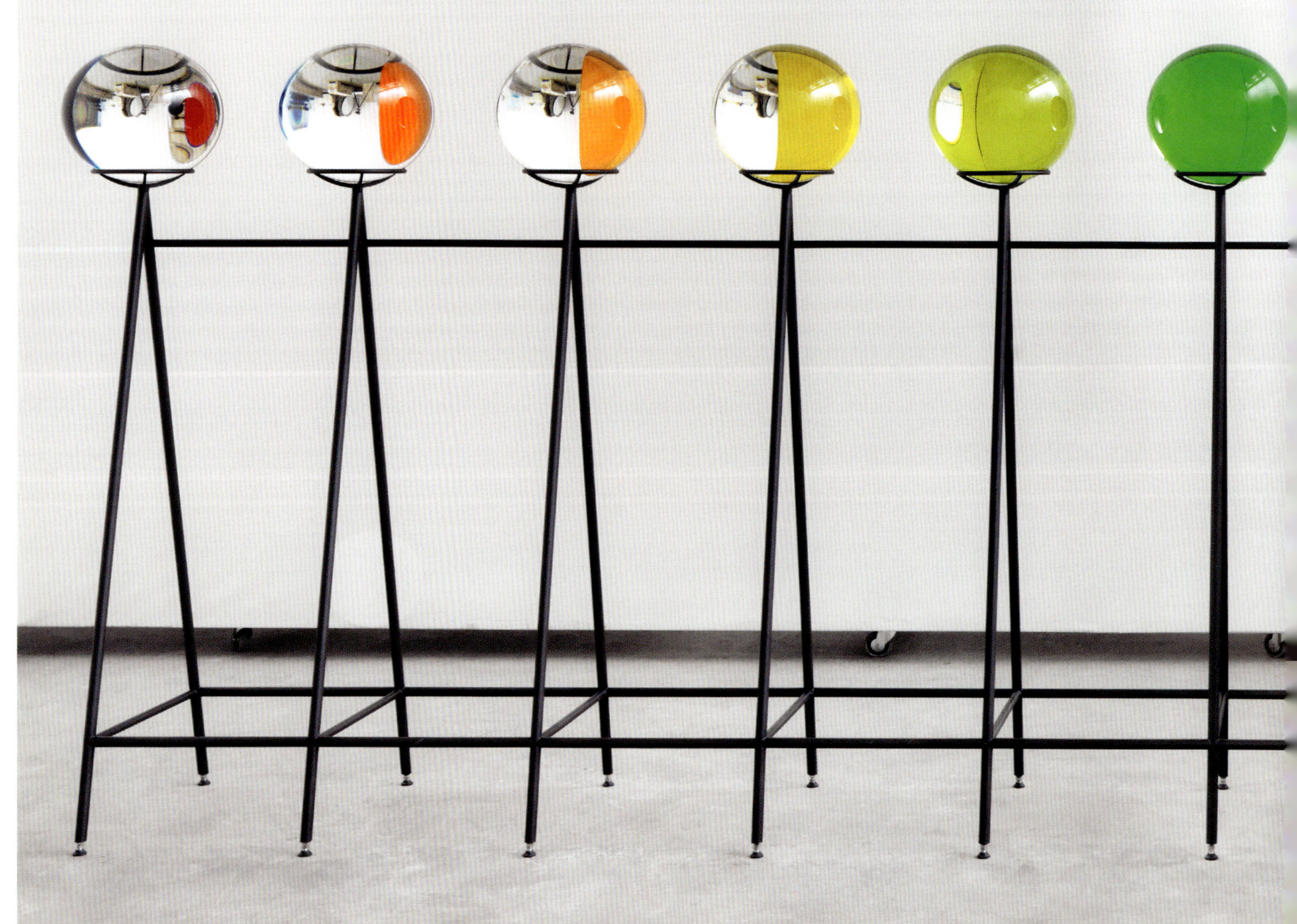

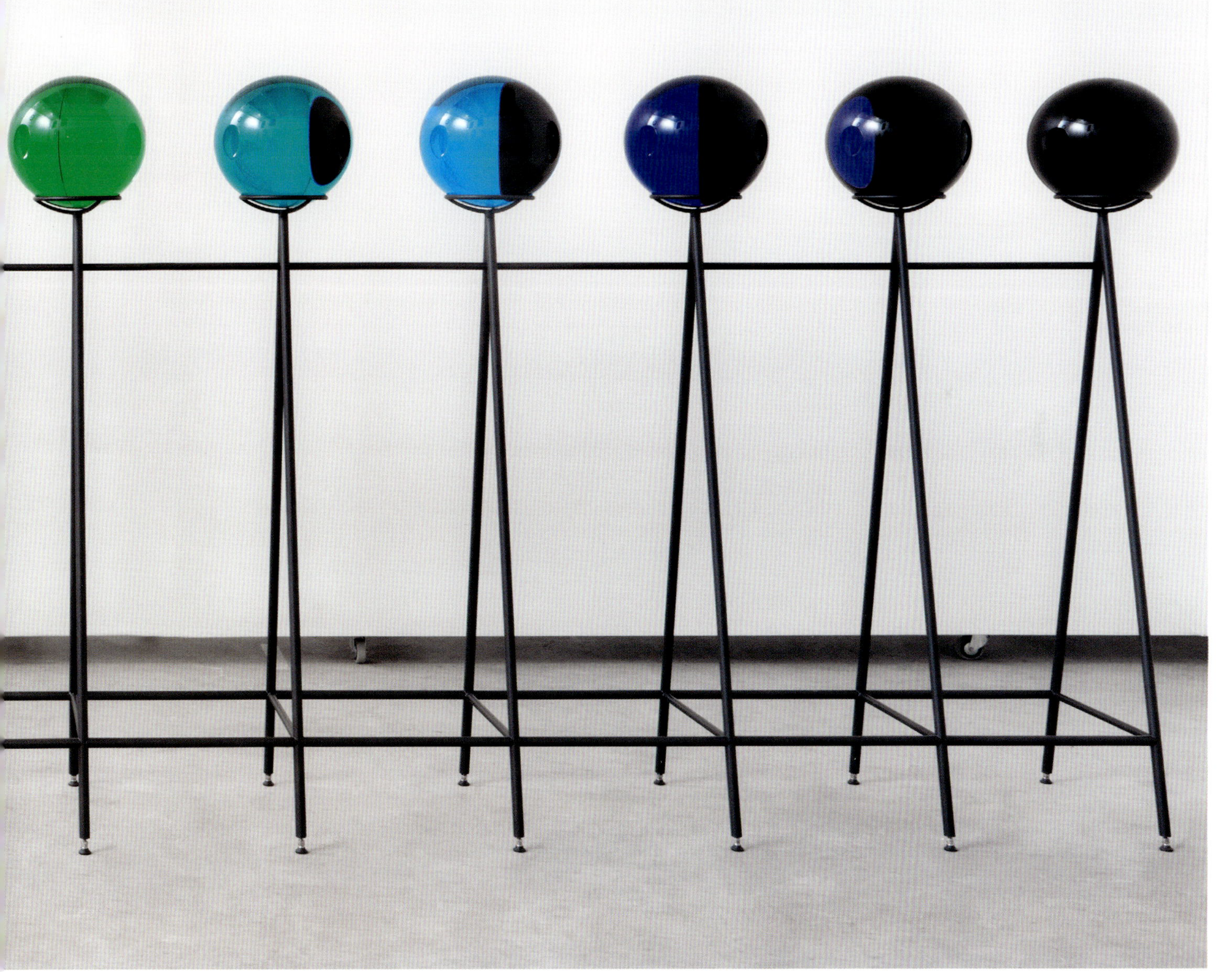

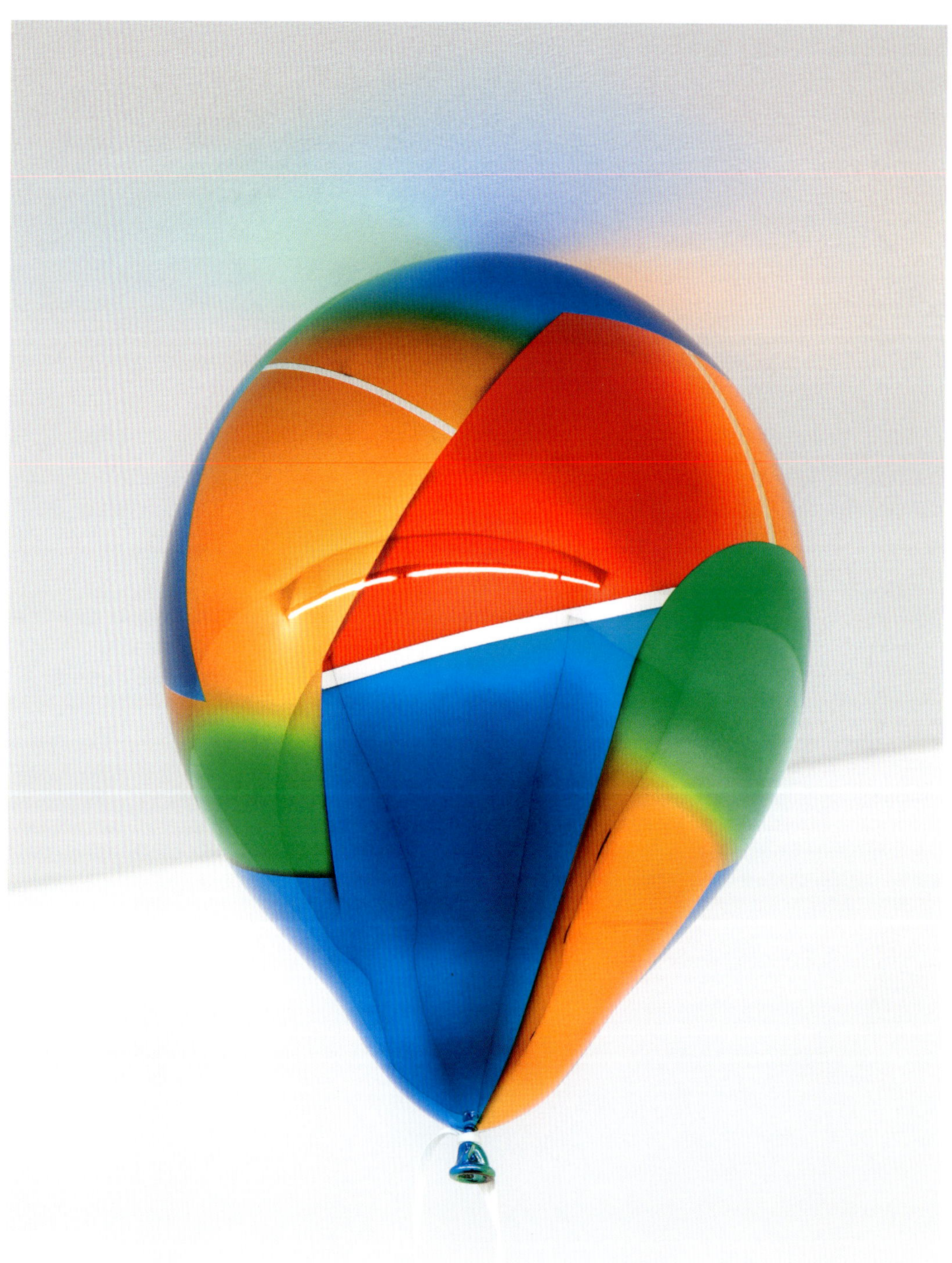

Jeppe Hein

Light Yellow, Medium
Blue and Dark Orange
Mirror Balloon   2019

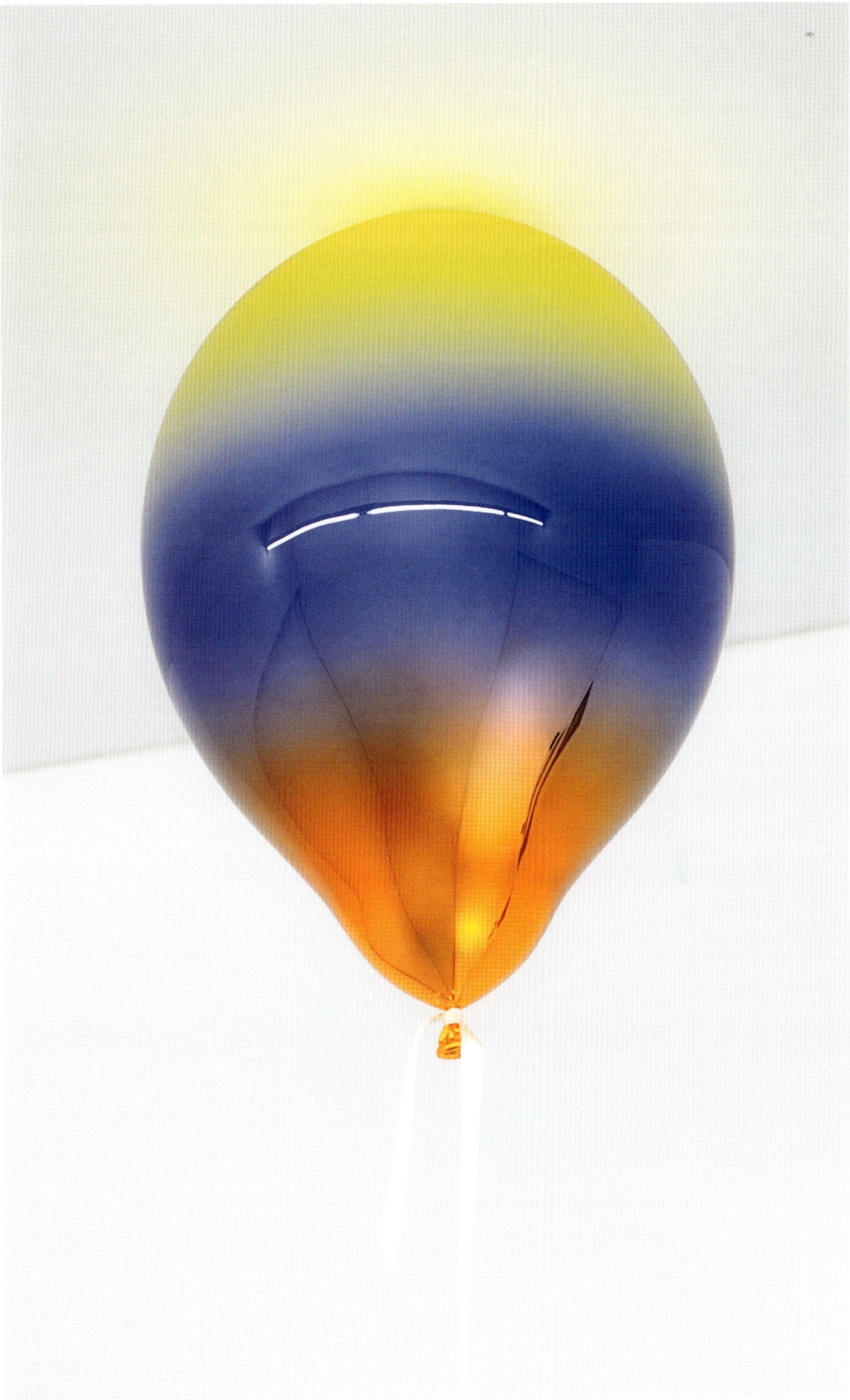

Jeff Koons

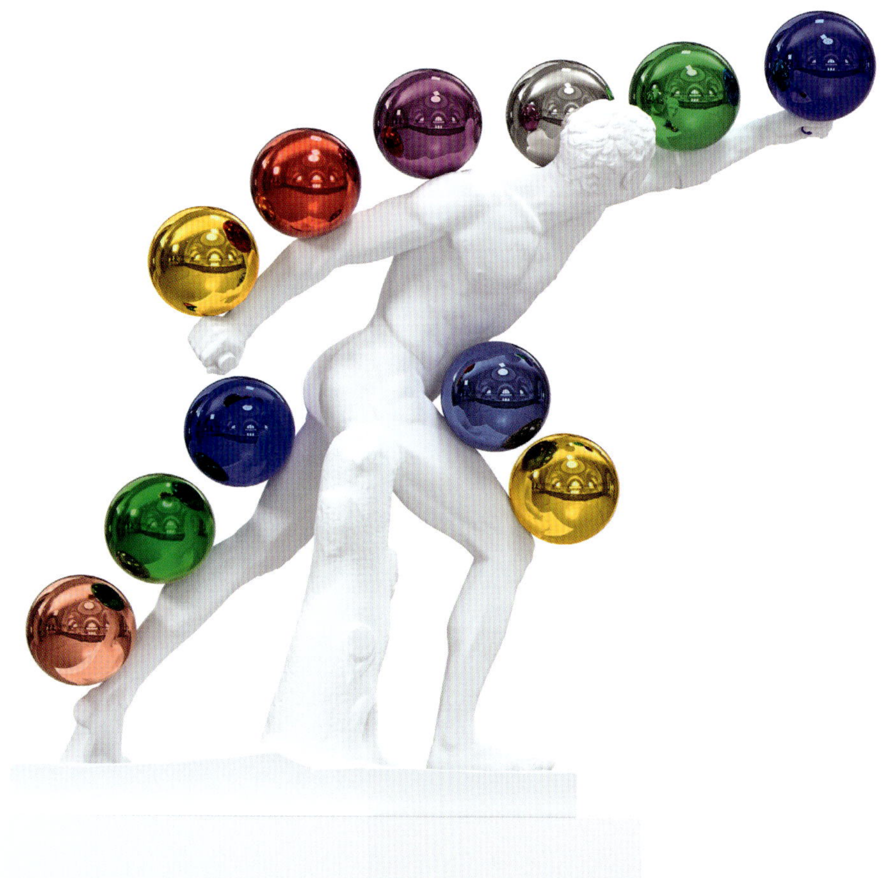

(Borghese Gladiator) Gazing Balls 2024

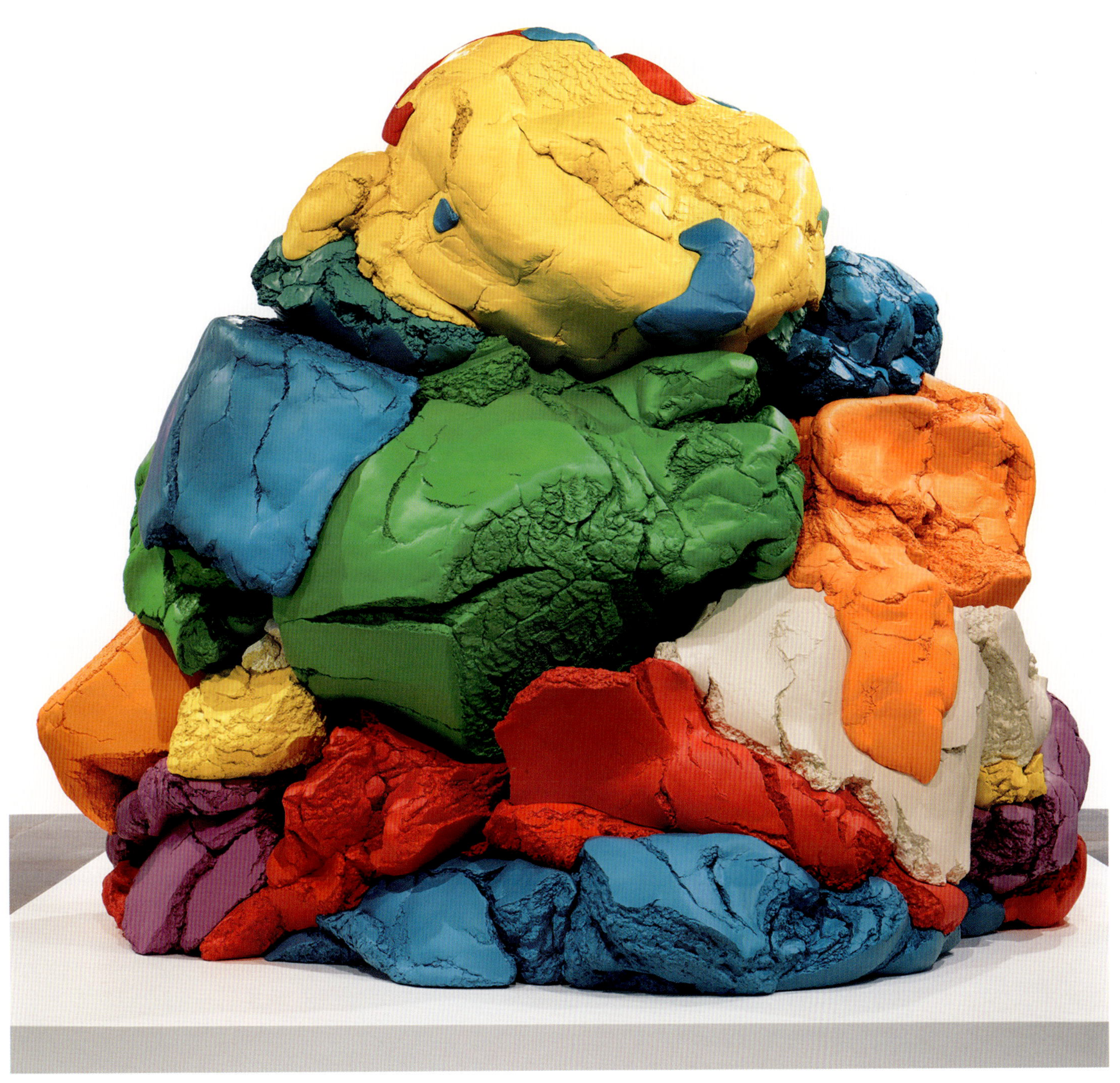

Mickalene Thomas

Resist 2017

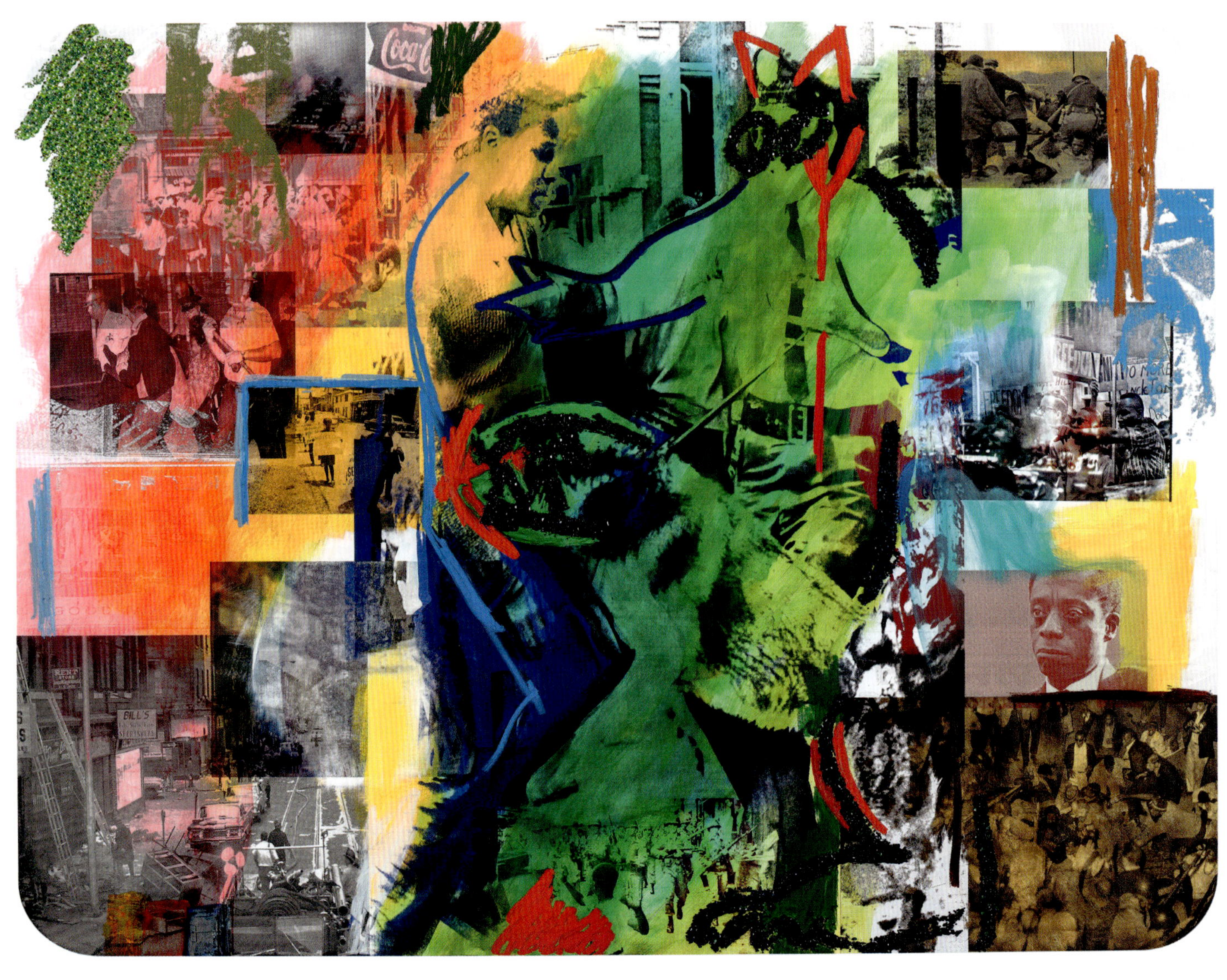

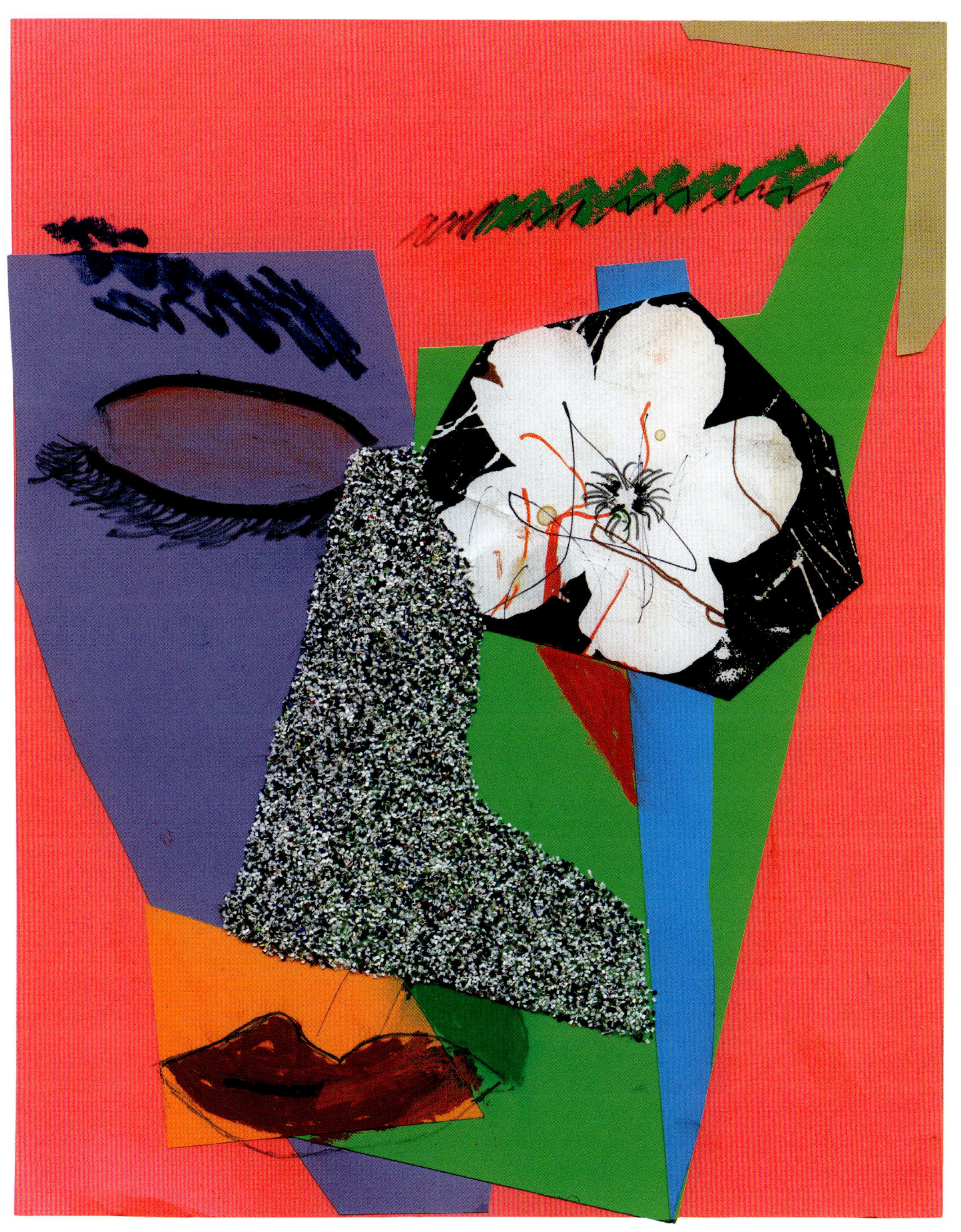

Untitled #10   2014

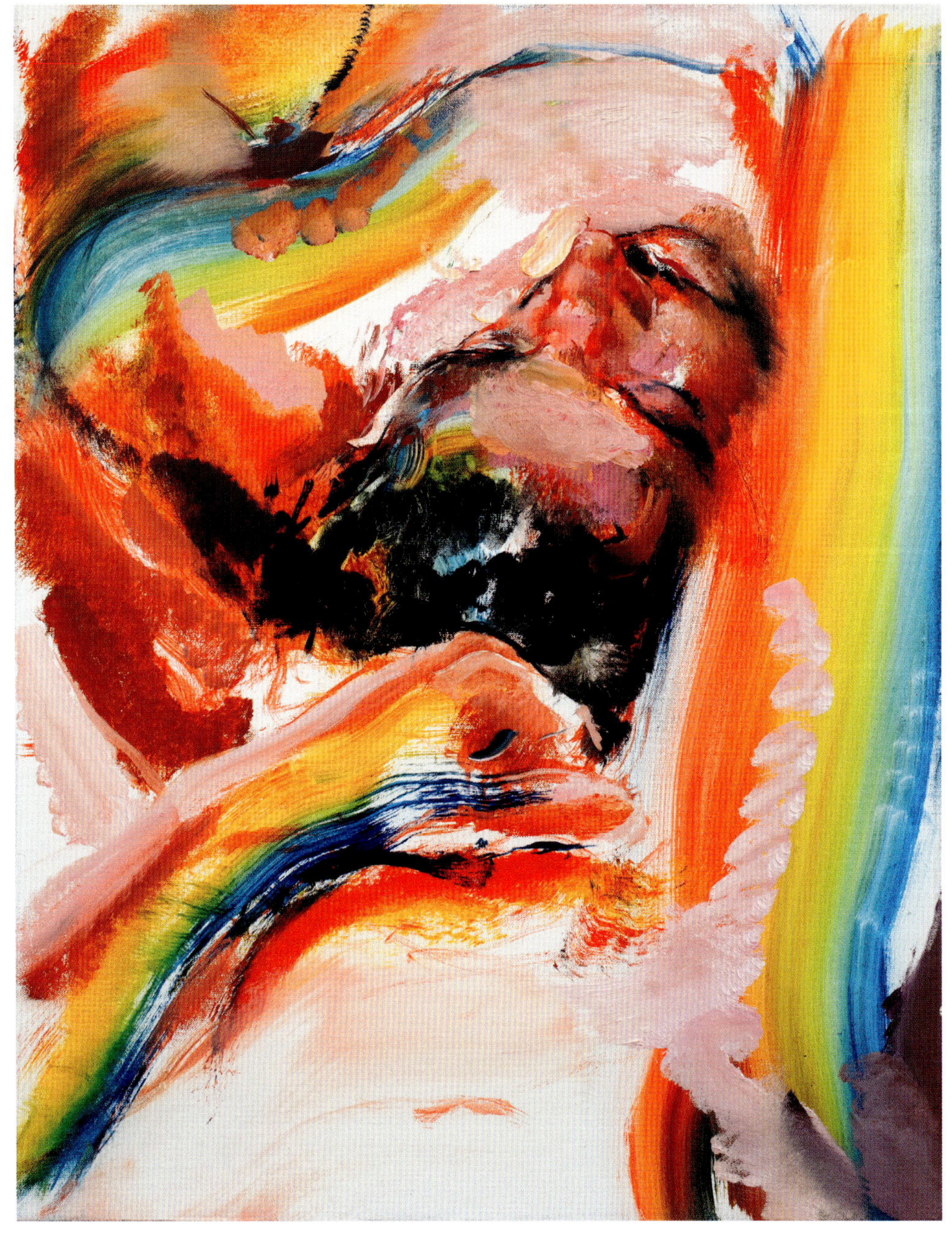

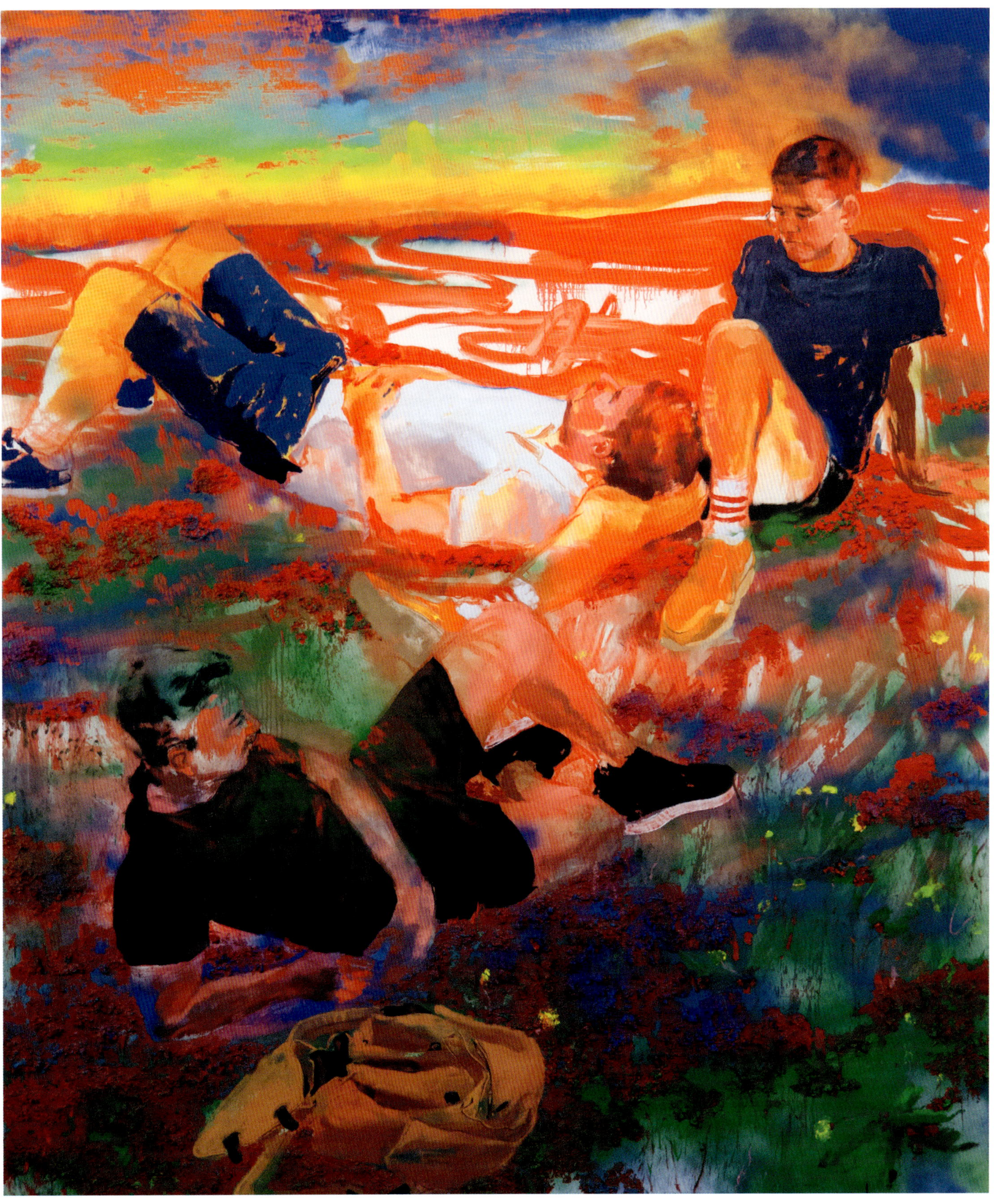

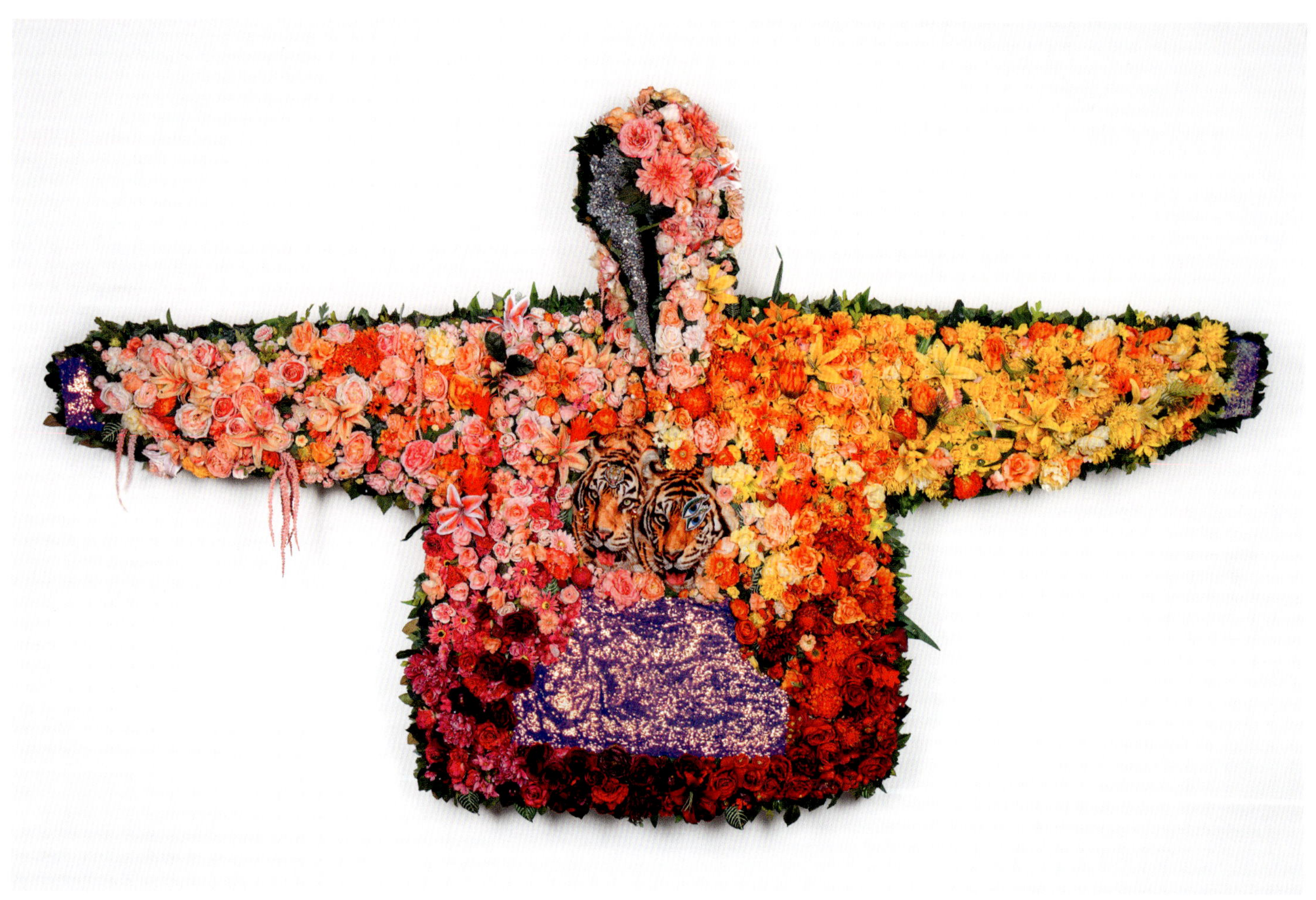

February   2019

Page of Wands   2020

Devan Shimoyama

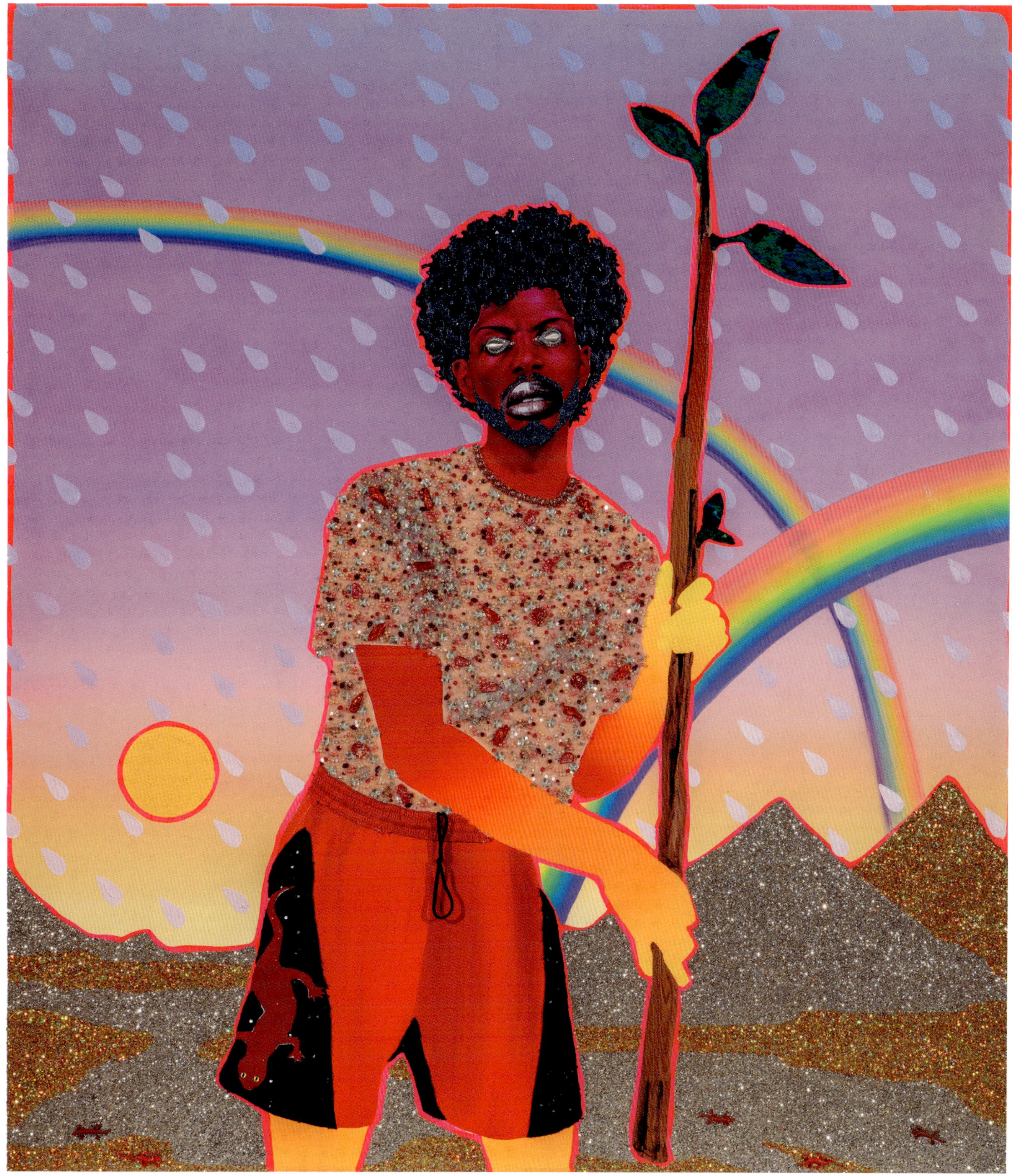

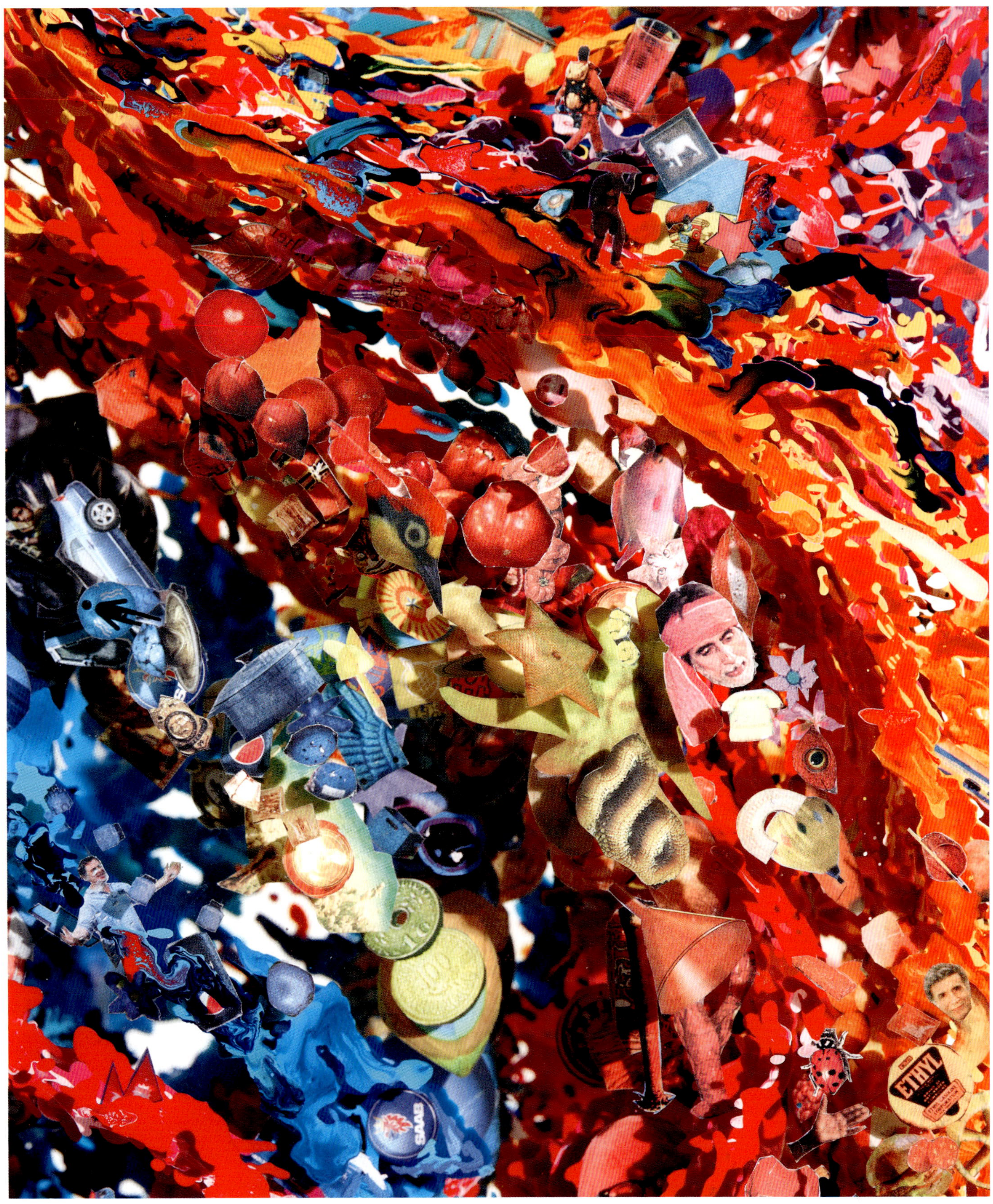

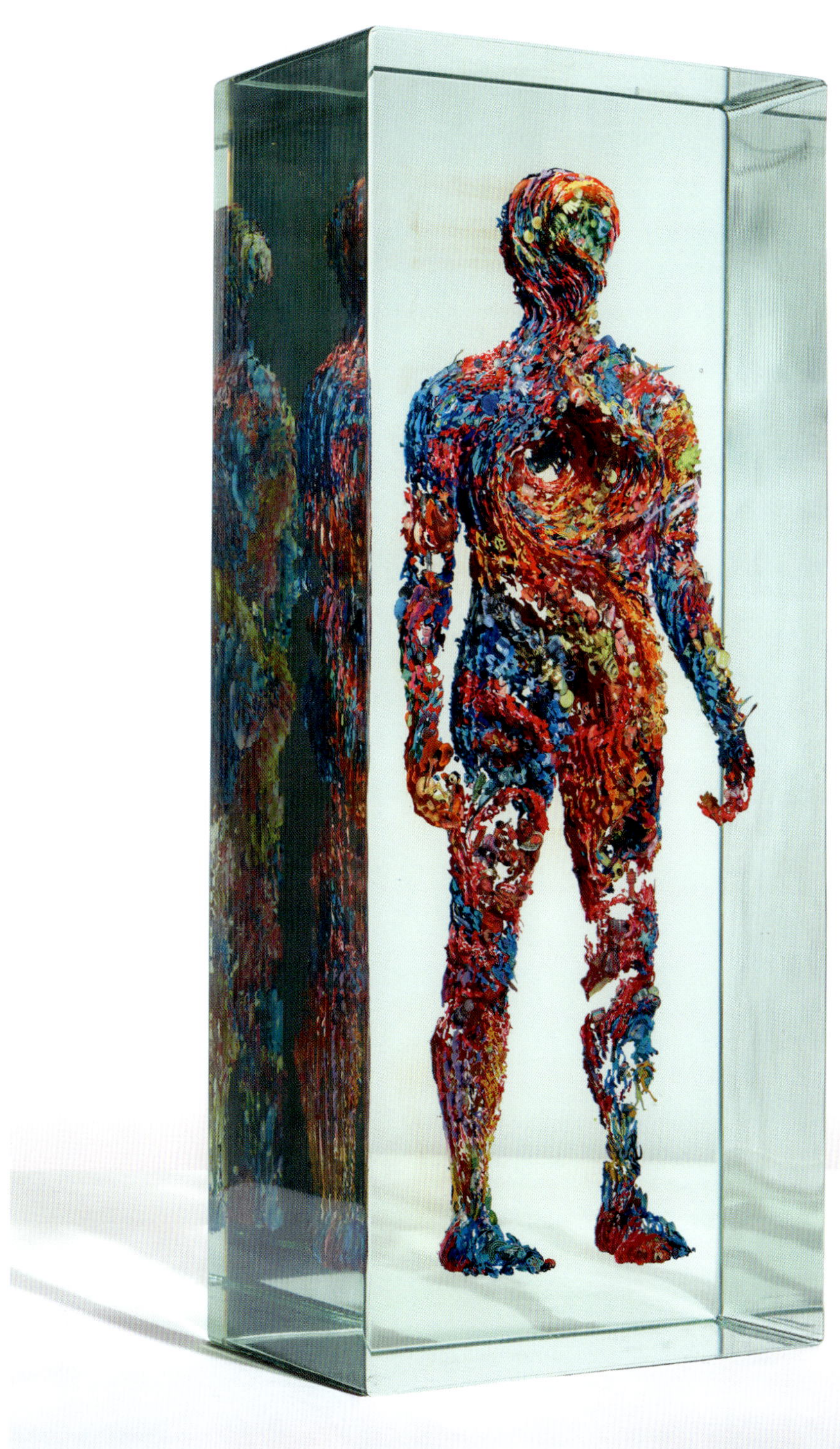

Unweave the Rainbow   2019

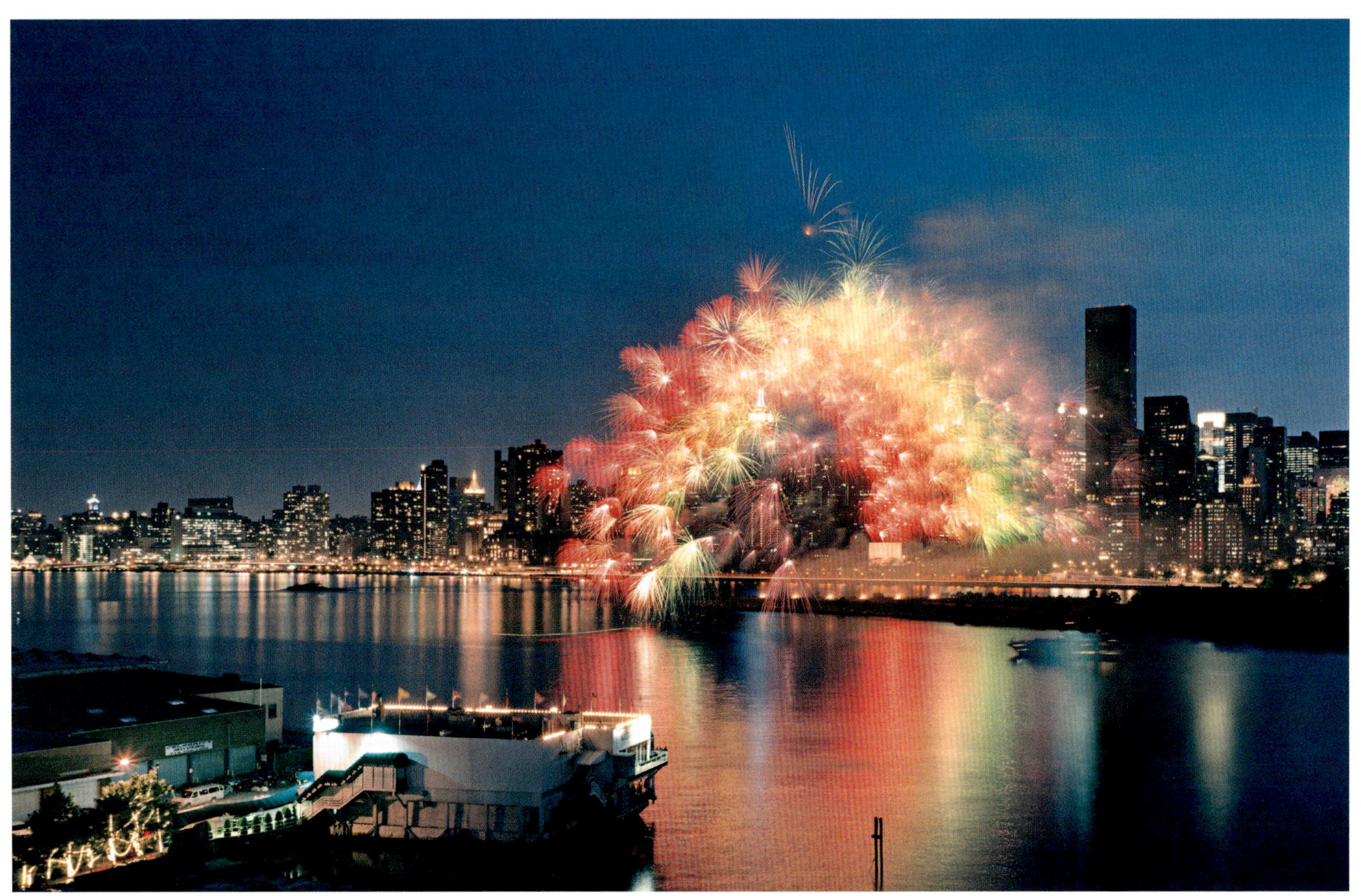

Transient Rainbow 2002

WE ARE: Explosion Event for PST ART 2024

Cai Guo-Qiang

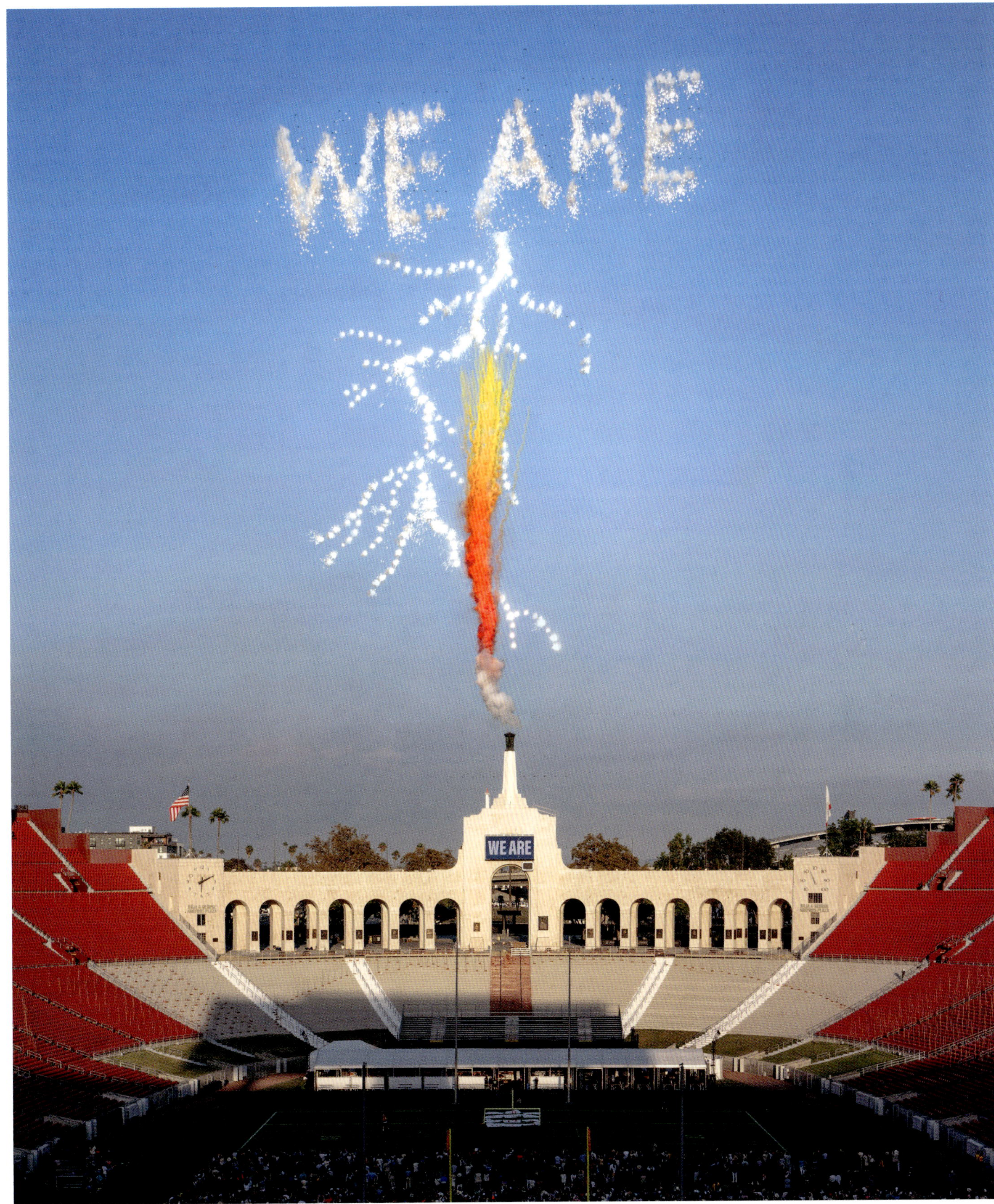

WE ARE
WE ARE

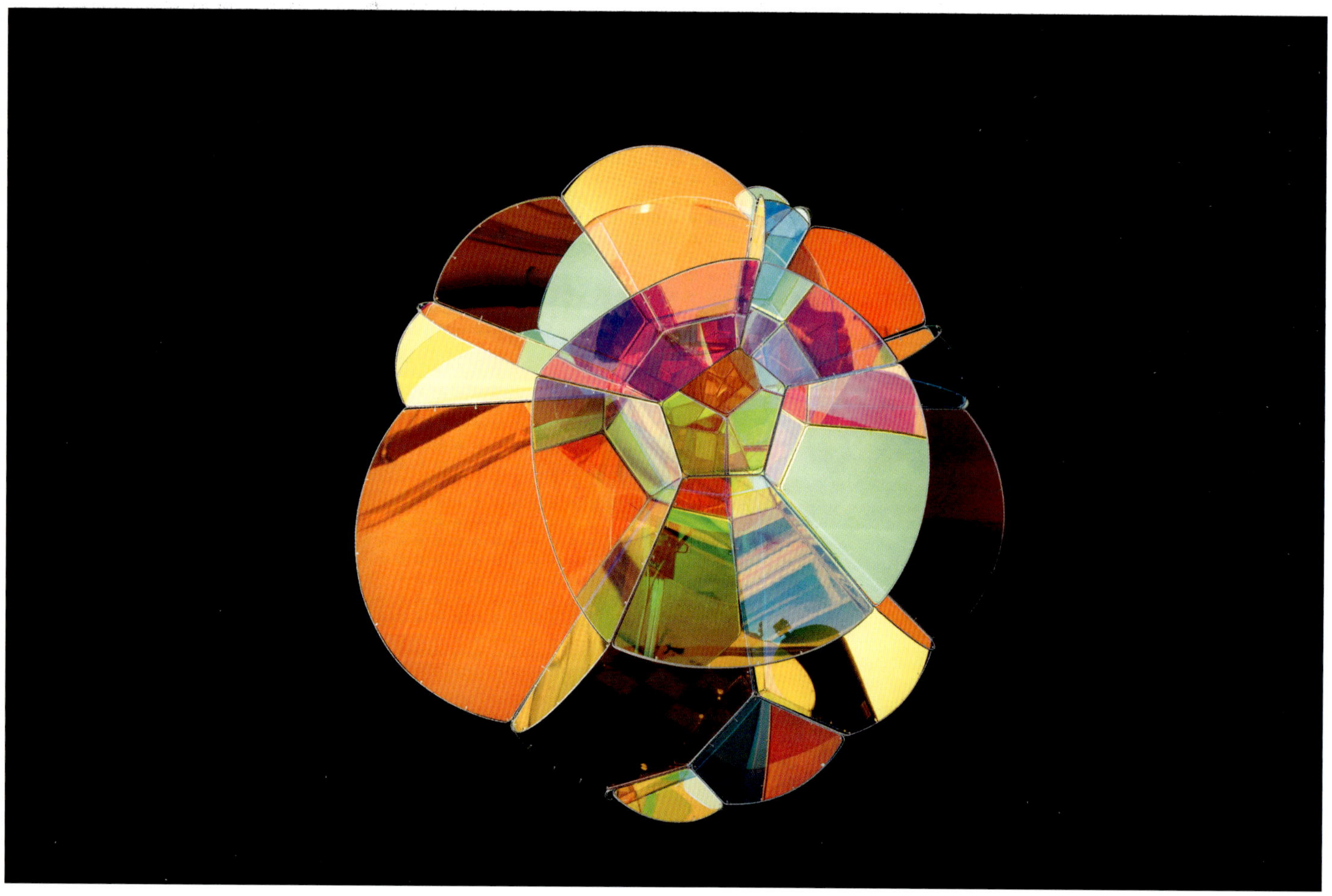

Foam SB 82/45p 2024

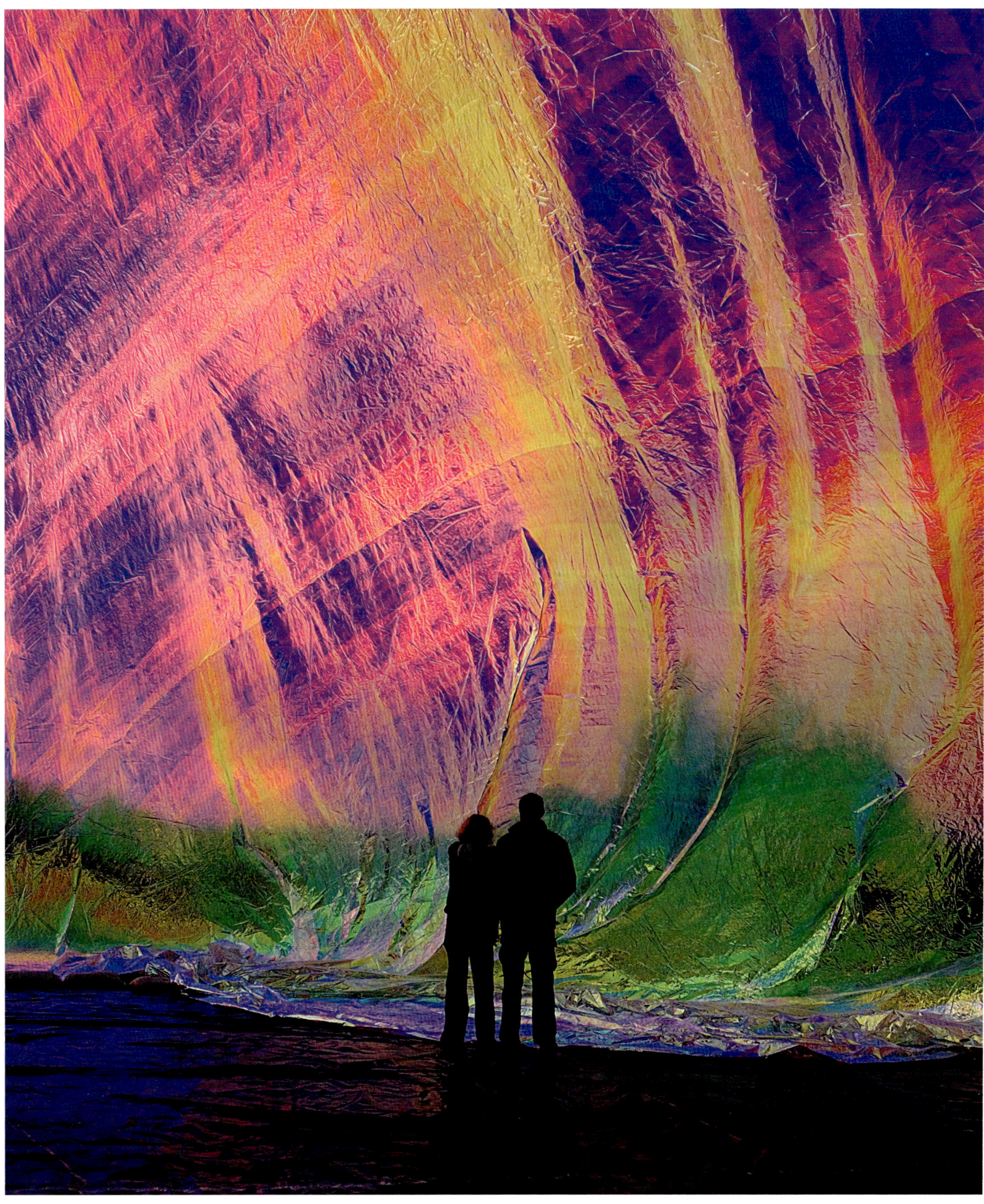

teamLab

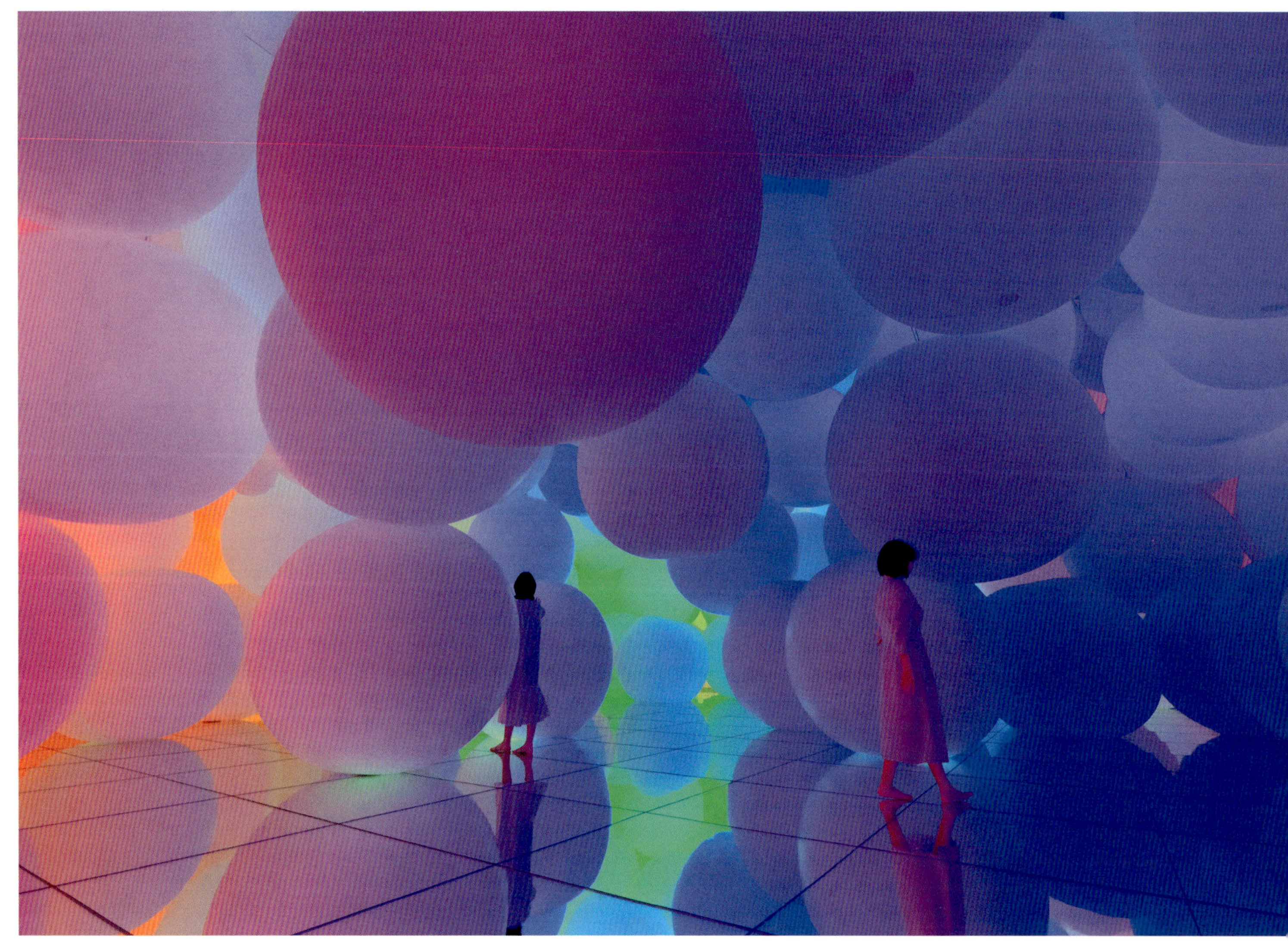

Expanding Three-dimensional Existence in Transforming Space – Flattening 3 Colors and 9 Blurred Colors   2023

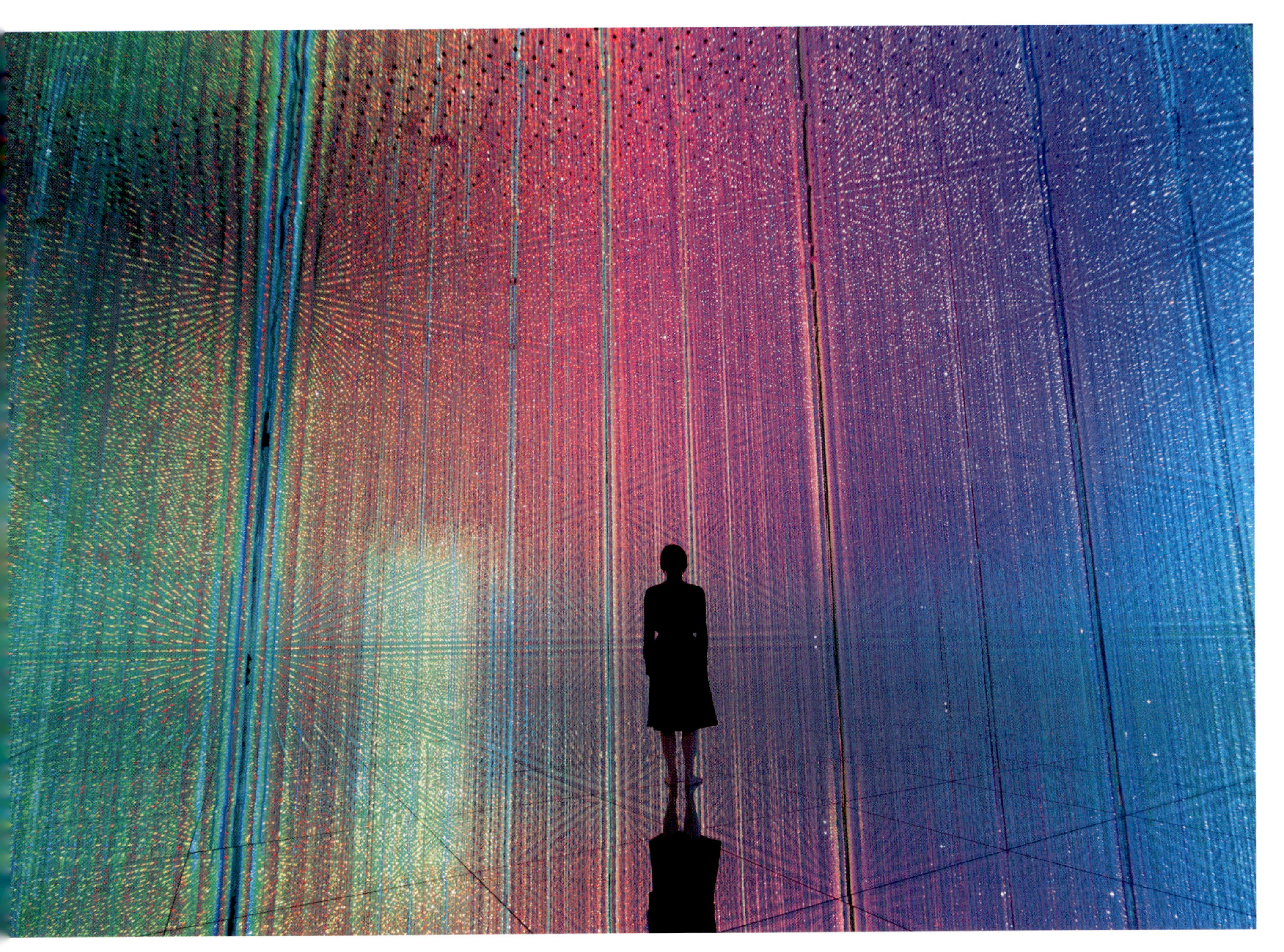

The Infinite Crystal Universe 2018

Janet Echelman

Noli Timere, Sculpture #1 2023

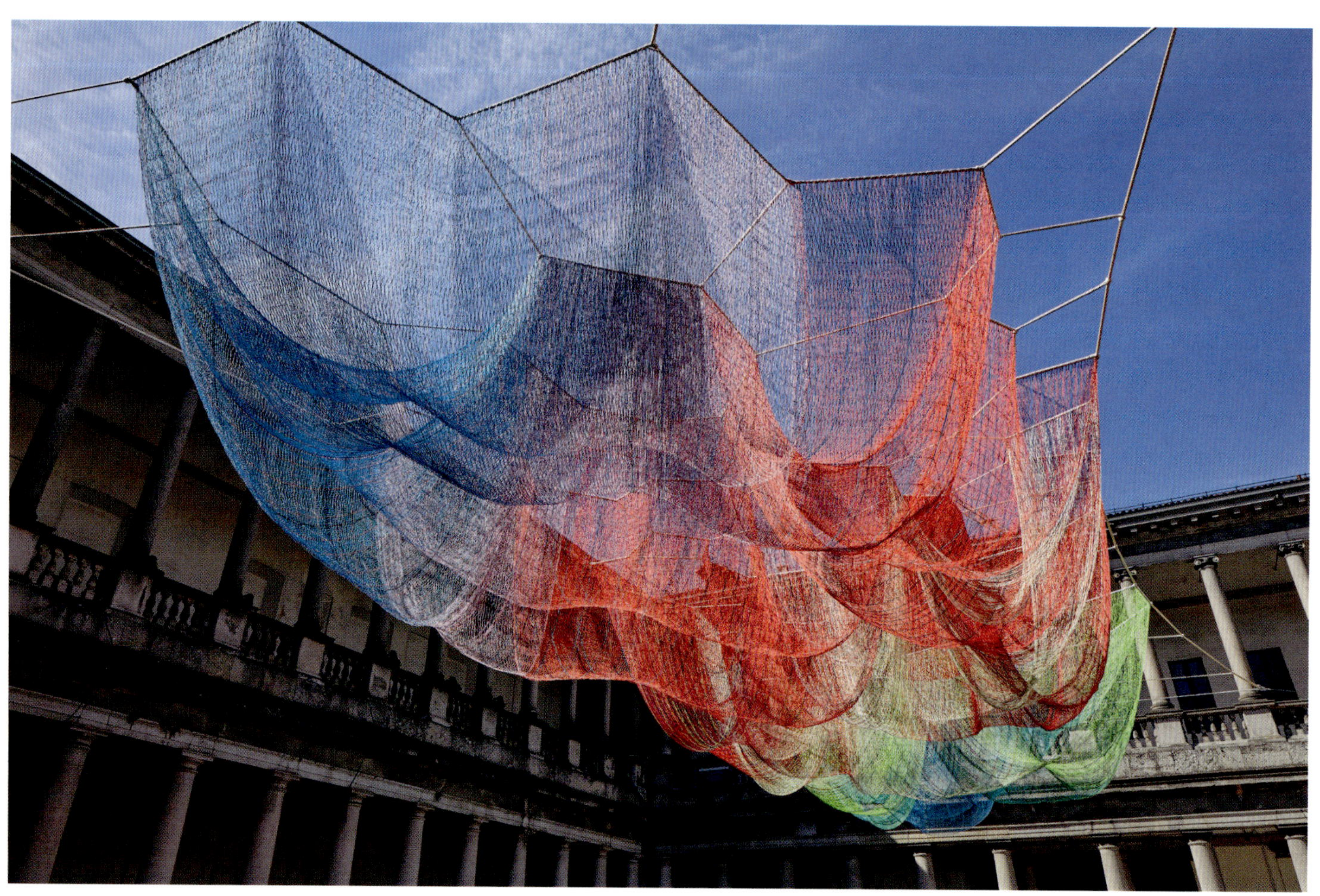

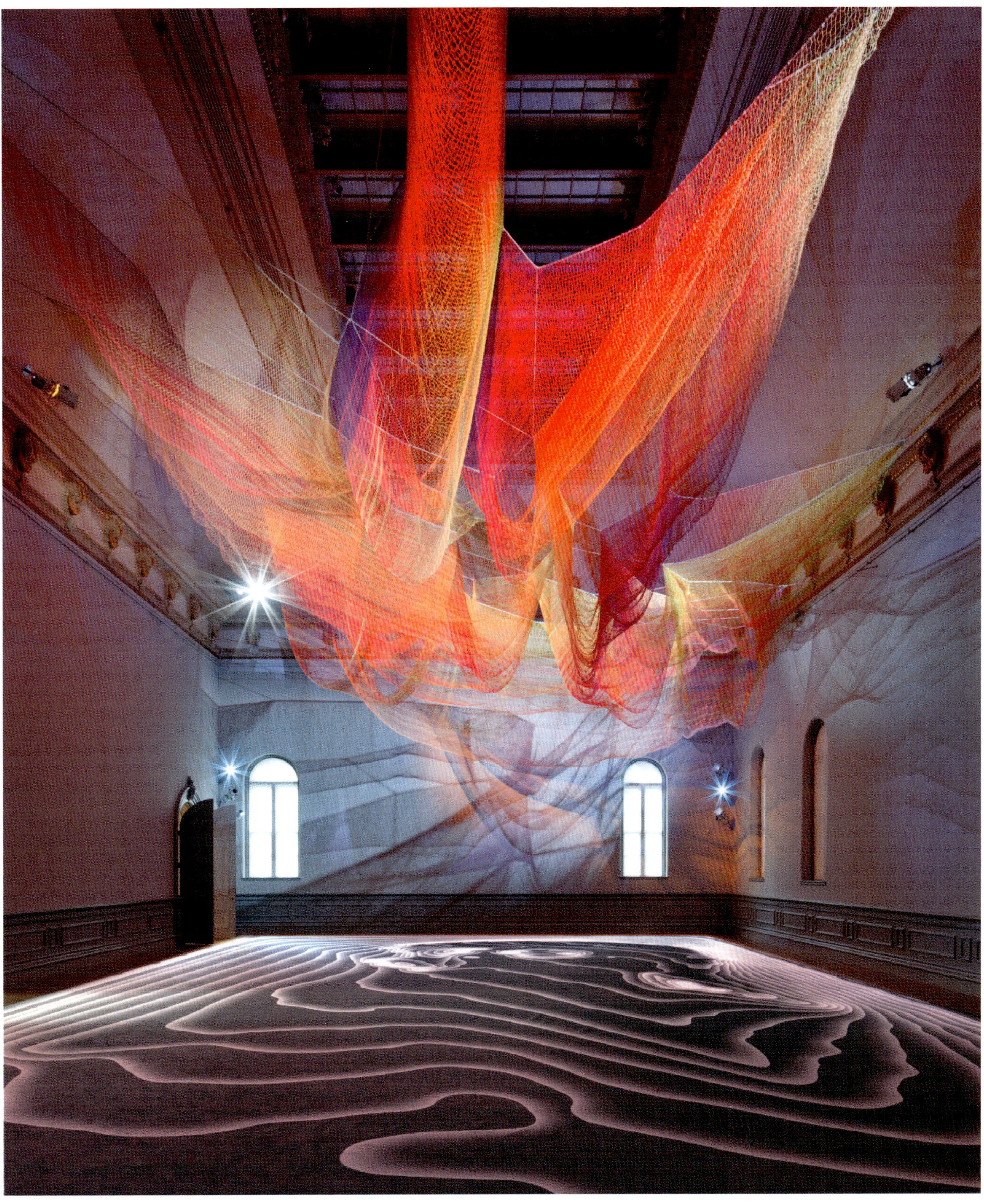

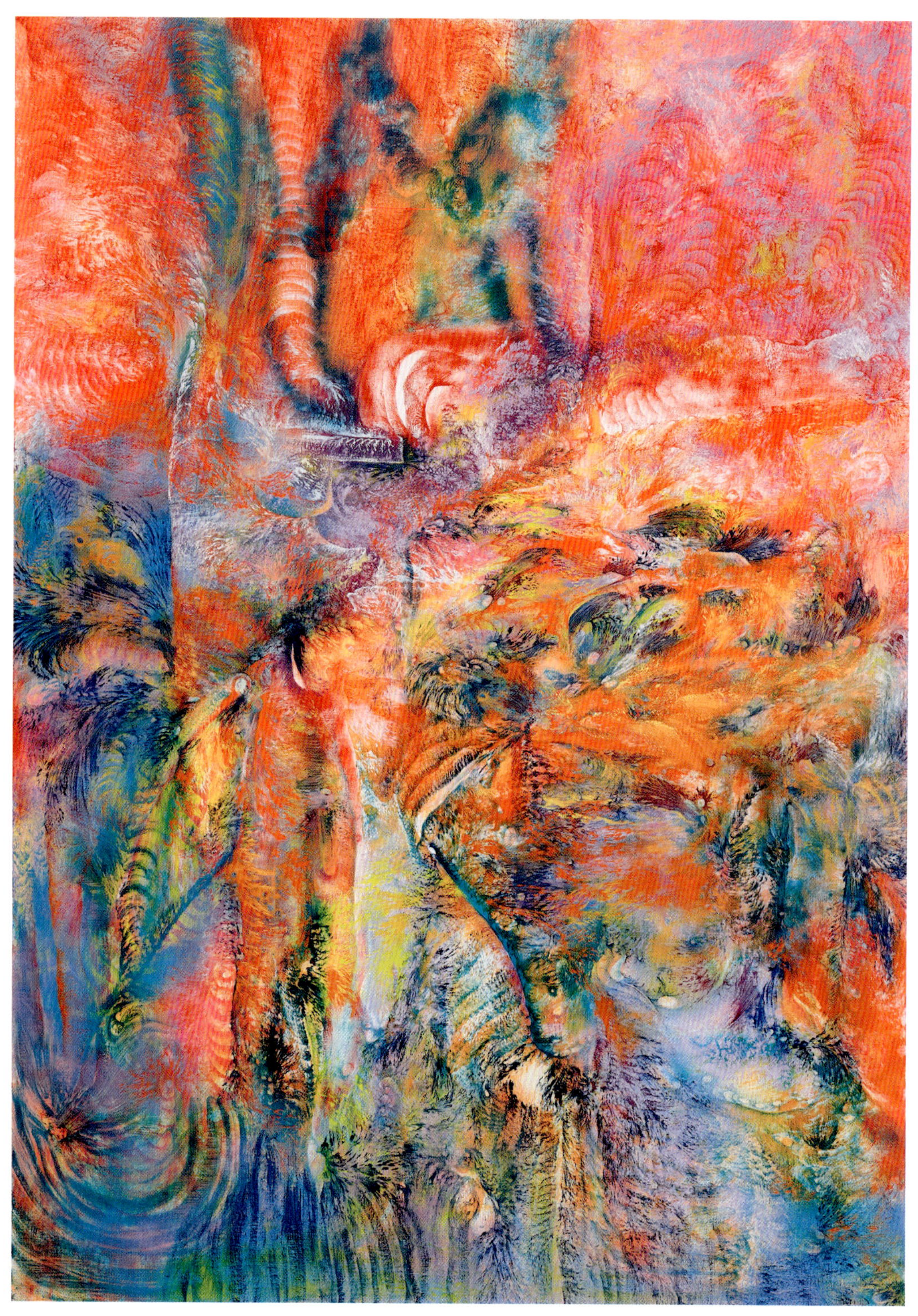

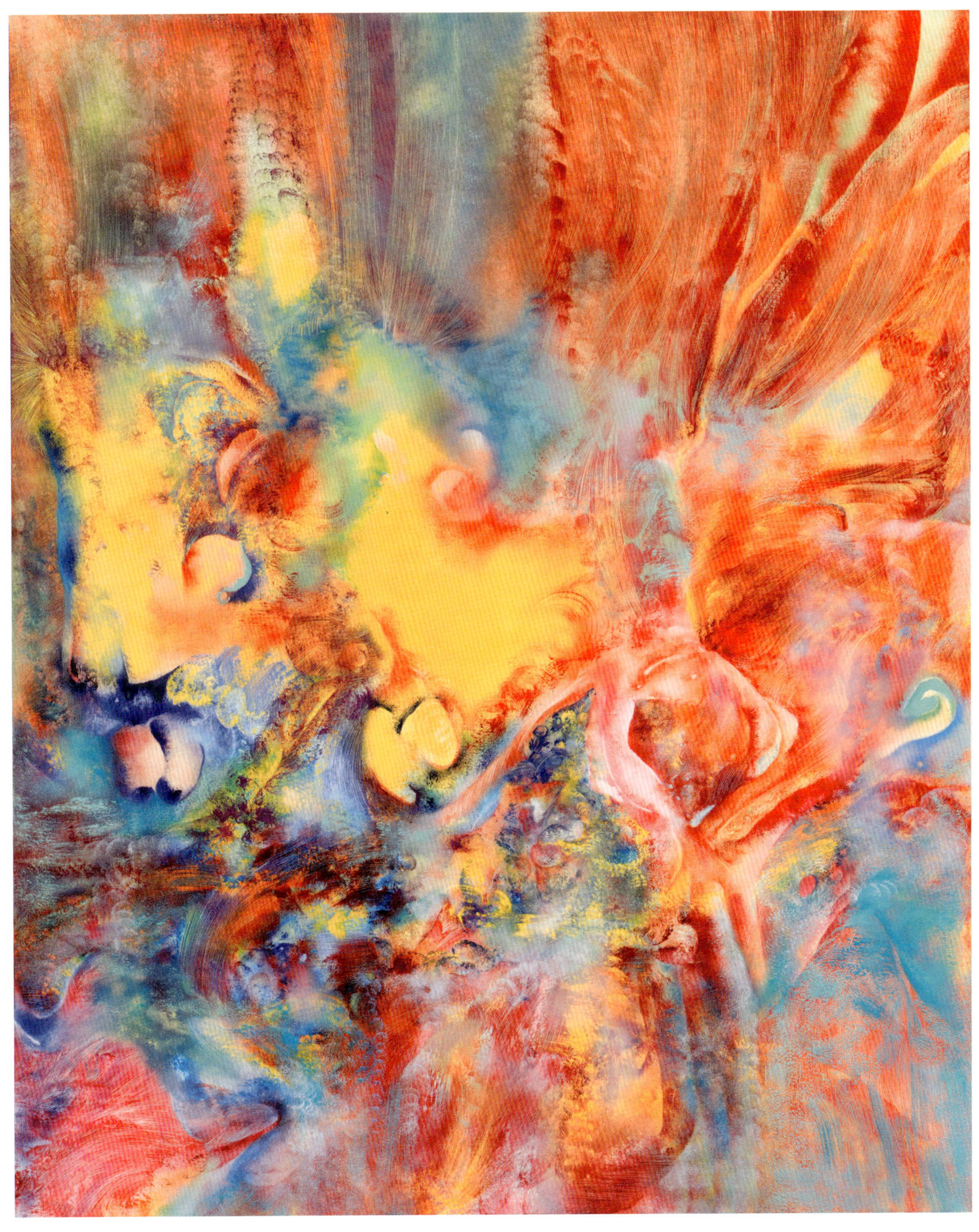

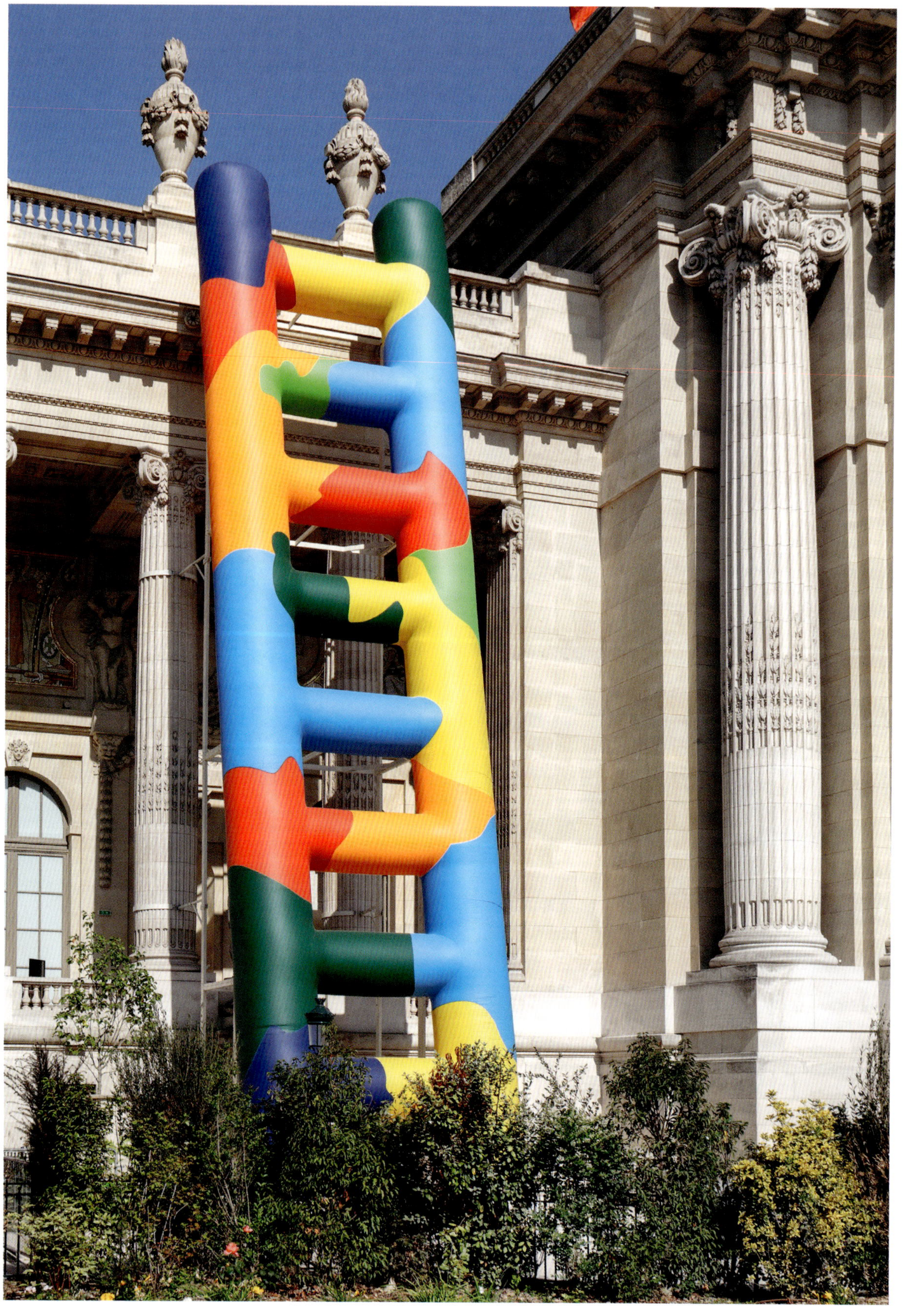

Paola Pivi

Installation view: *We are the baby gang* 2019

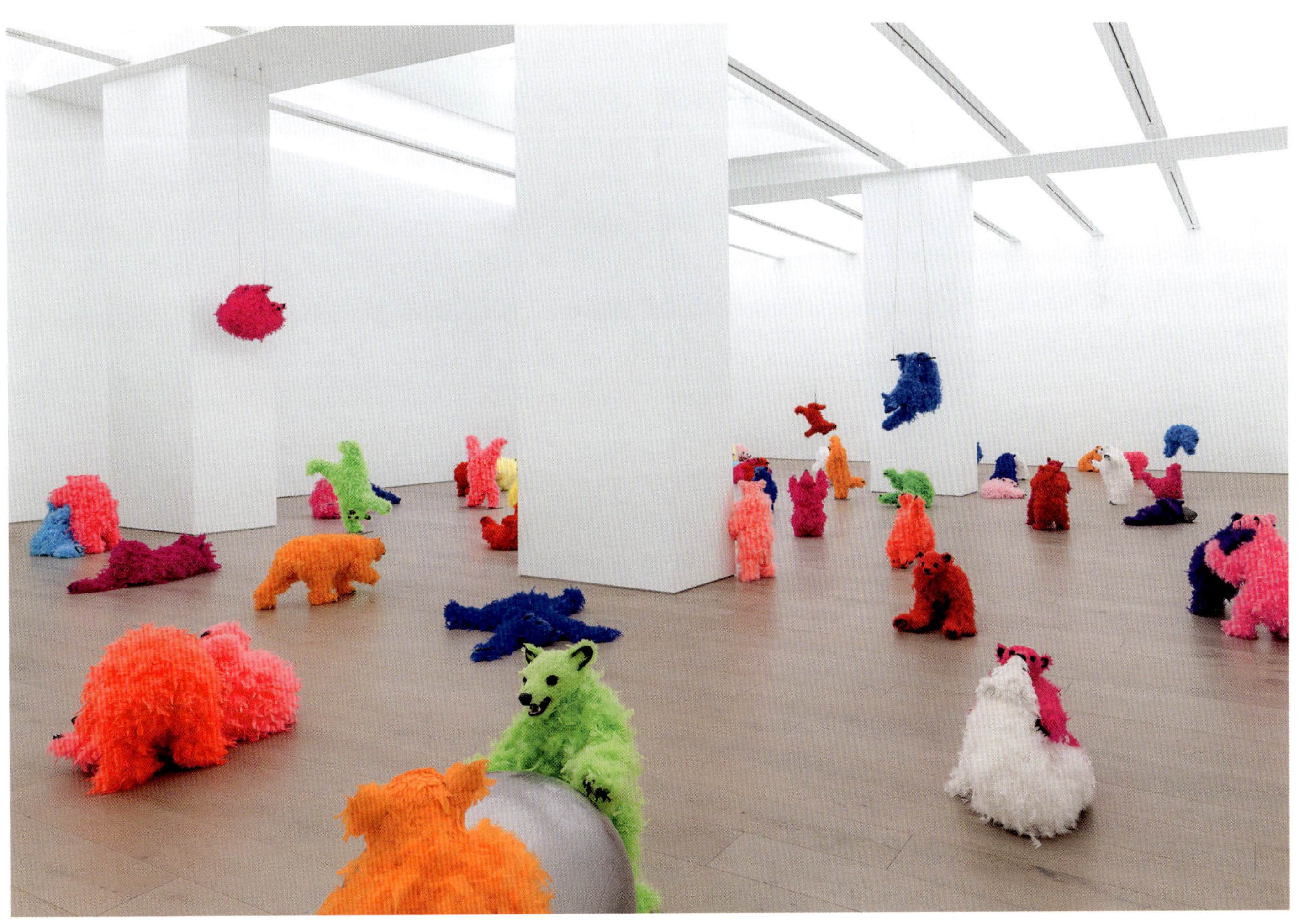

Tony Tasset

Rainbow   2012

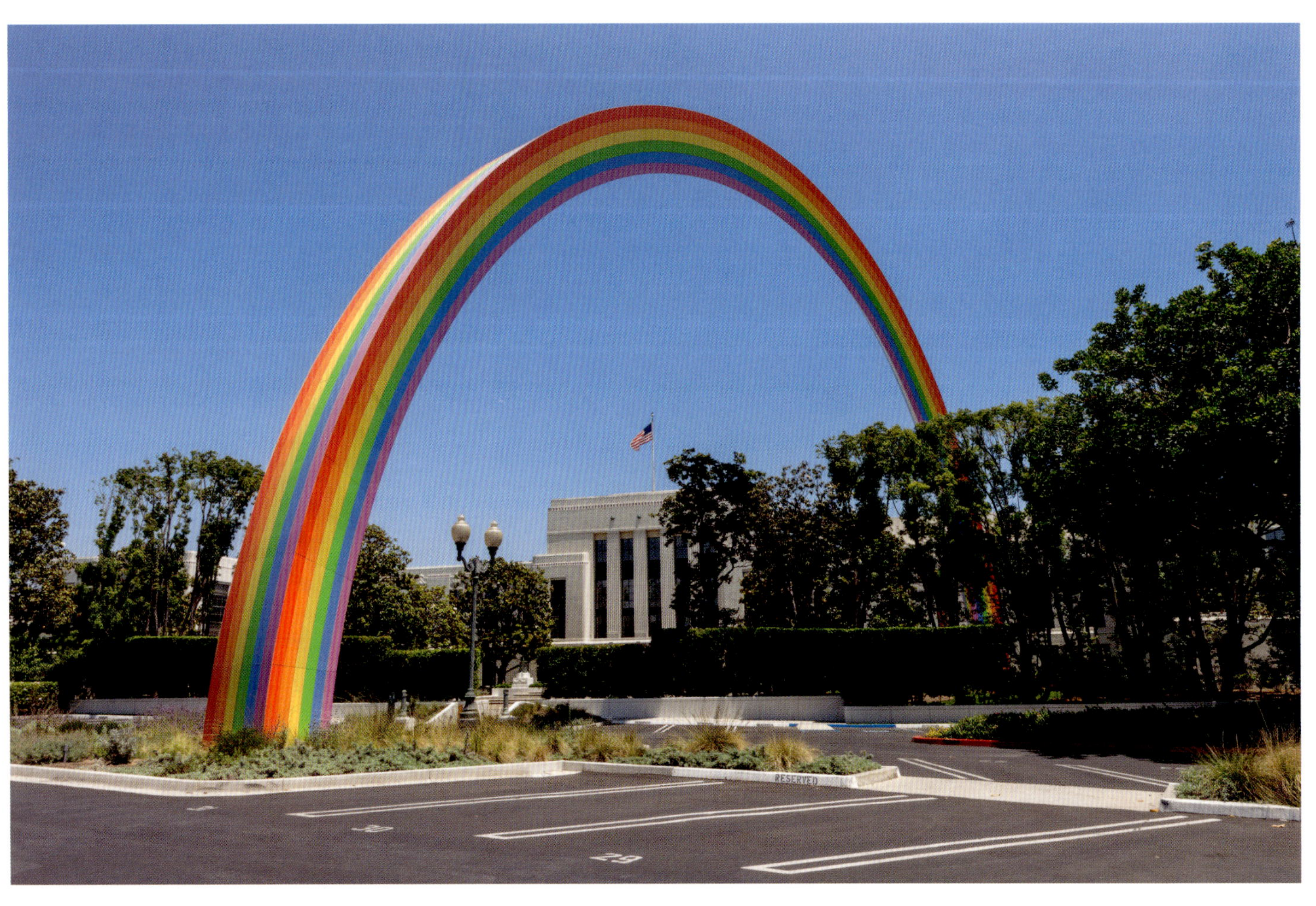

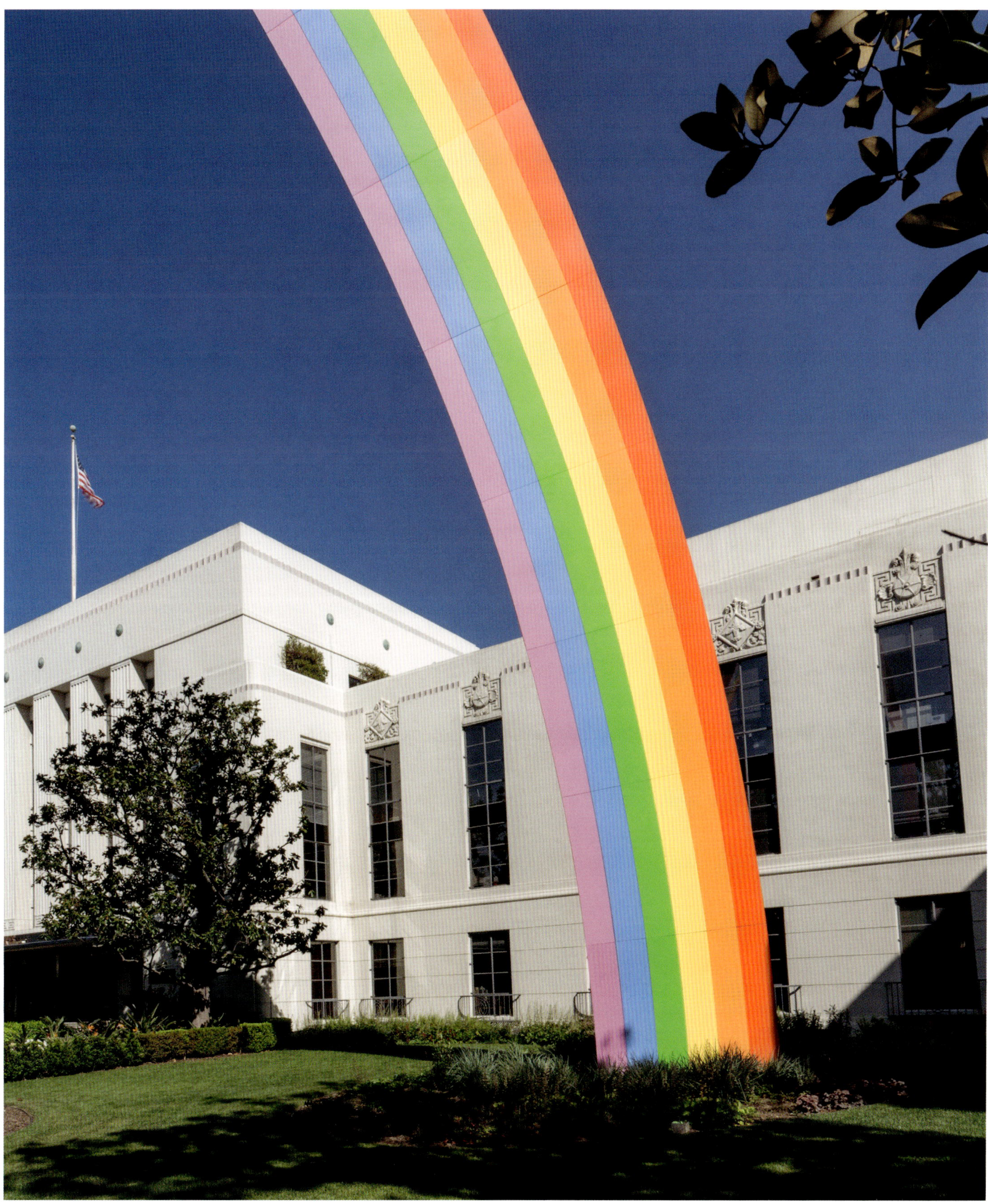

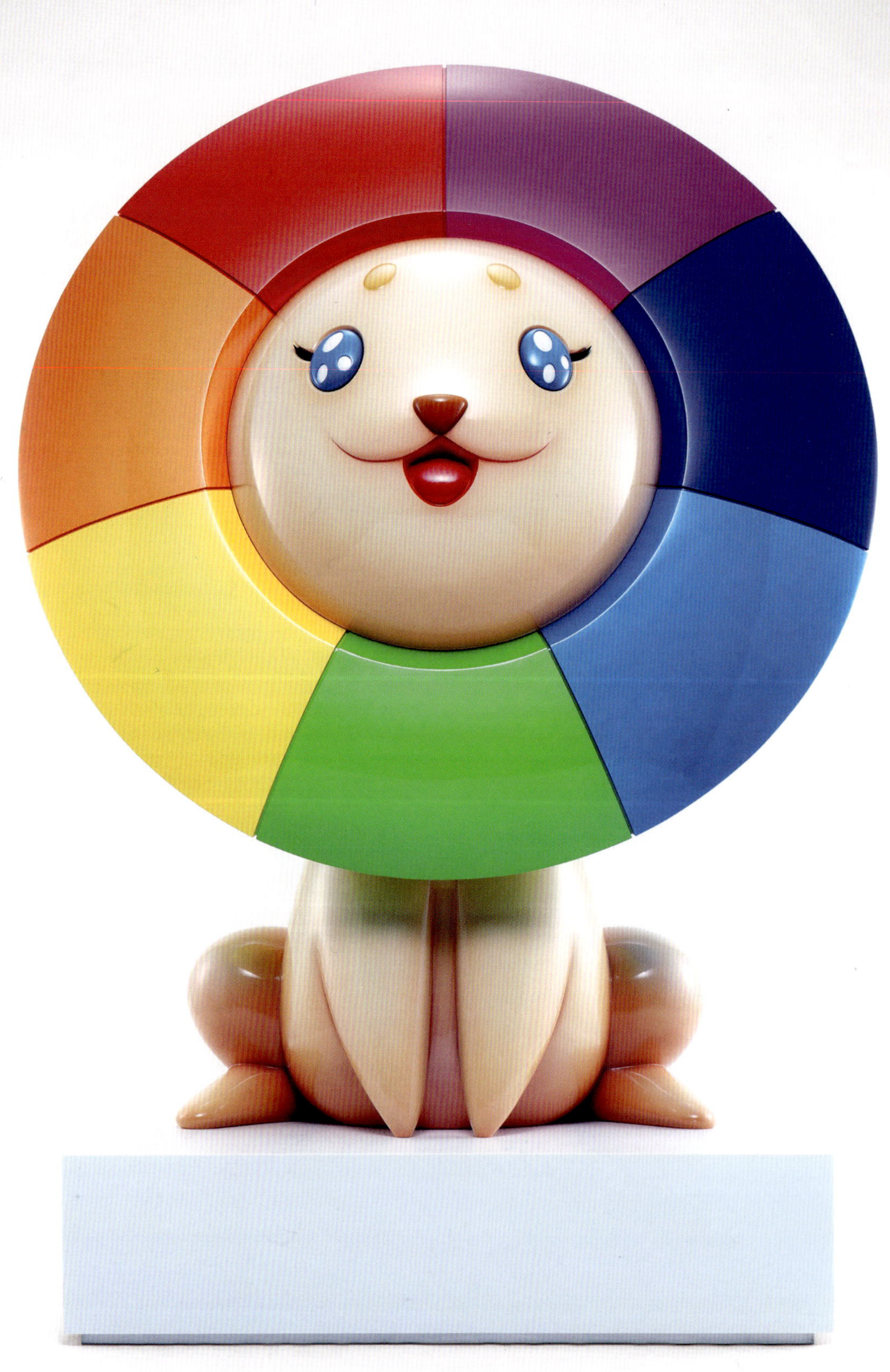

Takashi Murakami

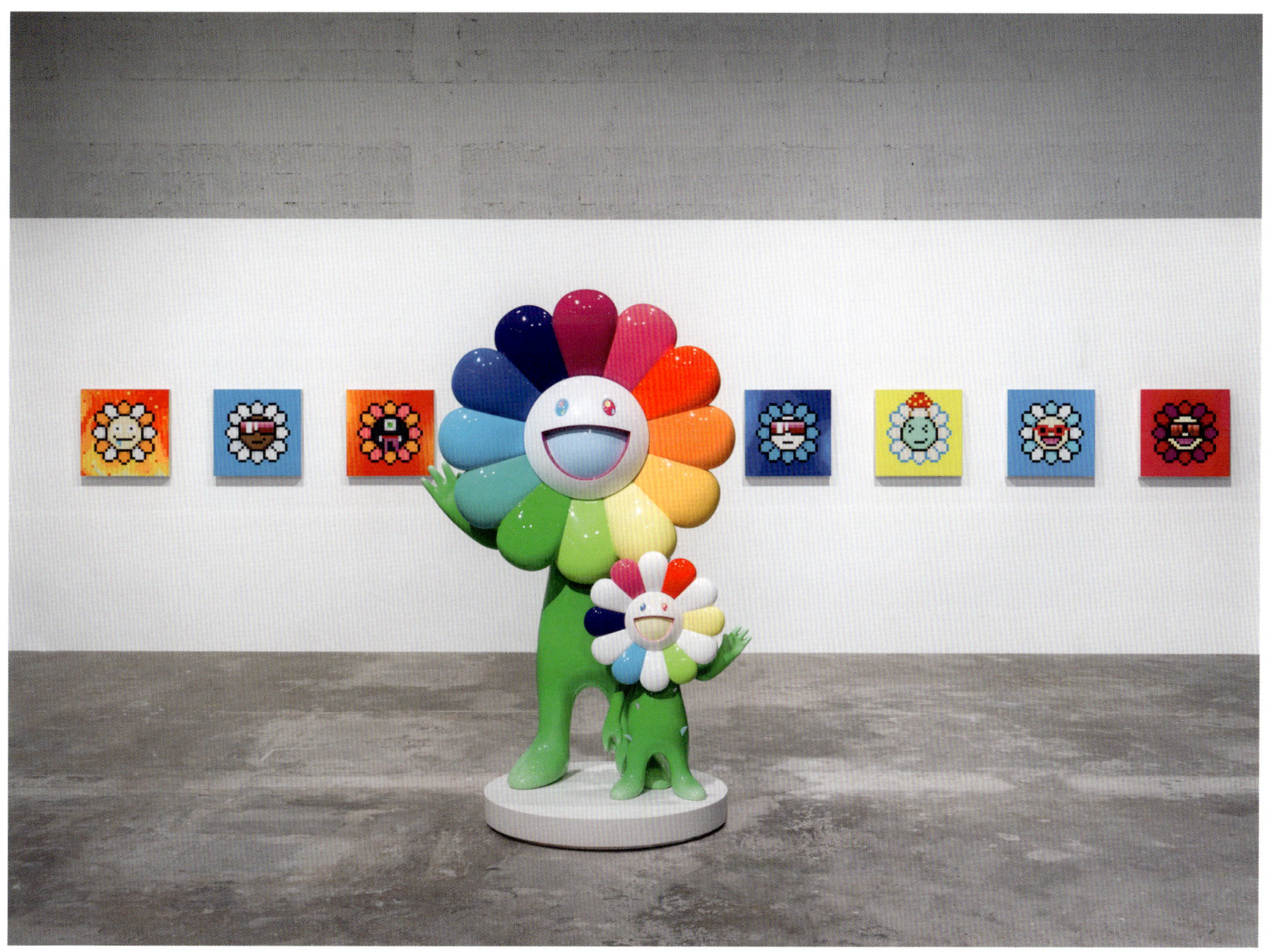

Together with the Flower Parent and Child 2021–22

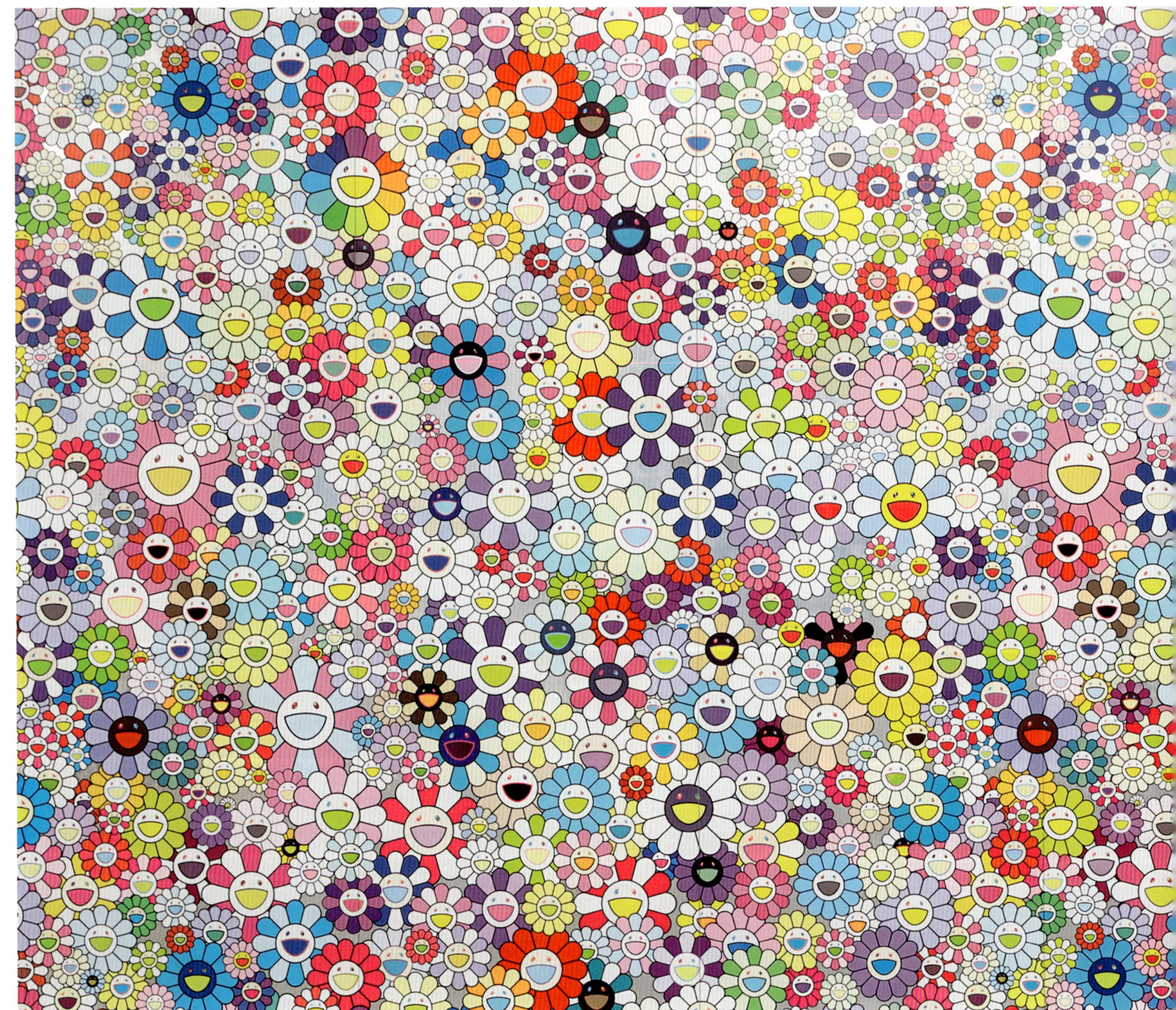

Untitled   2018

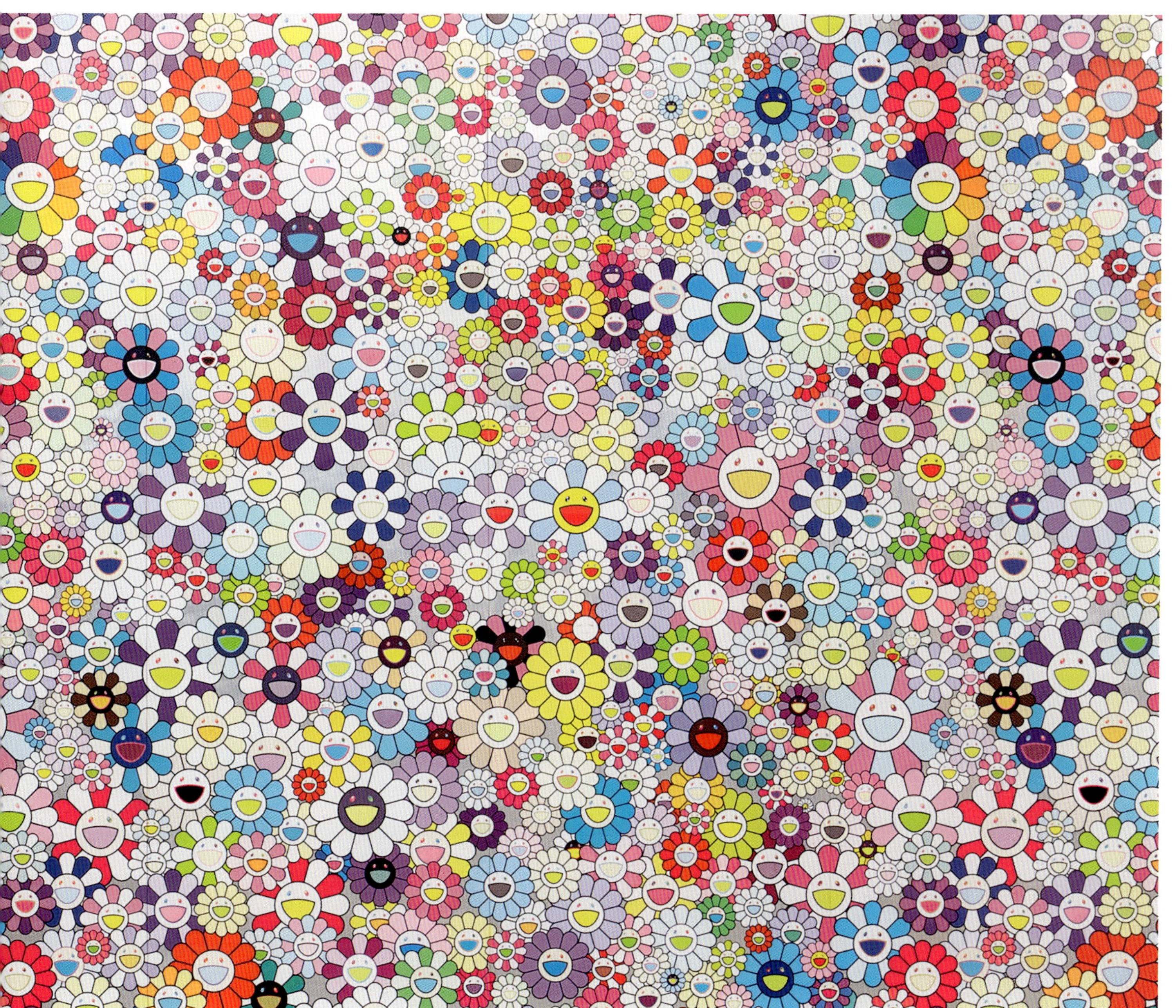

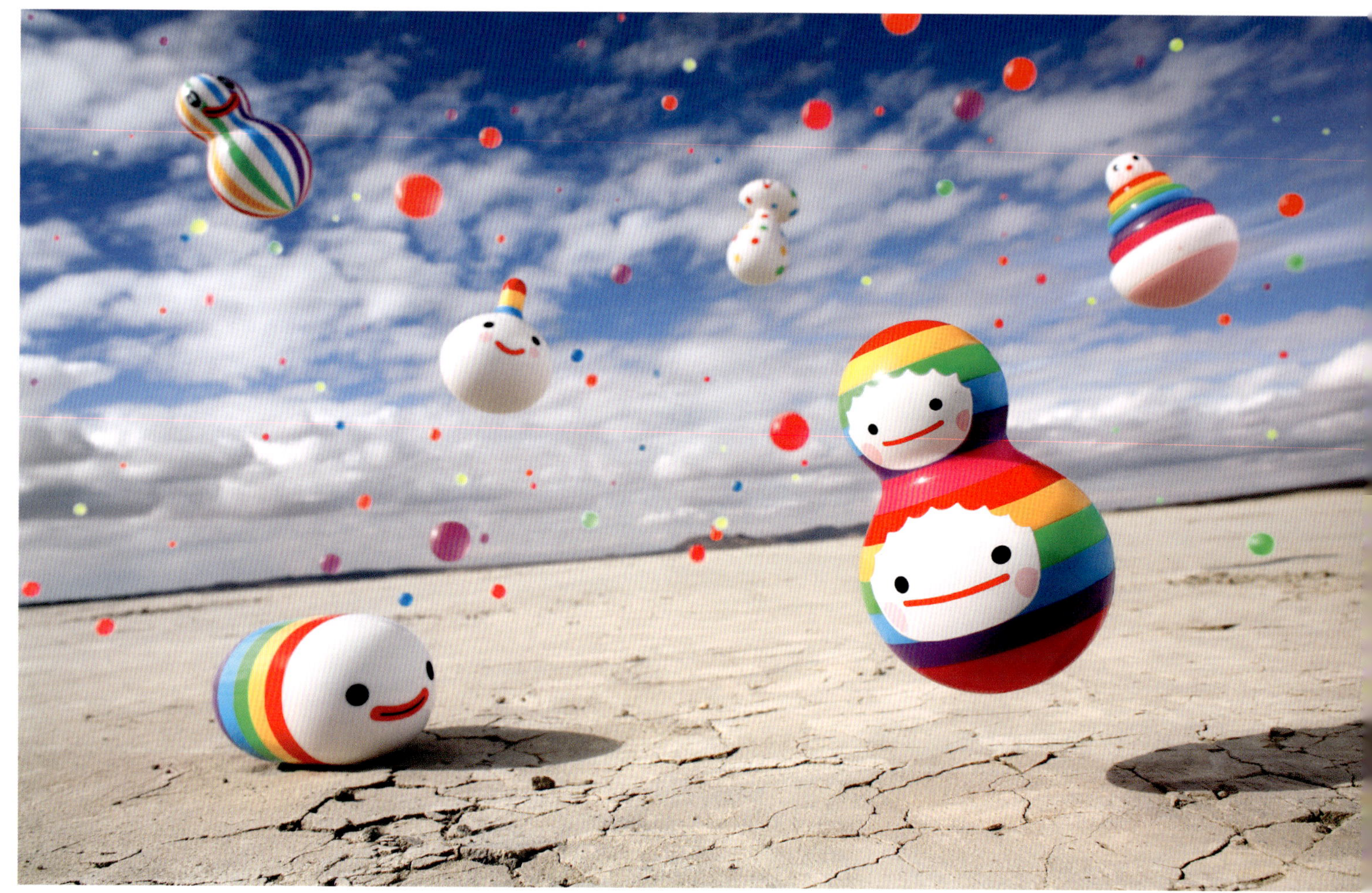

Weeble Wobble, Wish Come True   2006

FriendsWithYou

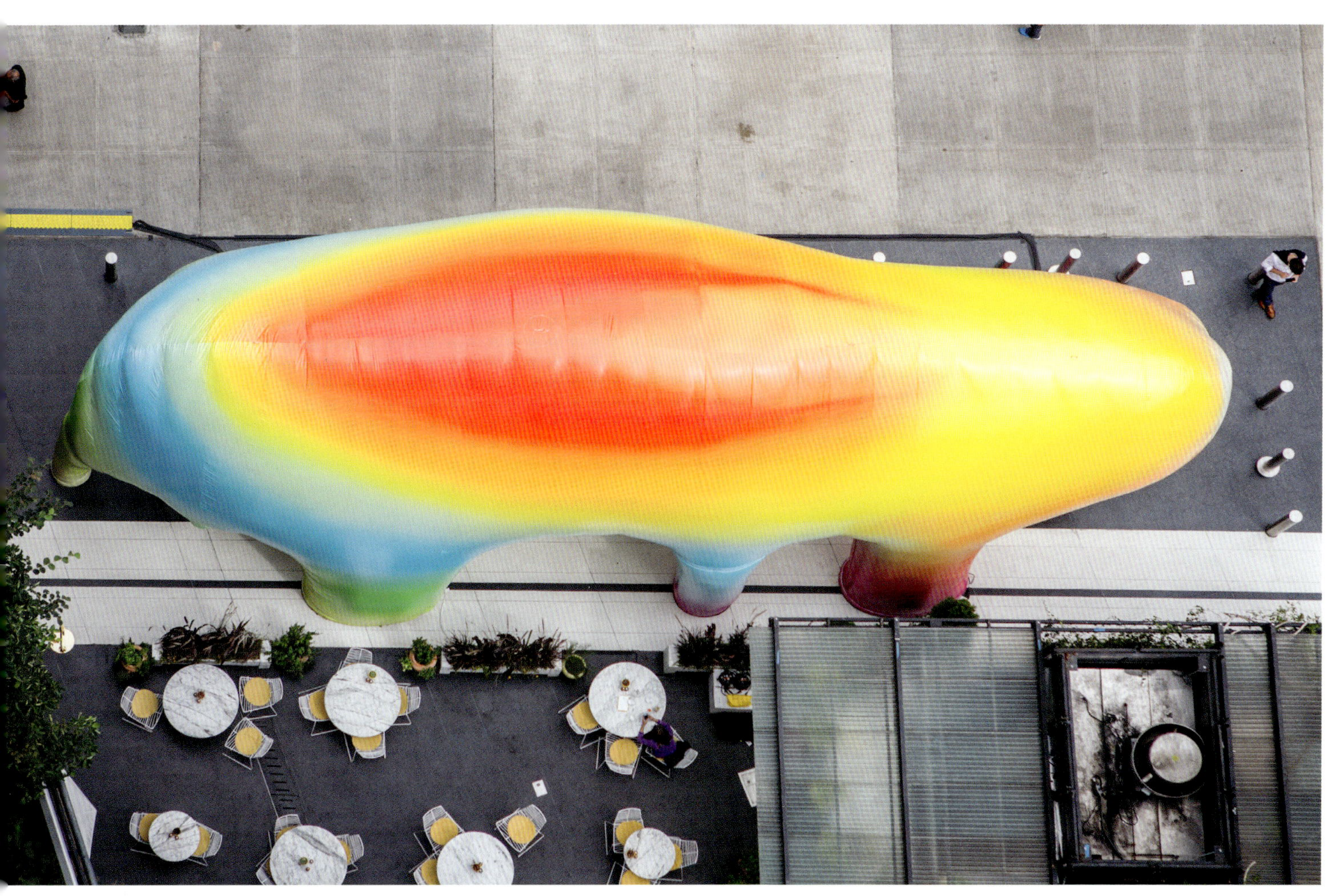

Light Cave 2014

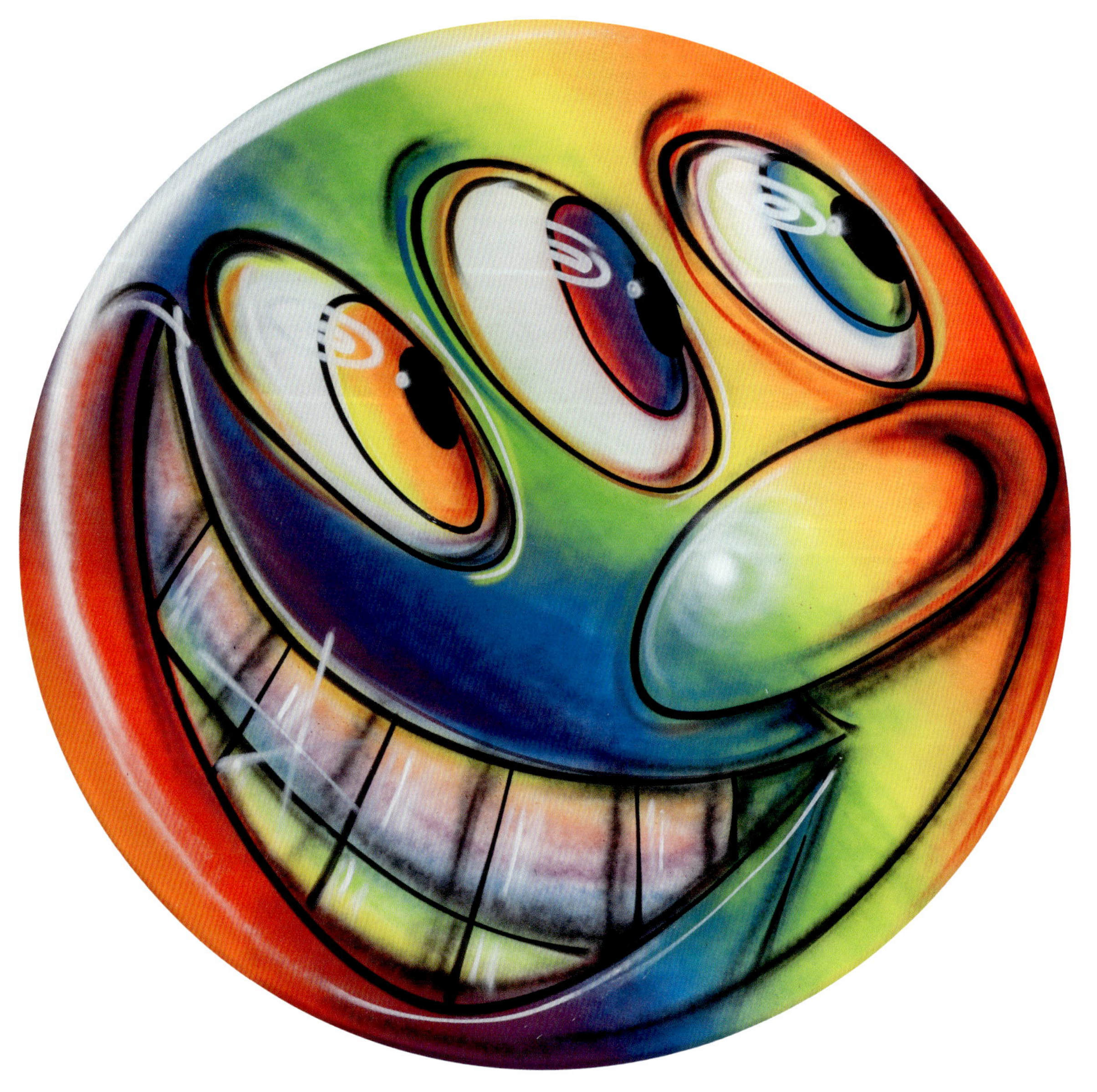

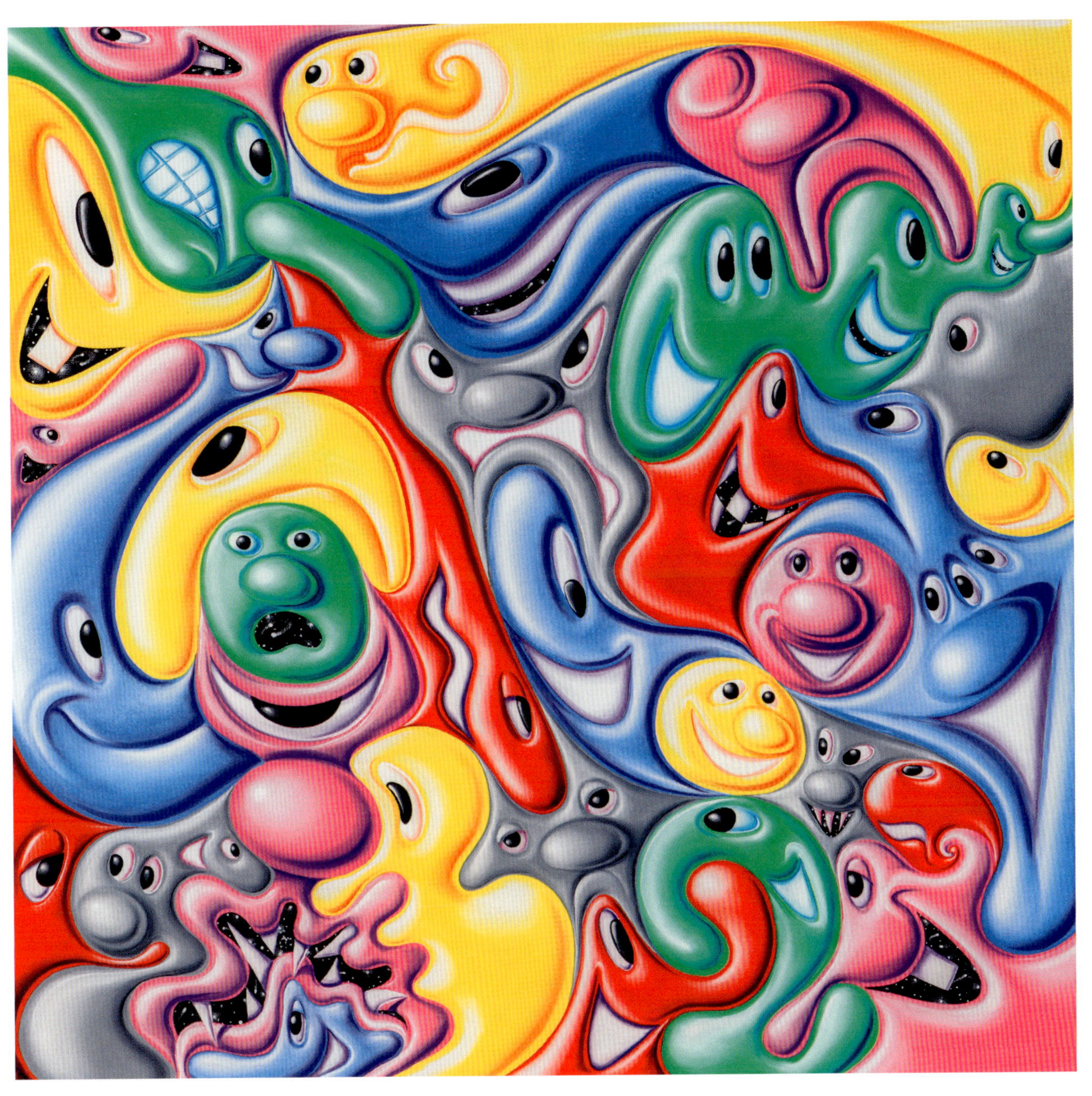

FACES IN PLACES 2016

Nina Chanel Abney

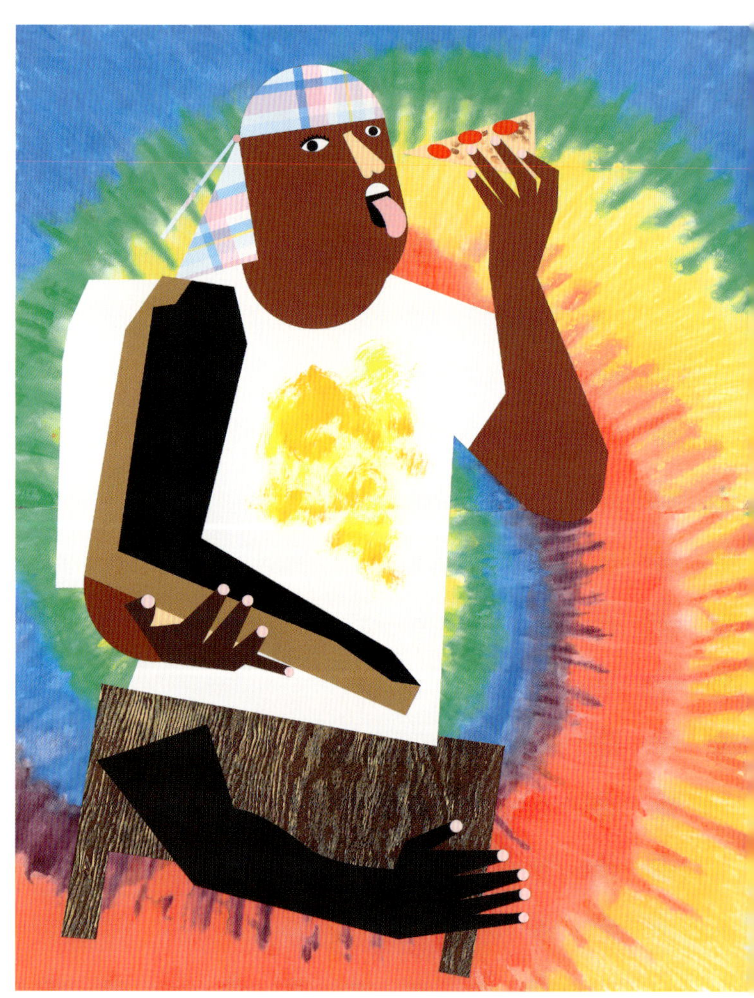

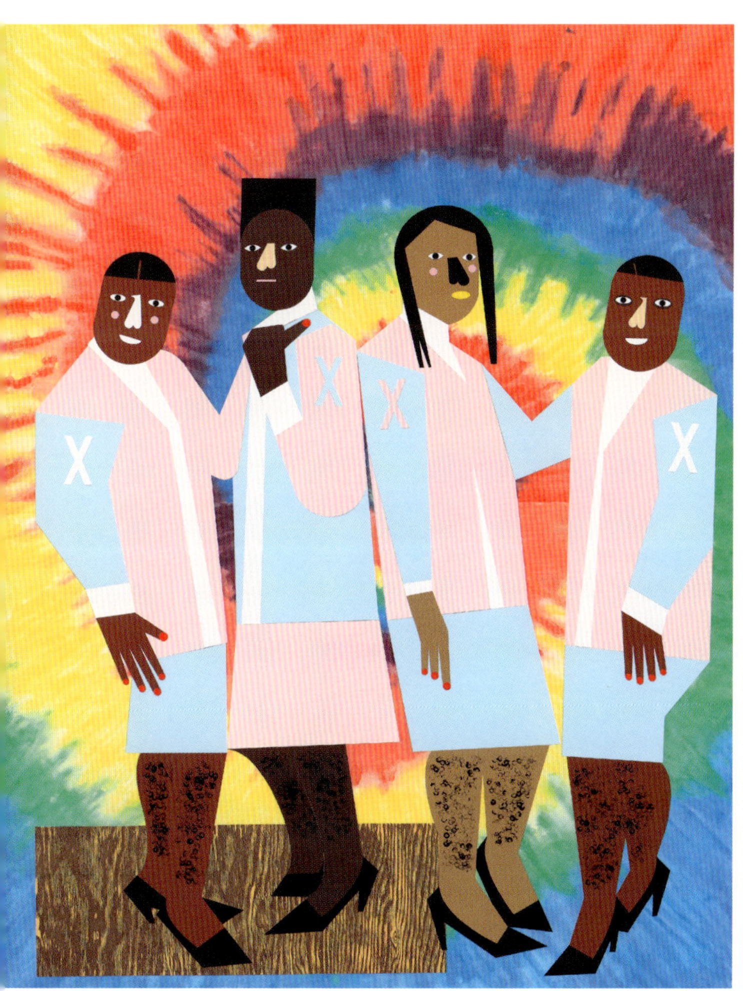
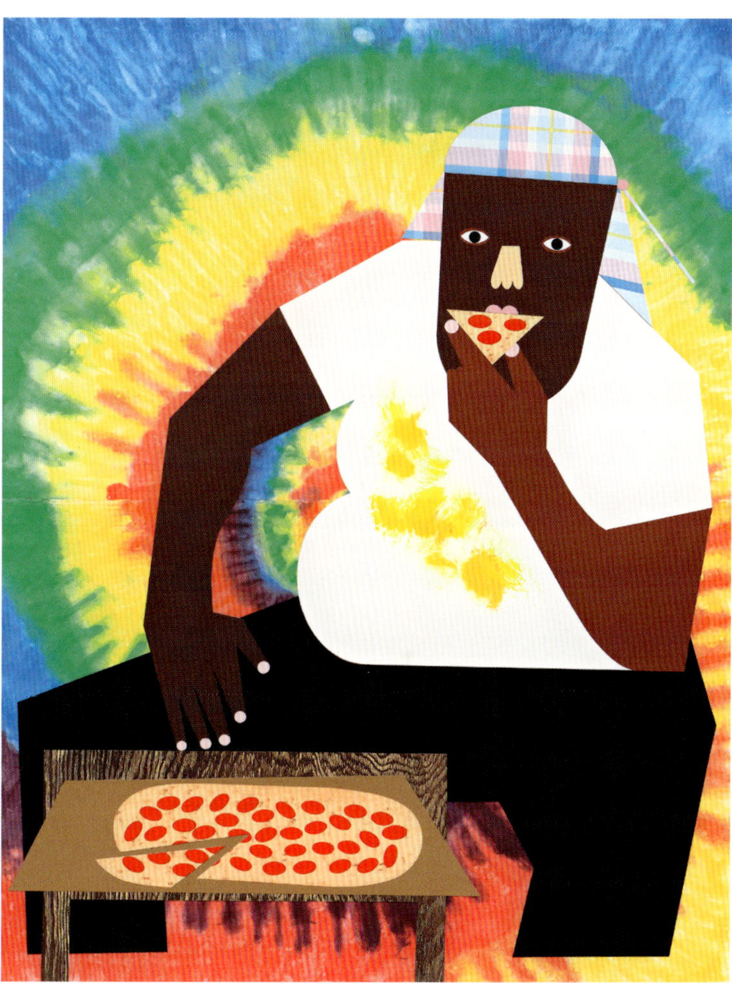

What I Wanted vs. What I Got 2022

Olaf Nicolai

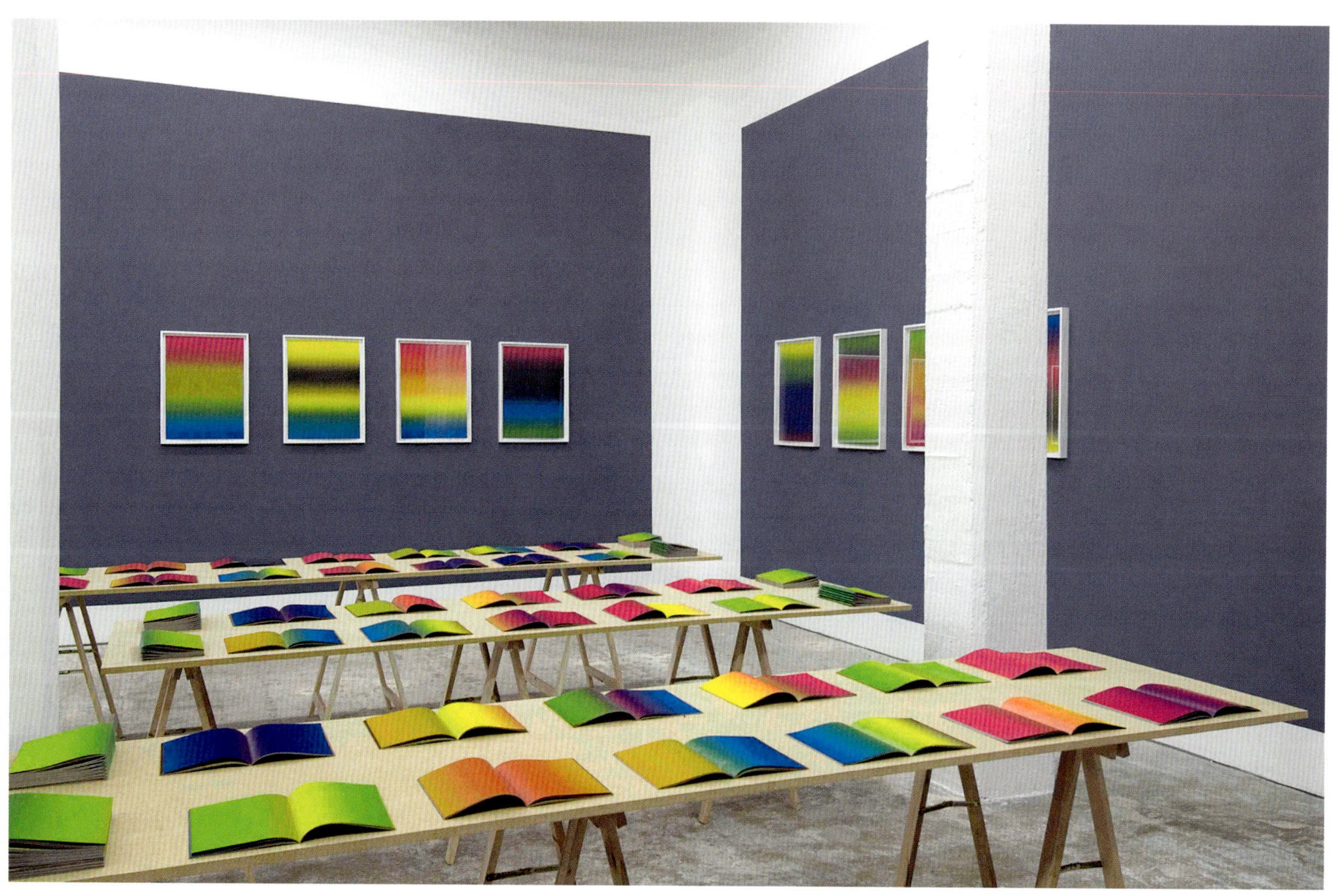

Considering a multiplicity of appearances in light of a particular aspect of relevance. Or: Can art be concrete? 2008

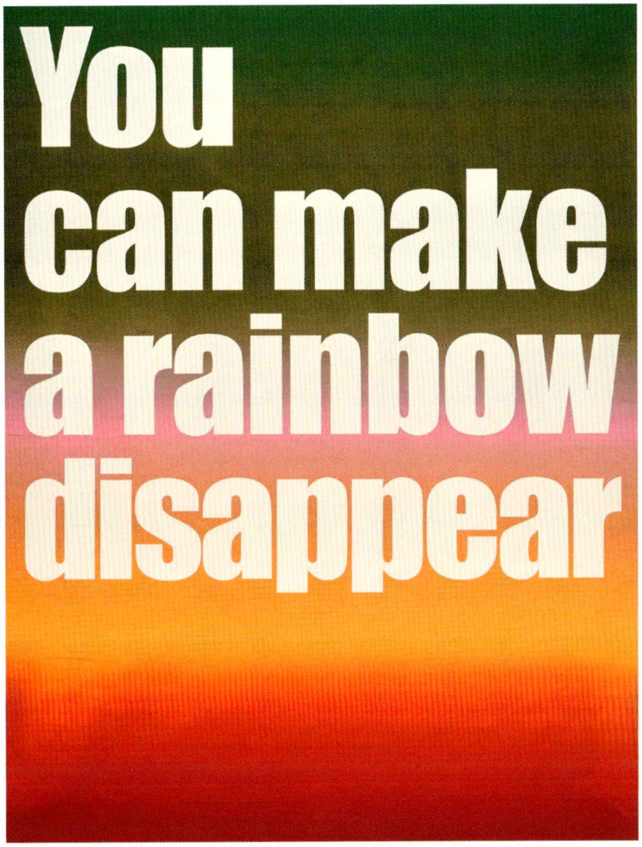

You
can make
a rainbow
disappear

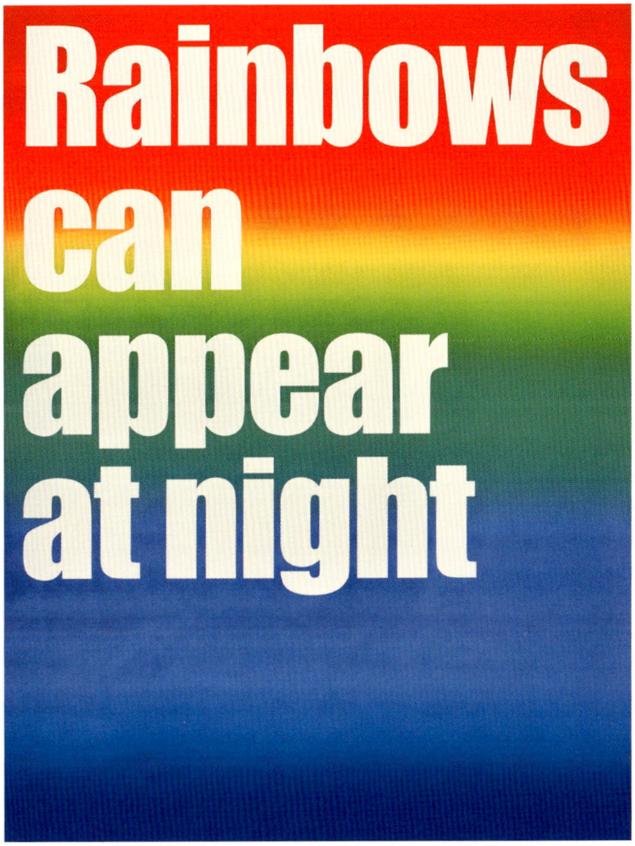

Rainbows
can
appear
at night

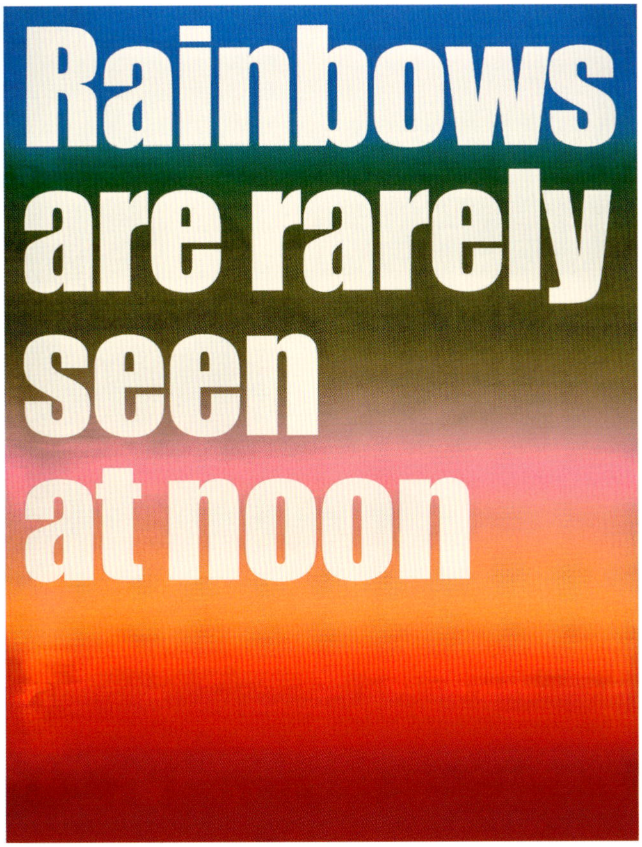

Rainbows
are rarely
seen
at noon

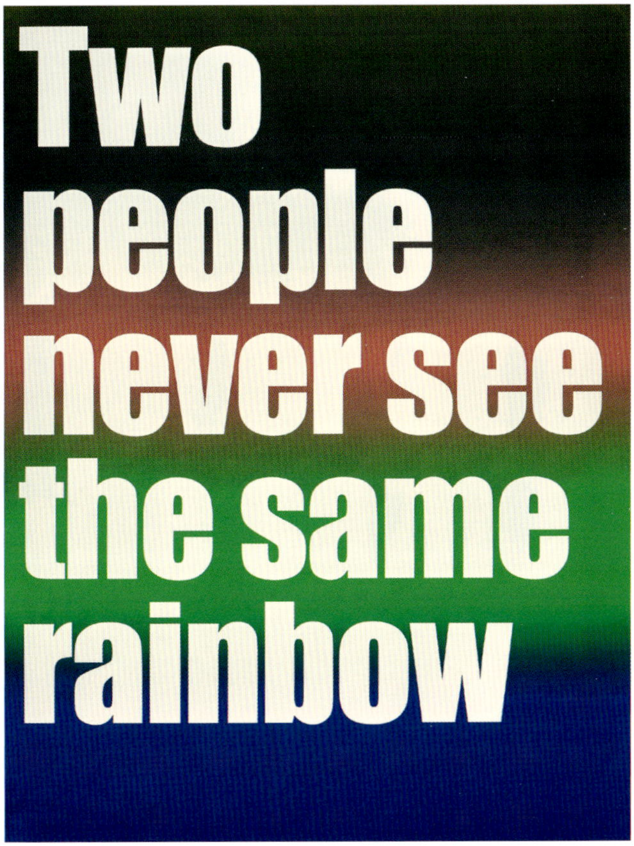

Two
people
never see
the same
rainbow

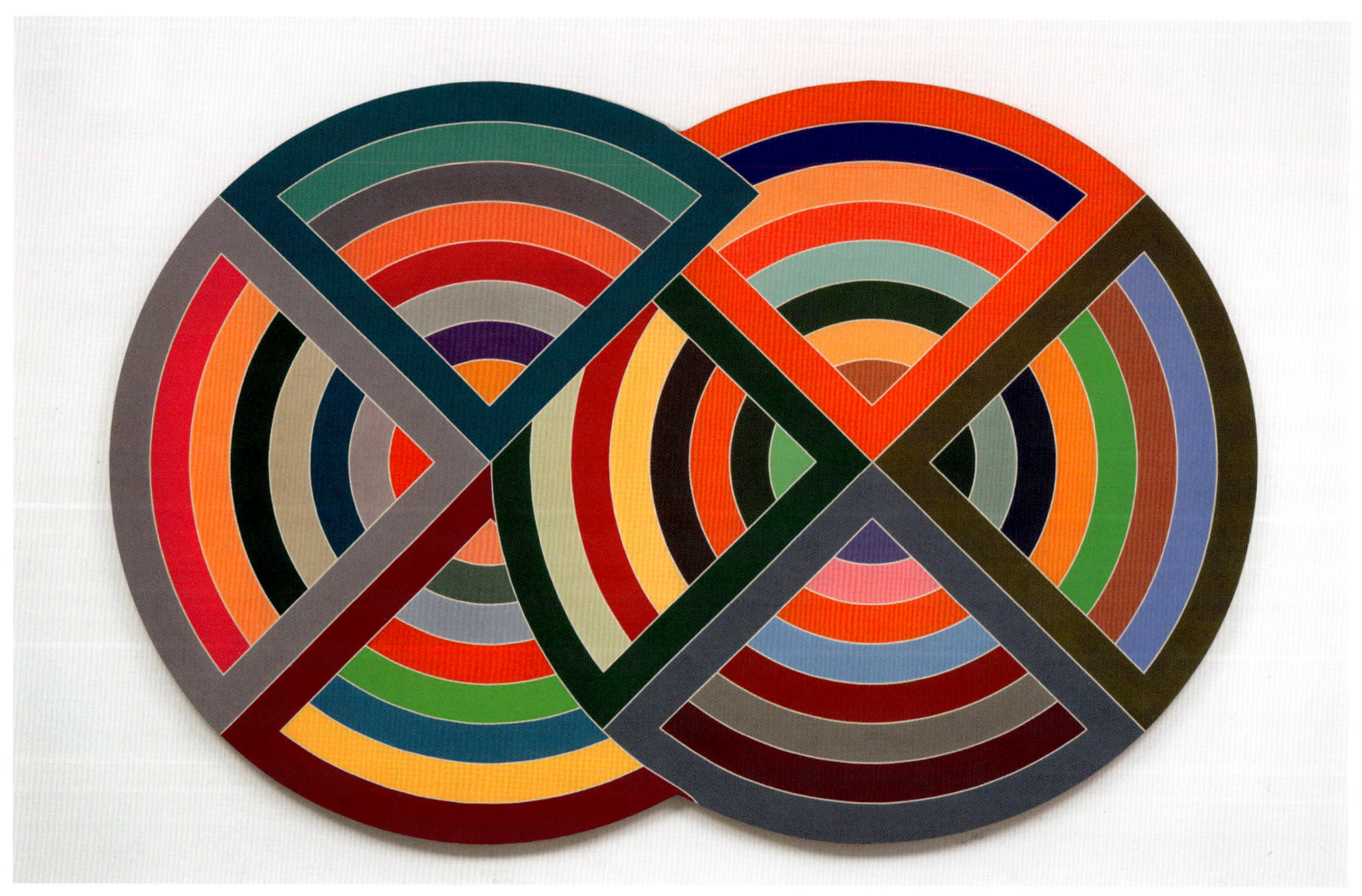

Firuzabad 1970

Frank Stella

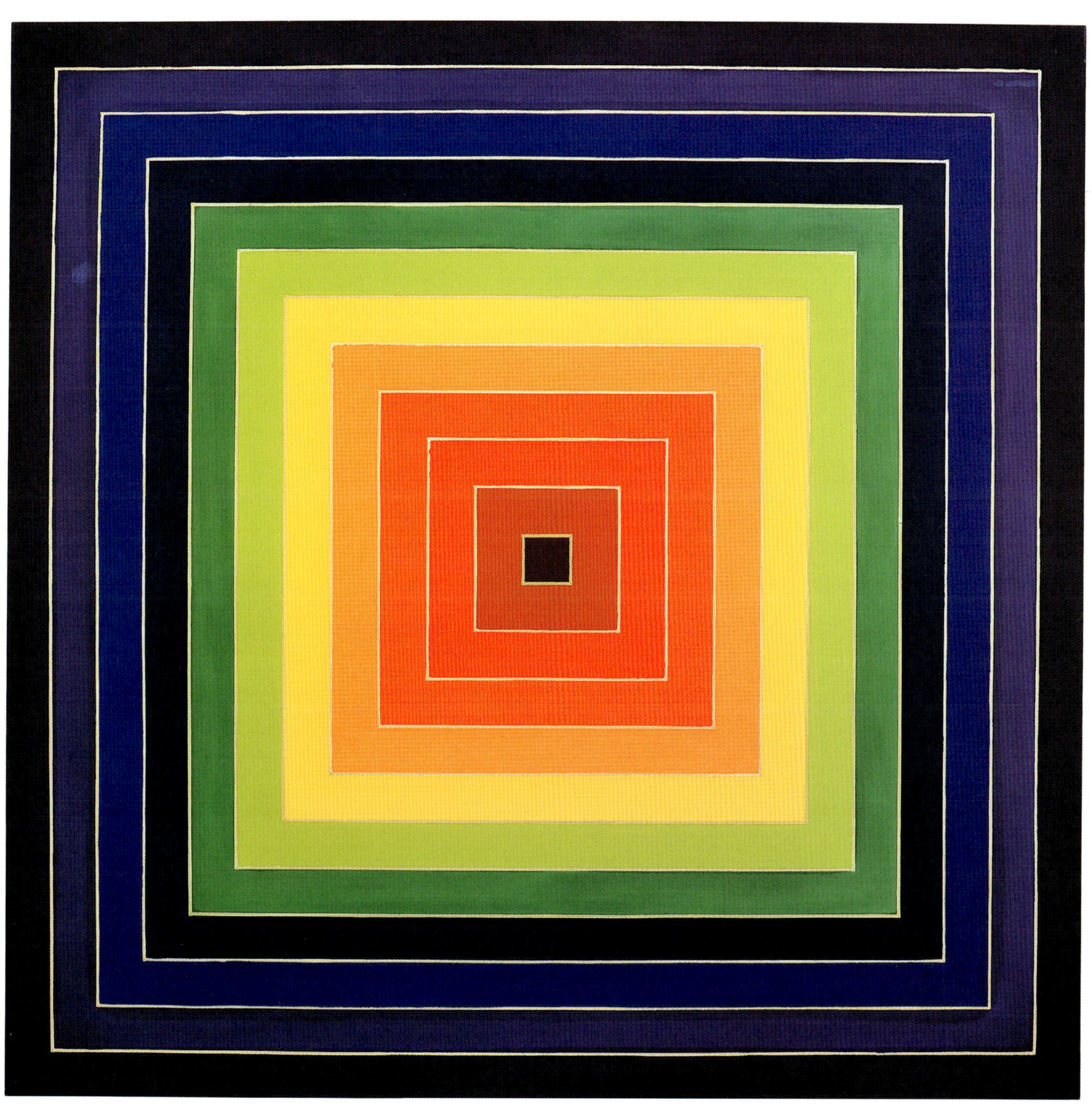

Untitled (Concentric Squares) 1974

Katharina Grosse

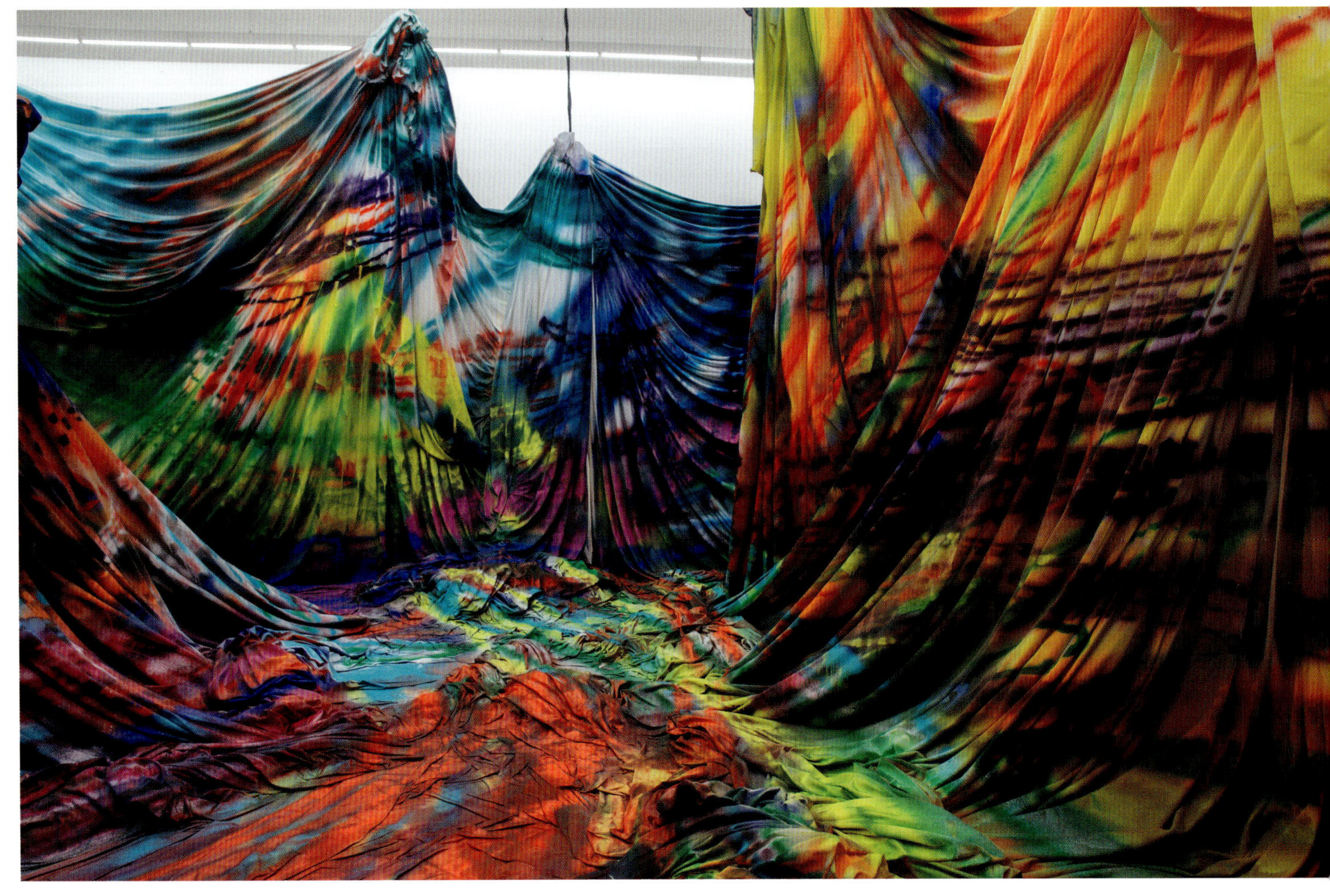

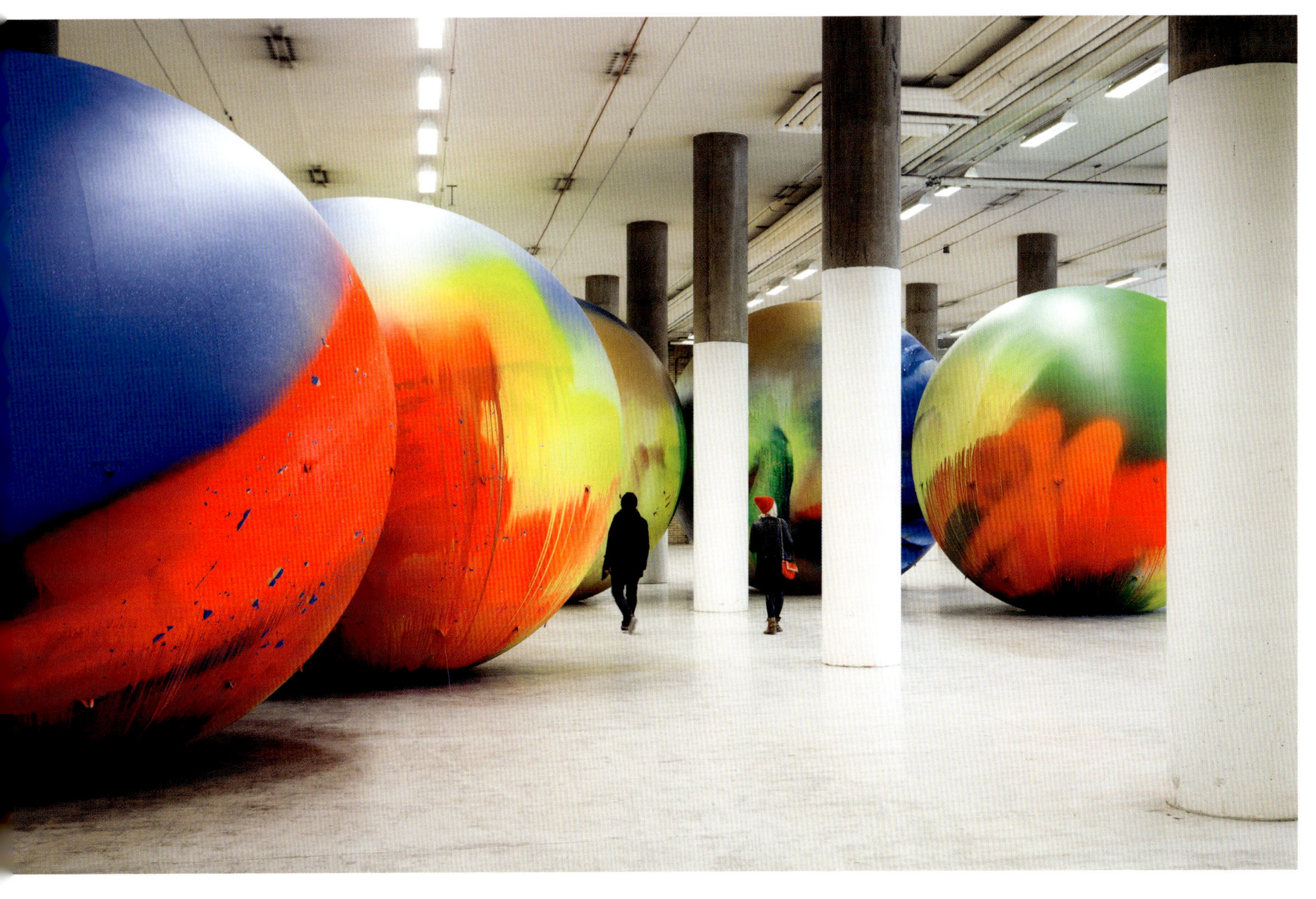

Rob Pruitt

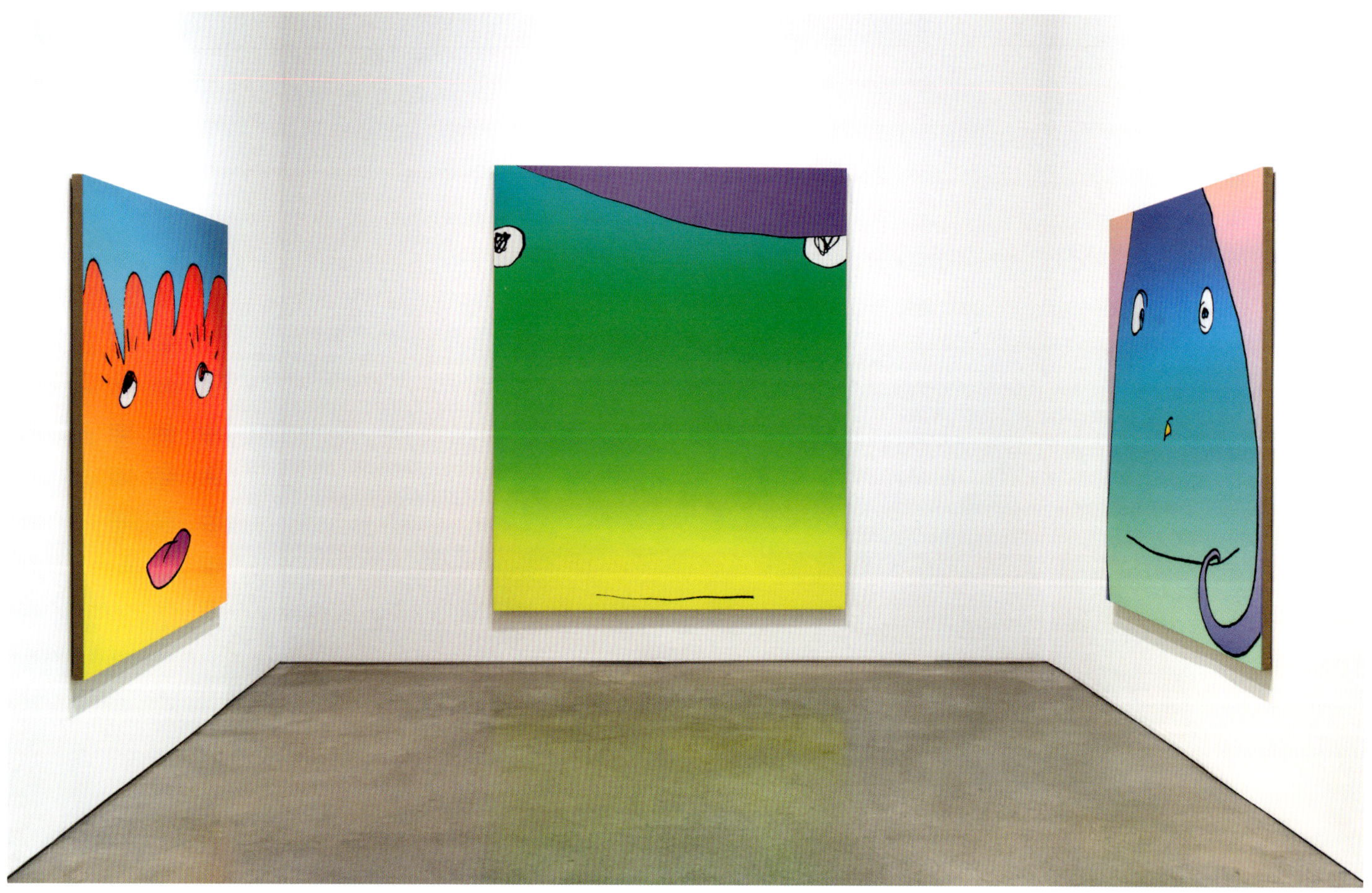

Installation view: *New Faces*   2022

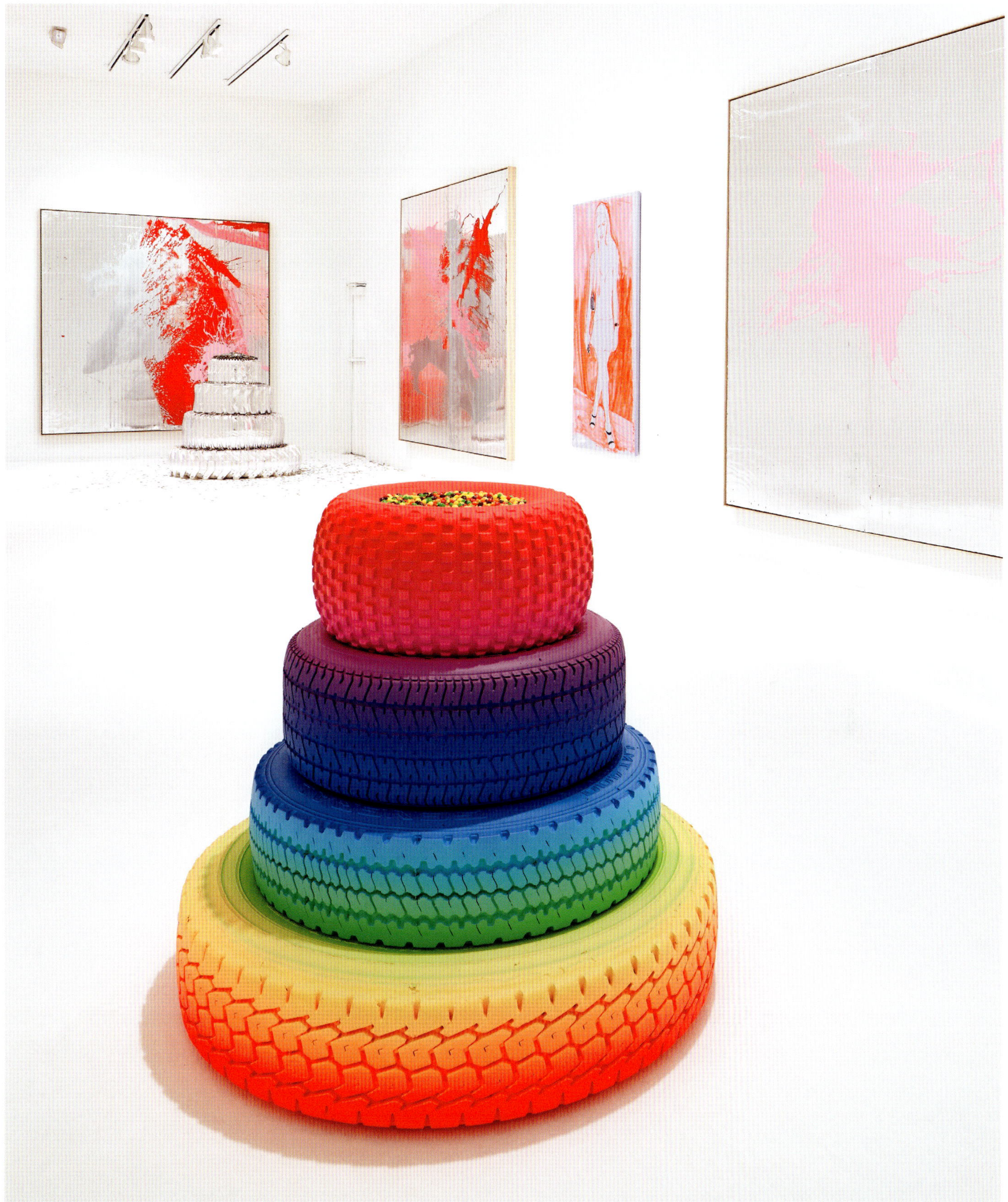

Josh Sperling

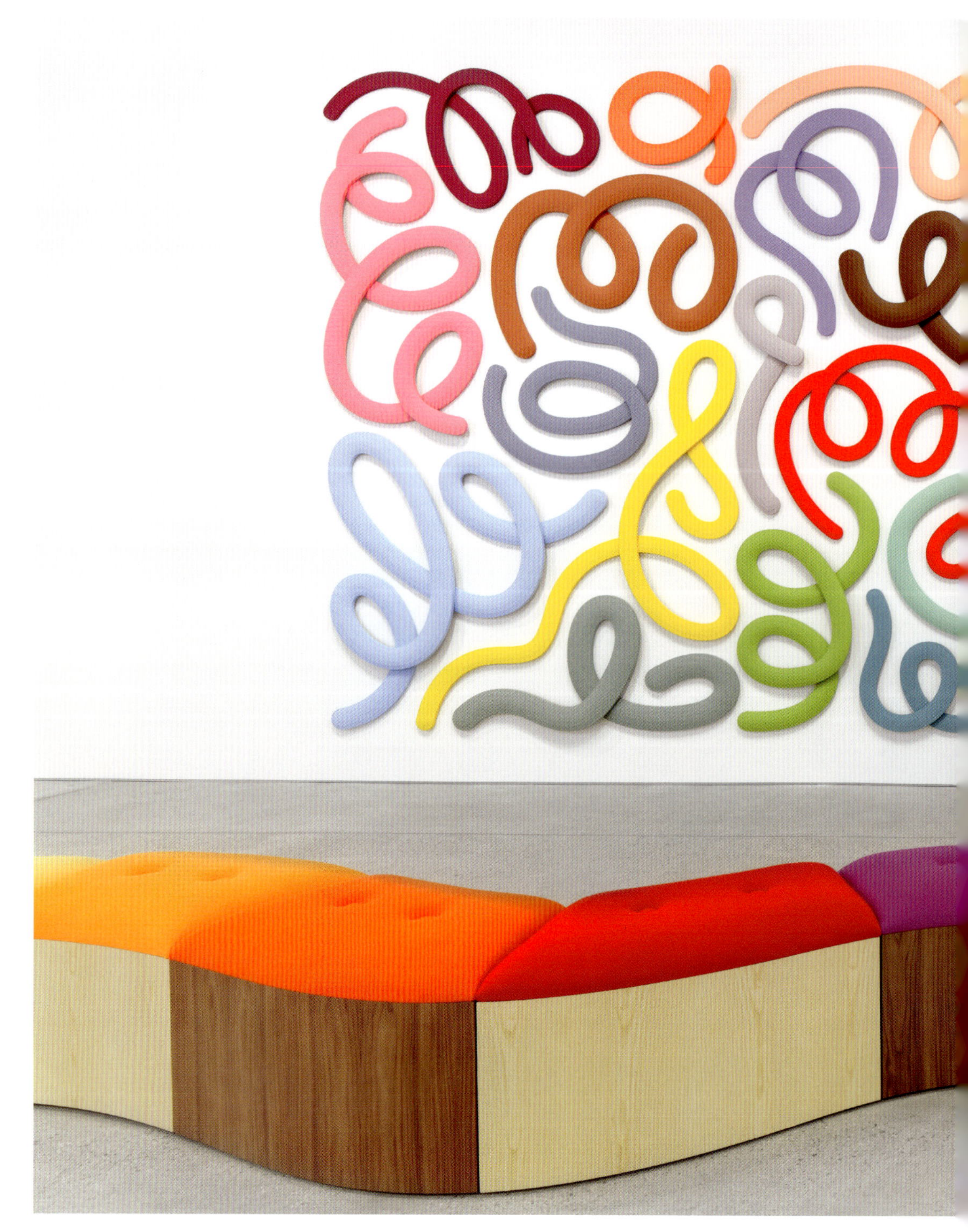

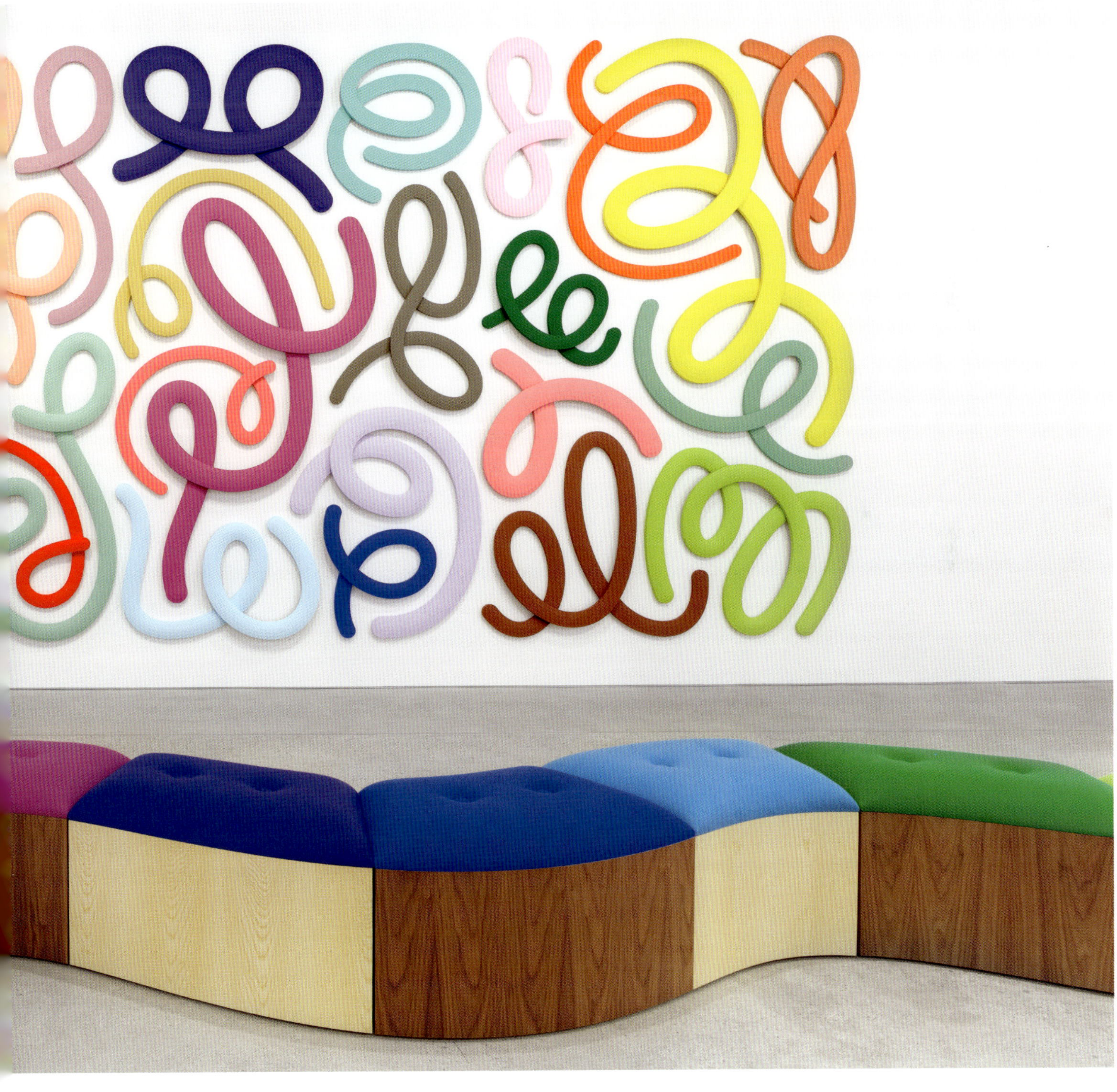

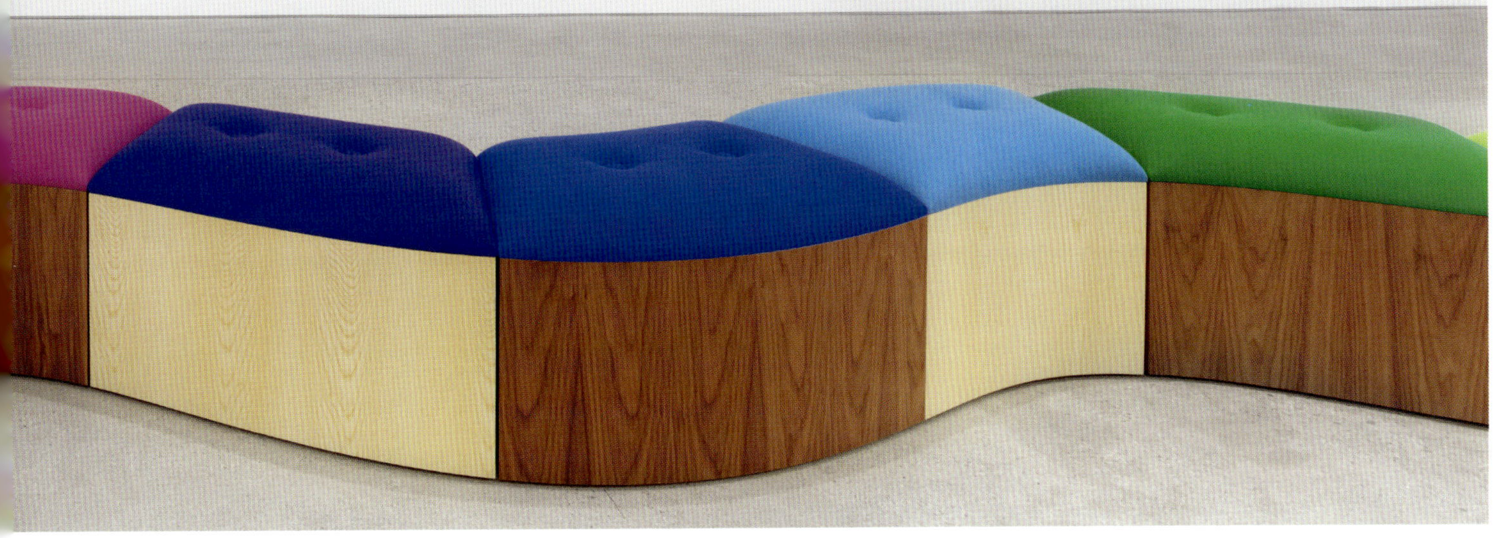

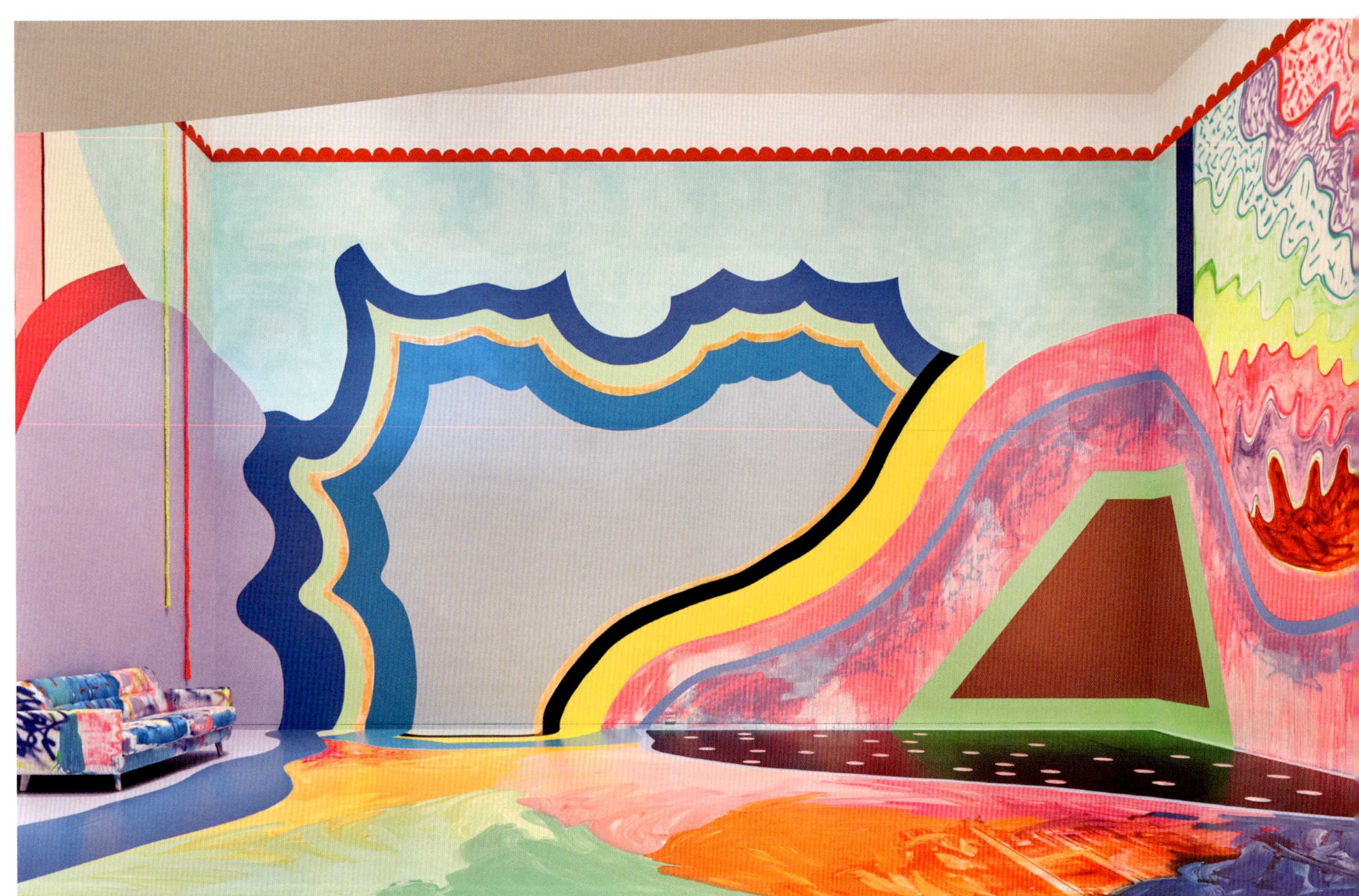

Day after day on this beautiful stage   2023

Sarah Cain

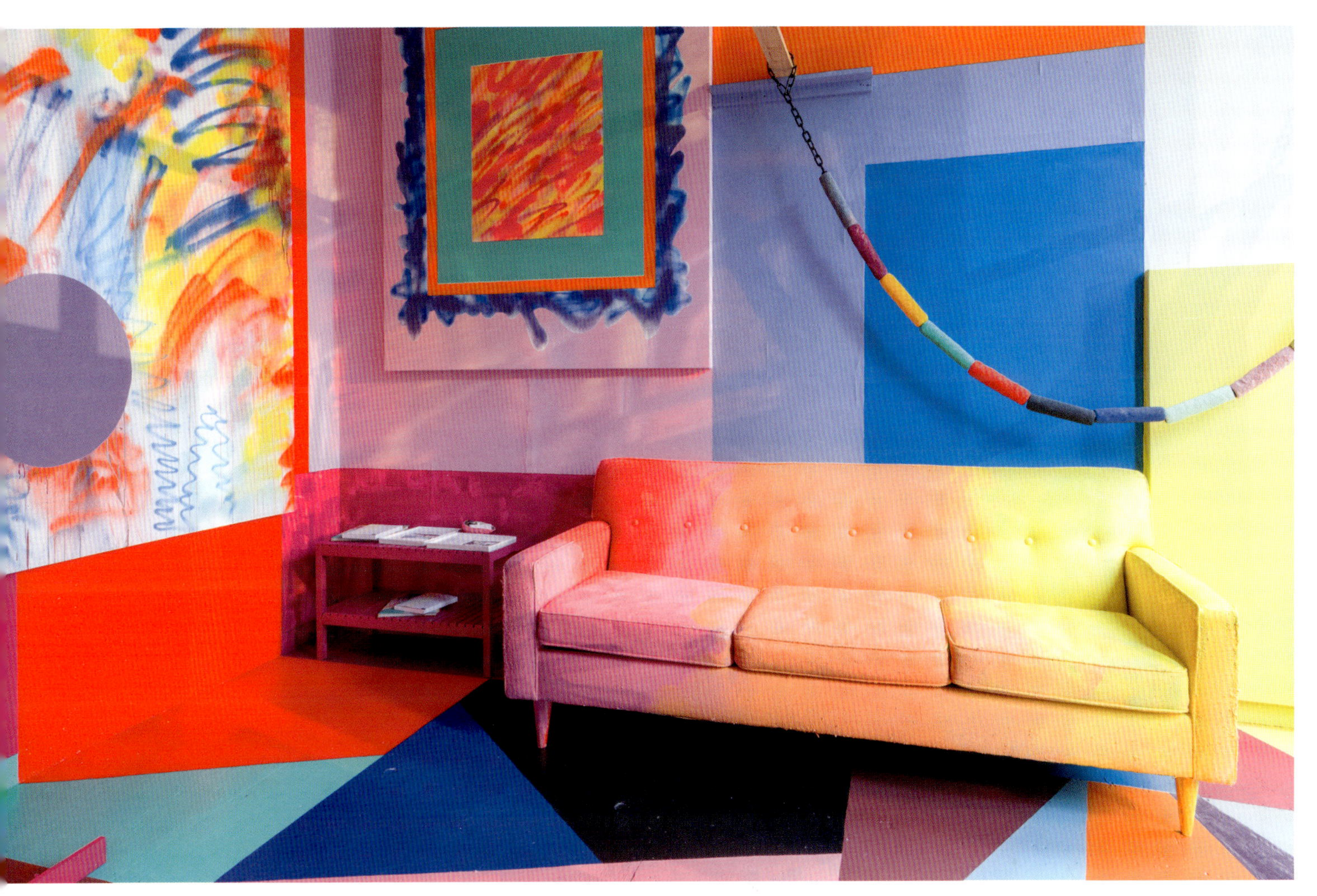

The Sun Will Not Wait 2019

Morag Myerscough

Dancing in the Sky   2024

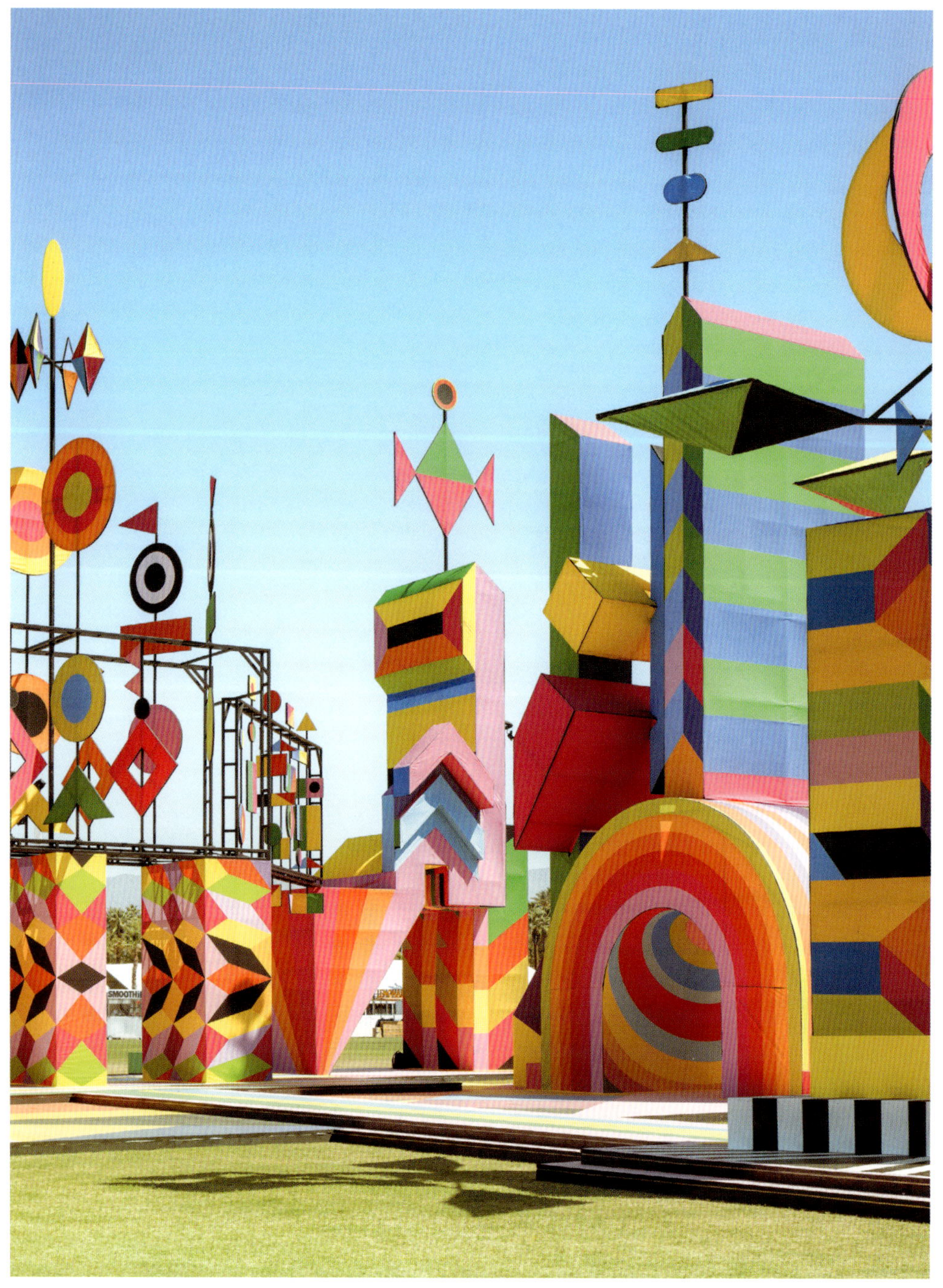

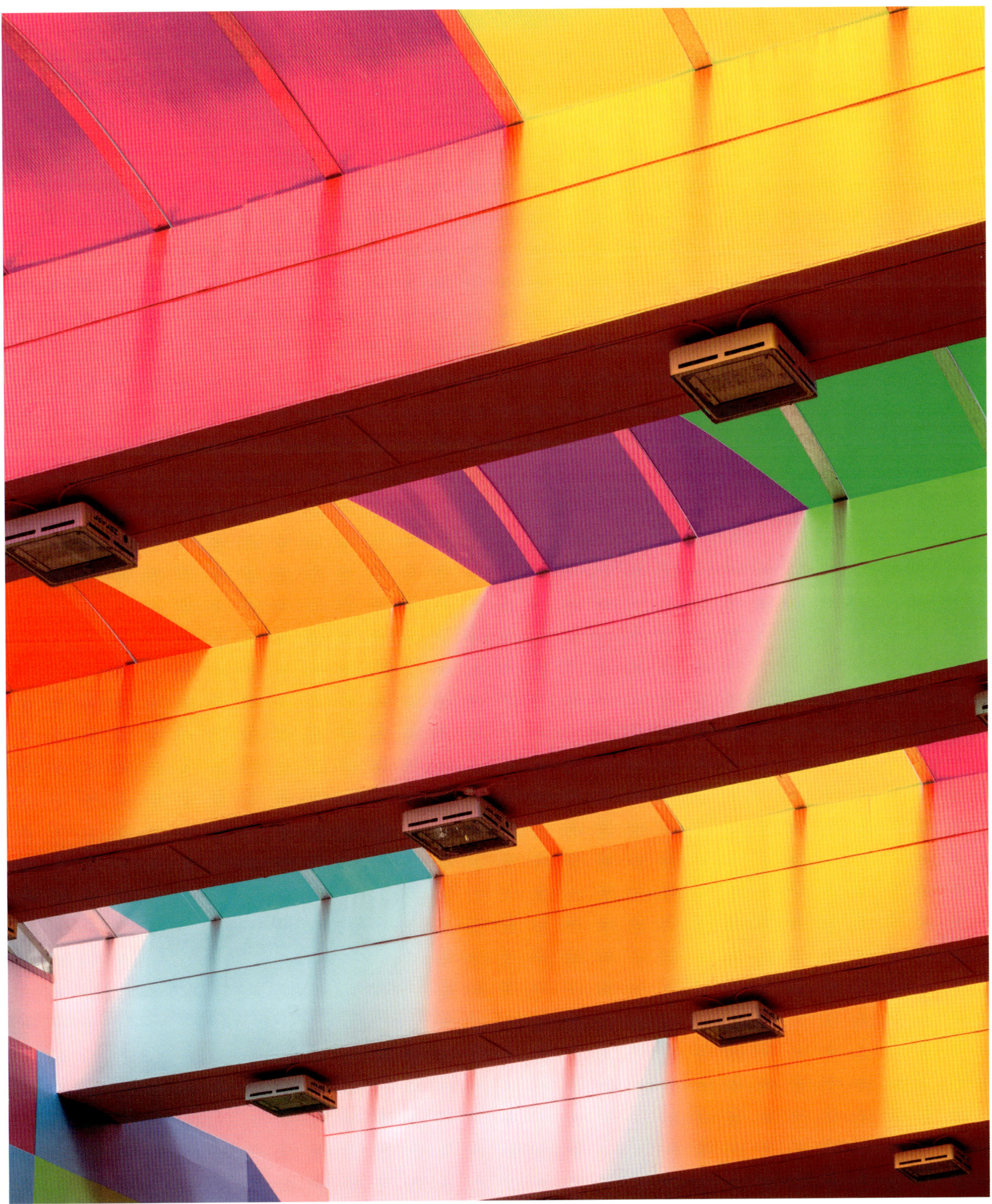

Yayoi Kusama

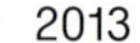

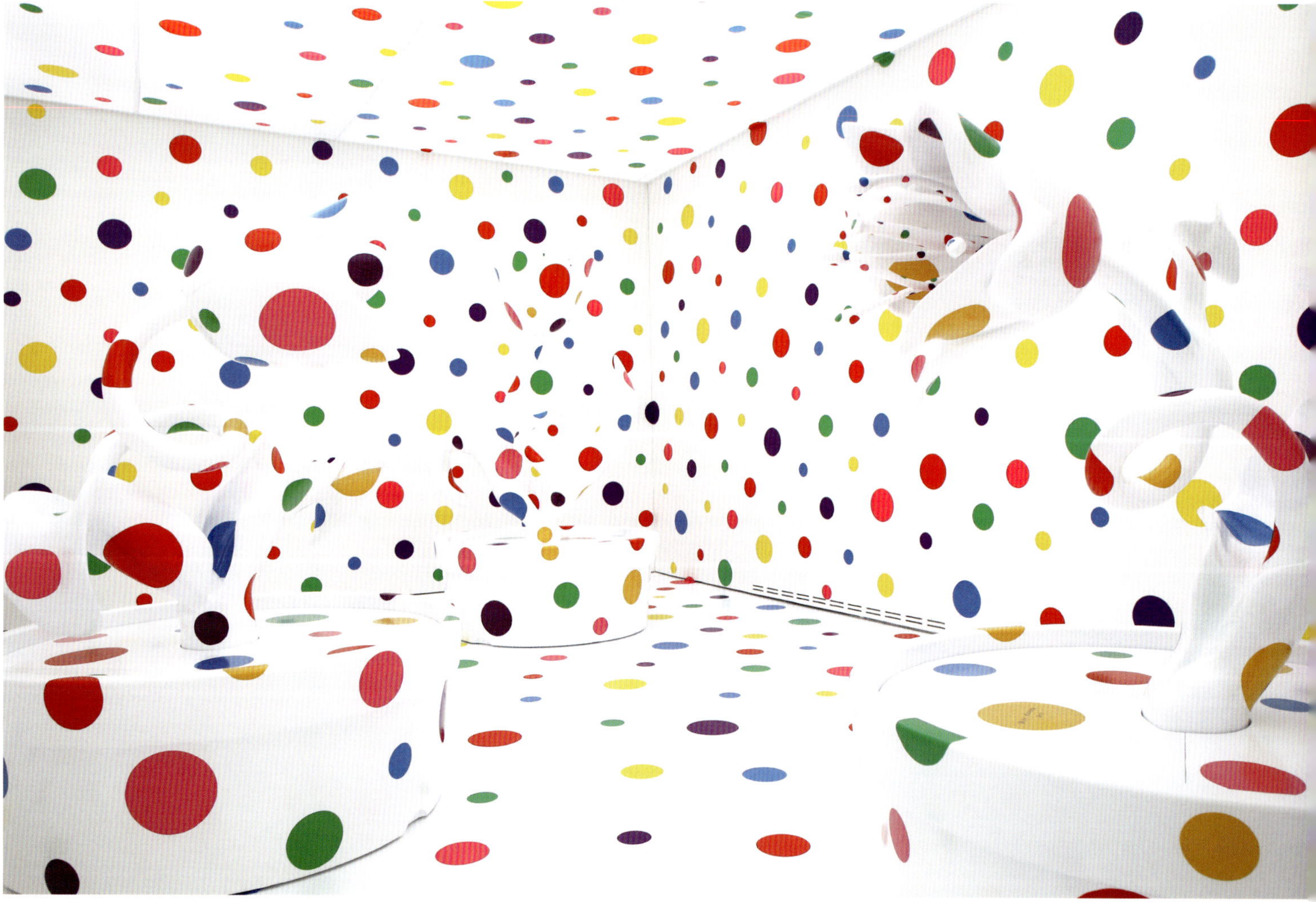

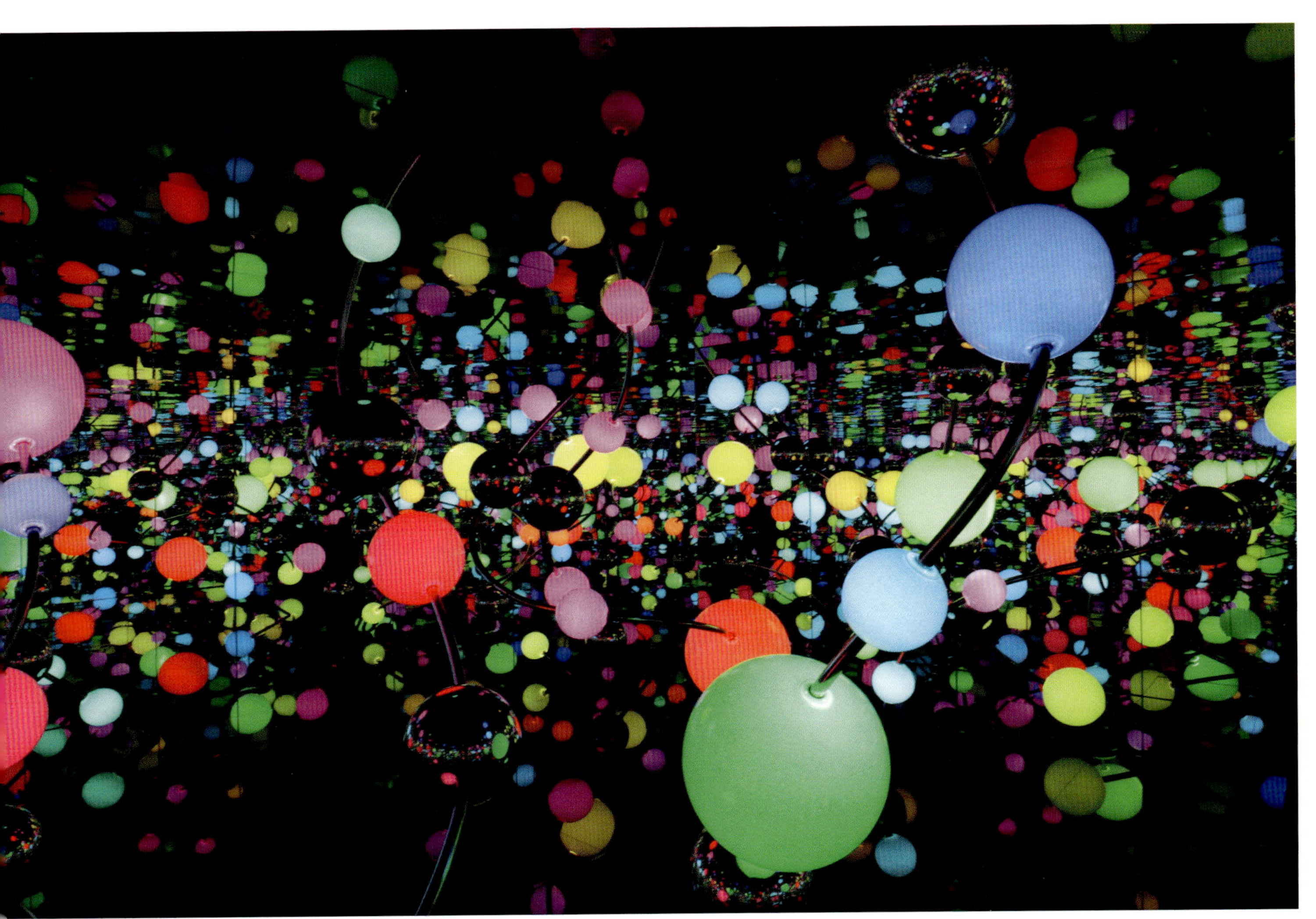

Jim Lambie

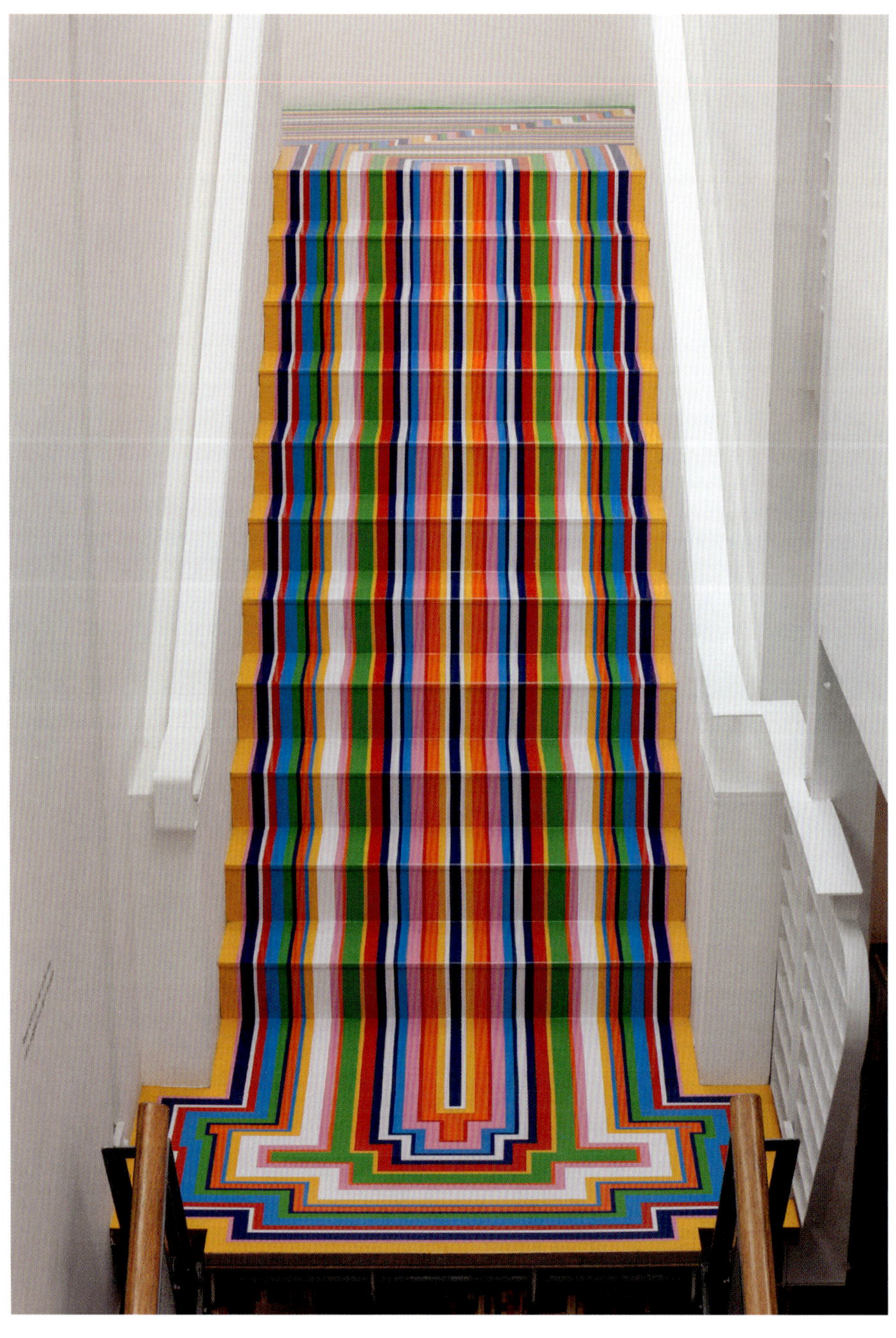

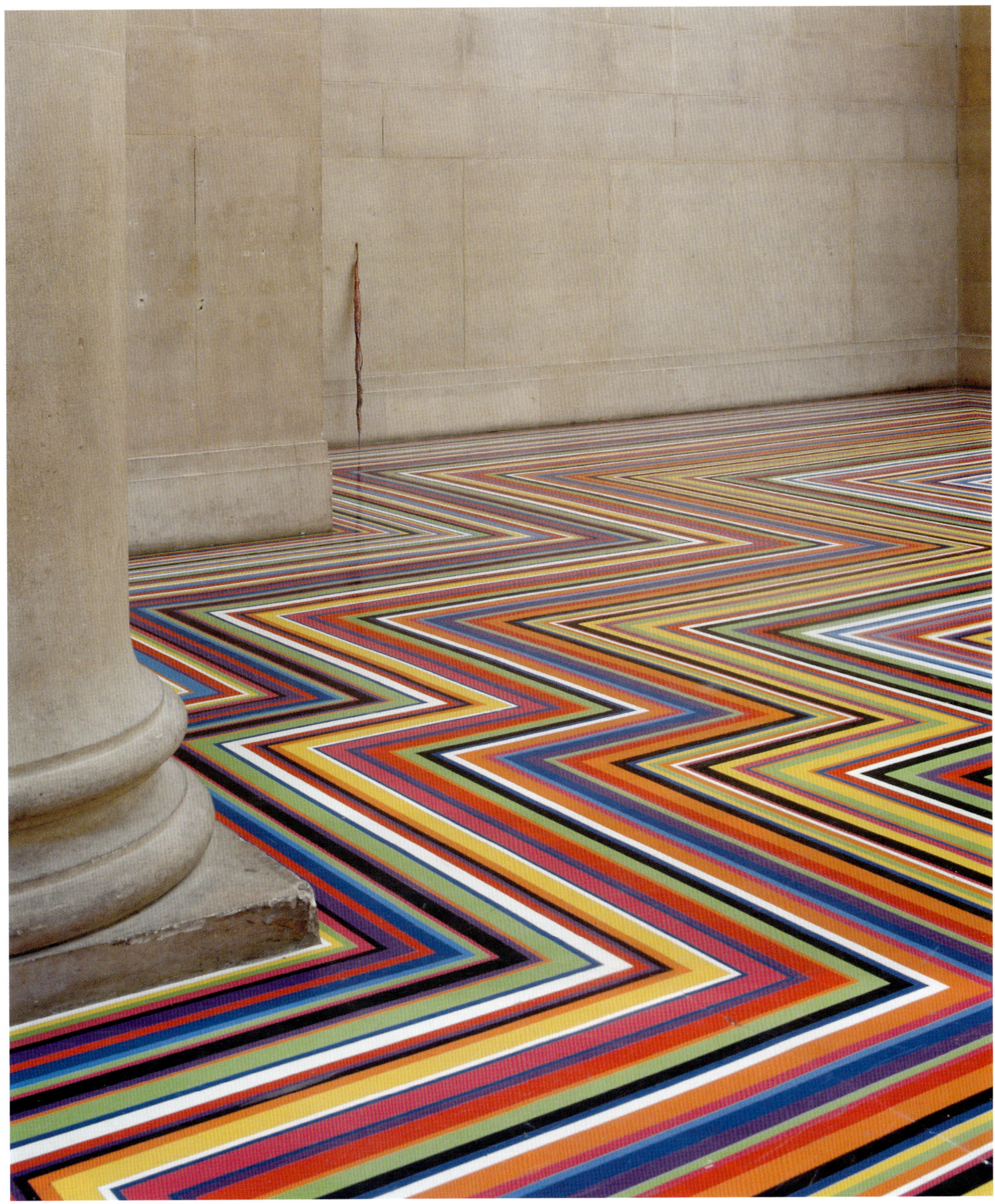

Vaughn Spann

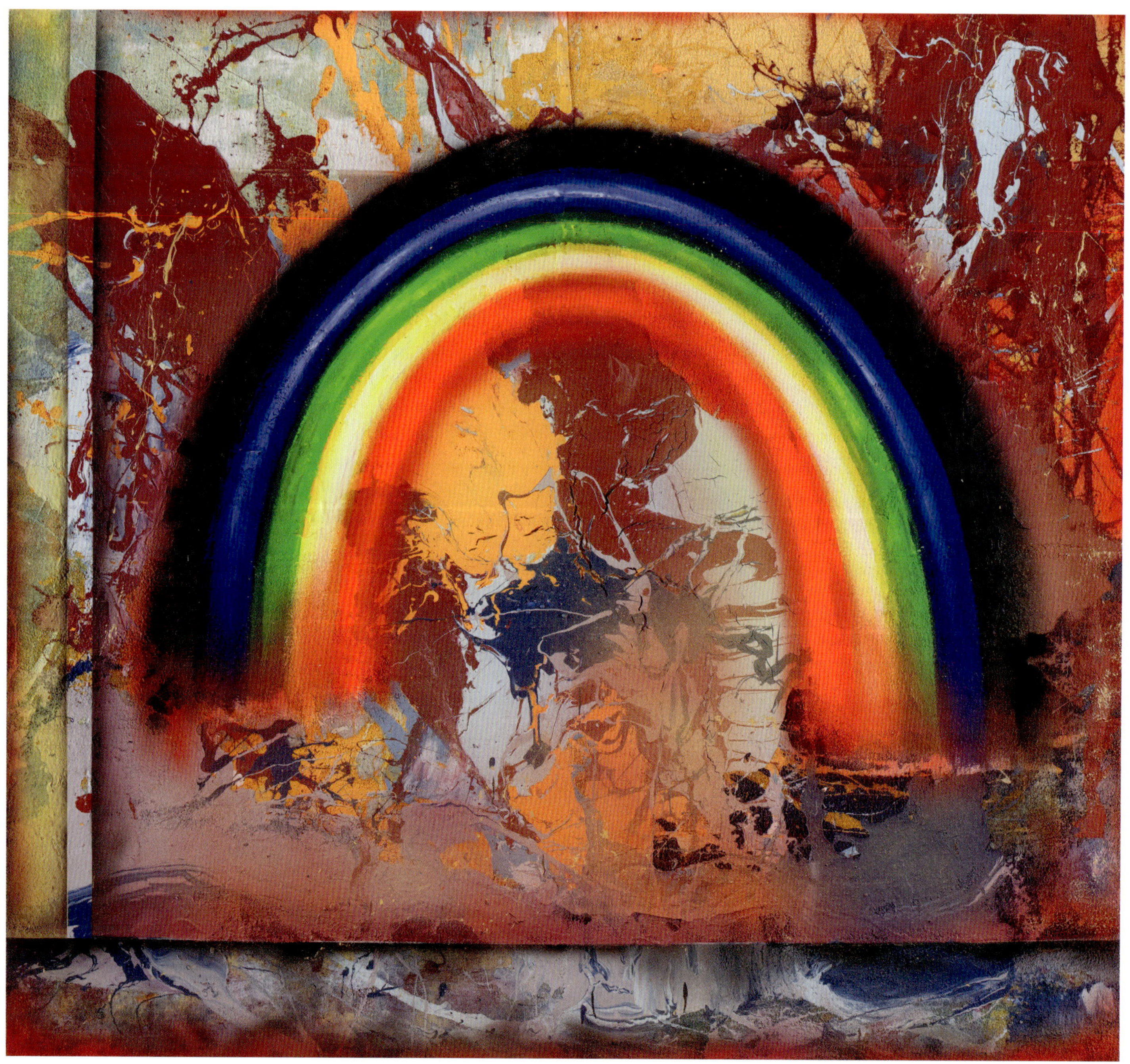

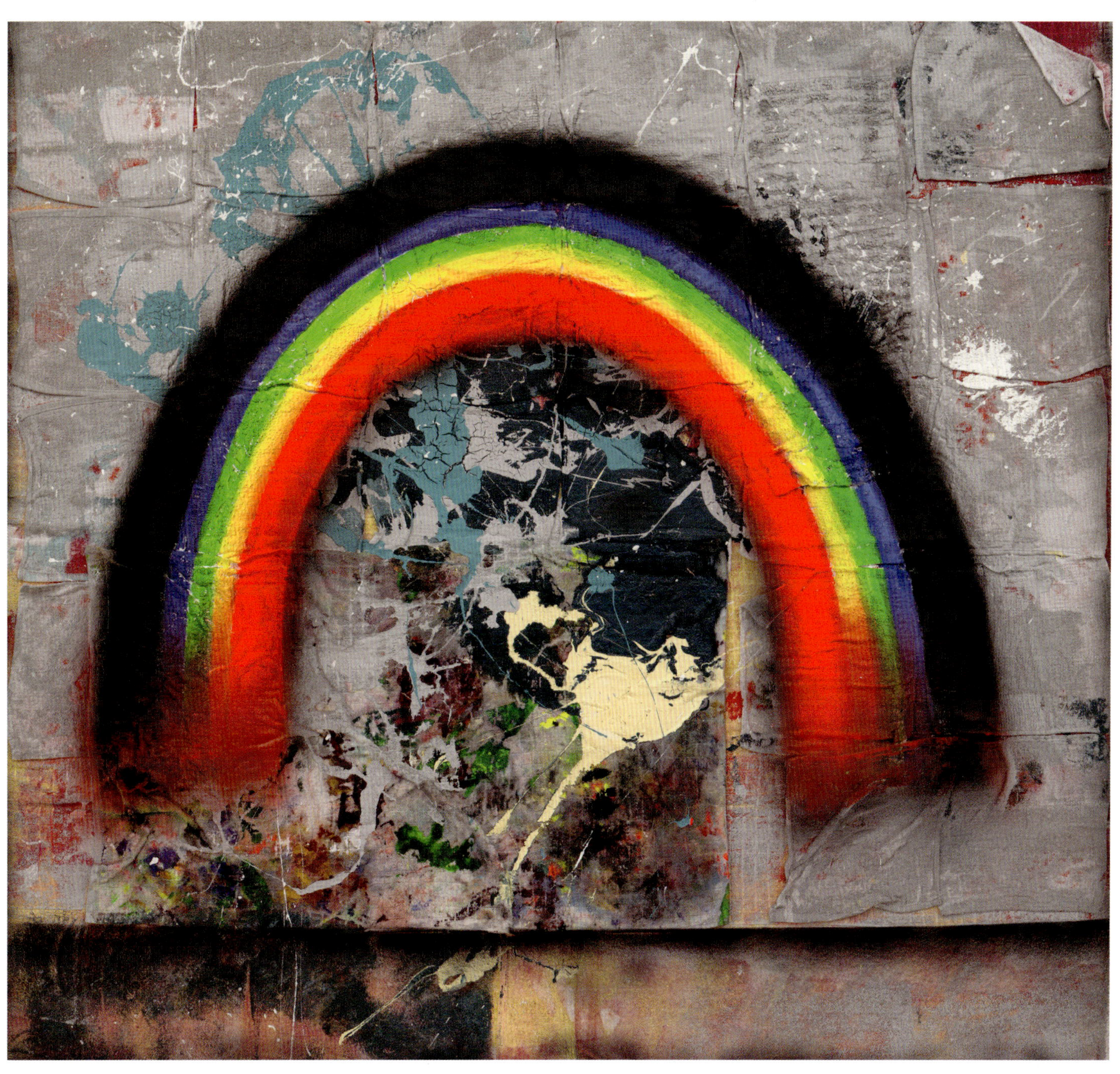

A New Chapter 2024

I've Been Walking

SHANTELL MARTIN

Yes, I've been walking this path, this line, for a long time.
From dark to light.
From imagination to making.

Yes, I've forgotten some of how I made my way here…
But every now and then, a drawing, a shape, a fragment of old work
brings me back…
Back to a version of myself I almost forgot.
A challenge I moved through.
A moment of becoming more ME.

Yes, like many of us, I didn't grow up with the freedom to speak
openly or share myself fully.
I was raised in a place where dreams weren't always supported.
Where communication was not encouraged.

Yes, recently I've been thinking about the things we don't need
permission for…
Walking. Drawing. Breathing. Being still.
The quiet things that change us anyway.

Yes, I'm grateful for drawing.
For paper and pens.
For the chance to make my own lines, my own curves, my own language.
To imagine new worlds
And to slowly, step by step, begin to live in them.

Yes, I've learned to trust that inner voice.
The one that travels from my head to my heart to my hand, and out into
the world.

Yes, the journey has been challenging.
Doors have closed, and still do.
But I keep finding windows to climb through.
I keep finding new paths.
And yes, I keep growing.

Shantell Martin

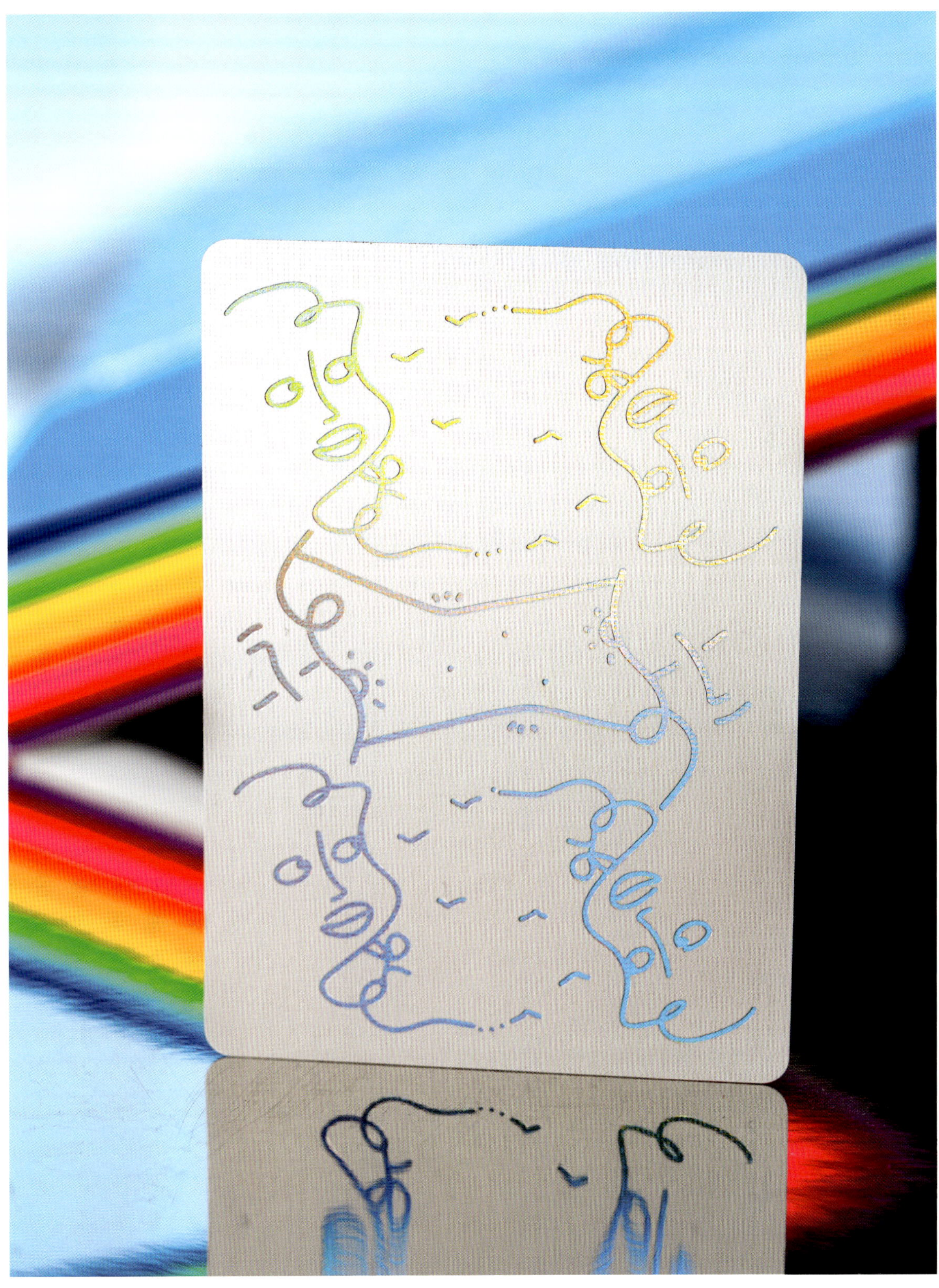

Nina Chanel Abney (pp. 220–21)
Born 1982, Harvey, IL. Lives and works in New York.

What I Wanted vs. What I Got, 2022
Collage on pigmented Pace Paper handmade cotton,
mounted on panel
Triptych, each 78 × 59 in. (198.1 × 149.9 cm)

Derrick Adams (pp. 52–53)
Born 1970, Baltimore. Lives and works in Brooklyn.

Floater 15, 2016
Acrylic and fabric on paper
50 × 50 in. (127 × 127 cm)

Style Variation 35, 2020
Acrylic paint and graphite on digital inkjet photograph
on Artex canvas in custom gold-leaf frame
96 × 59¾ in. (243.8 × 151.8 cm)

Hiva Alizadeh (pp. 90–91)
Born 1989, Kerman, Iran. Lives and works in Tehran
and London.

Untitled (light curls) (detail), 2021
Synthetic hair on canvas
25⅝ × 7⅞ × 1⅝ in. (65 × 20 × 4 cm)

Untitled (Mountain) (detail), 2023
Synthetic hair on canvas and wooden bar
70⅞ × 78¾ × 3⅛ in. (180 × 200 × 8 cm)

Monira Al Qadiri (pp. 144–45)
Born 1983, Dakar, Senegal. Lives and works in Berlin.

BENZENE FLOAT, 2023
Inflatable sculptures, air pump system
Dimensions variable
Installation view: *Mutant Passages*, Kunsthaus Bregenz,
Austria

Polly Apfelbaum (pp. 164–65)
Born 1955, Abington, PA. Lives and works in New York.

For the Love of Gene Davis, 2014
Hand-dyed and woven wool, wallpaper
4 carpets: 760 × 233 in. (1,930.4 × 591.8 cm) overall
Wallpaper: dimensions variable
Installation view: Temple Contemporary, Philadelphia, 2014

Halfpipe, 2018
Hand dyed hand-woven wool, cotton
139⅛ × 308¼ in. (353.5 × 783 cm)
Installation view: *Waiting for the UFOs (a space set
between a landscape and a bunch of flowers)*, Ikon Gallery,
Birmingham, UK, 2018

Firelei Báez (pp. 68–69)
Born 1981, Santiago de los Caballeros, Dominican Republic.
Lives and works in New York.

*Adjusting the Moon (The right to non-imperative clarities):
Waning*, 2019–20
Oil and acrylic on panel
114 × 78 × 1½ in. (289.6 × 198.1 × 3.8 cm)

Untitled (Temple of Time), 2020
Oil, acrylic, and inkjet on canvas
94½ × 132⅜ × 1⅝ in. (240 × 336.2 × 4 cm)

Kevin Beasley (pp. 72–73)
Born 1985, Lynchburg, VA. Lives and works in New York.

Garden Arches I, 2024
Raw Virginia cotton, polyurethane resin, Sharpie transfer,
fiberglass
51½ × 35¾ × 1½ in. (130.8 × 90.8 × 3.8 cm)

Garden Arches IV, 2024
Raw Virginia cotton, polyurethane resin, Sharpie transfer,
fiberglass
52 × 35¾ × 1½ in. (131.8 × 90.8 × 3.8 cm)

Jean-Baptiste Bernadet (pp. 118–19)
Born 1978, Paris. Lives and works in Brussels.

Untitled (Fugue), 2023
Oil and cold wax on canvas
90½ × 81½ in. (230 × 207 cm)

Untitled (Vetiver XVIII), 2015
Oil and cold wax on canvas
78¾ × 70⅞ in. (200 × 180 cm)

Lucy Bull (pp. 206–7)
Born 1990, New York. Lives and works in Los Angeles.

16:23, 2024
Oil on linen
86 × 68 × 1¼ in. (218.4 × 172.7 × 3.2 cm)

17:50, 2022
Oil on linen
68⅞ × 48⅛ × 1⅛ in. (174.9 × 122.2 × 2.9 cm)

Daniel Buren (pp. 54–55)
Born 1938, Boulogne-Billancourt, Paris. Lives and works
in situ.

Catch as catch can, 2014
Work in situ
Installation view: BALTIC Centre for Contemporary Art,
Gateshead, UK, 2014

Excentrique(s), 2012
Work in situ
Installation view: Monumenta 2012, Grand Palais, Paris

Cai Guo-Qiang (pp. 198–99)
Born 1957, Quanzhou, Fujian, China. Lives and works
in New York.

Transient Rainbow, realized on June 29, 2002, 9:30 p.m.
1,000 3-inch multicolor peony fireworks fitted with
computer chips
Explosion event realized over the East River, from Manhattan
to Queens
Approx. 15 sec.

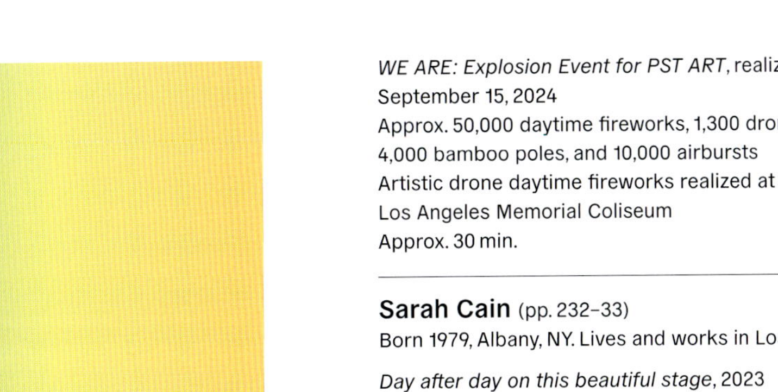

WE ARE: Explosion Event for PST ART, realized
September 15, 2024
Approx. 50,000 daytime fireworks, 1,300 drones,
4,000 bamboo poles, and 10,000 airbursts
Artistic drone daytime fireworks realized at the
Los Angeles Memorial Coliseum
Approx. 30 min.

Sarah Cain (pp. 232–33)
Born 1979, Albany, NY. Lives and works in Los Angeles.

Day after day on this beautiful stage, 2023
Paint on floor, walls, sofa, and rope
Dimensions variable
Installation view: Henry Art Gallery, Seattle, 2023

The Sun Will Not Wait, 2019
Paint on floor and mixed media canvases
Dimensions variable
Installation view: Honor Fraser, Los Angeles, 2019

Nick Cave (pp. 124–25)
Born 1959, Fulton, MO. Lives and works in Chicago.

Installation view: *The Let Go*, Park Avenue Armory, New York,
2018

Soundsuit, 2010
Human hair and mannequin
96 × 29 × 20 in. (243.8 × 73.7 × 50.8 cm)

Judy Chicago (pp. 104–5)
Born 1939, Chicago. Lives and works in Belen, NM.

Rainbow Pickett, 1965/2021
Matthews polyurethane paint on stainless steel
118¾ × 132 × 118¾ in. (301.6 × 335.3 × 301.6 cm)

Rearrangeable Rainbow Blocks, 1965/2022
Matthews polyurethane paint on stainless steel
Overall dimensions variable
6 pieces: 12 × 12 × 48 in. (30.5 × 30.5 × 121.9 cm)
6 pieces: 24 × 24 × 12 in. (61 × 61 × 30.5 cm)

James Clar (pp. 40–41)
Born 1979, Wisconsin. Lives and works in Manila, Philippines.

Binary Star, 2016
LEDs, filters, wires
74¾ × 74¾ in. (190 × 190 cm)

Time Bandits, 2018
LED lights with custom light filters, blinds, jumpsuit,
and artificial plant
Approx. 96 × 96 in. (244 × 244 cm)

Melissa Cody (pp. 168–69)
Born 1983, No Water Mesa, Navajo Nation, AZ.
Enrolled Member of the Navajo Nation. Lives and
works in Los Angeles.

Into the Depths, She Rappels, 2023
Wool warp, weft, selvedge cords, and aniline dyes
87 × 51½ in. (221 × 130.8 cm)

Scaling the Caverns, 2023
Jacquard wool tapestry, aniline dyed wool fringe
89 × 47 in. (226.1 × 119.4 cm)

Carlos Cruz-Diez (pp. 18–19)
Born 1923, Caracas, Venezuela. Died 2019, Paris.

Chromosaturation, Paris, 1965/2017
Installation with colored lights
Dimensions variable
Installation view: *Kinesthesia: Latin American Kinetic Art,
1954–1969*, Palm Springs Art Museum, CA, 2017–18

Ian Davenport (pp. 22–23)
Born 1966, Sidcap, Kent, UK. Lives and works in London.

Ariel, 2021
Acrylic on paper
72⅞ × 57⅛ in. (185 × 145 cm)

Poured Staircase, 2021
Acrylic on MDF and aluminum panel
Site-specific installation
Installation view: Chiostro del Bramante, Rome

Gabriel Dawe (pp. 176–77)
Born 1973, Mexico City. Lives and works in Dallas.

Plexus A1, 2015
Thread, painted wood, and hooks
25 × 12 × 40 ft. (7.6 × 3.7 × 12.2 m)
Installation view: Renwick Gallery, Smithsonian American Art
Museum, Washington, DC

Raúl de Nieves (pp. 74–75)
Born 1983, Michoacán, Mexico. Lives and works in Brooklyn.

The child (Gift), 2009–20
Mixed media
98 × 48 in. (248.9 × 121.9 cm)

The Fable, which is composed of wonders, moves the more,
2021
Fiberglass, epoxy foam, cement, resin, glue, and beads
95 × 29 × 75 in. (241.3 × 73.7 × 190.5 cm)

DRIFT (pp. 146–47)
Founded 2007, Amsterdam. Studio located in Amsterdam.

Meadow, 2017
Aluminum, stainless steel, printed fabric, LEDs, robotics
36⅝ × 8⅝ in. (93 × 22 cm) when closed
36⅝ × 47¼ in. (93 × 120 cm) when opened
Installation view (p. 146): Centrum Chodov, Prague, 2017
Installation view (p. 147): Stedelijk Museum Amsterdam, 2018

Janet Echelman (pp. 204–5)
Born 1966, Tampa, FL. Lives and works in Brookline, MA.

Earthtime 1.8 Renwick, 2015
Fiber, colored LED lighting, textile flooring, and historic
architecture
Fibers braided with polyester and UHMWPE (ultra-high-
molecular-weight polyethylene)
40 × 40 × 100 ft. (12.2 × 12.2 × 30.5 m)
Installation view: Smithsonian American Art Museum,
Washington, DC

Noli Timere, Sculpture #1, 2023
Fiber, buildings, and sky combined with colored lighting
Fibers braided with nylon and UHMWPE (ultra-high-molecular-weight polyethylene)
Dimensions variable, 73 × 26 × 12 ft. (22.3 × 7.9 × 3.7 m)
Installation view: Palazzo del Senato, Milan

Olafur Eliasson (pp. 182–85)
Born 1967, Copenhagen. Lives and works in Berlin.

Colour experiment no. 10, 2010
Oil on canvas
Diam. 94½ in. (240 cm)

Rainbow bridge, 2017
12 partially painted and silvered glass spheres (12 colors, black), steel, paint (gray)
66½ × 195¼ × 19¾ in. (169 × 496 × 50 cm)
Each sphere: diam. 11¾ in. (30 cm)

Whenever the rainbow appears, 2010
360 oil paintings on canvas
7 ft. 6½ in. × 43 ft. 10 in. (2.3 × 13.4 m)
Installation view: Israel Museum, Jerusalem, 2010

Edie Fake (pp. 56–57)
Born 1980, Evanston, IL. Lives and works in Twentynine Palms, CA.

Lost Path, 2024
Acrylic and gouache on wood panel
12 × 12 in. (30.5 × 30.5 cm)

Twist, 2024
Acrylic and gouache on wood panel
12 × 12 in. (30.5 × 30.5 cm)

Sam Falls (pp. 128–29)
Born 1984, San Diego, CA. Lives and works in Los Angeles and New York.

Untitled (Light Room B), 2014
Powder-coated aluminum panels and hardware, aluminum framed stained glass
96 × 34 × 34 in. (243.8 × 86.4 × 86.4 cm)

Untitled (Hartland, VT, Ferns 4H), 2013
Pigment on canvas
138 × 162¼ in. (350.5 × 412 cm)

Spencer Finch (pp. 102–3)
Born 1962, New Haven, CT. Lives and works in Brooklyn.

Rose Window at Saint-Denis (morning effect), 2022–23
LED fixtures, LED lamps, filters
Diam. 76½ in. (194.3 cm)

Spring Haiku (Cherry Blossoms, Brooklyn), 2022
LED fixtures, LED lamps, filters (2 three-foot fixtures, 1 four-foot fixture)
48 × 16 × 2 in. (122 × 40.6 × 5 cm)

Dan Flavin (pp. 20–21)
Born 1933, New York. Died 1996, Riverhead, NY.

untitled (in honor of Harold Joachim) 3, 1977
Pink, yellow, blue, and green fluorescent light
8 ft. (244 cm) square across a corner

untitled (for Ad Reinhardt) 2h, 1990
Pink, yellow, blue, and green fluorescent light
4 ft. (122 cm) wide

FriendsWithYou (pp. 216–17)
Founded 2002, Los Angeles.
Samuel Albert Borkson: Born 1979, Plantation, FL. Lives and works in Los Angeles.
Arturo Sandoval III: Born 1976, Havana, Cuba. Lives and works in Los Angeles.

Light Cave, 2014
Inflatable sculpture
25 × 55 × 14 ft. (7.6 × 16.8 × 4.3 m)
Installation view: The Standard, High Line, New York

Weeble Wobble, Wish Come True, 2006
Vinyl toys
Dimensions variable

Bernard Frize (pp. 48–49)
Born 1949, Saint-Mandé, France. Lives and works in Berlin.

Cuor, 2022
Acrylic and resin on canvas
59 × 51⅛ in. (150 × 130 cm)

Troe, 2019
Acrylic and resin on canvas
39⅜ × 31⅞ in. (100 × 81 cm)

Jeffrey Gibson (pp. 86–87)
Born 1972, Colorado Springs. Lives and works in Hudson Valley, NY.

DREAMING OF HOW IT'S MEANT TO BE, 2023
Acrylic on canvas, vintage beaded elements, vintage pinback button, glass beads, acrylic felt, and nylon thread in a custom painted frame
70¼ × 60¼ in. (178.4 × 153 cm)

Installation view: *Jeffrey Gibson: the space in which to place me*, US Pavilion, 60th Venice Biennale, 2024

Sam Gilliam (pp. 110–11)
Born 1933, Tupelo, MS. Died 2022, Washington, DC.

Double Merge, 1968
Acrylic on canvas
Left panel: 120 × 796 in. (304.8 × 2,021.8 cm)
Right panel: 120 × 852 in. (304.8 × 2,164.1 cm)

John Giorno (pp. 16–17)
Born 1936, New York. Died 2019, New York.

SIT IN MY HEART AND SMILE, 2019
Ink on linen
56 × 56 in. (142.2 × 142.2 cm)

YOU GOT TO BURN TO SHINE, 2018
Acrylic on canvas
112 × 112 in. (284.5 × 284.5 cm)

Katharina Grosse (pp. 226–27)
Born 1961, Freiburg im Breisgau, Germany.
Lives and works in Berlin.

Is It You?, 2020
Acrylic on fabric
19 ft. 8 in. × 44 ft. 3 in. × 41 ft. (6 × 13.5 × 12.5 m)
Installation view: Baltimore Museum of Art

Wizz Eyelashes, 2014
Acrylic on PVC
Dimensions variable
Installation view: Frihammen, Magasin 6, Magasin III Museum
for Contemporary Art, Stockholm

Mark Grotjahn (pp. 162–63)
Born 1968, Pasadena, CA. Lives and works in Los Angeles.

Untitled (Colored Butterfly White Background 10 Wings), 2004
Colored pencil on paper
69¾ × 47½ in. (177.2 × 120.7 cm)

Untitled (Full Color Butterfly 41.81), 2011
Colored pencil on paper
47⅝ × 38 in. (121.1 × 96.5 cm)

Jennifer Guidi (pp. 62–63)
Born 1972, Redondo Beach, CA. Lives and works
in Los Angeles.

An Essential Order (Goethe), 2019
Sand and acrylic on linen
202 × 236 in. (513.1 × 599.4 cm)

Your Colors are Eternal (Schiffermüller), 2019
Sand, acrylic, and oil on linen
144 × 2½ in. (365.8 × 6.4 cm)

Alteronce Gumby (pp. 140–41)
Born 1985, Harrisburg, PA. Lives and works in Bronx, NY.

Life in Rainbow, 2022
Gemstones, glass, and acrylic on panel
96 × 154 in. (243.8 × 391.2 cm)

Peter Halley (pp. 24–25)
Born 1953, New York. Lives and works in New York.

ANTESTERIA, 2021
Installation, digitally printed vinyl
Dimensions variable
Installation view: Museo Nivola, Orani, Sardinia

Lauren Halsey (pp. 84–85)
Born 1987, Los Angeles. Lives and works in Los Angeles.

auntie fawn on tha 6, 2021
Synthetic hair on wood
115 × 56 × 8 in. (292.1 × 142.2 × 20.3 cm)

Installation view: *Lauren Halsey*, David Kordansky Gallery,
Los Angeles, 2020

Zach Harris (pp. 122–23)
Born 1976, Santa Rosa, CA. Lives and works in Los Angeles.

Eclipse Eye, 2018
Carved wood, water-based paint, ink
39 × 35⅞ in. (99 × 91 cm)

Study for 20/20, 2016–17
Carved wood, water-based paint, ink
68⅛ × 47⅝ in. (173 × 121 cm)

Jeppe Hein (pp. 186–87)
Born 1974, Copenhagen. Lives and works in Berlin.

Colourful Mexico #03, 2021
Glass fiber-reinforced plastic, chrome lacquer (coral blue
IV, emerald, medium orange essence, ruby), magnet, white
smoke string
15¾ × 10¼ × 10¼ in. (40 × 26 × 26 cm)

Light Yellow, Medium Blue and Dark Orange Mirror Balloon,
2019
Glass fiber-reinforced plastic, chrome lacquer (light yellow,
medium blue, dark orange), magnet, white smoke string
15¾ × 10¼ × 10¼ in. (40 × 26 × 26 cm)

Damien Hirst (pp. 106–7)
Born 1965, Bristol, UK. Lives and works in Devon, UK.

Beautiful Fart in a Japanese Garden Painting, 2008
Household gloss on canvas
Diam. 48 in. (121.9 cm)

Cobalt Chloride, 2021
Household gloss on canvas
100 × 108 in. (254 × 274.3 cm)

Loie Hollowell (pp. 46–47)
Born 1983, Woodland, CA. Lives and works in Queens, NY.

Spectrum XVI, 2024
Oil paint, acrylic medium, Aqua-Resin, epoxy resin, and
sawdust on linen over panel
16 parts, each 12⅛ × 9 × 2½ in. (30.8 × 22.9 × 6.4 cm)

Alex Israel (pp. 92–93)
Born 1982, Los Angeles. Lives and works in Los Angeles.

Self-Portrait (Surf Shop), 2016
Acrylic and Bondo on fiberglass
96 × 84 × 4 in. (243.8 × 213.4 × 10.2 cm)

Wave, 2018
Acrylic on fiberglass
96 × 96 in. (243.8 × 243.8 cm)

Ann Veronica Janssens (pp. 42–43)
Born 1956, Folkestone, UK. Lives and works in Brussels.

Hot Pink Turquoise, 2006
Two 700/1000W halogen lamps, dichroic color filters, tripod

Peacock Blue, 2017
700/1000W halogen lamp, dichroic color filter

Installation view: *mars*, Institut d'art contemporain,
Villeurbanne/Rhône-Alpes, France, 2017

yellowbluepink, 2015
Artificial fog, artificial light, color filters
Dimensions variable

Sarah Anne Johnson (pp. 126–27)
Born 1976, Winnipeg, Canada. Lives and works in Winnipeg.

FMMTY, 2023
Pigment print with oil paint and gold leaf
40 × 59⅞ in. (101.5 × 152 cm)

FTA, 2021
Pigment print with oil paint
45 × 30 in. (114.5 × 76 cm)

Mike Kelley (pp. 108–9)
Born 1954, Detroit. Died 2012, South Pasadena, CA.

Deodorized Central Mass with Satellites, 1991/1999
Plush toys sewn over wood and wire frames with Styrofoam
packing material, nylon rope, pulleys, steel hardware and
hanging plates, fiberglass, car paint, and disinfectant
Overall dimensions variable

Memory Ware Flat #8, 2001
Mixed media on wood panel
70¼ × 46¼ × 4½ in. (178.4 × 117.5 × 11.4 cm)

Ellsworth Kelly (pp. 8–9)
Born 1923, Newburgh, NY. Died 2015, Spencertown, NY.

Spectrum VIII, 2014
Acrylic on canvas, twelve joined panels
250 × 230 in. (635 × 584.2 cm)
Installation view: Fondation Louis Vuitton, Paris

Krista Kim (pp. 136–37)
Born 1976, Toronto. Lives and works in Los Angeles.

Continuum, 2022
Video installation, .mp4 format
40 min.
Installation view: Aranya, China

Mirror of the Mind, v. 9, 2022
.mp4 delivered as NFT
8 min.

Kimsooja (pp. 148–49)
Born 1957, Daegu, Korea. Lives and works in Seoul and Paris.

To Breathe – A Mirror Woman, 2006
Site-specific installation consisting of diffraction grating film,
mirror, and sound performance *The Weaving Factory* (2005)
Installation view: Crystal Palace, Museo Reina Sofía, Madrid,
2006

To Breathe – Leeum, 2021
Site-specific installation with diffraction grating film
Dimensions variable

Jeff Koons (pp. 188–89)
Born 1955, York, PA. Lives and works in New York.

(Borghese Gladiator) Gazing Balls, 2024
Plaster and glass
72⅞ × 62⅝ × 54 in. (185.1 × 159 × 137.2 cm)
Edition of 3 plus 1 AP

Play-Doh, 1994–2014
Polychromed aluminum
124 × 152¼ × 137 in. (315 × 386.7 × 348 cm)
One of five unique versions

Taisuke Koyama (pp. 44–45)
Born 1978, Japan. Lives and works in Tokyo.

Installation view: *THE EXPOSED #4*, CASO, Osaka, 2009

Untitled (Melting Rainbows 061), 2010
Archival pigment print
43¾ × 29⅛ in. (111 × 74 cm)

Astrid Krogh (pp. 32–33)
Born 1968, Copenhagen. Lives and works in Copenhagen.

ORNAMENT, 2003
Neon, aluminum
102⅜ × 141¾ in. (260 × 360 cm)

IKAT II, 2011
Optical fiber, paper yarn, LED
78¾ × 98⅜ in. (200 × 250 cm)

Yayoi Kusama (pp. 236–37)
Born 1929, Matsumoto, Japan. Lives and works in Tokyo.

*Infinity Mirrored Room—The Eternally Infinite Light of the
Universe Illuminating the Quest for Truth*, 2020
Mixed media
111⅛ × 242⅛ × 242⅛ in. (300 × 615 × 615 cm)

With All My Love for the Tulips, I Pray Forever, 2013
Mixed media
Dimensions variable

Atta Kwami (pp. 58–59)
Born 1956, Accra, Ghana. Died 2021, UK.

Another Moment, 2019
Acrylic on linen
61 × 78¾ in. (155 × 200 cm)

Dzidzɔ kple amenuveve (Joy and Grace), 2021–22
Installation view: *Maria Lassnig Prize Mural*,
Serpentine North Garden, London, 2022–23

Jim Lambie (pp. 238–39)
Born 1964, Glasgow, Scotland. Lives and works in Glasgow.

Zobop Colour, 1999
Colored vinyl tape
Dimensions variable
Installation view (p. 238): The Fruitmarket Gallery, Edinburgh,
2014
Installation view (p. 239): *Days Like These: The Tate Triennial
Exhibition of Contemporary British Art 2003*, Tate Britain,
London, 2003

Doron Langberg (pp. 192–93)
Born 1985, Yokneam Moshava, Israel. Lives and works
in New York.

In my Lap 1, 2021
Oil on linen
18 × 24 in. (45.7 × 61 cm)

Kyle, Robert, and James, 2019
Oil on linen
96 × 80 in. (243.8 × 203.2 cm)

Lakwena Maciver (pp. 166–67)
Born 1986, London. Lives and works in London.

Julius Erving, 2022
Acrylic, vinyl, and polyurethane varnish on wood pane
79⅛ × 42⅛ in. (201 × 107 cm)

Larry Bird, 2022
Acrylic, vinyl, and polyurethane varnish on wood pane
81⅛ × 43¼ in. (206 × 110 cm)

Lift Your Head High, 2025
Hand cut plywood, acrylic paint
63⅛ × 63⅛ × 2¾ in. (160.3 × 160.3 × 7 cm)

Shantell Martin (pp. 242–43)
Born 1980, London. Lives and works in Los Angeles.

Shantell Martin x The Whitney Museum Shop Playing Cards,
2021
Playing cards with holographic, rainbow reflective foil on the
outer packaging and silver holographic foil on the back of
each card
Packaging printed using FSC-certified paper manufactured
with 100 % renewable green energy
3½ × 2½ × ¾ in. (6.4 × 8.9 × 1.9 cm)

Leslie Martinez (pp. 112–13)
Born 1985, McAllen, TX. Lives and works in Dallas, TX.

The Decorum of this Body, 2023
Paint rags, studio clothes, dried paint chips, charcoal,
coarse sawdust, pumice, acrylic on canvas
Approx. 60 × 75 × 8 in. (152 × 191 × 20 cm)

one hand knows where to meet the other, 2022
Fabric, paper, crushed charcoal, crushed rock, sawdust,
wood ash, iron oxide, and acrylic on canvas
60 × 48 × 4 in. (152 × 122 × 10 cm)

Tomokazu Matsuyama (pp. 170–71)
Born 1976, Takayama, Gifu, Japan. Lives and works in Brooklyn.

You, One Me Erase, 2023
Acrylic and mixed media on canvas
108 × 260 in. (274.3 × 660.4 cm)

Julie Mehretu (pp. 130–31)
Born 1970, Addis Ababa, Ethiopia. Lives and works
in New York.

Sumo, 2024
Ink and acrylic on canvas
96 × 120 in. (243.8 × 304.8 cm)

TRANSpaintings (mask), 2023
Ink and acrylic on monofilament polyester mesh framed
in an aluminum sculpture conceived by Nairy Baghramian
70 × 60 in. (182.9 × 152.4 cm)

Joel Mesler (pp. 172–73)
Born 1974, Los Angeles. Lives and works in East Hampton, NY.

Untitled (Love, Hate), 2020
Pigment on linen
80 × 70 × 1½ in. (203.2 × 177.8 × 3.8 cm)

Untitled (Mama), 2020
Pigment on linen
80 × 70 × 1½ in. (203.2 × 177.8 × 3.8 cm)

Untitled (Party time), 2024
Pigment on linen
76 × 72 in. (193 × 182.9 cm)

Untitled (Play the Hits), 2024
Pigment on linen
78 × 72½ in. (198.1 × 184.2 cm)

Beatriz Milhazes (pp. 26–27)
Born 1960, Rio de Janeiro. Lives and works in Rio de Janeiro.

Marilola, 2010–15
Aluminum; brass; copper; acrylic; enamel, polyester, and
paper flowers; resin; foiled paper; wood; hand-painted
enamel on aluminum
114⅛ × 110¼ × 16⅞ in. (290 × 280 × 43 cm)

O Esplendor, 2023
Vinyl adhesive on glass
23 × 36 ft. (7 × 11 m)
Installation view: *Beatriz Milhazes: Maresias*, Turner
Contemporary, Margate, UK

Justin Morin (pp. 98–99)
Born 1979, Mont-Saint-Martin, France. Lives and works
in Paris.

How to drape a rosa gammoca officinalis, 2015
Chromed steel and printed silk
118⅛ × 112¼ in. (300 × 285 cm)

How to drape the sound of waves, 2019
Chromed steel and printed silk
86⅝ × 74¾ × 7⅞ in. (220 × 190 × 20 cm)

Rosie Mudge (pp. 100–101)
Born 1988, Knysna, South Africa. Lives and works
in Cape Town.

Better off alone, II, 2022
Automotive paint and glitter glue on canvas
40⅜ × 28⅜ × 1⅝ in. (102.5 × 72 × 4 cm)

Future Reflections, I, 2024
Automotive paint and glitter glue on canvas framed in ash
Each: 67⅜ × 31⅞ × 1⅝ in. (171 × 81 × 4 cm)

Takashi Murakami (pp. 212–15)
Born 1962, Tokyo. Lives and works in Tokyo.

Together with the Flower Parent and Child, 2021–22
FRP, urethane paint, stainless steel, wood base
77½ × 48½ × 35⅜ in. (196.8 × 123.1 × 90 cm)
Installation view: Perrotin Dubai, ICD Brookfield Place, Dubai, 2022–23

Untitled, 2018
Acrylic and platinum leaf on canvas mounted on aluminum frame
7 panels, overall 118⅛ × 275⅝ in. (300 × 700 cm)

Yume Lion (The Dream Lion), 2009
Carbon fiber, acrylic, steel, and Corian base
75¼ × 50 × 43¼ in. (191 × 127 × 110 cm)

Morag Myerscough (pp. 234–35)
Born 1963, London. Lives and works in London.

Dancing in the Sky, 2024
Steel structure, digitally printed fabric, hand-painted plywood
60 × 100 × 100 ft. (18 × 30 × 30 m)
Installation view: Coachella Valley Music & Arts Festival, Indio, CA, 2024

Endless Ribbon Connecting Us, 2021 (permanent installation)
Hand-painted walls and transparent vinyl ceiling
19 × 180 ft. (6 × 55 m)
Installation view: Hertford Street, Coventry, UK

Olaf Nicolai (pp. 222–23)
Born 1962, Halle an der Saale, Germany. Lives and works in Berlin.

Considering a multiplicity of appearances in light of a particular aspect of relevance. Or: Can art be concrete?, 2008
Installation of 16 unique prints and 400 unique books
Each print: 26¾ × 18⅞ in. (68 × 48 cm)
Each book: 64 pages, 7⅞ × 6⅞ in. (20 × 17.5 cm)
Installation view: Galerie Hecey, Brussels

Rainbows, 2017
Silkscreen on paper
47¼ × 35⅜ in. (120 × 90 cm)
Edition of 5

António Ole (pp. 66–67)
Born 1951, Luanda, Angola. Lives and works in Luanda and Lisbon.

Township Wall (nº10), Düsseldorf, 2004
Found objects, wood, corrugated sheet metal and plastic, iron, and glass
141¾ × 378 in. (360 × 960 cm)

Jean-Michel Othoniel (pp. 152–53)
Born 1964, Saint-Étienne, France. Lives and works in Paris.

Pink Lotus, 2016
Pink mirrored glass, stainless steel
51⅛ × 59 × 39⅜ in. (130 × 150 × 100 cm)

Wild Pansy, 2017
Mirrored glass, stainless steel
118⅛ × 118⅛ × 78¾ in. (300 × 300 × 200 cm)

Ariana Papademetropoulos (pp. 142–43)
Born 1990, Los Angeles. Lives and works in Los Angeles.

Echoes of Nature Boy, 2019
Oil on canvas
84 × 105 in. (213.4 × 266.7 cm)

Espulsione dalla discoteca, 2020
Oil on canvas
90 × 120 in. (228.6 × 304.8 cm)

José Parlá (pp. 70–71)
Born 1973, Miami. Lives and works in Brooklyn.

ONE Union of the Senses, 2014
Acrylic, oil, enamel paint, and plaster on wood
16 × 90 ft. (4.9 × 27.4 m)

Paola Pivi (pp. 208–9)
Born 1971, Milan. Lives and works in Hawaii.

Untitled (ladder), 2021
Inflatable made of tarpaulin and blower
65 ft. 7⅜ in. × 16 ft. 4⅞ in. × 11 ft. 9¾ in. (20 × 5 × 3.6 m)
Installation view: *Euphoria: Art is in the Air*, Galeries Nationales du Grand Palais, Paris

Installation view: *We are the baby gang*, Perrotin, New York, 2019

Rob Pruitt (pp. 228–29)
Born 1964, Washington, DC. Lives and works in New York.

Installation view: *New Faces*, 303 Gallery, New York, 2022

Installation view: *Rob Pruitt: An American Folk Artist*, Aspen Art Museum, CO, 2013

Gerhard Richter (pp. 60–61)
Born 1932, Dresden, Germany. Lives and works in Cologne, Germany.

25 Colors, 2007
Enamel on Alu-Dibond
19⅛ × 19⅛ in. (48.7 × 48.7 cm)

Chair, 1985
Oil on canvas
78¾ × 78¾ in. (200 × 200 cm)

Ugo Rondinone (pp. 10–15)
Born 1964, Brunnen, Switzerland. Lives and works in New York.

clockwork for oracles, 2008
Mirror, color plastic gel, wood, paint
Dimensions variable

einundzwanzigstermaizweitausendundzehn, 2010
Acrylic on canvas plexiglass plaque with caption
Diam. 106¼ in. (270 cm)

Love invents us, 1999
Installation; translucent color foil on existing glass facade
Dimensions variable

Installation view: *seven magic mountains*, Public Art
Production Fund, Nevada Museum of Art, Las Vegas, 2016

Rafaël Rozendaal (pp. 88–89)
Born 1980, Amsterdam. Lives and works in New York.

Not Never No.com, 2018
Website
Dimensions variable
https://www.notneverno.com/
Installation view: *Double Pressure*, Centraal Museum Utrecht,
the Netherlands, 2019

Random Fear (with Mirrors), 2019
Installation
Dimensions variable
Installation view: *Trouble in Paradise: Collection Rattan
Chadha*, Kunsthal Rotterdam, the Netherlands, 2019

Sterling Ruby (pp. 178–79)
Born in 1972, Air Force Base, Bitburg, Germany.
Lives and works in Los Angeles.

SP184, 2011
Spray paint on canvas
160 × 160 × 2 in. (406.4 × 406.4 × 5.1 cm)

*TURBINE. YOUR LIGHT GROWS DARK BY LOSING OF YOUR
EYES.*, 2024
Acrylic, oil, and cardboard on canvas
96 × 126 × 2 in. (243.8 × 320 × 5.1 cm)

Thomas Ruff (pp. 38–39)
Born 1958, Zell am Harmersbach, Germany. Lives and works
in Düsseldorf, Germany.

Substrat 21 III, 2003
Chromogenic print with Diasec
73¼ × 113 in. (186 × 287 cm)

Substrat 34 I, 2007
Chromogenic print with Diasec
80¾ × 72⅞ × 2⅜ in. (205 × 185 × 6 cm)

Athi-Patra Ruga (pp. 28–29)
Born 1984, Umtata, South Africa. Lives and works
in Hogsback, South Africa.

The Future White Woman of Azania 1, 2012
Lightjet print
47¼ × 31½ in. (120 × 80 cm)
Edition of 5 + 3 AP

Thud of a Snowflake (detail), 2013
High-density foam, artificial flowers, fiberglass, steel,
polystyrene, fabric, rhinestones, automotive paint, glue
Flower figure: 55⅛ × 82⅝ × 16½ in. (140 × 210 × 42 cm)

Maja Ruznic (pp. 120–21)
Born 1983, Bosnia and Herzegovina. Lives and works
in Placitas, NM.

Deep Calls to Deep, 2023
Oil on canvas
100 × 150 in. (254 × 381 cm)

The Past Awaiting the Future/Arrival of Drummers, 2023
Oil on linen
99½ × 151½ in. (252.7 × 384.8 cm)

Tomás Saraceno (pp. 200–201)
Born 1973, Tucuman, Argentina. Lives and works in Berlin.

Foam SB 82/45p, 2024
Powder-coated stainless steel, iridescent plexiglass,
monofilament
Dimensions variable

Poetic Cosmos of the Breath, 2007
Iridescent foil, transparent foil
Dimensions variable
Installation view: 2nd International Artists' Airshow,
Gunpowder Park, Essex, UK, 2007

Kenny Scharf (pp. 218–19)
Born 1958, Los Angeles. Lives and works in Los Angeles.

FACES IN PLACES, 2016
Oil on linen with powder-coated aluminum frame
48¼ × 48¼ in. (122.6 × 122.6 cm)

KOLORZI, 2020
Spray paint on canvas
Diam. 70 in. (177.8 cm)

Sho Shibuya (pp. 96–97)
Born 1984, Fukuoka City, Japan. Lives and works in Brooklyn.

Sunrise from a small window, May 2020–ongoing (daily project)
Acrylic on newspaper
22 × 12 in. (55.9 × 30.5 cm)

Devan Shimoyama (pp. 194–95)
Born 1989, Philadelphia. Lives and works in Pittsburgh.

February, 2019
Silk flowers, beads, rhinestones, and sequins on fabric
with steel mount and frame
92 × 156 × 3 in. (233.7 × 386.2 × 7.6 cm)

Page of Wands, 2020
Oil, colored pencil, glitter, acrylic, sequins, beads, collage,
costume jewelry, and plastic salamanders on canvas
84 × 72 × 3 in. (213.4 × 182.9 × 7.6 cm)

Shoplifter (Hrafnhildur Arnardóttir) (pp. 50–51)
Born 1969, Reykjavík, Iceland. Lives and works in New York.

Chromo Sapiens, 2019
Synthetic hair extensions, soundscape by HAM
Site-specific installation
Installation view: Icelandic Pavilion, 58th Venice Biennale,
Spazio Punch, Giudecca

Hyperweb, 2023
Synthetic hair extensions and paracord
Site-specific installation
Installation view: Kai Art Center, Tallinn, Estonia

Phillip K. Smith III (pp. 138–39)
Born 1972, Los Angeles. Lives and works in Palm Springs, CA.

Lucid Stead, 2013
Existing homestead shack, aluminum, glass, LED lighting,
electrical components, unique color program
Dimensions variable
Installation view: Joshua Tree, CA

Three Half Lozenges, 2021
Existing historic windows, alupoly, aluminum, LED lighting,
electronic components, unique color choreography
396 × 120 × 6 in. (1,005.8 × 304.8 × 15.2 cm)
Installation view: *Phillip K. Smith III: Three Half Lozenges*,
Newark Museum of Art, NJ, 2021

Vaughn Spann (pp. 240–41)
Born 1992, Florida. Lives and works in Newark, NJ.

Beloved Bliss (Big Black Rainbow), 2022
Mixed media, terry cloth, canvas on aluminum stretcher bars
80 × 84 × 1⅝ in. (203.2 × 213.4 × 4.1 cm)

A New Chapter, 2024
Mixed media, terry cloth, canvas on aluminum stretcher bars
81 × 84½ × 2½ in. (205.7 × 214.6 × 6.3 cm)

Josh Sperling (pp. 230–31)
Born 1984, Oneonta, NY. Lives and works in Ithaca, NY.

Installation view: *Josh Sperling: Big Picture*, Perrotin,
Los Angeles, 2025

Jennifer Steinkamp (pp. 134–35)
Born 1958, Denver, CO. Lives and works in Los Angeles.

Retinal, 2018
Computer animation projected on architecture
35 ft. 4¼ in. × 12 ft. 9⅝ in. (10.8 × 3.9 m)
Installation view: *Souls*, Leeahn Gallery, Seoul, 2020

Pat Steir (pp. 64–65)
Born 1938, Newark, NJ. Lives and works in New York.

Rainbow Waterfall #1, 2022
Oil on canvas
108 × 108 inches (274.3 × 274.3 cm)

Rainbow Waterfall #5, 2022
Oil on canvas
108 × 108 in. (274.3 × 274.3 cm)

Frank Stella (pp. 224–25)
Born 1936, Malden, MA. Died 2024, New York.

Firuzabad, 1970
Synthetic polymer paint on canvas
119¾ × 180¼ in. (304 × 458 cm)

Untitled (Concentric Squares), 1974
Acrylic on canvas
80½ × 80½ in. (204.5 × 204.5 cm)

Matthew Stone (pp. 116–17)
Born 1982, London. Lives and works in the Wye Valley, UK.

Holding (Removed), 2019
UV-cured ink on linen
86⅝ × 70⅞ in. (220 × 180 cm)

La Danse Inachevée (Virtual Mix) I (after Matisse), 2024
UV-cured ink on linen board
47¼ × 47¼ in. (120 × 120 cm)

Hiroshi Sugimoto (pp. 180–81)
Born 1948, Tokyo. Lives and works in Tokyo and New York.

Opticks 094, 2018
Type-C print
46½ × 46½ in. (118.1 × 118.1 cm)

Opticks 250, 2018
Type-C print
46½ × 46½ in. (118.1 × 118.1 cm)

Do Ho Suh (pp. 82–83)
Born 1962, Seoul. Lives and works in London.

Installation view: *Do Ho Suh: Passage/s*, Victoria Miro,
London, 2017

Jet Lag (detail), 2022
Polyester and stainless steel
412⅝ × 130¾ × 11¾ in. (1,048 × 332 × 30 cm)

Sarah Sze (pp. 132–33)
Born 1969, Boston. Lives and works in New York.

Free Fall, 2021
Oil paint, acrylic paint, acrylic polymers, ink, aluminum,
diabond, and wood
84 × 106 × 3 in. (213.4 × 269.2 × 7.6 cm)

Installation view: *Sarah Sze: Timelapse*, Solomon R. Guggenheim
Museum, New York, 2023

Mika Tajima (pp. 174–75)
Born 1975, Los Angeles. Lives and works in New York.

Art d'Ameublement (Catoodden), 2021
Spray enamel, thermoformed PETG
90 × 65 in. (228.6 × 165.1 cm)

Art d'Ameublement (Onamu), 2021
Spray acrylic, thermoformed PETG
90 × 65 in. (228.6 × 165.1 cm)

Tony Tasset (pp. 210–11)
Born 1960, Cincinnati, OH. Lives and works in Sawyer, MI.

Rainbow, 2012
Steel, aluminum, and paint
94 × 188 × 8 ft. (28.7 × 57.3 × 2.4 m)
Installation view: Sony Pictures Entertainment, Los Angeles

teamLab (pp. 202–3)
Founded 2001.

*Expanding Three-dimensional Existence in Transforming
Space – Flattening 3 Colors and 9 Blurred Colors*, 2023
Interactive installation
Endless duration
Sound: Hideaki Takahashi
Installation view: teamLab Planets TOKYO

The Infinite Crystal Universe, 2018
Interactive light sculpture, LED
Endless duration
Sound: teamLab
Installation view: teamLab Planets TOKYO

Diana Thater (pp. 36–37)
Born 1962, San Francisco. Lives and works in Los Angeles.

Abyss of Light, 1993
Three video projectors, three media layers, Lee filters,
and existing architecture
Dimensions variable
Installation view: Los Angeles County Museum of Art, 2015

Installation view: *Diana Thater: the sky is unfolding under
you*, David Zwirner, New York, 2001

Mickalene Thomas (pp. 190–91)
Born 1971, Camden, NJ. Lives and works in Brooklyn.

Resist, 2017
Rhinestones, acrylic, gold leaf, and oil stick on canvas
mounted on wood panel
84 × 108 in. (213.4 × 274.3 cm)

Untitled #10, 2014
Paper collage, glitter, graphite, marker, and oil pastel
on archival board
11⅛ × 8⅝ in. (28.3 × 21.9 cm)

Fred Tomaselli (pp. 30–31)
Born 1956, Santa Monica, CA. Lives and works in Brooklyn.

March 16, 2020, 2020
Gouache, acrylic, collage, and archival inkjet print on
watercolor paper
11 × 12⅛ in. (27.9 × 30.5 cm)

Untitled, 2020
Leaves, photo collage, acrylic, and resin on wood panel
60 × 60 in. (152.4 × 152.4 cm)

Zoe Walsh (pp. 114–15)
Born 1989, Washington, DC. Lives and works in Los Angeles.

Drift and cling to shape, 2023
Acrylic on canvas-wrapped panel
40 × 30 in. (101.6 × 76.2 cm)

In the dust of summer, 2023
Acrylic on canvas-wrapped panel
72 × 90 in. (189 × 228.5 cm)

Mary Weatherford (pp. 94–95)
Born 1963, Ojai, CA. Lives and works in Los Angeles.

Blue Cut Fire, 2017
Flashe and neon on linen
117 × 104 in. (297.2 × 264.2 cm)

Coney Island, 2012
Flashe and neon on linen
103 × 83 in. (261.6 × 210.8 cm)

Liz West (pp. 34–35)
Born 1985, Manchester, UK. Lives and works in Manchester.

Our Colour, 2016
Site-specific installation: T5 fluorescent lamps, cellulose gels
Dimensions variable

Pae White (pp. 160–61)
Born 1963, Pasadena, CA. Lives and works in Los Angeles.

Noisy Blushes, 2020
Polished stainless steel, colored cable, and silk-screened
elements
167 × 166 × 132 in. (424.2 × 421.6 × 335.3 cm)

Dustin Yellin (pp. 196–97)
Born 1975, Los Angeles. Lives and works in Brooklyn.

Unweave the Rainbow, 2019
Glass, collage, acrylic
48¼ × 20 × 12½ in. (122.6 × 50.8 × 31.8 cm)

Tokujin Yoshioka (pp. 150–51)
Born 1967, Japan. Lives and works in Tokyo.

Rainbow Church, 2010/2013
Glass (500 crystal prisms)
Dimensions variable
Installation view: *Crystallize*, Museum of Contemporary Art
Tokyo, 2013

Spectrum, 2017
Glass (200 crystal prisms)
Dimensions variable
Installation view: Shiseido Gallery, Tokyo, 2017

Image Credits

All works © and courtesy the artist.

9: © Ellsworth Kelly Foundation, courtesy Matthew Marks Gallery. Collection Fondation Louis Vuitton. Artist commission; 10: Photo: Studio Rondinone; 11: Photo: Stefan Altenburger; 12–13: Photo: Gianfranco Gorgoni; 14–15: Photo: Studio Rondinone; 16: © Giorno Poetry Systems, courtesy Giorno Poetry Systems and Almine Rech; 17: © Giorno Poetry Systems, courtesy Giorno Poetry Systems and Almine Rech. Photo: Alessandro Wang; 18, 19: © Estate of Carlos Cruz-Diez. All rights reserved 2024/Bridgeman Images. Photo © Atelier Cruz-Diez, Paris / Palm Springs Art Museum/Lance Gerber / Bridgeman Images; 20, 21: © 2026 Stephen Flavin / Artists Rights Society (ARS), New York. Courtesy David Zwirner; 22, 23: Photo: Prudence Cuming Associates; 24–25: © Peter Halley. Courtesy Museo Nivola, Sardinia. Photo: White Box Studio; 26: © Beatriz Milhazes Studio. Photo: Eduardo Ortega; 27: © Beatriz Milhazes Studio. Photo: Thierry Bal; 28, 29: Courtesy Athi-Patra Ruga and WHATIFTHEWORLD. Photo: Hayden Phipps; 30, 31: Courtesy Fred Tomaselli and James Cohan, New York; 32: Photo: Kurt Hoppe. Collection Danish Arts Foundation; 33: Photo: Torben Eskerod; 34, 35: © Liz West. Courtesy the artist. Commissioned by Bristol Biennial; 36: © Diana Thater. Courtesy the artist and David Zwirner; 37: © Diana Thater. Photo: Fredrik Nilsen; 38, 39: © 2026 Thomas Ruff/Artists Rights Society (ARS), New York/VG Bild-Kunst, Germany. Courtesy the artist and David Zwirner; 40: Courtesy James Clar and Jane Lombard Gallery. Photo: Arturo Sanchez; 41: Courtesy James Clar and Jane Lombard Gallery; 42: Courtesy Wellcome Collection. Photo: Thomas SG Farnetti; 43: Photo: Andrea Rossetti, courtesy Esther Schipper and Institut d'art contemporain, Villeurbanne/Rhône-Alpes (IAC); 44: Photo: Taisuke Koyama; 46–47: © Loie Hollowell, courtesy Pace Gallery. Photo: Melissa Goodwin, courtesy Pace Gallery; 48: Courtesy Bernard Frize and Perrotin. Photo: Roman März; 49: Courtesy Bernard Frize and Perrotin. Photo: Ringo Cheung; 50: Commissioned by Icelandic Art Center. Photo: Elisabet Davidsdottir; 51: Photo: Anu Vahtra; 52, 53: © Derrick Adams Studio 2024; 54, 55: © DB-ADAGP Paris; 56: Photo: James Prinz, courtesy Western Exhibitions, Chicago; 57: Photo: James Prinz, courtesy Western Exhibitions, Chicago. Collection Zach and Laura Williams, Skokie, IL; 58: Courtesy the Estate of Atta Kwami. Photo: Hugo Glendinning; 59: Courtesy the Estate of Atta Kwami and Goodman Gallery; 60, 61: © Gerhard Richter 2026; 62, 63: © Jennifer Guidi. Courtesy the artist and Gagosian; 64: © Pat Steir, courtesy the artist and Hauser & Wirth. Photo: Elisabeth Bernstein; 65: © Pat Steir, courtesy the artist and Hauser & Wirth; 66–67: Courtesy .insofar art gallery; 68: © Firelei Báez. Courtesy Shah Garg Collection. Photo: Christopher Burke Studios. Image courtesy the artist and Hauser & Wirth; 69: © Firelei Báez. Courtesy Wilks Family Collection. Photo: Phoebe d'Heurle. Image courtesy the artist and Hauser & Wirth; 70–71: Collection ONE World Trade Center, New York City. Courtesy Parlá Studios; 72, 73: © Kevin Beasley. Courtesy the artist and Casey Kaplan, New York. Photo: Phoebe Dheurle; 74, 75: © Raúl de Nieves, courtesy the artist and Company Gallery, New York; 82: © Do Ho Suh.

Courtesy the artist and Lehmann Maupin, New York, Seoul, and London; 83: © Do Ho Suh. Courtesy the artist; Lehmann Maupin, New York, Seoul, and London; and Victoria Miro. Photo: Thierry Bal. 84: Courtesy Lauren Halsey and David Kordansky Gallery, Los Angeles. Photo: Allen Chen / SLH Studio; 85: Courtesy Lauren Halsey and David Kordansky Gallery, Los Angeles. Photo: Jeff McLane; 86: Artwork © Jeffrey Gibson, courtesy Sikkema Jenkins & Co., New York. Photo: Timothy Schenck; 87: Artwork © Jeffrey Gibson, courtesy Sikkema Jenkins & Co., New York; 88: Collection Centraal Museum Utrecht. Photo: Gert Jan van Rooij. Courtesy Upstream Gallery Amsterdam; 89: Photo: Job Janssen & Jan Adriaans. Courtesy Upstream Gallery Amsterdam; 90, 91: Courtesy The Flat-Massimo Carasi, Milano; 92: Photo: Martin Wong; 93: Photo: Jeff McLane; 94: Photo: Robert Wedemeyer; 95: Photo: Fredrik Nilsen Studio; 96, 97: © shoshibuya; 98, 99: Courtesy Justin Morin; 100, 101: © Rosie Mudge. Image courtesy SMAC Gallery; 102: © Spencer Finch. Photo: Gerhard Kassner, Berlin; 103: © Spencer Finch. Photo: Matthew Herrmann. © Hill Art Foundation; 104, 105: © 2026 Chicago/Woodman LLC / Artists Rights Society (ARS), New York. Photo: Elon Schoenholz; 106, 107: © Damien Hirst and Science Ltd. All rights reserved / DACS, London / ARS, NY 2026. Photo: Prudence Cuming Associates Ltd.; 108: © 2026 Mike Kelley Foundation for the Arts. All Rights Reserved / Licensed by VAGA at Artists Rights Society (ARS), NY. Courtesy Mike Kelley Foundation for the Arts; 109: © 2026 Mike Kelley Foundation for the Arts. All Rights Reserved / Licensed by VAGA at Artists Rights Society (ARS), NY. The Museum of Modern Art, New York. Partial gift of Peter M. Brant, courtesy the Brant Foundation, Inc. and gift of The Sidney and Harriet Janis Collection (by exchange), Mary Sisler Bequest (by exchange), Mr. and Mrs. Eli Wallach (by exchange), The Jill and Peter Kraus Endowed Fund for Contemporary Acquisitions, Anne and Joel Ehrenkranz, Mimi Haas, Ninah and Michael Lynne, and Maja Oeri and Hans Bodenmann. Digital Image © The Museum of Modern Art/ Licensed by SCALA / Art Resource, NY; 110–11: © 2026 Estate of Sam Gilliam / Artists Rights Society (ARS), New York. Dia Art Foundation and Museum of Fine Arts, Houston. Courtesy David Kordansky Gallery. Photo: Bill Jacobson Studio, New York; 112, 113: Photo: Paul Salveson, courtesy Leslie Martinez and Commonwealth and Council; 114, 115: © Zoe Walsh. Courtesy Yossi Milo, New York; 116: Courtesy Matthew Stone and CHOI&CHOI Gallery; 117: Courtesy Matthew Stone and JARILAGER Gallery; 118: Courtesy Jean-Baptiste Bernadet and Almine Rech. Photo: Nicolas Brasseur; 119: Courtesy Jean-Baptiste Bernadet and Almine Rech; 120, 121: © Maja Ruznic. Courtesy the artist and Karma; 122: Courtesy Zach Harris and Perrotin. Photo: Lee Thompson; 123: Courtesy Zach Harris and Perrotin; 124: © Nick Cave. Courtesy the artist and Jack Shainman Gallery, New York. Photo: James Prinz Photography; 125: © Nick Cave. Courtesy the artist and Jack Shainman Gallery, New York; 126, 127: © Sarah Anne Johnson. Courtesy Yossi Milo, New York; 128: © Sam Falls. Courtesy the artist and Galerie Eva Presenhuber, Zurich / Vienna. Photo:

Rainbow Dreams is a love letter to color, community, and hope. Throughout our careers, we've been consistently drawn to projects that bring artists together, and this book stands as a tribute to that collective spirit. We feel incredibly fortunate to have collaborated with amazing teams on one-of-a-kind projects, and we look forward to creating even more magic together in the future.

This book would not have been possible without the support and belief of so many. Our heartfelt thanks go to our brilliant editor, Simon Hunegs, as well as Paco Lacasta, Alexander Galan, Holly LaDue, and the incredible team at Monacelli/ Phaidon who believed in both rainbows and the love that shaped this project. And Danielle Strle, the original unicorn in our lives. We're deeply grateful to mentors Nick Makhatadze and Steph Dolgins, whose energy and guidance kept us empowered. And above all, thank you to our family and friends: your endless support and kindness truly mean everything.

In loving memory of Sergei Pashkovski

Research Collaborators:
Dr. Jeanne Dreskin
Sabeena Raj Khosla

Rainbow Contemporary Team:
Jaspre Guest
Ramzy Masri
Danielle Strle
Billy Zhao

rainbowcontemporary.com
rainbow-dreams.com
@rainbowcontemporary

Monacelli
A Phaidon Company
111 Broadway
New York, NY 10006

Phaidon Press Limited
2 Cooperage Yard
London E15 2QR

Phaidon SARL
55, rue Traversière
75012 Paris

phaidon.com/monacelli

First published 2026
© 2026 The Monacelli Press

ISBN 978 1 58093 712 2

A Library of Congress Control Number (LCCN) is available for this title.

Editor: Simon Hunegs
Production: Michael Vagnetti
Design: Lacasta Design

Printed in China

monacellipress.com

978 1 58093 712 2

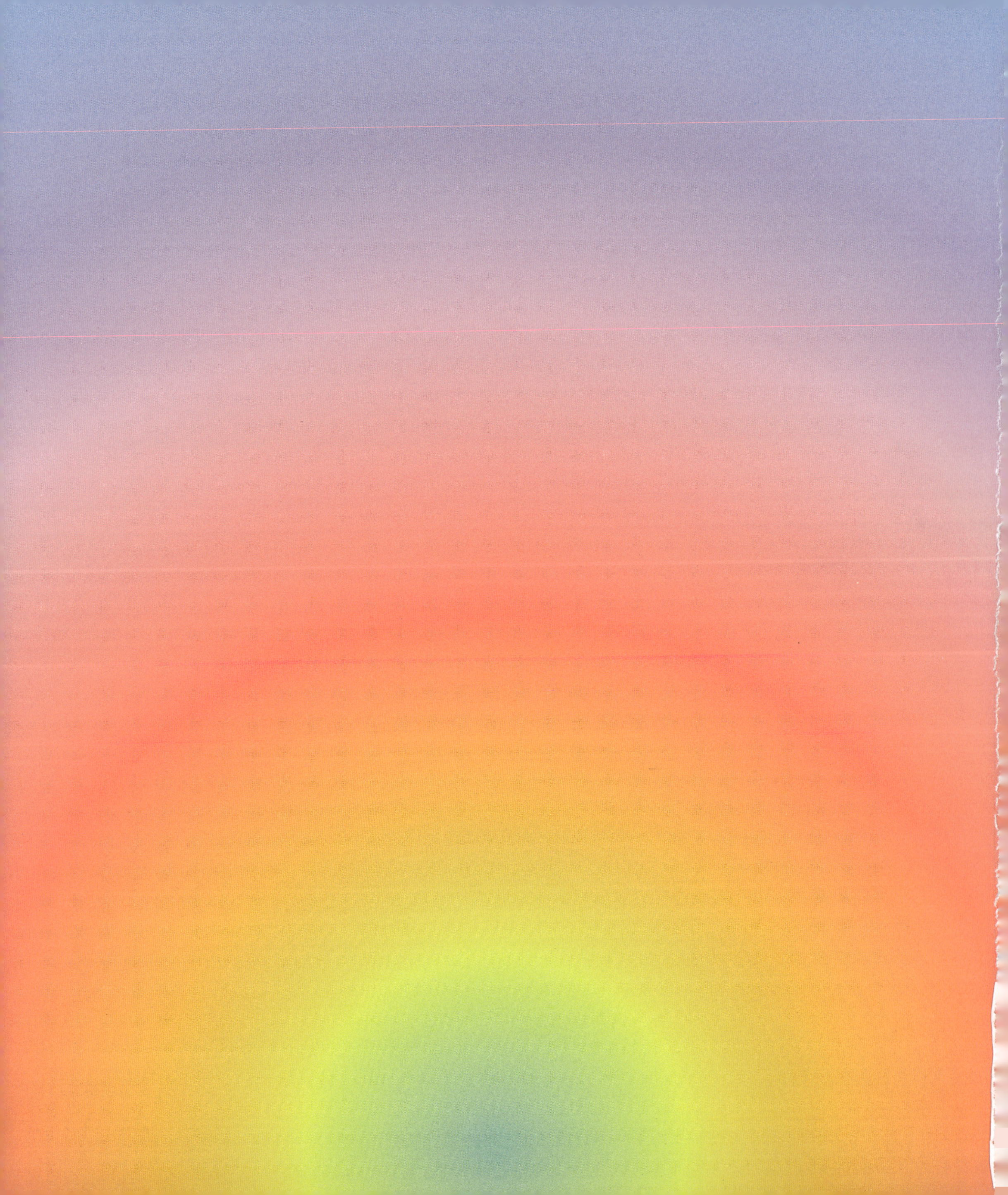